Vic and Sade on the Radio

Vic and Sade on the Radio

A Cultural History of Paul Rhymer's Daytime Series, 1932–1944

John T. Hetherington

McFarland & Company, Inc., Publishers
Jefferson, North Carolina

LIBRARY OF CONGRESS CATALOGUING-IN-PUBLICATION DATA

Hetherington, John T., 1970–
Vic and Sade on the radio : a cultural history
of Paul Rhymer's daytime series, 1932–1944 /
John T. Hetherington.
    p.   cm.
Includes bibliographical references and index.

ISBN 978-0-7864-6303-9 (softcover : acid free paper) ∞
ISBN 978-1-4766-1605-6 (ebook)

1. Vic and Sade (Radio program)   2. Radio broadcasting—
Social aspects—United States.   I. Title.
PN1991.77.V5H48 2014   791.44'72—dc23   2014010533

BRITISH LIBRARY CATALOGUING DATA ARE AVAILABLE

© 2014 John T. Hetherington. All rights reserved

*No part of this book may be reproduced or transmitted in any form
or by any means, electronic or mechanical, including photocopying
or recording, or by any information storage and retrieval system,
without permission in writing from the publisher.*

On the cover: Art Van Harvey (as Victor R. Gook) and
Bernadine Flynn (as Sade Gook) in a publicity shot for CBS Radio
(CBS/Photofest); microphone image by Yegor Tsyba © 2014 iStock

Printed in the United States of America

*McFarland & Company, Inc., Publishers
Box 611, Jefferson, North Carolina 28640
www.mcfarlandpub.com*

For Paul Rhymer, Art Van Harvey,
Bernadine Flynn, Bill Idelson,
Clarence Hartzell, and David Whitehouse

Contents

Preface	1
Introduction	3

PART I: THE MEDIA CONTEXT

Chapter One. Rhymer Is "Outstanding"	9
Chapter Two. The Birth of *Vic and Sade*	23
Chapter Three. "Something to be interested in": Daytime Radio	42
Chapter Four. The "ins and outs of modern life": Mass Culture and Its Critics	62

PART II: SOCIAL AND CULTURAL CONTEXTS

Chapter Five. Leisure: "It represents quite a problem"	73
Chapter Six. "Let's go to the picture show": Movies	106
Chapter Seven. "Seated on the davenport reading": The Role of Reading	121
Chapter Eight. "Where'd you copy that from?": Education	141
Chapter Nine. "Doing exactly the same thing": The Individual and the Community	160
Conclusion: Saying Goodbye	183
Chapter Notes	191
Selected Bibliography	203
Index	207

Preface

I grew up in the 1970s and 80s in a small farming community in western New York State, a place that offered little excitement for a growing boy. Fortunately, there was radio. As it did for the housewives who listened to radio in the 1930s, the medium provided a sense of community that I lacked; the on-air personalities became my friends, people I could call and talk to (read: annoy) during their listener-participation programs. And like those listeners of the 1930s, radio expanded my boundaries. I discovered a small station in Niagara Falls, New York, that brought me the sounds of the city's ethnic communities; and even more diverse sounds came to me from nearby Canada.

First was the blues. Thanks to a Sunday-night program that aired well past my bedtime I became acquainted with all the greats—Robert Johnson, Elmore James, Albert Collins, Sonny Boy Williamson, Big Bill Broonzy—and so many others, until one tragic day the program was gone. I don't remember what replaced it; I just knew I needed something else to keep me awake. The answer came from CHUM-FM, a Toronto station that that played *Theater of the Mind* on Sunday nights. The program was a mix of shows from radio's Golden Age—horror, thrillers, crime-dramas, and comedies—and I loved every minute of it.

The first classic show I ever heard, tucked in bed, headphones on, was *Boston Blackie*, the story of a former criminal turned detective; ever since that night I've had a soft spot for ol' Blackie. He was followed by the thriller *The Inner Sanctum* and the comedic foibles of *Fibber McGee and Molly*. There was more, but a ten-year-old had his limits—at least this one did—and eventually sleep overpowered me. I don't remember *Vic and Sade* ever being played on *Theater of the Mind*. If *Vic and Sade* wasn't played, it might have been because its format, a daily fifteen-minute program, simply didn't fit *Theater of the Mind*'s format.

I first learned of *Vic and Sade* sometime later from a battered copy of Raymond William Stedman's book *Serials*. I'm told people either love *Vic and Sade* or they hate it; there's no in between. I fell into the "love it" camp, and soon became obsessed. Paul Rhymer's comedy was absurd when few others were or knew how to be. Sure, there were other irreverent comedy programs, like the brilliant *Stoopnagle and Budd* and *Easy Aces*. But Rhymer and *Vic and Sade* were a less-obvious breed of humor. Rhymer took his listeners into a funhouse where their lives were reflected and refracted; whether it was through Sade's collection of washrags or her inventive, yet potentially deadly, homespun efforts to fix the washing machine. The fully human characters that populated Rhymer's show earned their title of "Radio's Homefolks." Vic, Sade, and their adopted son, Rush, provided the normalcy around which circled the often-understated absurdity of their friends and neighbors. This book, growing out of my love for *Vic and Sade*, explores some of the deeper meanings and themes beneath the absurdity and the humor.

I would like to thank the late Dr. Richard Hutton, a.k.a. "Dr. Sleetch"; his love of *Vic and Sade* and his extensive knowledge of the program were an inspiration and led me to delve more deeply into the genius of Paul Rhymer. I also wish to acknowledge Barbara Schwarz, Richard Cohen, and everyone in the Friends of *Vic and Sade*, whose tireless devotion has helped to preserve the show for generations to come.

I am indebted to Mark Lancaster for sharing his collection of wonderful photographs with me. As the great-nephew of Art Van Harvey, Mr. Lancaster helps to preserve his very great, great uncle's memory at www.artvanharvey.net. I am also indebted to the National Broadcasting Company for permission to reproduce their photographs, to the Wisconsin Historical Society for its tremendous research collections, to the Marr Sound Archives at the University of Missouri–Kansas City for making available to me previously unreleased *Vic and Sade* recordings, and to SUNY Empire State College for their generous support of my research.

Introduction

Early on the morning of June 29, 1932, NBC premiered (with little fanfare) a new daytime radio series, *Vic and Sade*, on fifteen of its stations. On paper there was little to distinguish *Vic and Sade* from any other program, at least not positively; particularly given the vast array of new programs that were premiering on the relatively new medium of radio. In essence, the program was about the daily lives of Victor Gook, a bookkeeper for a kitchenware company, and Sade, his wife. They would be, at least initially, the only two voices that audiences would hear. In time, though, these voices reached an audience of seven million, which included not only housewives, but also such notables as Ray Bradbury, Upton Sinclair, Ogden Nash, T.S. Eliot, the *New Yorker*'s James Thurber, and even President Franklin Roosevelt. But it didn't start out quite so impressively.

Vic and Sade was written by a young NBC continuity writer named Paul Rhymer. Rhymer was born in Fulton, Illinois, in 1905 and grew up at 708½ West Monroe in Bloomington, Illinois, where, for a time, he attended Illinois Wesleyan University. He withdrew following the death of his father. He then moved to 414 Virginia Avenue in Normal, Illinois, the name of the street where the Gooks would later live. Rhymer pursued a range of odd jobs, including one for the Chicago Alton Railroad; for many of the characters in *Vic and Sade* the railway would, in some way, be significant. Before entering radio, Rhymer had a brief stint as a reporter for the Bloomington *Pantagraph*. The position proved to be less a journalistic endeavor than a creative one for Rhymer, who was fired after it was discovered that he had fabricated sources. Although the practice didn't advance his career at the *Pantagraph*, in retrospect, given the vast number of characters that Rhymer would go on to create for *Vic and Sade*, it seemed that he possessed an irrepressible need to create—or fabricate, as the case may be.

"A paper moon": Paul Rhymer and the Creation of Vic and Sade

Prior to writing *Vic and Sade*, Rhymer had been a continuity writer for NBC, a role that entailed writing lines like, "And now the voices of the violins remind us 'it was only a paper moon.'"[1] However, Rhymer's assignments also provided the opportunity for more substantive and creative work, as we shall examine more fully in Chapter Two. One example of this is the *Keystone Chronicle*, a weekly series that Rhymer wrote, which aired Saturdays on the newly formed National Broadcasting Company. The program was first auditioned in November 1929 and was sponsored by the Keystone Steel and Wire Company of Peoria, Illinois, manufacturers of the Red Barn Fence. For much of the first year of the series seemed

Art Van Harvey (left) and Bernadine Flynn (right) dressed in character as Vic and Sade Gook in an undated NBC publicity photograph. The two actors would come to embody their characters and to identify with them over the twenty-five years of the show's history on radio and, later, television (courtesy Mark C. Lancaster, reproduced by permission of NBC/NBC Universal PhotoBank).

to concern itself with news about the use of "smart farming" within the community, with only the periodic story that had nothing to do with Keystone's galvanized fences. Eventually, however, characters and plots emerged within the galvanized plots. There was the paper's "star" reporter, Buck Huck Harkin, whose bumbling attempt to win the affection of Alice Dudley, daughter of the *Chronicle*'s editor, became a quaint storyline that spawned other entertaining developments.

As the popularity of radio grew throughout the 1920s, advertising agencies began recognizing the potential of the new medium to allow them to bring their clients directly into the consumers' homes. Advertising agencies began spending more and exerting more influence. As the *Keystone Chronicle* illustrates, sponsors were making their presence felt through more than just advertisements. Companies like Johnson and Johnson, Jell-O, and Procter & Gamble, among others, influenced content and specifically commissioned programs to suit and enhance their brand image with audience. As Michele Hilmes, professor of communication at the University of Wisconsin, explains of NBC's policy: "By 1932 the major point of creative control had shifted to the advertising agencies of major radio sponsors."[2] Hilmes adds that, by 1936, nearly all of the daytime and primetime programming was almost entirely outside NBC's direct control.

It was for Procter & Gamble, in fact, that Clarence Mesner, an NBC program executive, asked Paul Rhymer to develop a "family" program. The result, *Vic and Sade*, was presented to William Ramsey, who was in charge of programming for Procter & Gamble. The date was March 28, 1932, and Art Van Harvey and Bernadine Flynn were cast in the title roles. The episode finds Sade troubled because she believes that Vic's habit of reading the newspaper while they talk is a sign of trouble in their marriage. However, as Sade goes on at length about a neighbor's friend's upcoming nuptials while Vic attempts to read the latest "Pie Face Pete" comic strip, it's clear that Vic has not strayed from his marriage. Unfortunately, despite reassurances from Vic that "at the office I keep thinking, 'Oh boy, it won't be long now until I can go home to dinner and see the sweetest little wife in all the world,'"[3] Sade is not easily convinced and finds countless reasons to doubt Vic's affection. She admits to having gained a few pounds since marrying Vic, who helpfully points out, "Been about twenty, hasn't it, Sade?" Perhaps to endear Vic with potential audiences, the character adds that he "loves every extra pound you put on, just like my salary." Despite this, Sade confesses that she still feels insecure, saying, "I feel so stupid and unimportant and unnecessary. I'm like a piece of baggage or something you have to take care of all the time."

It's clear that Paul Rhymer was attempting to cater to the predominately female audience with an episode that featured a female character with whom they could identify; a housewife who genuinely loves her husband and who has the same sorts of concerns that many women would have. Further, having shown Sade's concerns to be unfounded, Vic becomes the ideal husband. Though he shares some of the audience's husbands' faults, this only makes him all the more real; what matters is the sensitive and humorous way that he addressed Sade's concerns—over and over again in the fifteen-minute episode. Despite the melodrama, Rhymer does incorporate hints of what will become his trademark humor. For example, Sade tells Vic that she heard about Tina Volk, the "one that wears the funny hats without any front teeth."

At another point Sade reads to Vic from the paper about a man who shot his sweetheart with a slingshot he borrowed from a small boy, using his own glass eye. Interestingly, given Paul Rhymer's past with the Bloomington *Pantagraph*, such incredible stories would become part of the press in *Vic and Sade*'s world.

As we shall see in Chapter Three, Procter & Gamble rejected *Vic and Sade*, only to pick it up two years later. In the interim, Clarence Mesner allowed it to air as a sustaining program, meaning one that did not have commercial support. In an interview conducted long after the program had ended, Bernadine Flynn, the actress who portrayed Sade, was asked about the program's early days. When asked whether it was clear from the start that they were on to something great, she replied that while she would want to say every episode was wonderful, she knew that probably wasn't the case, especially in the beginning. She recalled that she "didn't dislike it," but was not sure at the time what to make of it or what it would become.[4] Flynn's candid assessment appears accurate. As she notes, early episodes are "good" but at this early stage Flynn, Van Harvey, and Rhymer were still working to find Vic and Sade's voices. This, of course, is a necessity for any radio character, but in this situation it is particularly important, given that Vic and Sade are the only characters on the show at that time.

With the limitation of two characters becoming obvious, Paul Rhymer decided to add another member to the cast. Paul Rhymer drew upon the revelation that Vic and Sade were unable to have children of their own and introduced the character of Victor "Rush" Meadows, the son of one of Sade's sisters who was no longer able to care for him. Rush was to be played by eleven-year-old Billy Idelson, already a radio veteran, having appeared on *Gasoline Alley*, among other shows. It may not have instantly transformed the show, but Rush's presence brought out a new dimension of Vic and Sade. Sade now had something to worry about other than Vic, and although Vic may have attempted to hide his delight in Rush's arrival behind a curmudgeonly façade, his love for the boy—and his own boyishness—was apparent.

Through Rush, the program also began to incorporate an entire imagined community of eccentric figures with interesting names. Mary Frances Rhymer recalled her husband's "life-long love affair with Dickens"[5]; this appreciation is clearly reflected in the large number of characters who were part of *Vic and Sade*. Much attention has been placed on the unlikely, absurd, and even preposterous names that Paul Rhymer gave many of his characters: Hunky J. Sponger, Robert and Slobert Hink, Y.Y. Flirch, Vernon Peggles, Heinie Call, Mr. and Mis' Razorscum, to name just a few of the literally thousands of characters that populated *Vic and Sade*'s world. What few realize is that these names were not simply gimmicks; Paul Rhymer developed unique personalities, and those who had recurring parts were fully developed characters, a trait we will examine in this book's chapter on individuality.

One example of Paul Rhymer's attention to character development was Jake Gumpox, the Gooks' garbage man. Through Rush, Vic, and Sade, audiences knew Gumpox almost intimately; he resided in the Bright Kentucky Hotel, an establishment on the "wrong" side of the tracks. In 1937, listeners learned that Gumpox had tired of the single life and married a woman through an international marriage broker; he was now finally able to bring her to live with him. Gumpox, listeners learned, had overcome great obstacles in his rise to success in the world of garbage. He had worked hard to learn the business first-hand from the pros and had come to be more than a garbage collector: he was a garbage aficionado. His dream was to leave the small town in which he'd mastered the art of garbage collecting for "new fields to conquer."

One might suspect that the humor surrounding Mr. Gumpox, or similar characters, was that of the mocking variety. Not at all. One thing that is clear throughout the history of *Vic and Sade* is that the characters—at least those who were genuine—were treated with respect. As Paul Rhymer's widow noted, her husband "had an unerring eye for the falseness, whether in a person or a theatrical piece" and he resented any implication that his characters were "quaint," dismissing the claim that his show was "great folk writing" as patronizing.[6]

The respect accorded Mr. Gumpox was also extended to Howard, his horse. Rhymer developed as complete a story for Howard as he did for every other character. Howard was married to a horse down the street, but even such apparent domestic tranquility doesn't prevent Howard from engaging in self-doubt, something to which Rush was especially sensitive. It's not until Sade reveals that, in a fit of rage, Mr. Gumpox actually kicked Howard that Rush can truly appreciate the nature of the problem. Howard has always been self-conscious and, as Rush's friend Rooster Davis suggests, is "disappointed in life" given that his sister, Bernice, drives the milk carriage. Perhaps the kick was just one more blow to remind poor Howard of his lowly status.

"Talky talk": Mass Culture and Its Critics

By the time *Vic and Sade* debuted, radio was a fixture in 60 percent of American households. With the Great Depression, a nation that had once prided itself on rugged individualism now found its people more intertwined and dependent on one another. Radio defied physical boundaries, blurring the personal and private as it brought programs and sponsors directly into the home. Listeners were connected with their fellow Americans; they shared common experiences in a way that had never before been possible.

Broadcasting to a mass audience, radio programming did more than entertain listeners; it presented them with an American identity for the first time. Critics of radio, like economist William Orton and writer James Rorty, felt that instead of enlightening listeners, radio presented standardized program intended to appeal to the lowest common denominator. Radio programming, they believed, was an assembly-line process in which programs were created not for artistic reasons but for profit. As William Orton said when referring to movies, such a large output could only result in a limited number of "interesting" products.[7] Orton, Rorty, and others were concerned with more than just mediocre programming; they were concerned with its effects on audience. In order to appeal to the largest audience and reap the greatest profits, critics claimed that radio had diminished individuality by presenting a singular view of America that left no room for diversity. They feared that homogenized programming and public entertainments would limit the public's individuality, creativity, and curtail their ability to entertain themselves.

While critics rallied against radio programming, Vic and Sade managed to make fans of some of radio's harshest critics, including T.S. Eliot, Upton Sinclair, Ray Bradbury, Ogden Nash, James Thurber, Jean Shepherd, and Hendrik Wilhelm Van Loon, who regarded Rhymer's work as an example of "great folk writing."[8] *Harpers*, which frequently served as a voice for radio's critics, went so far as to call *Vic and Sade* "the most literate of all radio daytime serials," adding that it was "one of the few radio shows that is always consistently mature in conception and writing."[9] We will consider these critics' claims in greater detail in Chapter Four.

"Standing outside": Living in Mass Culture

Perhaps the easiest ways to understand *Vic and Sade*'s appeal to both the masses and the culturally elite can be explained by Bernadine Flynn, who played the role of Sade. Flynn commented in an interview that Rhymer "didn't stand outside looking in at anybody.... He was part of the human race; he enjoyed it, he delighted in it, the weaknesses, foibles, eccentricities ... he was not standing aside."[10] This philosophy is very different from that of most culture critics, who believed that average people were unable to make decisions for themselves and would ultimately follow the flock. This philosophy also found expression in Paul Rhymer's characters, who were intentionally designed to be part of the pageant of humanity. The Gooks and most everyone in the town had jobs, they went shopping, and they went to school. They enjoyed a range of leisure activities, from attending movies at the Bijou Theatre, to taking part in fraternal orders. This book will examine the many ways in which the world of *Vic and Sade* reflected and refracted the cultural context of its era and lives of the middle class in the Depression. As Ray Bradbury explained,

> Middle-class America, as it existed in the 1930s, was dramatized lovingly and forever by Paul Rhymer. [...] The world of Vic and Sade has *not* vanished from the world. It has changed somewhat, [but] a helluva lot of America still lives in small towns, and even those who have moved into the city have brought with them, genetically or otherwise, the temperament of Vic and Sade.[11]

Researching Radio

There are certain challenges in researching the history of radio, not the least of which is the dearth of existing material on many topics related to the medium. As Michele Hilmes explains in the *Radio Reader*, despite the fact that radio exercised far more influence on the norms and standards of American life than its successor, television, television has received markedly more attention.[12] To be fair, radio does not make it easy for the researcher; the majority of shows are unavailable, scripts have been lost or destroyed, and many cast members have long since died. This is certainly the case with *Vic and Sade*. In 1932, at the time the program begin airing, it was broadcast live; it was not recorded until 1937. Despite the fact that the Wisconsin Historical Society, in Madison, houses more than thirty boxes of the show's scripts, countless episodes were destroyed by Procter & Gamble, leaving many gaps. Finally, at the time this is being written, only one member of *Vic and Sade*'s cast survives: Dr. David Whitehouse, who played Russell in the final seasons.

This book is an exploration of some of the themes and ideas found within one of the greatest radio programs ever to grace the air, and now forgotten by so many. The show represented how Americans lived at the time, regarding leisure, entertainment, education, community, and so much more. These subjects will be explored in the context of Depression-era America and through the opinions of the era's elitist critics, who always thought they knew best. This study is limited to *Vic and Sade* in its first and longest-lasting incarnation, as a daily daytime radio program, from 1932 to 1944. It will not include the program's three later incarnations: an irregularly scheduled daytime show in 1945, which featured numerous new characters; a short-lived weekly thirty-minute nighttime serial in 1946, which had a live audience; and two short-lived television programs (1949 and 1957), both of which necessitated major format changes that redefined the program and moved it away from its original concept.

While *Vic and Sade* was the best-written comedy on radio and an example of the finest American comedy writing in general, it also provided an interesting critique of life in the mass society that had been fostered by the Great Depression. At a time when critics of radio and mass culture were portraying Americans as mindless sheep being herded from one vice and entertainment to another, Paul Rhymer was depicting the human race through the lens of a nice family who lived "halfway up in the next block."

PART I : THE MEDIA CONTEXT

One. Rhymer Is "Outstanding"

So proclaimed the November 13, 1929, edition of Illinois Wesleyan University's student newspaper, the *Argus*, in an article that celebrated Paul Rhymer and another alumnus, George Redman, both of whom had recently obtained jobs in radio with some level of success. Rhymer had attended the college in the mid–1920s, meeting his future wife, Mary Frances, and preparing for a future career as a writer. However, his father's illness forced Paul to leave the school before taking his degree. He parlayed his school connections into a career, however, when a fraternity brother helped him land a low-level writing job at NBC in Chicago.

The article points to Rhymer's work for sponsors such as "Studebaker Champions, Williams Oil-O-Matics [sic], Ted Fiorito [usually spelled Fio Rito] and his Edgewater Beach Hotel Orchestra as well as other music productions." Rhymer had also written what the paper described as "a series of vaudeville shows" for the radio and that he was also preparing his first "dramatic" series, *The Keystone Chronicles*, to be set in a small-town newspaper office. The student authors hail Rhymer as part of the "new school of playwrights" plying their trade in an "untried field," the exciting medium of radio. For the student writers at the *Argus*, radio seemed to be a treasure trove of reward, a field of immeasurable potential. They looked forward to a day, not far off, when broadcasting would mature and the "radio play" would surpass the offerings of the "current legitimate theatre."[1] For the *Argus*, the *Keystone Chronicles*, to debut that December 7, was a program of "untold possibilities," and the fitting culmination of an alumnus's glamorous first year with NBC.

However, Rhymer's radio life hadn't been entirely the type of artistic bohemian existence students imagined. At the time, Rhymer was a continuity writer for the National Broadcasting Company, a position and title borrowed from the more glamorous world of movies, that was about as low down on the scale of writing prestige as one could get. It was, in those days, the stepping stone toward upward mobility in the radio world. In the world of the cinema, continuity writing evolved from the need to explain to the crew how to set up shots and connect scenes together—"with Iris in's and Dissolves, Fade-outs, and Pan Downs's [sic]— and all the other technical phrases which are the continuity writer's private stock-in-trade," as *Vanity Fair* explained to its readers in 1922.[2] In radio, which had no pictures, the continuity writer's job was a step up, since his or her work would actually be read by an announcer and *heard* by audiences, describing for them what they might have seen had radio been a visual medium. However, little of it would be terribly memorable. Mary Frances would later explain that much of her husband's work as a continuity writer consisted of writing lines such as "And now the voices of the violins remind us 'it was only a paper moon'"[3] and similar filler. The writers, who worked together in cubicles in the Continuity Department, considered many of these filler lines to be quite silly, and they competed with each other to devise the most outrageous. Rhymer took great pride in scripting a line so silly that a distinguished Shakespearean actor waved the script in the air and told Rhymer, "I will *not* read this line."[4]

Yet despite the sometimes trivial nature of this position, Mary Frances stressed Paul's good fortune of having found employment during the Great Depression. And he made a success of it—so much so that the management of NBC assigned him to write programs after only six months, a high honor for a continuity writer and one fully worthy of an adulatory write-up in his alma mater's newspaper.

The *Argus* article served a dual purpose: paying respect to Redman and Rhymer while also highlighting Illinois Wesleyan's ability to train students for modern careers in the new medium of radio. As stated in the article, Rhymer had an impressive résumé for a continuity writer, but this only hinted at the work that was to follow. His early work, prior to *Vic and Sade*, both his short stories and his continuity writing, offers insight into the themes that the young writer would explore, as well as the evolution of his characters and humor. Paul Rhymer exercised his creativity in ways that his contemporaries were unable to match.

At the same time that young Rhymer was beginning his radio career, he was also exploring the literary world, seeking any outlet for his storytelling. However, as his radio duties increased, his output of literature sputtered and stopped, and eventually he must have recognized that his talents worked best in the broadcast medium. Rhymer had begun his story-writing career while still in high school, where he found much success. In 1924, Rhymer's short story "Reflection Marvelous" received Honorable Mention in Bloomington High School's annual Merwin Cup contest and appeared in the school's yearbook, *Aepix*. "Reflection Marvelous" is the story of Timothy Moore, a privileged high school sophomore who has "contracted a case of that common yet insidious malady—swelled head" and "had never experienced grief, hunger, necessity or the desire to amount to something."[5] Timothy's life is irrevocably changed when, thanks to a life of excess, he contracts tuberculosis. As he struggles to regain his health, Timothy undergoes a metamorphosis. From a boy who once wore a studied look of "boredom and world-wisdom" assumed an "an expression of good-will, joviality and even happiness,"[6] he became studious and parents thought him a suitable role model for their sons. Timothy even took to the airwaves, conducting a radio program called *The Wind from the Rockies*.

In short, the "giant of evil, that devastator of humanity, that deceitful pet whom we find all too late has sharp claws concealed under soft paws,"[7] tuberculosis had proven to be a mirror through which Timothy Moore had been given the opportunity to see himself as others had seen him. Whether due to Paul Rhymer's age at the time it was written, or perhaps by design, "Reflection Marvelous" is notable in its lack of cynicism and its abundance of hope—characteristics that would not be readily apparent in some of Rhymer's other manuscripts. "Reflection Marvelous" finds Rhymer visiting the theme of physical challenge and loss; however, in this instance the ending is unequivocally a happy one, complete with Timothy Moore's marriage to the "sweetest and most intelligent person in the world," and having the "the most successful law business in the Southwest."[8]

The following year, Rhymer would win the Merwin Cup with an entry entitled "Crilotte and the Engineer." It is interesting to note when reading the story, the protagonist of which is a cab driver, that Paul Rhymer would himself be occupied in that line of work in the not too distant future. "Crilotte and the Engineer" is an almost exuberant love story in which cab driver Joe Martin, for whom the "sound of the working engine was music to his ears, the feel of the wheel in his hands was a joy, and the sensation of swiftly moving cords under him made a warm place in his heart" finds something that rivals his love of engines: Crilotte

Franklin, a young woman just out of high school, who startles Joe because he "never thought a jane [sic] could moon-eye me like this."[9] Yet "moon-eye" him she does, and marriage would seem imminent were it not for the fact that Joe insists on getting "enough filthy lucre to keep both of us from living as cheaply as one," despite Crilotte's protestations that the "love in a cottage" is not without appeal to her.[10]

The apparent solution to the "filthy lucre" issue comes in the form of an automobile race with a $20,000 prize. Joe and Crilotte work tirelessly to fix the perfect race car for Joe's engine, only to have him break his arm while finishing work on it just hours before the race. In what must have seemed a bold endorsement of gender equality, not just for the period but also for the publication, Crilotte takes Joe's place during a hazardous four-hour race and comes tantalizingly close to winning. Despite the loss, Crilotte still saves the day when she reveals to Joe that, in her self-assumed role of his future wife, she had sold his engine for $30,000, leaving Joe to do "the only logical thing."[11]

Although Rhymer does not spell out precisely what the "logical thing" to do was, the reader can make certain assumptions. Beyond the fun of the story, and even in spite of Joe's accident and the treacherous race, this story points toward the strong female characters that Rhymer would depict in upcoming professionally published stories, like "Hen" and, in a different context, the character of Sade. These are women who can race cars, run ranches, or repair washing machines using newspapers, elastic braces, and molasses.

Four years later, at the end of his college career, Rhymer once again turned to story writing, perhaps dreaming of a literary career as he prepared for life after college. In September 1928, "Hen" appeared in *College Humor*, a publication begun by Collegiate World Publishing in 1920. By 1928, the popular magazine boasted such contributors as Groucho Marx, F. Scott Fitzgerald, Zelda Fitzgerald, and Heywood Broun. By the time Paul Rhymer contributed "Hen," appearing in *College Humor*'s pages could guarantee an audience of 800,000 readers, even at the seemingly high cover price of thirty-five cents[12] in an era when *Popular Mechanics*, for example, sold for twenty-five cents and *Time* for fifteen.

"Hen" is the story of Bill, a physically disfigured railway worker whose tall tales initially appear to be a means of compensating for his shortcomings. Ultimately, however, readers learn that Bill's seemingly ridiculous stories may well be true.

Bill Crane's very name is itself a ruse, as Bill's real name is Thorton Royal Crane, a five-foot-tall man with three missing fingers, "the first and second on his right hand and the thumb on his left hand."[13] As the narrator explains, one was lost in an industrial accident, the second while he was showing off. Bill Crane is more evasive about the fate of the third finger: "I'll admit I was a fool, but I'm never going to admit just how big a fool I was."[14]

Crane seems determined to relate self-aggrandizing stories that leave readers wondering what is fact and what is fantasy. He is also prone to alienating those around him by making "revolting remarks," guaranteed to send dinner companions reeling from the table.

The majority of Crane's tales revolve around his amorous feelings toward the wife of a ranger, Henrietta, whom he calls "Hen." "She knocked me down once with a left hander," he recalls. "She did it 'cause I took a piece of pie after she told me not to."[15] Unrequited love, it seems, is the only kind of love he knows. Undeterred by Hen's rebuff, Crane only pursues her more aggressively: "I used to bring her kids candy, and once I bought her husband a shirt."[16]

Crane likely believes his chances with Hen improve when her husband is shot in the back and dies. Despite a search, led by Crane, there was no success in finding a perpetrator, though it is implied that it was, in fact, Crane who fired the fatal shot. Immediately after

In the 1920s and 1930s, there was a thriving market for short fiction in magazines. Paul Rhymer tried his hand at publishing in fiction magazines, but he discovered his true calling in scriptwriting instead (Library of Congress).

her husband's death, Hen assumed the responsibilities of the family farm. Soon thereafter, Crane asked for her hand in marriage, a proposal she flatly refused. "I asked her to get married every chance I got," Bill tells the narrator, "but she always turned me down. I just sat around and pined—all I had to do anyway."[17] More bad luck befalls Hen when her farm burns to the ground and her cattle escape, acts for which her would-be suitor takes credit, confident that they were justified by his love. These revelations startle his listener, who asks incredulously: "You stole the cattle!"

"Yeah, got run outta town," he answers remorselessly. He then adds with some relief: "I'm right' glad I got run out in a hurry. [...] I mighta confessed to burnin' the house."[18]

All of Crane's efforts had been directed at convincing Hen to marry him as a last resort. "She certainly was a wonderful woman," he says wistfully. When asked if the shooter was ever apprehended, he says, "I don't recollect as they ever did."[19]

In many ways, "Hen" hints at the long-winded tales that Sade's uncle Fletcher would tell years later; rambling and, at times, nonsensical, it derives its humor from the improbable extremes to which Crane is willing to go to secure the love of a disinterested party, and the nonchalant manner in which he approaches his actions. In this case, Rhymer attempts to exaggerate the humor by juxtaposing the tall tales and grandiose efforts of a small man within what would otherwise be common circumstances. "Hen" also features the use of dialect humor, which would become a staple of *Vic and Sade*; dialog is written as the characters would speak:

> "Goin' to town," I inquired.
> "No."
> "What are you dressin' for then?"
> "Just to be doin' something."[20]

Although "Hen" is somewhat primitive in development and execution, the style would become a staple of Rhymer's later work. The character of Crane also introduces into Rhymer's work an element of physical disfigurement, something that would become a regular theme in this early period.

"Hen" was accompanied by a brief, humorous autobiographical sketch that showed Rhymer was able to view himself in the same humorous light as his characters. In the sketch, Rhymer writes of his move from Fulton, Illinois, to Bloomington, and his subsequent enrollment in Illinois Wesleyan University. It was at the university, he continues, that he "wore wide pants" and "broke the intercollegiate record by four dates in one day." In addition to that admirable feat, he boasts of having "an immense vocabulary."[21]

Rhymer produced another dark comedy set in the railroads in "Yella," a story submitted to, but not published by the *Forum*, a prestigious New York literary magazine (it had published William Faulkner's "A Rose for Emily" in April 1930) that would go out of business at the end of 1930. Paul Rhymer submitted "Yella" to the *Forum* from the address he used prior to 1932, so it seems likely to have been written around 1929 or 1930. Again, it features the tall tales of Bill Crane; however, this time the emphasis is on a character called McClaughry, who was renowned for his machismo: "He could whip two men when he was giied, and three when he was sober," Crane reported to his attentive audience. "He was strong same like an ox, too. Could carry a signal motor up a twenty-five-foot pole with one arm ... he was a tough monkey."[22]

Despite the feats of strength and bravery recounted by Crane, McClaughry could not overcome the battle he waged with his nervous stomach when confronted by the woman he loved.

> Every time McClaughry saw this girl he got sick to his stomach. She was uncommon pretty, too, and Bill could a had her, I think, bein' as he was a big, good lookin' cuss, but he couldn't even get a glimpse of her without getting' awful sick. He was crazy about her, too. Used to talk about her in his sleep, and rehearse meetin' her.[23]

McClaughry was unable to conquer his malady and, after a torturous attempt at meeting his dream girl that left him thinking "she was so disgustin' as to make him sick," he committed suicide courtesy of the Number Two train. His remains were collected by "two calm gents and a couple of undertakers."[24]

Although the story was greeted with a rejection form from the editors of the *Forum*, stating that the story "does not prove available for our magazine" some hope came in the shape of a handwritten note reading, in part, "Rather clever and rather amusing, but not sufficiently so."[25] The editors did, however, invite Rhymer to try them again sometime, though, of course, it was not to be since the magazine, which tried to buy a new lease on life during the Depression by merging with the *Century* in the spring of 1930, ceased to publish shortly thereafter.

In another story, "Adjustment," amputation would play a significant role, continuing the author's apparent fascination with deformity and disfigurement. The short story appeared in the October 1931 edition of *College Life*, a publication "full of snappy, peppy, and breezy stories, cartoons, and jokes." At a quarter an issue, its chief virtue was that the fiction magazine sold for less than its competitor, *College Humor*. In this case, Rhymer attempted to write a "dramatic interlude of gripping power," which produced mixed results.[26] "Adjustment" is the tale of Lewis Crane, college all-star, who lost his arm while rescuing another teen. At a party in his honor, Lewis attempts to come to terms with his loss.

> Lewis groaned and tried not to listen. He was going to be pitied! Who was he to be pitied? Why, just last year he could take on any two men in the university in a rough and tumble bout; he had run away with the popularity contest; he had dated Cynthia McClaughry consistently. Pitied![27]

At the same time he is forced to face rejection from Cynthia, the object of his affection. It is after she rejects him that the story reaches its intended dramatic climax, as the pair narrowly escapes an automobile accident:

> Just then a car bore down upon them from the opposite direction, a large car with undimmed, extra-brilliant lights. Lewis and Cynthia looked at each other. They stopped laughing. In the eyes of both were great tears. Lewis saw something besides tears in Cynthia's eyes. And then the boy put his left arm around the girl. And the girl stopped the car and put two arms around the boy and strained him to her. And then both laughed a little, and finally, a great deal as, facing each other, they found understanding.[28]

Rhymer then gives Lewis his happy (albeit slightly contrived) ending, not out of pity, but love. While one accident took something from him, another (near) accident gives Lewis that which he desires. However, stepping away from his forte, Rhymer seems awkward; the tale stumbles and the strain of writing a serious piece is apparent; the results fail to live up to the publication's promise of "snappy, peppy, and breezy writing." Ironically, though, snappy, peppy, and breezy would be an apt description of the type of writing that would help Rhymer rise from continuity writer to full-fledged writer at NBC.

Making Transitions

The dark side of Paul Rhymer's humor didn't disappear as he moved from short stories to radio plays. He remained interested in human curiosities and anomalies, but soon found himself mining these themes, not as a student or aspiring writer, but as a commercial writer—

both literally and figuratively—when he was offered the opportunity to begin developing scripts for actual programs, not just the filler read by announcers. Rhymer seized the opportunity and began developing ideas that ranged from the conventional to the absurd. His first major production fell close to the conventional end of the spectrum.

When Rhymer was profiled in the *Argus* in 1929, the article focused on what they described as his "upcoming" *Keystone Chronicle*, a "series of dramatic productions"[29] set in a newspaper in a small town, not unlike his own hometown of Bloomington, Illinois. *Keystone Chronicle* was situated in the paper's small office in the home of its editor and his daughter and focused on small-town gossip and the program's sponsor, Keystone Steel and Wire Company.

Keystone Chronicle was, at first, a striking example of the level of control that sponsors exercised over their programs. Sponsors' efforts were initially limited in radio's early days, as the networks feared a more aggressive approach would be regarded by listeners as an intrusion. However, as sponsors increasingly recognized the power of the new medium their efforts grew bolder. Eventually, products came to play a major role in many programs and, in some cases, the program was actually secondary to the product. This was the case in early episodes of the *Keystone Chronicle*, which was first auditioned (the early term for a test episode or pilot) in November 1929. These shows exemplify the sponsor's ability to shape program content. Consider the following dialog:

> DUDLEY: Got that ad, I see. Read it; let's hear what it's like.
> BUCK (*READS*): "Red Barn Fence" helps you do a better job of farming. That's the fence with the Red Brand Top Wire. That means the fence is made of Copper Bearing. "*Galvan-nealed*" and will last years longer than regular galvanized wire—Get it at Henry Gates' Hardware Store.[30]

In other instances the pitch was somewhat less obvious, but clear nonetheless:

> MILLER: And you're *still* hammering along. That's the way with a lot of farmers. They work and work and work and it's darn far few of 'em that go along that go along as fast as they ought to. I've been reading in the Keystone Steel and Wire Company "Farm Planning" book about a fellow in Albert Lea, Minnesota—Theodore Torgeson—who started out farming with a horse and wagon and today owns a hundred acres of debt. He was a bright chap.[31]

Moore's fellow farmer, Miller, leads him into further discussion regarding the virtues of planning and the highly useful Keystone Steel and Wire Company "Farm Planning" book. Their discussion becomes one of, if not *the*, dominant theme of the program. This was to be expected, as the program—one of the first serials to use a written script—originated in the Continuity Department at NBC and was intended to use Rhymer's skills as a continuity writer to create a program as, essentially, "filler" between the advertising messages.[32]

By setting the *Keystone Chronicle*'s offices in the Dudleys' home, Rhymer is able to plausibly compensate for the lack of news generated at the paper with gossip and family events. Indeed, aside from the occasional bit of town gossip or reports of community events gathered by "star reporter" Buck Harkin, the paper was primarily concerned with developing strong advertising copy for Red Barn Fencing. In addition to Buck's weekly phone conversation with Red Barn representatives, during which he detailed the advantages of their product and "farm planning" system, editor Jim Dudley was an outspoken advocate for the product and it benefits, proselytizing to anyone who would listen. Although the approach of integrating spokespeople as characters would later be used with great success by the likes of Harlow Wilcox touting Johnson's Wax on *The Fibber McGee and Molly Show*, the heavy-handed tactics found in early episodes of *Keystone Chronicle* left little room for entertainment. Often, nearly a quarter of the script was devoted to discussion of the Red Barn Fence and farm planning.

There was some irony in the fact that Rhymer was writing a program about a newspaper. It had not been long since he had been dismissed from the *Pantagraph* after editors discovered he was fabricating sources. Rhymer, of course, realized that making up dialog for imaginary characters was a portable skill, one that was better suited to fiction writing than news writing.

Gradually (and wisely) the program's approach shifted. The Red Barn Fence ad copy was still reviewed and listeners were reminded by the announcer to write to Keystone for their complimentary copies of farm-planning booklets; but, the show began to emphasize characters and simple plots, particularly the "love" triangle between the perpetually inept star reporter, Buck, Alice Dudley, whose periodic singing and piano playing offered a respite from talk of fences and farming, and a sensitive poet called Rhiny. Despite the highly structured context, Paul Rhymer's wit and, at times, irreverence, began to shine through. In one scene Buck is approached by a book salesman whose volumes contain the knowledge of the world:

> SALESMAN: Can you tame a lion, make ice cream at home, perform a minor operation, make a speech on short notice shingle a roof, operate an airplane, mix concrete, embalm a corpse...?
> BUCK: I can't do none of them things.
> SALESMAN: You can never tell when you might be called upon to do some of them.[33]

The salesman continues to list useless trivia, which Buck immediately shrugs off with a "Naw." He remains steadfast until the salesman reveals that that, in addition to containing 457 ways of making money, the volumes also contain sure ways of getting girls: "With these books *any* woman will succumb to your blandishments. Simply follow the directions, and the one you adore will be craving your patronage."[34] With that encouragement, Buck relents, certain that he will finally win the love of Alice.

For the most part that characters in *Keystone Chronicle* remain one-dimensional, a fact that can be attributed to the program's highly structured format. That aside, it is possible to see Paul Rhymer working in a refined setting over an extended period of time and introducing small touches of irreverence with his characters in a believable manner. This comes through at times, such as when Buck inadvertently displays his romantic ineptitude as he tries to compete for the love of Alice with Rhiny, the pretentious, poetry-writing romantic. In one episode, Buck presents Alice with a series of birthday gifts, ranging from a dog, a dress, and a gallon of perfume, all of which mortify her. Only when Alice learns that Buck has paid for her gifts by agreeing to parachute from an airplane does she manage to appreciate his efforts. In another episode, the well-intentioned Buck, inspired by a recent sermon, decides it is his mission to bring happiness and light to all around him, regardless of how annoying his actions may prove.

In the spring of 1930, Alice's sanctimonious aunt Hassie was introduced. Hassie disapproved of everything, and liked no one. Her presence also emphasized the generation gap that existed between she and the rest of the cast. As the characters on *Vic and Sade* would later do, Hassie brought many off-mic acquaintances to the show; in her case, discussing the acquaintances served to illustrate parables. Though she often digressed, she did, eventually, make a point. In the March 15, 1930, episode, for example, Hassie attempts to prove to Buck that "children should be seen and not heard," a feat she accomplishes by telling the tale of

Emil Walters's son Sherlock, who threw a tomato at the milkman. This milkman, she mentions apropos of nothing, "didn't make a go of the blacksmith business," then adds, "I personally don't think he'll ever make a go of anything." Having established Emil's age and the career path of his victim, Hassie proceeds to be a strong advocate for the woodshed as an "institution," calling for it to be "revived with pomp and pageantry."[35]

Although rural Americans had allegedly become "intensely interested" in the *Keystone Chronicle*, according to *Big Farmer* magazine,[36] the show ended in 1931. More commercial message than lively serial, it left its creator looking for a more creative and humorous outlet.

Moving Toward Humor

During the run of the *Keystone Chronicle*, Rhymer continued to develop new, more interesting material. In one particularly innovative script, dated August 29, 1930, *The Busyman Program* (also labeled *The Busy-Man Program*), is a parody that takes an average day's radio programming and condenses it into a single program, hosted by "Maham Grackamee," an obvious anagram of NBC's popular broadcaster Graham McNamee. The faux announcer astutely notes, "You haven't time to sit around listening to nasty old radio programs. Of course not. You have work to do." He then proceeds to briskly guide listeners through a dizzying variety of miniature programs that demonstrate Rhymer's ability to capture the essence of then-current media.

With the sound of a starter's pistol, listeners are treated to the finer things at a breakneck pace. True to its word, the program moves swiftly, first through orchestral interludes and messages from absurd sponsors, including the Spunkwater Brothers, makers of "roots, herbs, garbs, barks" and other natural products, and Stein Brothers' Apple Butter Company. This transitions to an educational segment in which unwitting listeners are subjected to truncated lessons in Double Dutch before hearing near-apocalyptic weather reports of "cyclones, tornadoes, wind, rain, lightning and thunder" in an area never revealed—all read at a breakneck pace.

The script further reveals Rhymer's fascination for disfigurement, pairing this theme with topical parody. The *Busyman Program* presents Mother Merriwell (possibly a parody of Mother Moynihan, from Irna Phillips's popular soap opera *Painted Dreams*) in a special segment for children:

> Hello, folks, this is Mother Merriwell with you again. Everybody happy? Good! Now what do you think Mother Merriwell has for you today? Would you like you to know how to amputate your leg at home? *Would* you, kiddies? It's *such* fun! And perfectly safe, too. Go out in the barn and get daddy's nice axe. Place your leg across a chair and...[37]

At this point Mother Merriwell is interrupted by a symphony orchestra playing innocuous music.

As the *Busyman* programming continues, Lucullus Rogers hosts a sporting event (of sorts) in the operating room of the aptly named Cutmore Hospital, where the doctors and nurses engage in what could best be described as a battle with a patient "who is looking fine" at the start of the procedures, but who is unable to withstand the enthusiastic practitioners' cheer: "Say 'ah' 'ah' Sis-Boom, Bah—Cutmore Hospital Rah, Rah, Rah!"[38] As the doctor begins his work, Rogers reports that the floor is dripping in blood, in "glorious patterns" no less. There is a frenzy of excitement as the patient struggles in vain: "Fight, doc!" Rogers yells. "He's operating with a lot of pep now. Looks like it's the doctor's day. He's working like mad! He's going! The patient can't stop him! Yeah! The patient died. Hooray!"[39]

One should not get the idea *The Busyman Program* consisted entirely of debauchery; it covered a gamut of topics and offered prospective listeners absurdist humor, all within a single script. The culturally inclined businessman could benefit from brief and rapidly interrupted operatic segments and a production of "High Fever" by the Snappy Shakespeare Players, which is interspersed with melodramatic romance with hog futures so that business and art share equal priority. Rhymer would reference Shakespeare time and again through the years of *Vic and Sade* and also in an unproduced undated short routine for the *National Farm and Home Hour*. *The Busyman Program* is a microcosm of the era's radio programming; it highlights the commercialization of the medium as well as its sensationalized content while still being written for potential broadcasting.

Rhymer also worked to inject humor in his continuity writing, especially for some of NBC's comedy programs, including *The Three Doctors* starring Russell Pratt, Ransom Sherman, and Joe Rudolph, a trio of comics who were popular in the 1920s. The comedy team later had a regular segment on NBC's *Club Matinee* on WMAQ out of Chicago, which Ransom Sherman hosted. Rhymer's introductions set the stage for Pratt, Sherman, and Rudolph, while at the same time exercising his increasingly well-honed sense of humor:

> Good afternoon, ladies and gentlemen. Grinding up its loins, so to speak, and hoping for the best, the National Broadcasting Company brings you *The Three Doctors*, formerly the *Minneapolis Symphony Orchestra*, who will at one and the same time present a radio program, grow a mole just above the right temple, and imitate a bathtub half filled with water. The Three Doctors, Pratt, Sherman, and Rudolph…[40]

Rather than writing mundane introductions and exits, Rhymer crafted playful, witty material that, in some instances, foreshadows the dialog that listeners would be experiencing on *Vic and Sade* less than one year later. In the opening to the October 15, 1931, episode of *Club Matinee*, the announcer, Charles Lyon, states, "He who addresses you now feels a small catch in his throat, a tremor in every bodily muscle, and a warm little glow way down deep inside." He goes on to explain that the Three Doctors are there to provide "all sorts of microphone machinations, including japes, dodges, and jingles, not to mention songs, dances, and other features of that kidney."[41] It's easy to imagine Victor Gook going on a similar verbal spree while teasing Sade after returning home from the office.

As seen in the *Keystone Chronicle*, in some programs, a sponsor's product played a substantive role; in *Fibber McGee and Molly*, for example, spokesperson Harlow Wilcox brought Johnson and Johnson products front and center. Paul Rhymer, however, took a different approach in presenting Orange Crush to listeners of the *Three Doctors*:

> RANSE: Just the kind of charming warm Sunday morning for a heaping big drink of refreshing a … refreshing … a … a …
> RUSS: Precisely. A refreshing drink of Apple Smash.
> RANSE: No—not Apple Smash. To the contrary, this is just the kind of charming morning for a refreshing drink of … of … Pomegranate Punch … a …
> RUSS: Drat it … Cranberry Cramp…[42]

Ranse and Russ continue to speculate on precisely which drink would be perfect on a "charming warm Sunday morning" and eventually forget the name of their radio program. It is not until the end of the segment that someone says, "Naw, I think it was Orange *Crush*." A similar

Orange Crush, seen here at a 1926 industrial exposition, was one of many companies that sponsored radio programs and used them to promote their products. Paul Rhymer worked to make the commercials entertaining while still reminding listeners of *The Three Doctors* to buy Orange Crush (Library of Congress).

approach to promoting Orange Crush can be found in other scripts. Unfortunately, there is no record of the sponsor's reaction to these advertisements. However, this form of advertising, which essentially distracts the audience into receiving the advertiser's message by burying it amid a sea of entertaining jokes, is not very far removed from the "entertaining" commercials of today—or televised product placement. Rhymer, however, would occasionally get into trouble due to advertisers' demands. After one 1933 *Vic and Sade* episode implied that canned foods could spoil once opened (Rush and Vic were making dinner from cans but got caught up talking and left them open on the counter, prompting them to head out for hamburgers, worried that the food had gone bad from "staying in the cans"[43]), the American Canned Foods Association protested to NBC. The New York office, it seems, had sent word to Chicago that a future episode needed to subtly promote the virtues of canned food, appealing specifically to Rhymer's "brilliant" work in continuity—and that the network required copies of all future scripts to monitor for unintentional offense to future network sponsors.[44]

During this same period Rhymer worked on a children's radio program, *Smokey Rogers: Fire Chief*, that featured a popular clown in the Chicago region. Each week Smokey would offer his audience a new story that illustrated the power and dangers of fire. In one episode, for example, Smokey recounts the story of Jimmy, a young boy who feels that fires are fun and take place for his own entertainment. However, Jimmy's attitude changes when his own home catches fire due to a bracket chimney, and Jimmy's younger sister is nearly trapped in the blaze. Having experienced firsthand the effects of fire, both Jimmy and his father learn their respective lessons: Jimmy, the dangers of fire; his father, the danger of bracket chimneys. The idea of fire as a form of entertainment would recur in the November 23, 1933, episode of *Vic and Sade*, in which the neighborhood gathers to watch a smoldering fire at the Kreiders.' The fire has resulted in the "the most excitement we've had around here in a long time."[45] Though a tragedy for victims of the fire, the sensationalistic nature of the event appeals to the onlookers because, as Sade explains, "It's just the way people are made, the way they're made."[46]

Rhymer tinkered with many story ideas before being awarded his own program, and he continued to do so even afterward. His drafts varied in innovation and creativity. One script, dated April 25, 1931, entitled "The Barbershop Philosophers," establishes what may have been an audition for a series. The script follows the antics of two barbers, Elmer and Will, who also happen to be philosophers by night. The short script plays off the "rube" humor popularized by Chester Lauck and Norris Goff in *Lum and Abner* (1931–1954), the story of two scheming Southern "rubes" who ran a small town general store, and, to a lesser extent, *Bushwood Mercantile Company* and the *Si and Elmer* program. In the case of *Lum and Abner*, Lauck and Norris drew upon their own experiences growing up in Arkansas in much the same way that *Vic and Sade* and *Keystone Chronicle* reflected Paul Rhymer's experiences in the Midwest.

Rhymer's attempt to mimic the "rube" style was flawed. While the dialect mirrors the popular perception of rural speech, the humor is forced and contrived. The two barbers retire "after the day's shaving and shearing and searing is done, to soothe the jaded sprit with the delights of song and the fruits of deep reflection."[47] These reflections include pondering the wisdom of "Edgar Allan Shakespeare's" views on music, and their discussion of "Colonel Shakespeare's" philosophy on music's ability to "soothe a horse of a different color." Such musings provides the perfect opportunity for a musical interlude featuring "The Spanish Cavalier." Perhaps recognizing the flaws in "The Barbershop Philosophers," Rhymer tried again with "The Barbershop Boys," an unfinished one-and-a-half page script featuring Will and Elmer playing songs and discussing relationships.

As he struggled to develop a winning concept for his own series, Rhymer continued his continuity writing, which included, among other things, a two-page proposed script for a humorous sketch to air on the *National Farm and Home Hour*, a government-sponsored agricultural discussion and variety program known as "the farmer's bulletin board."[48] Despite being deemed "pretty good, Paul" by NBC programming executive Frank Mullen, the network doubted whether it was appropriate for the farm program, and it was easy to see why.

The script's conceit is for a twenty-four-act play with forty-five cast members entitled "Romeo and Juliet Were Two Young People Who Needed an Automobile Pretty Bad and So They Went and Bought One Like Any Two Young People Who Need One." We are informed at the play's opening that twenty-three of the forty-five parts will be played by Donahue Montgomery. The two-page script is to be performed by two actors, credited as Bruce and Wolf. The pair assumes the roles of the play's ensemble. While the script is both absurd and clever, it also could be accused of containing a good deal of filler: the entire title, "Romeo and Juliet Were Two Young People Who Needed an Automobile Pretty Bad and So They Went and Bought One Like Any Two Young People Who Need One," appears no fewer than five times in the space of two typewritten pages, totaling perhaps two minutes of airtime.

"Three Deathbeds in a Row": Later Experiments

At a time when he was writing at least five scripts per week for a program that would air daily, he still found the time to create new, unrelated radio plays. A couple of examples give the flavor of these extracurricular adventures. One was *A Deathbed Romance*, a play written in 1933 from a treatment he had developed sometime before. Two versions of the script exist, with some differences. While NBC executives thought the script would make a fine series, especially for a pharmaceutical sponsor, the show was never produced. The play is a charming, if conventional, story of Doctor Gray, a small-town physician.

Back from a late-night house call, Dr. Gray finds himself recounting his first days in town as a doctor and how he not only saved "three deathbeds in a row" but also "annexed the sweetest wife in the United States" to the young drugstore clerk.[49] Gray recalls that, on his first night in town, he encountered a retired physician who had become a hypochondriac, Colonel Allen R. Donaldson, and his daughter, Sylvia, with whom Dr. Gray is immediately enamored. Colonel Donaldson challenges Gray, although not medically. His brushes with death pose little threat as Gray discovers upon making a follow-up visit to his patient:

> GRAY: He was upstairs dying in a frightful agony ... that's what he told Sylvia ... but I happen to know while he was drawing his last few gasps he was also playing poker with a couple of cronies of his. (*THEY LAUGH.*)[50]

As the colonel continues to insist that he is dying, Dr. Gray finds himself drawn to the beautiful Sylvia: "Perhaps it wasn't quiet ethical of me, but while the colonel was supposedly expiring upstairs his physician was in the rose-arbor telling his daughter that she had lovely eyes."[51] Only when Dr. Gray springs on the colonel (and Sylvia) the news that he and Sylvia are marrying does the colonel rouse from his deathbed and free himself from the shackles of death.

Written not long after *Vic and Sade*'s debut, *A Deathbed Romance* bears a resemblance to early episodes of *Vic and Sade*; its humor is subtle and situated in an everyday context. While the play does demonstrate Rhymer's versatility as a writer, the writing is conservative and lacking the absurdity and irreverence that dominated so much of his early work.

One of the more peculiar pieces to be found in Paul Rhymer's papers is a script for an episode of *The Mickey Mouse Theater*. The script initially appears to be a satire; it doesn't follow the format of Disney's *Mickey Mouse Theater of the Air*, which began airing in February 1938 and ran until May of that year to promote the release of *Snow White and the Seven Dwarfs* (from 1937). The script centers on two children, Grace and Bill, who bring images of Mickey and Minnie Mouse to life by tracing them from a picture book. Upon springing to life, Mickey announces that it's time for his birthday party. He promptly orders the children to trace all of his other friends, including Samuel Seal, Alex Alligator, Horace Horse, George W. Giraffe, and a menagerie of others so that they, too, can come to life and join the fun. Assuming that they will be guests at Mickey's party, Bill and Grace eagerly comply, only to be informed by their hero that they are not invited to the shindig: "You can't join the party, children," he explains. "Flesh and blood folk can't go to Mickey Mouse parties." Though disappointed, Mickey's discrimination proved fortunate for the children as the party erupted into a savage depiction of the food chain, with each animal consuming smaller prey, and only the celebrity mouse couple surviving:

> LITTLE GIRL GRACE: Oh, Bill, Emma Elephant swallowed everybody at Mickey Mouse's Birthday party!
> LITTLE BOY BILL: I bet she didn't swallow Mickey and Minnie!
> [...]
> (*FUNNY LITTLE WHISTLE TOOTS*)
> MICKEY: You're right, Bill!
> MINNIE: You're wrong, Grace![52]

After the ruckus, Mickey and Minnie are "fine and dandy" and looking forward to their next party.

Despite the satirical nature of the script, it is impossible to dismiss it solely as folly. In a July 1938 letter from the Story Department of Disney Productions John C. Rose refers to his familiarity with Rhymer's work (though not this script) and says, "We secretly hoped that someday we could get you out here with us." He goes on to say that "having mentioned your name to the gang, including Walt Disney, it seemed high time that I get a line on your future plans."[53] There is, unfortunately, no record of Rhymer's response to Disney; perhaps he feared spending his days creating rodent versions of *Vic and Sade*, or his affection for the show he had created outweighed the potential of being a name behind someone else's animated creation. Perhaps he wrote this *Mickey Mouse* script as a humorous rejoinder to the Disney offer and what he likely saw as the restrictions he'd face as a Disney writer.

Summing Up

In 1931, preparing to launch his own show, Rhymer could look back on an impressive body of work in his short time working for NBC. The influence of mass culture is apparent in much of this early work. Scripts like *The Busyman Program* reflect and parody the sensationalized nature of a culture that was, according to its critics, intended to appeal to the lowest common denominator. The unproduced script for "The Barbershop Philosophers," with its stab at "rube" humor, is an attempt to emulate popular programming of the day. Similarly, his later effort, *A Deathbed Romance*, found Rhymer assuming a writing style not unlike that found in romance magazines and the growing daytime radio market. As he was to do in *Vic and Sade*, Rhymer used his forum (or potential forums) as a means to critique the absurdities of radio broadcasting.

While these efforts were not successful in that they did not become long-running series, they did lay the groundwork for Rhymer's most important work, the program that would define his legacy, that of the creator of the longest, most sustained interrogation of mass culture and its effect on everyday American life.

Two. The Birth of *Vic and Sade*

Shortly after the conclusion of *Keystone Chronicle* and *Smokey Rodgers*, Rhymer was approached by NBC's Clarence Mesner to produce a family program for Procter & Gamble. At this stage of the radio industry, sponsors had taken a more active role in programming decisions and had grown increasing powerful, not only suggesting program content or personalities but also requesting that entire programs revolve around their products. Dutiful employee that he was, Paul Rhymer set out to create the family fare that Procter & Gamble requested. Given the nature of *Vic and Sade* and the relationship he would eventually come to have with the program—single-handedly writing each of the program's more than 3,500 episodes—one would think that Rhymer enthusiastically embraced the opportunity. Not so. According to Esther Shultz of the *Chicago American*, "So little did Mr. Rhymer like the job that pressure had to be put upon him before he would continue it."[1] Others confirmed Rhymer's reticent attitude toward the project, noting that he would hide behind his newspaper to avoid discussing the project.

The typical process for launching a new show involved preparing an audition for key decision makers. These auditions were similar to the contemporary television pilot, a chance to preview a program and evaluate its potential for success. It was also a means of making necessary changes and doing some fine-tuning. On March 28, 1932, the audition tape of *Vic and Sade* was broadcast to an audience that consisted primarily of NBC executives like Paul Rhymer's boss, Clarence Mesner, and P&G's director of programming, William Ramsey.

The program featured only two voices: Art Van Harvey, in the role of Victor Gook; and, in the role of his wife, Sade, Bernadine Flynn. (Van Harvey and Flynn would eventually be paid about $600 a week apiece when the show went to series.) Flynn had had a long career, relatively speaking, that began in Madison, Wisconsin, where she studied drama under Zona Gale, a novelist and playwright whose work focused on local themes. Flynn eventually found herself on Broadway, which *Radio Stars* magazine explained "helped [her] to get into radio." Following her time on Broadway she decided to make the move to Chicago, reasoning, "I might have a better chance in Chicago—not so much competition!"[2] Art Van Harvey had a very different introduction to radio—and to acting. He had spent much of his professional life in advertising before turning to brokerage services, then vaudeville and, finally, radio, largely as a result of the economic upheaval of the period. Born Arthur H. Van Berschot in 1883, he had always dreamed of being an actor, despite his mother's belief that actors were the devil's emissaries.[3] Both actors would become so identified with their roles that Flynn once said that she did not know where Sade ended and she began; for his part, Van Harvey answered to "Vic" from the NBC staff for the series' entire run.

The characters these two actors portrayed were multifaceted from the beginning, though they would continue to develop over time. In 1942, shortly after *Vic and Sade*'s tenth anniversary, *Radio and Television Mirror* offered readers "*Vic and Sade* in Living Portraits." Their descriptions of Vic and Sade provide both an idea of how the characters were then presented and a contrast with their present and future selves. Victor Gook, the *Mirror* proclaimed, was a "delightful, amazing and wholly down to earth fellow with the wonderful quality of always being able to say and do the things that coat small town trouble." The adulatory description went on to note that "Vic is more like an overgrown boy than a man." Sade, on the other hand, "combines a certain lecturing toughness around her family with an inner nature that is actually timid as a rabbit."[4] That timidity, however, won't prevent her from telling Vic when he's engaged in a "darn fool scheme."[5] Paul Rhymer's own 1935 assessment provides more insight into the program's early period and the way he first imagined his husband-and-wife team. In his assessment, Rhymer paints Vic as a man who is "content" despite the fact that he is unlikely to advance at Consolidated Kitchenware beyond his present position. Rhymer continues:

> Somewhat of a braggart at home, he is the greatest of citizens at work and among his men friends. A good and loyal worker, he is well liked.... For his wife he has a deep and enduring affection, together with a vast admiration which he would just as soon not know about.[6]

According to Rhymer, Sade is "beginning to realize" that she is no longer a girl; a realization she that she doesn't entirely understand. Rhymer, reflecting the gendered-biased roles of the period, noted that she "was in the dark about most things that are going in the world." However, Rhymer added that "in her own kitchen she's as deft, wise and capable as any human being could be."[7] Sade, though not denying an interest in anything outside of her home, does suggest a limited understanding and intellect, something she fears could ruin her relationship with Vic.

We see hints of Rhymer's descriptions in the early episodes; certainly Vic shows an indication of what Rhymer refers to as a "brisk sense of humor and an eye for the ridiculous."[8] The script for *Vic and Sade*'s audition reveals early indications of what is to come in the series. The episode, like so many of *Vic and Sade*'s, was set in the couple's home; though it would be years before it would be described as the "small house halfway up in the next block," it seems a safe assumption that it was the same Virginia Avenue place the Gooks would call home for seventeen years; a home likely modeled after Paul Rhymer's own, at 414 W. Virginia Avenue, in the Bloomington, Illinois, suburb of Normal, where he had lived until 1929. The prairie foursquare home with its stucco façade and tile roof remains today much as it did when *Vic and Sade* first aired.

Another similarity between the audition episode and later episodes is Vic's insistence at reading the newspaper while Sade tries to converse with him; a fact that is evident in Vic's non-sequitur responses. This was the case in the following scene in which Sade has just finished telling Vic about a rather sensational newspaper story in which a man shoots his sweetheart with a slingshot. Sarcastically, Sade asks Vic what he plans to shoot her with.

VIC: (*NEWSPAPER CRINKLES AS IT IS LOWERED TO HIS LAP*) I said yes.
SADE: "Yes" what?
VIC: Whatever you said.
SADE: What did I say?[9]

Sade's response was curiously overwrought: "Vic Gook, you haven't the slightest idea in the world what I said."

This photograph from Art Van Harvey's personal collection shows the actor, as Vic, with Bernadine Flynn, portraying Sade. The two would perform the roles more than 3,500 times (Mark C. Lancaster/ The Art Van Harvey Collection).

A reasonable allegation, but Sade seems to feel this is symptomatic of a larger problem: "We grow further apart every living day." She compares them to a couple she and a friend saw at the Bijou who led separate lives. Unfortunately for Sade, Vic has turned once again to the newspaper. Despite Vic's attention to the paper, he possesses a certain disdain for it, a fact that is likely derived from Rhymer's own attitude toward the press. Indeed, disdain for the press and, in particular newspaper writers, would become an ongoing theme.

Sade's anger is replaced by insecurity, which Vic tries, in his way, to placate Sade by telling her, "You're the best looker in the county and you've got more brains than a *horse*,"[10] a compliment by which Sade is especially taken.

There is, throughout the audition script, a sense of melodrama that overwhelms the almost-tentative humor. The mix, apparently, did not appeal to Procter & Gamble, who rejected it. Despite this, Clarence Mesner decided to give *Vic and Sade* a chance. He allowed it to run on NBC as a sustaining program (meaning without commercial support) as part of the network's fledgling daytime schedule.

Week One: Vic and Sad(e)

Throughout much of *Vic and Sade*'s first week, the program was an, at times, awkward mix of humor and melodrama. The uncomfortable combination reflected several challenges with which Paul Rhymer was faced. First, *Vic and Sade* was only the second "serial" to join NBC's daytime schedule, the first being the well-established *Clara, Lu, and 'Em* which had been transplanted from the nighttime schedule, where it had enjoyed considerable popularity. Second, the formula for daytime serials had yet to be established. *Betty and Bob*, the clones it would inspire, and the assembly-line soaps of Frank and Ann Hummert were still to come. Perhaps more to the point, it seems that Paul Rhymer did not have a clear vision for *Vic and Sade*. Rhymer had been asked to create the program for a specific commercial purpose—a family show designed to promote products—but he now found himself with, if not complete freedom, then considerably more than he'd initially been given to make the program his own. The results were uneven.

Vic and Sade premiered on June 30, 1932, at 8:15 a.m. Central Time, over fifteen stations on the NBC Red Network. Although it might have hope for a better position on the daytime schedule and the opportunity to be heard on more stations, it was at least a start.

The premiere episode began with that age-old source of both comedy and drama: the mother-in-law. In this case, as one might expect, it was Sade's mother, and her visit to the Gook household was fueling a breakfast-time argument. The script reveals a more assertive Sade, again complaining about Vic's tendency to sit and converse from behind the daily paper. Vic blusters about his own mother, who, having lived on a farm, never knew the sort of leisure time that Sade's mother has. (While the couple is bickering, Mother is asleep in their bedroom.)

There seems to be a good sparring rhythm between the two: Vic's bluster is always normally far worse than is intended, though he clearly derives no pleasure from the presence of his mother-in-law; Sade, apparently, is more than willing to defend her mother and her duties as a wife. That is until Vic, almost without recognizing it, strikes a blow that cuts at the heart of Sade's pride in house and home: her ability to maintain adequate levels of preserves. Having run out of one type of preserve, she offers him another, raising her already put-upon and cantankerous husband's ire to a new level: "A swell way to run a household. What do you do? Put samples on the table?"

Vic's demeanor is only made worse when Sade urges him to be quiet to avoid disturbing his sleeping mother-in-law, prompting Vic to explain the hardships placed upon man by the outer world: "During the day a man has to be diplomatic, polite, obsequious, hypocritical..."[11]—all constraints, Vic implies, women do not have. Tortured by the outside world, Man, particularly Vic, should be free from such pains once at home. Yet, thanks to the davenport, Vic has been forced to no end of pain so that he might accommodate Sade's mother, who has taken his bed.

Sade, who had been strong throughout the comical battle, now reverts to the melodramatic ways that she had illustrated in the audition episode. She begins crying as she offers Vic another egg, this one cold, as is the coffee she pours. Whether or not Sade's tears are genuine they have a manipulative effect as Vic quickly recants his previous statements; he and the davenport get along fine, and cold eggs and coffee are delicious.

But none of Vic's concessions are sufficient. Sade admits that she was crying but not for the reasons Vic thinks. "Darling," she attempts to explain, "you're my husband and *you* are my home. Don't you see, Vic, this house—this breakfast table—they're my kingdom— my *business* and I love *them*, and I love *you*."[12] But as quickly as Sade has contrived a cause for sadness and a reason for joy the true topic of their trouble, at least for Vic, once again emerges and the pair resumes their fight.

The episode was, in part, a situation comedy, with Rhymer following the standard structure: the mother-in-law who, despite not being seen or heard, is a source of trouble for the young married couple; a young husband who is insensitive to his wife's efforts, and the wife who wilts under criticism. Whether Sade's response is for comedic effect, or an attempt to interject melodrama into an episode that was light on plot, is unclear. What *is* clear is that, in the days that follow, Sade is depicted as a frequently unhappy character.

In the following day's episode, for example, she has laid dinner out for Vic so she and her mother can go shopping downtown. Aside from Sade's peculiar observation to Vic that "you must roll around on that floor down at that office the way you soil your clothes,"[13] the scene is marked by what would become a hallmark of *Vic and Sade*: Vic attempting unsuccessfully to tell a story while Sade interrupts with orders or otherwise ignores him. In this case, Vic proudly attempts to tell Sade about his boss's interest in his hat. Sade, meanwhile, finds it difficult to leave Vic, acting at once like a newlywed who feels that the only place she belongs is at her husband's side. At the same time she demonstrates a mix of anxiety and insecurity that would suggest her marriage is in jeopardy.

> SADE: (*BACK AGAIN*) (*MAKES HER PRESENCE KNOWN WITH SOME SUCH SPEECH OR OTHER*).
> VIC: Hi, Sade. What now?
> SADE: (*LAUGHS A LITTLE*). Oh, nothing. Here! (*GOOBER*)
> VIC: Oh,—forgot to kiss the old man goodby, huh? 'Bye, Sade.[14]

Minutes later, Sade finds cause to rush in again, this time to check on the stove, which she was convinced was on fire. Sade's frequent delays in keeping her appointment with her mother lead to a fight between the two.

> SADE: Our marriage is a mess and it's your fault.
> VIC: It's *your* fault. It was *you* who didn't keep the appointment with your mother. Not *me*. You had to stick around and see that your grownup husband got his dinner. Treatin' me like a baby!
> SADE: You oughta be treated be like a baby. You're too silly to take care of yourself.[15]

Sade, having determined a woman should never let herself "be too devoted to her husband," prepares to leave Vic and never return, a statement to which Vic, not wishing to be coddled, offers no objections. The pair says their goodbyes and prepare to part forever. It's not until Sade sees that Vic has cut himself on a can of sardines that she is drawn back to her husband. Meanwhile, her mother is now safely residing in a hotel.

The Gooks are, at this point, portraying the quintessential serial couple: blissfully happy at the start of a meal, on the verge of divorce by dessert, and reconciled after. All they were lacking was the pretense of genuine conflict. There were no villainous Lotharios wooing Sade, and Vic demonstrated no desire to do much of anything, let alone find another woman, in these early episodes. Even the ubiquitous mother-in-law, despite her role in history as a home wrecker and purveyor of trouble, provided no real sense of malice because Rhymer had yet to develop what would become one of his trademarks: the off-mic character who, despite never being heard, is a full-fledged presence. (In time, this trademark would be so famous that the rare spoken line by someone other than the main cast—e.g., Mr. Gumpox's "Hello, Mr. and Mrs. Gook" to celebrate the show's sixth anniversary—became a news story in the radio columns of 1938.)

The real culprit may have been dwelling in the Gooks' own home. While, in later years, Sade would be cast as a proud, homemaking anti-intellectual with little patience for "talky talk," in these earlier episodes Sade appears sensitive regarding her intellect. As the July 4 episode opens, she is struggling with a book lent to her by a neighborhood friend, Mis' Fisher; at the same time she is forced to feign laughter over a joke Vic relays from the newspaper that she doesn't understand. Sade relays that she has been attempting to read a book entitled *The Bridge of Saint Louis Bay*, which she has deemed "kinda nonsense."[16] However, Sade appears to have been biased before she began reading.

> SADE: I told her when she gave it to me—I was leafing through it, ya know—there aren't any pictures—that I didn't think I'd get interested ... it's a kind of a little book, isn't it? Got some of the craziest stuff in it.[17]

Although she is dismissive of the book, Sade's feelings of inadequacy become clear as she talks with Vic, noting that she was never able to interest herself in reading in school. She is impressed, however, by Vic's voluminous consumption of literature.

> VIC: Read most books, though [...] *Les Misérables*, *David Coppersmith* ... *all* that stuff ... used to enjoy it, too.
> SADE: (*AFF.*) Uh-huh. I never got interested much. Guess I'm *awful* ignorant.[18]

If Sade's lack of self-esteem is the culprit hiding within the Gook household, it is not unassisted. The chauvinistic gender roles of the time are not without blame. As Vic comforts her, "Oh, no, you're not, kiddo. You got lots a good horse sense."[19] Sade then needn't worry about literature or loftier pursuits; her "horse sense" would be sufficient to guide her through the necessary tasks. Sade is delighted at what she perceives as a compliment until Vic, demonstrating that he isn't as clever as he believes, goes too far.

> VIC: Ya know, Sade, sometimes I feel like I wish I was more like *you* ...
> SADE: Like *me*?
> VIC: Yeah, like you. There ain't much satisfaction in bein' a *brainy* type ... just keeps a fella keyed up and on edge.[20]

With that, Vic transformed flattery to a further means of fueling his wife's insecurity. Sade, however, listens with interested as Vic describes the nature of life as an "intellectual gink," a burden with which he is all too familiar. For Sade, the conversation isn't enough.

> SADE: Vic, don't you think it's too bad that we can't think of anything to talk about?
> VIC: (*SURPRISED*) Hunh?[21]

Sade wonders how two people who should really share "one life" have so little to talk about, a remark that only serves to puzzle Vic. Sade explains:

> SADE: And now ... well, you don't bother to tell me what happened at the office because you think I wouldn't understand. And I know you don't care about *my* gossip. [...] I know it isn't very interesting stuff to an intellectual gink like you.[22]

Although Vic explains that they *have* been talking, Sade's concerns seem to extend beyond conversation; her problem is "I'm just awful happy," and, for Sade, that happiness is cause for concern, and perhaps an indicator of problems to come:

> SADE: Oh, I can't think of anything worse than you tiring of me, Vic. Why, there's nothing worse in the *world* [...] and it frightens me to think there's nothing for us to talk about.[23]

We finally learn that Sade's foe is internal. "Guess I'm just jealous," she confides to Vic. "Jealous?" he says with little interest.

> SADE: Yes—jealous of everything you do and think about that isn't connected with me. I guess I want to absorb every bit of you. I don't want any of you to be left over for anybody else.[24]

Her possessive confession behind her, Sade goes on to explain the "sinking feeling" she had when she thought that she and Vic had nothing to talk about.

Vic, assuming the role of ideal husband, explains that they may not be full of "gush and talky talky," the "kids' stuff" they one experienced; however, now they had something different—"a sort of feeling," one that defies words, at least for Vic who is "an ordinary duck walking down the street or buying a cigar. I'm *nobody* particularly. But I'm somebody *here*."[25]

Things do not remain calm at the Gooks for long, as Sade prepares to host Vic's boss, Mr. Ruebush, whom she unfortunately seems more prone to call Mr. Rubbish, thanks to Vic's after-work grumbling. Sade has been preparing for the event all day with a mixture of excitement and trepidation, and treats Ruebush's visit like an impending royal visit. This provides another opportunity for her insecurities to serve as her foil. She worries that there are too many forks on the table and, more significantly, she worries that she will seem "silly and stupid." She is also positive that she will "sink through the floor if anything went wrong."[26]

This, of course, meant that something does go wrong for Sade. And, despite the fact that she doesn't sink into to floor, she is able to hide upstairs while her guest waits outside. Sade's dilemma is not related to the meal she has prepared (though it *will* ultimately suffer) or her lack of intelligence. Rather, Sade faces a fashion catastrophe. Eager to please and impress Ruebush, Sade decides to wear the blue dress she was wearing when she married Vic. Unfortunately, she waits until the last minute to change, only to realize that it no longer fits.

The farce continued in the following day's episode, with the Gooks sitting in the dark bickering about how to avoid their intended guest. Though ridiculous, the comedic nature of the episode reveals Paul Rhymer's intentions for the program—after a little more serious business was taken care of.

"Inarticulate and cramped"

The July 7 episode marked what would be turning point for *Vic and Sade*—the program and the characters—but the change was not immediately clear. As the episode opens, Sade sits on the porch swing admiring the "garden of stars" the summer evening has brought and admonishing Vic for not being as poetic as he used to be:

> VIC: Used to be poetic? Never wrote a poem in life. Oh, yes I did too. Wrote a poem once to read at the Bookkeeping Department Banquet. [...] "The bookkeeping department is the department for me. The only place in the Consolidated Kitchenware Company worthwhile, by gee."[27]

Undeterred by Vic's lack of poetic prowess, Sade coerces her husband to join her on the porch swing, where, after observing passing neighbors, Sade confesses that there's something she wants to ask Vic: "It's ... well ... Vic, are you really intending to buy an automobile?"[28] Sade's question was reasonable given that the Gooks were somewhat behind the times. By 1927, 54 percent of those living in cities with populations greater than 100,000 had automobiles and "by 1929 almost 27 million cars were on the road."[29] For a chief bookkeeper, Vic wasn't keeping up with his peers. While Vic assumes that Sade is eager to "get a machine and tear around," Sade has something altogether different in mind:

> SADE: I want to adopt a child.
> VIC: Adopt—a—*child*?
> SADE: Yes, Vic.[30]

Sade's talk of an automobile now made sense as her proposition eliminated the possibility of car ownership, which had become a symbol of entry into the white-collar middle-class and conferred a certain social status, along with embodying what Madison Avenue and the middle-class alike agreed was the heart of the American dream.[31] Vic greets Sade's proposal unenthusiastically: "The idea is preposterous. Adopting a baby!" But Sade, who clearly has a specific child in mind, is quick to correct Vic that she hadn't said a baby, but rather a child, a distinction that Vic finds inconsequential. Despite her sometimes melodramatic and even irrational behavior in the past, Sade is clear in her motives for wanting a child:

> SADE: Vic there'd be *three* of us. And each of us would have two to love. As it is, Vic, you and I just love each other so much ... and all we've got is that, and it leaves us kind of *inarticulate* and *cramped* sort of.[32]

Sade's words were not merely her plea for a child, but also Paul Rhymer's concession: Writing a daily program for two characters had left him with few creative options, resulting in a program that was cramped and, at times, inarticulate. Like Sade, Rhymer knew that adding a baby was not the right move as it would add little beyond the occasional sound, a strategy that future serials would find disastrous. It would, for example, be little Bob who was blamed for the demise of *Betty and Bob* through what Stedman refers as "the Children in the Closet Syndrome," noting that "children seldom fulfilled their natural role in daytime radio drama. They were usually brought into a story to create difficulty for their parents or guardians."[33] Rhymer's expanding family, however, would be different. The child would have a voice, a personality, and a presence. However, that is not to say that the introduction of a child wouldn't pose some difficulty, particularly given Vic's resistance. Yet here we see Sade's cunning and ability to influence events when confronted with what is most important to her:

> SADE: ... and a little girl.

Much to Sade delight, Vic responds in a curmudgeonly manner:

> VIC: Little girl, nothin'. Little *boy*.[34]

Sade had purposely suggested a girl, knowing that Vic's reaction would help draw him in to adopting a boy, for it was, listeners will learn the following day, a little boy that Sade had in mind. She tells him about Mary Meadows, a school friend with three children, two girls and one boy, who happens to be named for Vic. What's more, Sade says, young Vic is a bit of a roughneck and a baseball player, two facts that cause Vic to light up with glee. Seeing the possibility to relive his own youth, he tells Sade that she should invite young Vic over after all, only to learn that she already had; he would be arriving the following week.

Change in a Rush

On July 14, 1932, eleven-year-old Victor Rush Meadows joined the Gook family. He was played by young Billy Idelson, who was already a veteran radio actor, having played the role of Skeezix in the radio adaption of *Gasoline Alley*, a popular comic strip, not long before. Much later in life, he explained that he "hated" radio acting. He was less than pleased to dis-

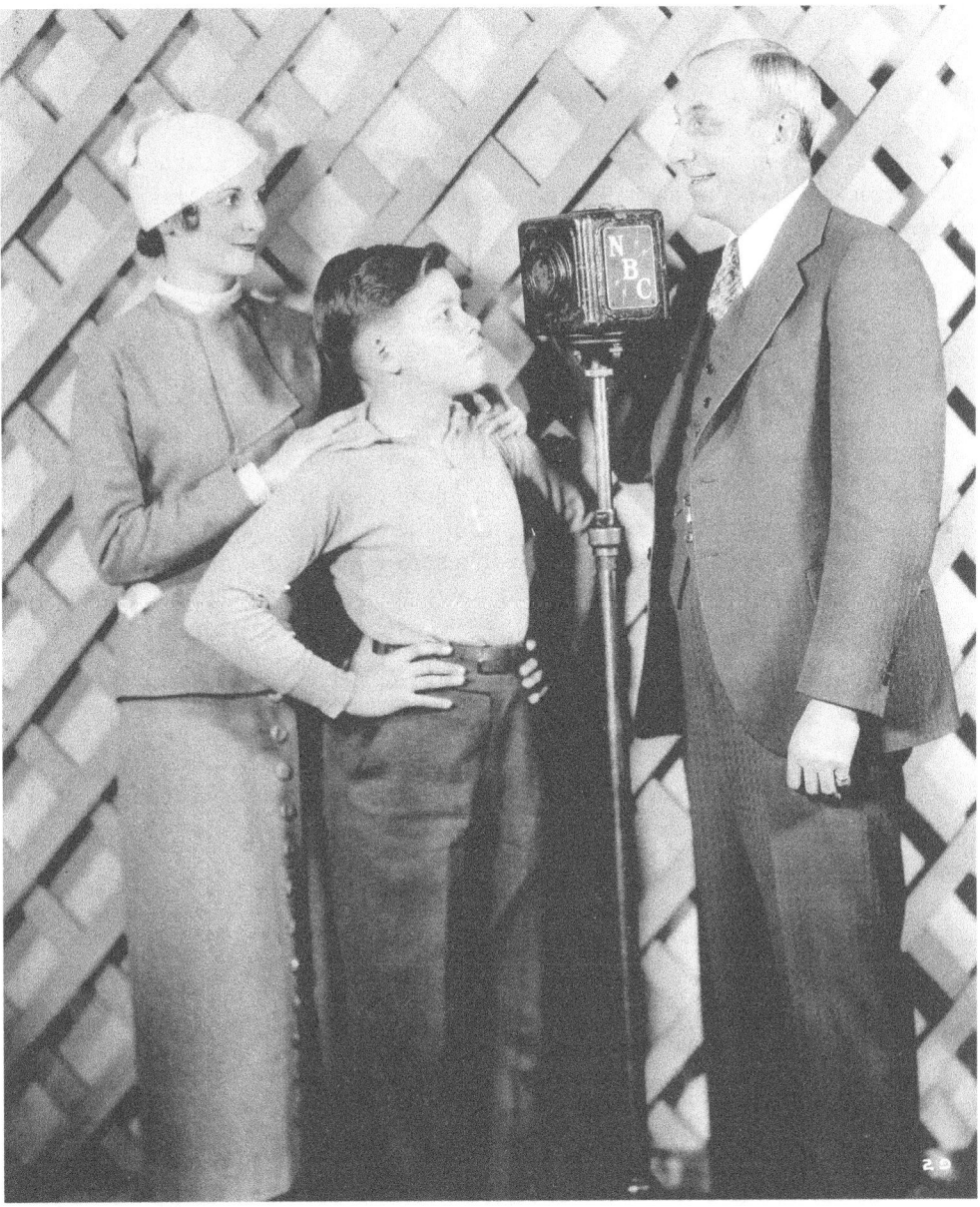

Rush (Bill Idelson, center) became the third voice on *Vic and Sade* and helped to expand the program's world by giving Vic and Sade another person to interact with and another window onto the larger world beyond the "small house" (courtesy Mark C. Lancaster, reproduced by permission of NBC/NBC Universal PhotoBank).

cover his mother and father had accepted a role for him on an NBC show he'd never heard of: "But I hit the ceiling. I wouldn't go! She calmed me down—it was to be for only four days. I gave in. But it was only for four days."[35] While Mrs. Idelson may have been telling her son the truth, his role on *Vic and Sade* would extend through his 1942 departure for military service in the war. Bill Idelson would be the last new cast member added until 1940, when Clarence Hartzell, who had filled in for an ailing Art Van Harvey, as Uncle Fletcher, became a permanent cast member due to his popularity with audiences. (In 1943, David Whitehouse replaced Idelson, who had been drafted, originating the role of Russell, the orphaned nephew of Vic's boss, Mr. Buller, whom the Gooks take in.)

Arriving at the darkened house that first night, Victor utters his only line of the episode: "Hello..., anybody home? [...] Hey, mister, wake up, wake up, c'mon." In introducing the young Vic, Paul Rhymer instantly opened a range of storylines that would never have been possible with the show's initial limited premise. The boy's character served as a reminder of the hardships so many Americans were facing, but also of the fact that the Great Depression had not impacted every American equally. The Gooks, though not wealthy, made a decent middle-class living: they rented a house, Vic had a good job, and they even prepared to buy an automobile. The life of Sade's friend, Mary Meadows, who was unable to care for her son, stands in stark contrast.

Vic and Sade, along with their adopted son, needed to adapt and adjust, and this also allowed for new dimensions of the husband-and-wife team to be heard. The early twentieth century had found many children separated from their families, as Victor had been. Damian McElrath, in his book on the well-known alcoholism researcher Dan Anderson, recounts the early life of the young Anderson, whose stepmother sent him away from Minneapolis to live with relatives in a small town in rural Minnesota, following the death of his father in 1936.[36] Even President Herbert Hoover had grown up in similar circumstances. When he was six years old, Herbert's father died and, unable to raise three children alone, his mother sent her son to live with an uncle in Oregon.[37] Although the fate of Victor's father is never stated, Hoover's story closely parallels Rush's.

Young Victor was understandably homesick, something neither Vic nor Sade was sure how to handle. Shortly after Victor arrives at the Gooks' residence, Sade wakes up Vic to tell him that the boy is homesick and is sobbing in bed. After they've calmed him down, Vic mentions that he has a bicycle that no longer fits him and he doesn't know what to do with it.

> VIC: It's a dandy bicycle, too ... coaster brake ... siren horn ... tool kit ... saddle seat ...
> VICTOR: (*GASPS INVOLUNTARILY*) Jimminy! It's a peach!
> VIC: Don't know where I could sell it, do you Vic?
> VICTOR: How much was it?
> VIC: I paid more for it, but I used it already so I guess I can't get such a fancy price. A nickel takes her.
> VICTOR: *I'll* buy it. *I* got a nickel.
> VIC: Where's the nickel? I'm not handing anything out on credit.[38]

The deal allowed Vic to make his new son feel better while also establishing a *faux* curmudgeonly persona that would continue for years to come. Later, while addressing the issue that father and son shared the same first name, Vic maintained the curmudgeonly façade that his new son enjoyed rather than feared. Vic established a proprietary claim on the noble name, but this was of little consequence to young Victor, who was already prepared to move on:

Clarence Hartzell (far right) as Uncle Fletcher joined the cast when Art Van Harvey became ill in 1940, and David Whitehouse (far left), as Russell, arrived in 1943 after Bill Idelson was drafted to serve in World War II (courtesy Mark C. Lancaster, reproduced by permission of NBC/NBC Universal PhotoBank).

VIC: Say, it's a funny thing, Vic. My name's the same as yours.
VICTOR: Uh-huh.
VIC: Well, nobody's coming in *here* named Vic. I had the name first and I'm gonna *keep* it. Understand?
VICTOR: (*LAUGHING*) Yes, sir.
VIC: Is there anything else you'd like to be called—besides Vic?
VICTOR: (*EAGERLY*) Yes, call me "Rush."
VIC: Rush?

VICTOR: Yes, that's my middle name. I like it.
VIC: (*BELLIGERENTLY*) Ya don't like "Vic," huh?[39]

Rush also, as radio chronicler Raymond William Stedman explains, brought "his own offstage characters to enliven the proceedings."[40] Indeed, after a somewhat claustrophobic beginning, Rhymer was deftly integrating characters into the program without listeners ever hearing their voices. These included Smelly Clark, Blue-Tooth Johnson, Rooster Davis, Nicer Scott, and of course, Rush's dog, Mr. Albert Johnson, who "suffered from astigmatism and could not bark."[41] Instead, Mr. Albert Johnson would communicate with a periodic "woosh" sound. *Radio Stars* elaborated on the canine character's role on *Vic and Sade*, noting that the "weird dog that suffers from astigmatism" did more than just "swoosh" in lieu of barking. Rush and Mr. Albert Johnson "often feel discredited, but the backyard and basement yield them a rich and interesting life."[42] Other characters who were discussed but never heard included Rush's girlfriend, Sydney Call, and her brother, Heinie; and neighbors Freeman Mason and Mrs. Hall. While little Bobby on *Betty and Bob* was a barnacle, weighing the program down and limiting its options, Rush did just the opposite on *Vic and Sade*. Together, the Gooks embarked on a program that, unbeknownst to them, would be very different from any other daytime program.

"Just by writin' a check": Creating a Middle-class World

It would be difficult to underestimate the importance of setting in radio drama. While in some instances the setting of a drama (or a comedy, for that matter) was little more than a backdrop upon which actions took place; in others, the setting was a character unto itself. In these cases the setting of a story had its own strengths, weaknesses, and moods. It was in those programs in which setting was fully developed that it stood on the front line along with the show's major players. In the case of *Vic and Sade*, Paul Rhymer brought to the show a unique setting drawn from his own experiences in the middle-class neighborhoods of Bloomington, Illinois, that were a world away from the tony surroundings of the upper-class world of *One Man's Family*.

For twenty-seven years, beginning on April 29, 1932, listeners began visiting Sea Cliff in San Francisco, home of the Barbours on *One Man's Family*, along with Sky Ranch, the Barbour family dairy ranch and vacation spot located outside of Sea Cliff. With its views of the Golden Gate Bridge, rolling fog, and subsequent booming foghorns, the Barbour family home became a familiar place for avid radio listeners. It was easy to envision Father Barbour's library with its oft-lit fireplace, Paul Barbour's book-filled study, and the garden that Father Barbour nurtured. The homes of other Barbour family members—Jack and Betty, Hazel and Dan, Claudia and Nicky, and their myriad children—were scattered throughout the city. These locations were more than mere backdrops, they were extensions of the characters and, at times, characters themselves, inflicting their will and influencing the paths of the Barbours. The San Francisco fog itself was a major player, at once an isolating and insulating factor as it separated characters and brought them together as if by a whim. It was, for example, the dense fog of Sea Cliff that caused Clifford's accident that caused him to lose his memory and, along with it, fifteen years of his life, redefining his character. The Barbours' home, grand and illustrative of their wealth, could wield similar power as it united the family even during its greatest trials while, on occasion, repelling guests with its intimidating stature.

Bloomington, Illinois, served as the model for *Vic and Sade*'s home town. Here we see a panorama of the city as it looked in Paul Rhymer's youth, and as it was depicted in the series (Library of Congress).

Vic and Sade's hometown may not have exercised its role in quite so dramatic a fashion, but its role in the program cannot be overestimated. Although it was most assuredly modeled after Rhymer's hometown of Bloomington, Illinois—evidenced from its proximity to Normal and the Kickapoo River to its daily newspaper, the *Pantagraph*, to the names of buildings and streets, and even to the use of Paul Rhymer's own Bloomington phone number 2572-X for the Stembottoms—the city was left nameless throughout the series, a fact that lent itself to listener identification.[43] The Gooks, for all intents and purposes, lived in "any town," with the "small house halfway up in the block."

Unlike so many of their daytime peers, the Gooks did not exist in a bubble, sequestered from those who were different than themselves. Their friends and acquaintances ranged from vagrants and garbage men to foundry and rail workers, from secretaries and homemakers to those in upper management. Their town included upper-class neighborhoods and a literal "wrong side of the tracks," replete with less-than-desirable housing and no shortage of tenants. The Gooks associated with all levels within their society, though, admittedly, Sade seemed a bit uncomfortable when dealing with those not within the middle- or working-class.

As created by Paul Rhymer, the Gooks were proudly and decidedly a middle-class family. Vic worked as an accountant for the Consolidated Kitchenware Company and, by July 12, 1932, was able to work his way to chief accountant, a position that allowed him to frequently work from home. Although their financial security was not always certain, with Vic's job being threatened shortly after his promotion, Sade was never forced to seek work outside of the home, and Rush was able to attend high school.

Vic's position stood in stark contrast to that of many of those around them, particularly Sade's family, who see Vic as the "biggest biggity-big there ever was" because he works for a "monstrous big company" that they believe has "trillions and trillions of dollars." They admire him for having a white-collar job with an "elegant office," for dressing up for work every day and for "takin' trips on business every place in creation." Vic was also able to get the family's furniture "cash down, just by writin' a check."[44] Despite their decidedly middle-class status, the Gooks did not own either a house or an automobile. The reasons for Vic and Sade renting their Virginia Avenue home rather buying it are never explicitly stated; however, home ownership was not to be taken for granted. Large down payments, between one-half and two-thirds of the purchase price in some cities, and short-term mortgages of less than eleven years made home ownership a virtual impossibility for many Americans of the time.[45] By the 1930s, the housing market began to see a change, thanks to "blossoming economy of the 1920s and large investment in housing by entrepreneurs." The private sector was soon witnessing a real estate transformation with millions of unions being added annually to the housing stock, rapidly reversing the downward trend of previous decades.[46] The growth in home ownership was dealt a setback with the stock market crash of 1929. As George S. Masnick explains, "The bank failures, personal bankruptcies, and high unemployment that characterized the Great Depression caused rates to drop by more than 4 percentage points (from 47.8 percent to 43.6 percent) between 1930 and 1940. During the early 1930s, mortgage foreclosure soared to around one thousand a day and half of the country's homeowners were in default."[47]

As Paul Rhymer understood, for families like the Gooks, renting was a better option. Although social scientists Robert and Helen Lynd, studying town life in the 1930s for their *Middletown in Transition: A Study in Cultural Conflicts*, observed a distinction between renters and home owners regarding permanency, with only 11.6 percent of Middletown renters remaining in their homes for five years or more, compared to 82.2 percent of homeowners.[48] The Gooks appeared to have made a commitment their Virginia Avenue abode.

Other renters, including some of the characters featured on *Vic and Sade*, lived more transitional existences. Vic's friend Hank Gutstop, despite remaining in one town, personified the life of the transient, demonstrating "distinct elements of survival value to the individual, living in a culture characterized by rapid change, in his learning to 'travel light' and to put on and off the physical paraphernalia of living as readily as he does his coat."[49] Gutstop, who transitioned from one job to another amid long periods of unemployment, took up residence in the Bright Kentucky Hotel, located quite literally on the "wrong side of the tracks" and home to the town's more disreputable characters, such as B.B. Baugh, Raymond Beerman, Roy Delfeeno, and Rishigan Fishigan from Shishigan, Michigan. Gutstop, along with many of his friends, was equally likely to be found sleeping in the courthouse yard or in the railroad platforms. Regardless of his lowly reputation, Gutstop is part of the community. However, he exists mainly on the outer fringes, frequenting the Lazy Hour Pool Hall and the Royal Thorne Twenty-Five Cent Barber-Shop, an establishment set within an "English basement," and warming himself by the radiators outside of Yamilton's. When he is able to afford the membership dues, he serves as the Exalted Little Dipper of the Sacred Stars of the Milky Way, Drowsy Venus Chapter.

Despite the Gooks' long-term residency on Virginia Avenue as tenants of Mr. Erickson, a landowner who resides on W. Mulberry Street, renting was not without significant shortcomings. Just as with many renters, Vic and Sade's difficulties were, for the most part, caused by their landlord. Although they expressed no plans to leave it, Erickson still regarded the property as his to do with as he pleased and when he pleased. In January 1942, Erickson informed Sade that he would be storing paint in their already-overloaded basement. The paint was for the Scotts' house, which he has agreed to paint before the Gooks.' Sade worries that saying no to her landlord will further delay the possibility of having her house done, thus denying them the pride of home she desires and deserves.[50]

Vic and Sade were continually reminded of the fact that their home was not really their own. This was certainly the case in 1941 when Erickson offered them the opportunity to have new wallpaper, as long as it is one of the patterns chosen by his daughter, Beulah. Among the "beautiful, beautiful wallpaper" selections Erickson presented the Gooks with were a "rich restful emerald color" that Vic suggests will induce "involuntary shakes and shudders"; a pattern featuring gorillas—or apes—which Beulah claims is "a touch of whimsy" that will cause guests to "appreciate your originality and humor"; alternating pink and purple stripes; a pattern featuring three little monkeys in the "hear no evil, see no evil, speak no evil" poses; "a dainty design and a pleasing color contrast" featuring purple splotches on a bright yellow background.[51] This offense, however, is rather mundane in comparison to some of the landlord's other deeds. In 1941, for example, he gives the Gook home to his daughter as an anniversary present. As part of the occasion he had wanted to have Rush appear dressed as Cupid, presenting Beulah and her husband with a card and the house wrapped in a red ribbon. As it happened, Erickson's gift would prove an empty gesture as he did not give Beulah the deed to the house. Still, the act alone sent a clear message to the Gooks that their home could be taken from them at any time.[52]

Such details helped to create a world with which middle-class listeners could identify.

"Kicked around"

Longtime *Vic and Sade* announcer Bob Brown, contrasting the program with the rest of daytime fare, once noted the program was "an island of delight in a sea of tears." Whatever similarities it shared with its daytime neighbors, *Vic and Sade* was decidedly different from any anything that surrounded it. As daytime serials with their melodrama, diseases, and romantic entanglements came to dominate daytime radio by 1936, *Vic and Sade* provided a valuable alternative for both the network and fans. In 1940, the *Chicago Times* reported that women were complaining about the glut of more the more than seventy-six serials that cluttered the airwaves; the article was quick to add: "There are 12 [favored] programs mentioned by 40 percent of women listeners queried, namely *Vic and Sade* and daytime's perennial quality programs, *The Goldbergs*, *Pepper Young's Family*, and *Road to Life*, programs that listeners felt sent positive, life-affirming messages."[53] By then, *Vic and Sade* had already achieved a strong following. *Radio Stars* reported in 1935 that frenzied fans postponed their shopping trips to listen to the program: "In the Black Hills of Dakota all business stops for 15 minutes" because "every last inhabitant" is a fan.[54] But, between 1932 and 1935, popularity could take a little show only so far. Even after Clarence Mesner made the decision to continue *Vic and Sade* following Procter & Gamble's rejection, the program still faced two serious challenges to achieve, if not success, then at least stability. First, it needed a sponsor.

For much of its first three years *Vic and Sade* aired as a sustaining program, paid for by the network from the profits of sponsored programs. While sustaining programs were viewed as typically being of a higher quality than sponsored programs, they were also often financially strained and prone to cancellation. As Darrell Ware explains in his aptly titled 1935 article "Kicked Around," the show's sustaining status put it in a precarious situation; NBC was obliged to force it to move every time a commercially viable, sponsored program sought their time slot and "was cancelled for any special event that came along."[55] The show changed slots fourteen times in just over two years, until finally Procter & Gamble offered them a five-year contract. But it was not easy.

One sponsor lasted only two months, in 1934. An unusual eight-week period of sponsorship from Ironized Yeast did little to solidify the show's position or time slot; in fact, the program went through four time changes during this eight-week sponsorship. The company had promised to make the sponsorship permanent, but did not do so. In the fall of the previous year, the John F. Jelke Company, makers of Jelke's Good Luck Margarine, sponsored the program for thirteen weeks. Though Jelke had no discernible impact on the content of the program, as can be determined from existing scripts, they did begin using the Gook family in contests and promotions. One included a collection of "100 Prize-Winning Hints" from listeners, offering time-worn advice such as, "To prevent rugs from slipping on floors sew old rubber jar-rings on the underside of the rugs" from a Mrs. Minnie Dietz, of Chicago; and, "If you fill your ice-cube trays with water and put cookie-cutters in the water, you will have attractive little designs" from Mrs. Elinor Sheldon, also of Chicago.[56]

This pamphlet was sent to listeners "compliments of Vic, Sade, and Rush" (though one would suspect that Rush and Vic would have had far less to do with the folksy promotion than Sade). The collection further identified Sade, and her family, with everyday listeners struggling to maintain their home. Unfortunately, *Vic and Sade* did too good a job selling Jelke's margarine. Its success in promoting the butter substitute came at an unfortunate time: a price war over butter drove margarine costs below the break-even point, causing huge losses to the sponsor. Every time *Vic and Sade* came on the air, Jelke lost money from tremendously increased margarine sales to the show's fans. Jelke officials could not wait for their thirteen-week contract to expire, and they wasted no time breaking away from *Vic and Sade*, never to return.

As soon as *Vic and Sade* gained its first sponsor, Paul Rhymer left his $50-a-week network job to become a freelance writer, in which capacity he would write for the rest of his life. His first loyalty was now to his show and to his sponsor, for which he would eventually be paid about $50,000 annually.[57] As a result of leaving the official employ of NBC, Rhymer lost his cubicle in NBC's Chicago offices, as well as his network typewriter. He had to rent a small desk and a typewriter for his own apartment, which he used from then on. So long did he keep the rental that the original owners eventually stopped billing him for the machine, apparently determining that he had already paid its value several times over. Rhymer's one-room apartment (and, later, his house), much to his wife's dismay, began filling with carbon copies of his scripts, bundled every month or so and tied up with a used necktie. He would then buy a new tie for the new month. (In time, the accumulated paper would weigh so much that his wife would need to have special crates constructed to haul the scripts away to the Wisconsin Historical Society, after her husband's death.[58]) Rhymer told interviewers that he squirmed and struggled with each script, seeing the difficulty as equal to its goodness, and that his African American maid Ethel helped him with everyday details, like the size of fat ladies' shoes and the name of the kitchen tool that strains applesauce.[59]

Despite these conditions, *Vic and Sade* "plugged away," "ready to be anyone's football" and, in the process, built a core of support from fans willing to listen at whatever time it aired and purchase whatever product sponsored *Vic and Sade*. As Ward explains, "With two black eyes" from failed sponsorships, it was beginning to look unlikely that *Vic and Sade* would find a permanent sponsor, despite being a favorite with critics and fans.[60]

Fortunately for Rhymer, Flynn, Van Harvey, and Idelson, in November 1934 Procter & Gamble, recognizing the quality and fan devotion to the program—not to mention its ability to move product—offered it a five-year contract. That contract would form the foundation for a nearly fifteen-year relationship. P&G would do more than Jelke had to build a relationship with the show's audience. While Jelke had distributed a household-hints booklet, P&G, for example, distributed a map of the Gooks' hometown (which would forever remain nameless), allegedly drawn by Rush Gook. Offering a map premium was popular and used by many programs, including *Little Orphan Annie* and *Amos 'n' Andy*. Among other promotions, they gave listeners the opportunity to win $10,000 by finishing Sade's sentence: "Use Crisco and only Crisco for fried cakes and pies and fried food because...." Bernadine Flynn (Sade) also hosted a war-time news program sponsored by Crisco. While the program did contain news of the war read by Flynn's co-host, her role was primarily limited to providing household hints and recipes—including one for boiled bologna cubes.

In time, *Vic and Sade* would become so popular that, in different years, Procter & Gamble broadcast it on both NBC and CBS. To accommodate this schedule during the summer and fall of 1938, the show's three actors—Art Van Harvey, Bernadine Flynn, and Bill Idelson—gathered at NBC's broadcast center in the Merchandise Mart in the morning, did their show, and then rode over to CBS's studios at the Wrigley Building in eighteen-year-old Idelson's new car for the afternoon broadcast.[61] The show would air on the two networks again, from 1939 to 1942.

Vic and Sade became wildly popular because it managed to serve two masters: It engaged

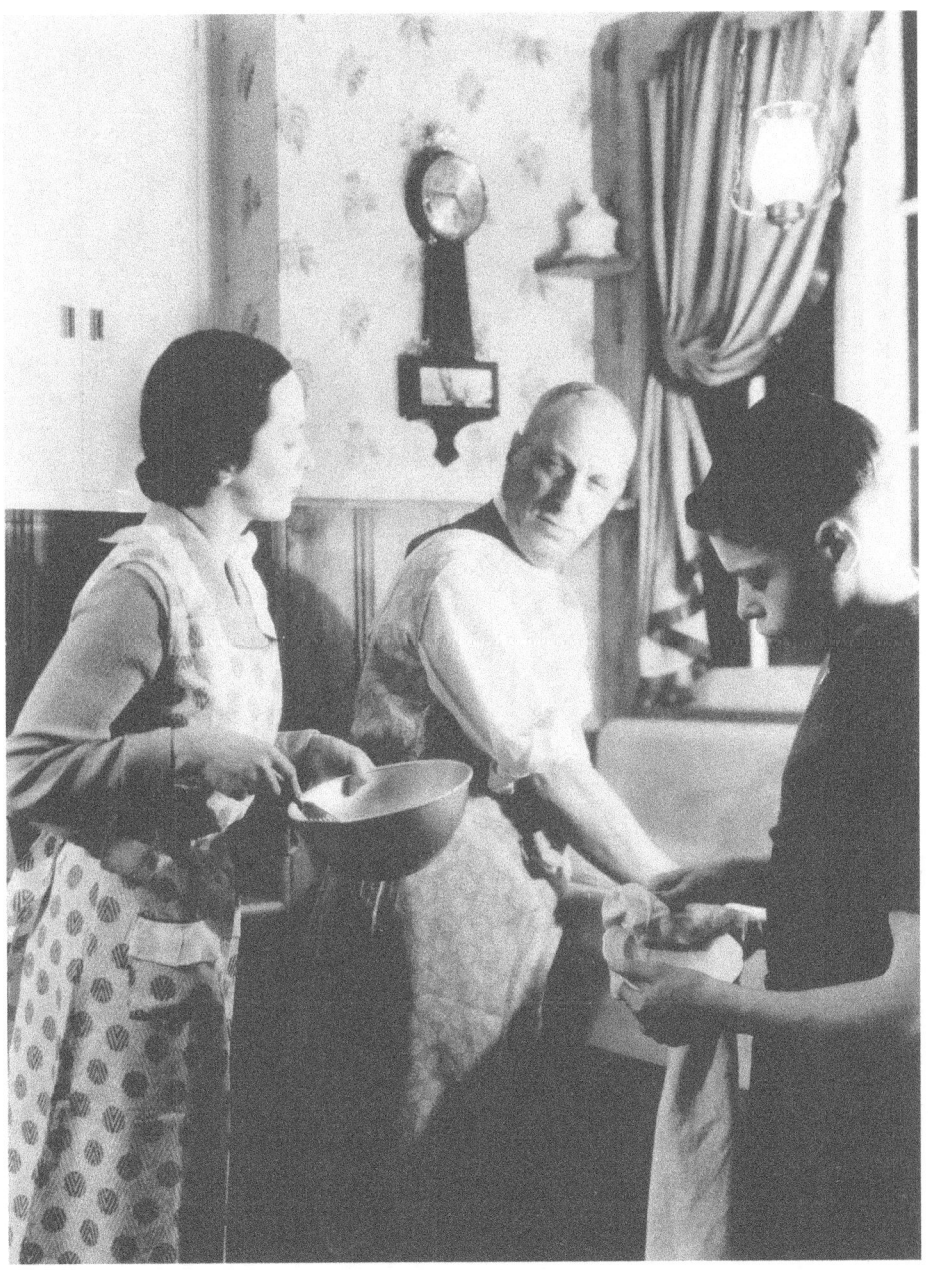

In this photograph from Art Van Harvey's personal collection we see the Gooks doing dishes after a hearty dinner. Thanks to sponsorship by Procter & Gamble's Crisco, *Vic and Sade* was able to stay on the air (Mark C. Lancaster/The Art Van Harvey Collection).

During the period when *Vic and Sade* aired on both NBC and CBS, the three cast members traveled from their morning broadcast at NBC's Merchandise Mart studio (seen here) to CBS's Wrigley Building studio in Bill Idelson's car for the afternoon broadcast (courtesy Mark C. Lancaster, reproduced by permission of NBC/NBC Universal PhotoBank).

Advertisers often distributed promotional tie-ins for popular radio programs. This map of the Gooks' hometown was sent out by Procter & Gamble around 1936; it offers a montage of the most beloved characters and locations from the series (reproduced by permission of Procter & Gamble).

its audience as a radio program in a media landscape, a product to be consumed and to serve as a vehicle for promoting the consumption of still more media and, especially, advertisers' products. However, within the world of the show, Paul Rhymer created a universe that reflected and refracted the cultural landscape in which the show's audience lived.

It is first to the broader landscape of daytime radio that we now turn.

Three. "Something to be interested in": Daytime Radio

When *Vic and Sade* took to the air in June 1932 the daytime schedule had yet to embrace the genre that would become known as the "soap opera." Daytime radio throughout the 1920s and early 1930s was, for most broadcasters, almost an afterthought. The typical daytime schedule would consist of several hours of miscellaneous programming, ranging from live operatic performances to pre-recorded music. Some, like WEAF in New York, began with "Health Exercises," while others included themed talk programs on a variety of topics. In most cases these daytime schedules were limited, some concluding as early as 8:30 a.m., others stretching until 11:15, leaving a void in much of the broadcast day. According to a study conducted in 1931, the previous year almost 63 percent of all radio programming was music, with literature (plays and adaptations of novels) making up 12 percent, educational programming at 21 percent, religion at 2.5 percent, and "novelties" (including serials) just 1.5 percent of all broadcast hours.[1]

As early as 1922, WEAF in New York had engaged in an "experiment" to demonstrate the viability of commercial radio. Sponsors began to realize the lucrative nature of the new medium that allowed them to reach larger audiences than previously imagined. Sponsors could now bring their message directly into the homes of their customers, and influence the programs that they listened to in the process. The WEAF "experiment" began at a studio on the top floor of Gimbel Brothers Department Store, in New York City, when the head of *Broadcast Advertising Magazine*, G.F. McLelland, paid $100 to talk for ten minutes about the value of advertising and public relations. McLelland then offered to send a copy of the speech to any interested listeners, a technique that advertisers would use throughout the Golden Age of radio to gauge listenership and enthusiasm. McLelland received "about ten telephone calls and fifteen letters and postcards, among them a prospective client."[2] Sponsors, of course, were naturally drawn to nighttime radio: It had larger audiences (families were listening together), it could reach greater distances, and it had a greater variety of programming. The phenomenal success of Freeman Gosden and Charles Correll's *Sam 'n' Henry* in 1926 and 1927, which, due to contractual issues was renamed *Amos 'n' Andy* in 1929, erased any doubt of radio's commercial viability. Other programs, like *Rudy Vallee's Fleischmann's Yeast Hour* demonstrated that radio could provide sponsors with both profits and power.

Sponsoring the Homemaker

The world of daytime radio was filled not with drama and comedy but with programs focusing on home economics and cultural matters. Despite the allure of nighttime radio to the potential sponsor, some, like Chipso soap, saw the potential of reaching housewives as early as 1923.[3] Chipso sponsored *Ruth Turner's Washing Talks*, a concept that Procter & Gamble would use some years later with Mrs. Reilly and Ivory Soap during *Vic and Sade* and other programs. The U.S. Department of Agriculture also recognized radio's ability to reach the homemaker and sponsored its own program beginning in 1926, *Housekeeper's Chats*. The program was hosted by "Aunt Sammy," who happened to be the wife of Uncle Sam. Rather than endorse a product, for eighteen years, five times a week, fifteen minutes a day, Aunt Sammy and a cast of regulars offered listeners tips on everything from household repairs to cleaning, gardening, and cooking.[4] Listeners learned to make such favorites foods as succotash, brioches and chicken fricassee, along with more exotic delicacies, including one called "scalloped cabbage, spaghetti, and cheese," for which listeners were instructed to boil broken spaghetti for twenty minutes and coat it in a béchamel sauce, hot sauce, cabbage, and American cheese before baking the whole concoction for half an hour.[5]

Looking at a *New York Times*' "Today on the Radio" column for the date of *Vic and Sade*'s premiere, June 29, 1932, there is little escapist fare to be found. Instead, we find a range of titles and topics that included "Beatrice Mable—Beauty Talk" at 10:00 a.m. (WJZ 760), "Food Talk—Miss Julian Heath" 12:00 (WJZ 760), and "Airplane vs. Dog Sled—Merle H. Guise, Explorer" 3:15 p.m. (WJZ 760). At 4:30 p.m. listeners could be enlightened by "Southern Authors and Poets" with Hugh Gordon Miller, attorney. That same day listeners could be treated to "The Cheer Up Club" at 5:45 a.m. on WMCA, followed by "Beauty Talk," at 9:30 a.m. listeners could hear a talk on "Modern Living," followed an hour later by "Graphology Talk." On WEAF 660 listeners could find similar fare, including, at 10:45, "Cooking Talk with Betty Crocker" and at 11:15, "Household Institute." All three stations broadcast musical interludes throughout the day, from organ recitals to opera to "Hillbilly Songs" (WEAF, 660, 9:30 a.m.).

In 1932, NBC committed $1 million to bring new talent to daytime radio, and the president of NBC, M. H. Aylesworth, predicted "more varied program material [and] a further advance in artistry" for the upcoming year.[6] It would not be long before daytime's typical programs took a back seat to what would quickly become the dominant force in daytime radio, the soap opera. In an environment dominated by interview and advice programs, the promise of an entertaining drama must have seemed like a welcome respite from the concerns of the day.

On the Dial: Vic and Sade's *Contemporaries*

Although it would be among the first programs to be considered a soap opera, *Vic and Sade* would not be alone on the dial for very long. Daytime radio was soon inundated with a wide variety of soap operas, which by the 1940s had already garnered a bad reputation (discussed below). The most famous definition of a soap opera is probably the one put forth by James Thurber, near the dawn of the genre.

> A soap opera is a kind of sandwich, whose recipe is simple enough.... Between thick slices of advertising, spread twelve minutes of dialogue, add predicament, villainy, and female suffering

in equal measure, throw in a dash of nobility, sprinkle with tears, season with organ music, cover with a rich announcer sauce, and serve five times a week. [...] It is the hope of every advertiser to habituate the housewife to an engrossing narrative whose optimum length is forever and at the same time to saturate the consciousness with the miracle of a given product, so that she will be aware of it all the days of her life and mutter its name in her sleep.[7]

In the simplest of terms, a soap opera is a daytime dramatic serial, which derives its name from the sponsorship of household cleaning products. Typically, these dramas consisted of "fictitious domestic crises and troubles [which are] characterized by little action and much sentiment."[8] In order to understand *Vic and Sade*, it is important to view it in the context of its time. Given the vast body of soap operas that would come to occupy the daytime dial it would be impossible to detail them all. Instead, a sampling of programs must suffice.

"Slap me silly": The Predecessors of the True Soap

The earliest of these programs tended to focus on the everyday situations familiar to the audience; in time, however, soap operas would develop into melodramatic fantasies. The first of these shows, and one actually sponsored by a soap company, had debuted less than two years before *Vic and Sade*. *Clara, Lu, and 'Em*, fresh from its successful run on radio's nighttime schedule, had begun in June 1930, on WGN in Chicago. The program was the brainchild of three Northwestern University sorority sisters, Louise Starkey, Isabel Corrothers, and Ellen King. Low-key and often humorous, *Clara, Lu, and 'Em* bore little resemblance to the heightened, melodramatic soap operas that would follow it in the years to come, as can be seen by this excerpt from a 1935 episode:

> CLARA: Gee, I wonder if we should have gotten the waffle iron. I don't know if I will ever get over a certain feeling of heaviness over us not getting her that waffle iron.
> 'EM: That's too bad. I realized how you felt, yet it does seem better for us to give her a wedding present she can use on her trip.
> CLARA: Oh, I know, it would be too much for her to carry a waffle iron all over Europe. Actually, she couldn't get any use for it except at home, but I did think him and her could have had waffle irons for breakfast. Er, waffles—waffles? Well waffles, yeah. Sounds funny to me, don't it?
> 'EM: Well no. Not to me it don't.[9]

There are obvious similarities between *Vic and Sade* and *Clara, Lu, and 'Em*; both are, for the most part, light-hearted serials that deal with the commonalities of everyday life, albeit from different perspectives.

Similarly, the often-overlooked comedy *Cecil and Sally* (1930–1933) is another forerunner of the serial, though not quite a soap opera. First broadcast as *The Funniest Things* in 1928 on KYA,[10] the program reflects the same low-key approach as *Vic and Sade* and *Clara, Lu, and 'Em* as it follows the development of the young title characters' relationship. Again, the plots are driven by simple, often humorous, events. In this scene from an undated episode, Cecil attempts to appease Sally after forgetting a gift she had made for him:

> SALLY: Wait, Cecil, wait a minute. You forgot something.
> CECIL: No, I didn't; goodbye.
> SALLY: Cecil, your sweater. You forgot it. It's under the counter here.
> CECIL: Well slap me silly, I nearly forgot. Hey, don't.
> SALLY: Well you asked me to slap you. (laughs)

CECIL: Would you like a nice black eye?
SALLY: (laughs) I like brown ones better.

Threats of domestic abuse aside, *Cecil and Sally* bears a striking resemblance to *Vic and Sade* and *Clara, Lu, and 'Em:* All three shows center on a small number of characters, with careful attention to their interaction, and each program is also driven more by dialog than by plot. However, *Cecil and Sally* differed from the type of serial that would develop into the soap opera. Instead, it focused on humorous skits rather than an attempt to build a world in which its characters would have adventures, be they realistic or fantastic.

Another early serial drama, *Just Plain Bill* (1932–1955), continued radio's attempt in the early serials to create everyday characters who participated in situations familiar to the (presumed) listening audience. *Just Plain Bill* premiered in September 1932 on the CBS radio network. The program was the story of Bill Davidson, "the barber of Hartsville, the story of a man who might be living right next door to you,"[11] described as a "homespun philosopher and helpful neighbor."[12] A program about a barber seems an unlikely addition to daytime radio and an even more unlikely success; however, the "proprietor of the Hartville barbershop seldom had time to lather many faces—he was too busy patching up marriages, stifling the urges of citizens to commit suicide or murder, solving crimes of major and minor proportions and, in essence, being the guardian of his community."[13] Presumably, CBS felt that audiences would feel comfortable with a character holding a familiar, working-class job. Again, like *Vic and Sade*, this program dealt with everyday situations, small-town life, and working-class lives. In that context, it's interesting to recall Paul Rhymer's philosophizing barbers, Elmer and Will from "The Barbershop Philosophers," a script that was much less successful in its approach to the same situation.

Bill wouldn't be the only radio character offering sage advice to the residents of his town; he would soon be joined by *Ma Perkins* (1933–1960). Like Bill Davidson, Ma would come to possess a gentleness and patience that would brand her "America's mother of the air." Of course, Ma Perkins didn't start out that way; she began as a "combative old hen"[14] before transforming into an "eternal busybody and do-gooder,"[15] who would spend much of her twenty-seven years on the air striving to solve the problems of the residents of Rushville Center. In so doing, *Ma Perkins* began the transition toward melodrama that would quickly overwhelm the soap-opera genre. While *Ma Perkins* generated its fair share of tears and crises, it moved at a decidedly slower pace than many of its peers, allowing for characters to engage in lengthy dialogs, much as *Vic and Sade* was doing in a more humorous way. While, to some, this was an "extension of the ancient art of storytelling" and a means of offering listeners "helpful hints to daily living," others believed it to be "tired bilge, intensifying human frustration in its calculated attempts to bring temporary relief by dredging emotional sewers."[16]

But these programs were not quite what we think of when we hear the phrase "soap opera." None of these was filled with melodrama; none involved characters with lives of great wealth, or adventure, or romance. *Clara, Lu, and 'Em* and its peers aimed to entertain through presenting a slice of life, much like *Vic and Sade*, though never with the same mix of humor, wit, absurdity, and likeability as Paul Rhymer's show.

Making Soap

In October 1932, NBC's Blue Network introduced what could easily be thought of as daytime radio's first *real* soap opera, *Betty and Bob*. The program featured all of the melodramatic, outrageous, emotional traits that James Thurber associated with daytime drama. Initially starring Don Ameche as wealthy Bob Drake, *Betty and Bob* thrived on melodrama in a tale of a secretary of "humble origins" who falls in love with her wealthy boss, the heir to a great fortune.[17] The drama is compounded when Bob loses his fortune after falling in love with Betty, and the pair is forced to start over. "The plot lines revolved around love, hate, hubris, jealousy, greed, betrayal, divorce, and madness, just what an escapist America wanted to hear during the Great Depression."[18]

Audiences embraced *Betty and Bob* as they "surmounted everything: divorce, misunderstanding, the interference of other people, and sometimes the worst of all foes, the passage of time."[19] The couple even survived insanity, as shown in a recording of an undated episode where even upright Bob Drake, forced to work in the steel trade as foreman on a bridge, could be pushed to the breaking point: "I'm going crazy, I'm going out of my mind…." Bob frets over his son being taunted by his peers because his father is crazy: "That would fix everything, I'll kill myself!" As one might predict, only Betty's love can save Bob: "You're my world, my whole world," Betty reassures him. "I'll always love you; I always have and I always will."

The program gave audiences a type of romantic, dramatic fantasy they had never been heard on the nascent medium and, in doing so, proved that a radio serial need not be comedic in order to be successful. *Betty and Bob*, rather than *Vic and Sade*, would become the model for the dozens of soaps that would soon overtake the daytime airwaves. It also marked the first daytime soap opera from Frank and Anne Hummert, two of the most prodigious producers of radio programming. By the time *Betty and Bob* premiered in 1932, the Hummerts had already had success with daytime's *Just Plain Bill*, *Judy and Jane*, and the popular children's serial, *Little Orphan Annie*. By 1939, the Hummert production "mill" was responsible for producing no fewer than fifty serials a week,[20] including the highly successful *Backstage Wife*, *Young Widder Brown*, *The Romance of Helen Trent*, and *Stella Dallas*. Their brand of serial drama grew so successful that the soap opera would come to dominate the air—and cause some to complain that nothing was on *except* soap operas.

A Series of Serials

By 1933, the radio serial had established a place for itself on radio's schedule, with two of what would become the genre's longest-running soaps debuting within months of one another in 1932–1933, and an ever-expanding number of serials in following years. The first of these soaps, however, harked back to the simple, relatable, small stories of *Clara, Lu, and 'Em* rather than the pioneering melodrama of *Betty and Bob*, though it would grow increasingly dramatic in time.

Broadcast from 1932 to 1959, *Pepper Young's Family* was a beloved daytime institution, written by Elaine Carrington. Originally broadcast as *Red Adams*, with Burgess Meredith in the title role, the program changed its title to *Red Davis* at the behest of its sponsor, Beechnut Gum, who did not like having the name of one of its competition, Adams Gum, mentioned in the program. Later, the show would settle on *Pepper Young's Family*.[21] The program dealt with issues easy for listeners to relate to, especially as it was broadcast in a time when "most serials were melodramas of preposterous scope," like *Betty and Bob* and its imitators.[22] By contrast, *Pepper Young's Family* could turn a walk to school into a dramatic event. That said, there was genuine, often realistic drama in the program, such as the time the Youngs faced the threat of losing their home when patriarch Sam Young lost his job and was forced to look for work out of town. Although *Pepper Young's Family* utilized many of the themes characteristic of the genre, it was also an anomaly in its wholesome and simplistic nature. That did not stop the show from including some "fantastic" storylines, such as Peggy Young's engagement to the wealthy Carter Trent, and other situations which were sometimes handled with a dash of treacle borrowed from the more melodramatic soaps.

While the Youngs faced their share of problems other character faced tumult and treachery as well as not always successful romantic entanglements. Helen Trent, the heroine of the popular *Romance of Helen Trent* (1933–1960) is a prime example of the situations in which soap-opera characters—particularly starlets—could find themselves. Billed as the "real-life" story of a woman who carries on undaunted even when "life mocks her, breaks her hopes, dashes her against the rocks of despair" to prove that "because a woman is thirty-five, or more, romance need not be over." Helen did this not only for herself, but for "so many women" who also sought romance after the age of thirty-five.

Helen may have proved that romance was possible, but given the nature of her exploits it would seem unlikely that she inspired others to seek it out. In one storyline, Gil Whitney, the man Helen loved, has been tricked into marrying another woman, while a short time later she is framed for the murder of her ex-boyfriend. In yet another development, Gil Whitney is confined to a wheelchair and refuses to marry Helen until he can walk. On another occasion, one of Helen's "suitors" would trap her in a tower and shoot and seriously wound her beloved Gil Whitney.[23] Despite the obstacles that confronted Helen in her attempts to find love and happiness, it is worth noting that her romances did not go awry because of Helen's own faults, but because of the machinations of others.

Helen wasn't the only woman on daytime radio with romantic woes, nor were hers the worst. Her contemporaries were adept at becoming involved with scoundrels, liars, or, as was most likely, married men. Nora Drake, nurse and heroine of the late 1940s serial *This Is Nora Drake*, helped to highlight the dearth of single men in soaps when she fell in love with Dr. Ken Martinson. But "being burdened with most of the emotional instabilities of serial drama males,"[24] he married nurse Peggy King, who promptly set about to make his life a misery. Nora Drake pined over Martinson for five years until King fell prey to an assassin, freeing him to be with Nora. It wasn't always the man who was married in these scenarios, as *Backstage Wife*'s Mary Noble illustrates. Mary was the wife of what the show called the "matinee idol of a million other women," Larry Noble, in "the story of what it means to be the wife of a famous star." A Hummert drama airing from 1935 to 1959, it follows a similar theme to that of *Betty and Bob*, with Mary, a girl of humble origins from Iowa, coming to New York seeking a bright new future. Yet despite being the "perfectly named serial heroine," Mary was "attractive to men, especially unbalanced ones."[25] It was this, combined with Larry Noble's philandering, that helped to keep the Noble's marriage in an almost perpetual state of flux. However, as radio chronicler Stedman explains, there was reason for Larry Noble's jealousy, given Mary's faithful nature:

> She just could not avoid lunatics. No doubt about it, *Backstage Wife* had daytime radio's best selection of deranged villains. Helen Trent, it is true, had to fend off some obsessed schemers, but Mary Noble's pursuers were much more desperately in need of medical attention. They seemed mild enough at first, but sooner or later they made things most unpleasant for Mary. They threatened her life, drugged her Ovaltine, left her to die in lonely places, and even threw acid on her face. They were not very nice chaps.[26]

Treachery did not exist in romantic entanglements alone. *Stella Dallas*, another production of the Hummerts' mill and "perhaps the most excruciating melodrama on radio,"[27] featured another heroine who had married above her class. Although the program, based on the popular Olive Higgins Prouty novel and the 1937 Barbara Stanwyck film, would focus on a mother's love for her daughter, Stella still found time for adventure and intrigue that extended well beyond the experiences of most listeners. She became an amateur detective, using her skills to protect her beloved daughter from mysterious strangers and terrible threats. To be sure, Stella Dallas was not easily intimidated by such threats, taking an assertive role in combating them. Her confidence was justified as Stella "could, while bound, escape entrapment in a skyscraper by dangling darning thread she had extracted from her purse until it attracted the attention of a passer-by far below."[28] On one occasion, Stella became embroiled in a case that would lead her all the way to exotic Egypt, as preserved in a recording of an undated episode. Below, the show's narrator is speaking:

> In Washington with her daughter, Laurel, and Laurel's husband, Dick Grovenor, Stella Dallas is falsely accused by Dick's mother, Mrs. Grovenor, of stealing an Egyptian mummy. Stella, however, through Jeff Kentrall, an underworld acquaintance of Stella's old admirer, Ed Munn, discovers the real thief to be Rashid, the twin brother of her friend Sheik Ahmed, whom Mrs. Grovenor is sponsoring in society; and Stella upsets Rashid's scheme to get $15,000 from Mrs. Grovenor. To save Ahmed's family honor and avoid embarrassment for Mrs. Grovenor, Stella agrees to keep the matter a secret upon Rashid's promise that he will keep out of their way in the future. Now it's the next night in Laurel's apartment, and Stella is having after-dinner coffee with Laurel and Dick.

In the end, Stella would find herself in a precarious situation in a submarine at the bottom of the Suez Canal—about as far from the house halfway up the next block as one could get.

But not all programs were full of danger and tears. In the same year that they launched *Stella Dallas*, another Hummert creation took to the air, this one the comedic tale of a daydreaming automobile mechanic who aspired to be an inventor. *Lorenzo Jones* (1937–1955) ran for eighteen years on NBC. It invited listeners to "smile a while with Lorenzo Jones and his wife, Belle," and made what was, for daytime radio, the seldom heard promise of "more smiles than tears," recalling nothing so much as the often-heard promise on *Vic and Sade* inviting listeners into the program by telling them "it's time to smile again." With so many soap operas dishing out emotional upheaval, listeners apparently needed to be informed when something different was about to air. In addition to being relatively unique in its comedic content, *Lorenzo Jones* was a rarity in daytime radio for its depiction of the working class rather than the leisure class, something it shared with programs like *Just Plain Bill* and *The Goldbergs*.

Many of the show's smiles came from Lorenzo's bumbling, though creative inventions which included a teapot with three spouts so that guests could be served weak, medium, and strong tea, a pep tonic caused consumers to struggle to keep anything down[29] as well as the Lorenzo Jones Lie Detector, among many others. There were some successes for him, including a device taken for granted today, the outdoor vacuum cleaner; however, that particular invention was greeted with ridicule. His perpetual foot warmer received a considerably more positive response; however, in true Lorenzo form, he lost the proceeds from the device. Mostly, Lorenzo's inventions worked out more along the lines of his waterless washing liquid, which forced him to bury a week's worth of linens because of the stench his solution created.

Like *Vic and Sade*, *Lorenzo Jones* brought a certain absurdity to daytime radio, allowing for a respite from the melodrama of the day. Radio historian Jim Cox correctly notes similarities between *Lorenzo* and the nighttime radio program *Fibber McGee and Molly*.[30] Both James and McGee had big aspirations but lacked the ability to bring these dreams to fruition. One might compare Fibber McGee's closet, always bursting with odd items, with Lorenzo's mind, which is bursting with odd and interesting ideas and inventions just waiting to get out. To that end, one could draw a connection between Lorenzo's contraption-filled mind and the irreverence of Victor Gook as he teased and sometimes befuddled his family, or the often-confusing Uncle Fletcher with his endless array of colorful characters and anecdotes. However, what is perhaps most worth noting is that *Lorenzo Jones* and *Vic and Sade* stand out as isolated islands of humor in a wide sea frothing with soap bubbles.

"Friend to millions": Soap Operas and Audiences

Radio executives understood that daytime programming needed to appeal to primarily female audiences since they assumed that men would be too busy working to listen, and that bored housewives would be the majority of those tuning in. Daytime radio, therefore, in its effort to capitalize on its predominately female audience, often produced programming intended to be a "companion, teacher, wet nurse, and friend to millions of women throughout America."[31] As we have seen, of all the many forms of programming tried by 1931, it was the soap opera that would ultimately prove most popular and most profitable, giving sponsors a new type of programming that encouraged women to listen throughout the day.[32] By 1936, 55.3 percent of the daytime schedule was comprised of serial programs, pushing out or severely limiting most other types of shows.[33]

Several factors contributed to the dominance of the soap opera, beginning with the public's acceptance of radio. The listening audience had embraced the relatively new medium, allowing programming and advertisers to reach consumers directly in their homes. Moreover, advertisers became increasingly involved in the development of programs, as was the case with Procter & Gamble, which had originally auditioned and rejected *Vic and Sade*. Advertisers were not merely sponsors; they were often producers. Further, because many women accepted and performed the roles of mother and housewife, sponsors and broadcasters were better able to craft programming that appealed to these women, especially escapist soap operas.[34]

The response to these programs was overwhelming. Since the medium's earliest days, listeners found themselves making connections to the voices emanated from their radios. Soap opera characters in particular became important and relevant to audience members, many of whom regarded them as friends. Most listeners could not (or did not) distinguish real people from actors playing parts,[35] and it was not uncommon for listeners to send their on-air friends gifts and cards or offer advice regarding their latest predicament.[36]

Regarding on-air personalities as friends was not a phenomenon limited to soap operas; these "ethereal relationships were important to many listeners."[37] The 1930s WJZ radio personality Norman Brokenshire recounted being inundated with fan letters that sometimes took the form of "books, candy, jars of homemade cookies, pressed flowers, clippings from local newspapers, jewelry."[38] In some instances, listeners perceived their relationships as being far more intimate than they were in reality. Brokenshire describes one occasion in which he was confronted by the husband of an "ardent radio fan" who had sent him a large number of letters to which he had not responded. The unrequited correspondence had, according to the husband, driven the woman to the brink of distraction. Sifting through the "ardent

Radio quickly became Americans' preferred method of learning about their world. In this 1929 photograph, technicians set up radio equipment to broadcast the inauguration of Herbert Hoover (Library of Congress).

love letters," he and the husband worked together to craft a response, suggesting that "a radio personality was not worth such emotional sacrifices."[39] This distracted wife was far from alone. Many who listened to soaps identified with the characters and embraced them as friends and as reflections of their own aspirations, ideals, and self-images.

Identification and Soap Operas

According to theorist Kenneth Burke, we are driven by a need to overcome the separateness caused by being members of different classes. Even though we may not be identical, in as much as our interests are joined we can identify with each other. This overlapping of interest, Burke explained, allowed two parties to become "substantially one."[40] As early as the 1940s, Rudolf Arnheim noted that serials invite identification through a "variety of means," but mostly through "narrative art."[41] Arnheim explained that two elements essential to the audience's ability to identify with a character were that character's role and the amount of time the audience was exposed to him or her:

> The central position of a character invites the listener to perceive and evaluate the plot situation from the point of view of this person. Identification is furthered by the sheer quantity of time devoted to a character and by the amount of insight given into what the person thinks and feels. Physical, intellectual, and ethical perfection, social power and prestige must also promote identification very strongly. Furthermore, there is the factor of resemblance: a middle-aged housewife will identify herself more readily with a middle-aged housewife, etc.[42]

Burke delineated several forms of identification. One category had an individual identify with another through property that is either shared or coveted. Another is identification through ideals, wherein two individuals share beliefs and attitudes. A third is formulistic identification, in which formal devices awaken an expectancy of collaboration. For our purposes, we will explore identification through property and idealism to better understand the relationship of the audience to serials. Within these forms of identification Burke proposed several strategies, including the common ground strategy, in which identification is made by emphasizing the shared beliefs and interests between the parties; the transcendent "we" which conveyed the commonality between the sender and the receiver; and identification through dissociation, in which two parties are united through a shared enemy.

When considering programs like *Vic and Sade* and *Pepper Young's Family*, it is easy to see how average, working-class listeners would have identified with the Youngs and the Gooks. Both families had modest homes: the Gooks rented theirs and, for a time, so too did the Youngs. The Gooks lived in a small, nondescript house on a block that, for all intents and purposes, could be the listener's. The Gooks also did not own another piece of coveted property—a car. Sade regularly darned socks and was concerned about how household funds were spent. Neither family had a "household staff." Sade Gook and Mary Young prepared the family meals. Listeners could also identify with those who inhabited property they did not own, but wished they did. Many, despite the troubles that followed them, could identify with the likes of Mary Noble, or Lora Lawton, relishing their rags-to-riches stories and feeling confident that they could find happiness in their place.

Some might have identified with *The Life of Mary Southern*'s titular character through idealism. Mary, who had been a dutiful housewife, found herself in the dual role of corporate president when her family began marketing bottled water. Mary is so devoted to her causes that she turns down a role in a "major" motion picture. For the housewife aspiring to do and be more, yet not sacrifice her family, Mary could have been an ideal, of sorts, proving that it was possible to do it all without sacrificing those you love.

The average housewife also found much to identify with in Sade Gook, and indeed in 1940, the Women's National Radio Committee's "Daytime Serial Survey" revealed that American women deemed *Vic and Sade* their favorite program in large part because it featured "people like ourselves." Like the average listener, Sade worried about how money was spent and frequently had to reel her husband in from buying unnecessary goods, and teaching her son the value of a dollar. In an episode aired on September 7, 1934, she refused Rush's request for a slip-over coat, saying, "Little boys with poor fathers hafta be out of date sometimes." Sade even thinks twice before buying new washrags, making sure to comparison shop. Sade also had insecurities with which the "average" housewife could, no doubt, identify. She was not, for example, as educated as Vic or some of her friends, something that could, at times, be a source of anxiety for her. On August 5, 1933, Sade, along with Vic's help, was entertaining "fancy folks," friends of Ruthie Stembottom, who were coming to visit.[43] We learn that the pair had been cleaning since eight a.m.. Sade points out that one of the ladies married a "real educated fella" who is so important he left for Hawaii on their wedding day.

Sade has clearly gone all-out to impress her guests, setting out her best dishes and keeping Vic at home for his superior conversational skills, so that she can impress those she perceived to be her superiors. Unfortunately, as the episode drew to a close, Rush returned home from playing General Lee with cotton glued to his face and chest! Many listeners could easily identify with Sade's position of having to entertain people who could be judging them.

On February 22, 1935, Sade planned a luncheon with lady friends, including Mis' Brighton and Mis' Chilly. At the same time Vic invited his boss, Mr. Ruebush, for an aromatic meal of beef punkies and limber-schwartz cheese, an idea that mortified Sade. These ladies, Sade explained, "ain't no ordinary ladies," to which Vic countered, "Mis' Brighton an' Mis' Chilly must be terrible thin-skinned women—terrible shallow hypocrites—terribly fully of false and contemptible pride."[44] Determined to impress her elite friends, Sade continued to forbid Vic from entertaining Mr. Ruebush, even if he did so in a different room. Only when Sade discovers that Mis' Brighton and Mis' Chilly actually enjoy beef punkies and limber-schwartz cheese does she relent.

Sade was also a wife who experienced many of the same situations as that of a typical housewife. She loved and was devoted to her husband, but, like most wives, she was forced to nag him in order to get the lawn mowed, the snow shoveled, and other chores accomplished. The June 15, 1936, episode illustrates precisely why nagging both Vic and Rush would be necessary at times. The pair is returning from work and school, respectively, when they spot the "ominous" lawnmower on the front lawn. Having plans to watch a particularly contentious bowling match at the YMCA, they lie to Sade, telling her that there are "problems" with the mower and that the lawn will have to wait until it is fixed.

Most women have dealt with someone like Sade's "friend," Mis' Applerot. Mis' Applerot was the pretentious, domineering and all-knowing member of the Ladies' Thimble club who talked "biggity-big talk," and Sade resented her. Listening to a particular episode from 1940, in which Sade is reduced to tears after Mis' Applerot reconfigures the Gooks' furniture to give them a "1940 style," it would be easy for a listener to identify through dissociation; relating to a shared "enemy," the listener is then joined with her.

Given the myriad ways avid listeners could identify with soap-opera characters, it is hardly surprising that they made such close connections to these characters, sending letters, cards, gifts, and words of advice.[45] Identification was also strengthened by the fact that radio brought these characters directly into the home in a way that was unprecedented. Soap-opera characters were in listeners' homes, their living rooms, kitchens, and bedrooms. They accompanied them as they worked and rested. They shared their day. But for many critics, audiences and characters had come to spend far too much time together. In fact, many came to see daytime radio—especially its soap operas—as a serious social problem.

"I won't listen"

When *Vic and Sade* came on the air, the daytime schedule offered listeners a range of programming, including music, cooking, fashion, and educational programs; but now, less than ten years later, listeners looking for enlightenment would have to hope that designer Stella Dallas might share some fashion secrets or that Ma Perkins would let them in on a recipe. In 1941, a "woman's serial" could be heard in all but one quarter-hour of daytime when, between 5:30 and 5:45 the children's serial *Jack Armstrong, The All-American Boy*, offered an alternative.[46] The relief provided by *Jack Armstrong* is clearer when one takes into account the fact that, for a total of four hours of the broadcast day, anyone tuning into network radio would have no choice but to listen to a soap opera. During twenty-six of the thirty-two quarter-hour periods of the broadcast day, at least two soap operas were heard, and in six of those quarters three were broadcast.[47] The soap suds were overflowing and overwhelming daytime audiences.

Not everyone was happy about wading through this immeasurable tide of suds. To many pining for the organ music that preceded soap operas or for those hoping to catch an educational or cultural program, the situation was unacceptable. Some began to demand air time for culture, education, news, and programs other than soap operas. One listener, Elsie Scott, in her March 10, 1938, letter to the *New York Times*' radio editor, spoke for many women:

> To the Radio Editor:
> There are too many silly serial stories fed to intelligent housewives hour after hour, morning and afternoon. One scans the published announcements hoping against hope for something with a bit of intellectual stimulation, and pouncing with glee on an occasional fifteen minutes devoted to some good chamber music, or a brief summary of current events. Why can't we have more of this sort of thing? Why not good programs about travel or gardens as well as the obvious one covering national and international problems, music, and literature?
> ELSIE SCOTT,
> Providence, R. I.[48]

By 1940, at least some of these disgruntled listeners had joined forces to take on broadcasters and sponsors for a new, more balanced, program schedule. The result was the "I Won't Listen" campaign organized by the domestic relations department of the New Rochelle, New York, Women's Club. The department, under the leadership of Mrs. Everett L. Bernard, hoped to spread their message of opposition to "cheap love dramas" throughout the state and to the National Federation of Women's Clubs. Mrs. Bernard said that the committee objected to the "serial romances that are flooding the air in the morning and afternoon."[49]

Writing in the Dubuque, Iowa, *Telegraph-Herald*, another "I Won't Listen" supporter explained the modern woman's listening needs, noting that most women were interested in self-improvement in a number of different contexts, including their appearance and their budgets; many were also interested in bettering their children's education. This was a new age, she wrote, and "Papa no longer leaves Mama home when he goes to a ball game, or when he sets out for a game of golf."[50] Therefore, programs dealing with international affairs and politics would also be welcomed by the modern woman so tired of hearing about Helen Trent's romances and about how *Portia Faces Life*. Even the FCC chair, James L. Fly, weighed in on the controversy, admitting in 1943 to having an "aversion" to soap operas and other programs that "fill the long daytime hours with highly emotional, cheap forms of droolery."[51]

While the "I Won't Listen" campaign did garner attention (reaching as many as thirty-nine of the forty-eight states, according to Mrs. Bernard), broadcast executives were quick to defend soap operas. Speaking before a symposium of representatives for the Westchester County women's clubs, WMCA executive vice-president, Donald S. Shaw, informed the women gathered that "dripping love dramas" were good business and were necessary to pay for those quality programs that couldn't pay for themselves.[52] Shaw's defense was echoed by others in the broadcasting industry, including the president of the Mutual Broadcasting System, Edgar Kobak, who would later note that soap operas offer tremendous appeal to "shut-ins [and] the busy housewife."[53]

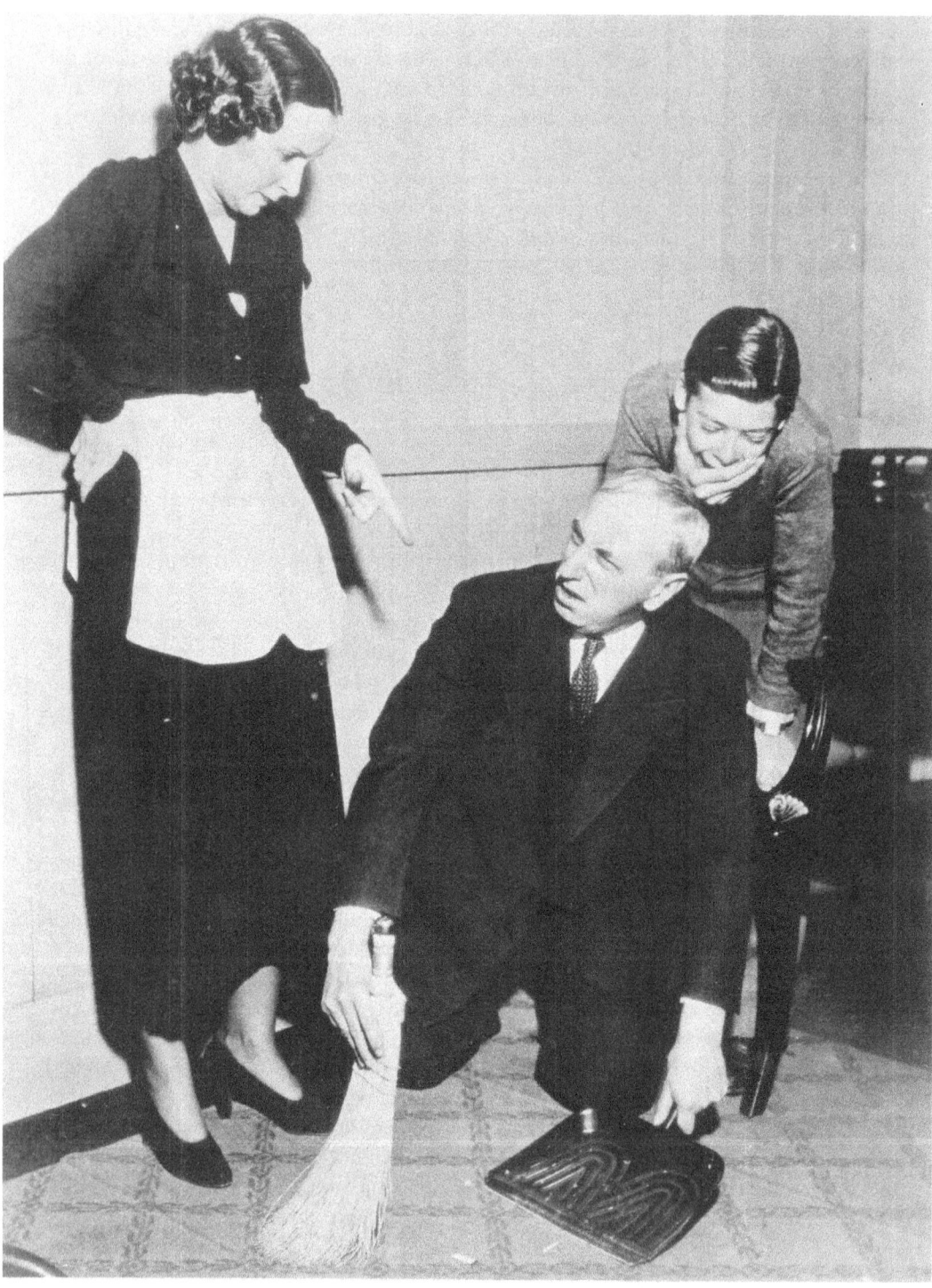

In this photograph from Art Van Harvey's personal collection we see Vic, Sade, and Rush in a brief domestic dust-up. The low-stakes domestic incidents of *Vic and Sade* contrasted markedly with the "highly emotional, cheap forms of droolery" condemned by critics like the chairman of the FCC, James L. Fly (Mark C. Lancaster/The Art Van Harvey Collection).

The 1940 Westchester County Symposium provided an opportunity for those present, including the publicity director for WHN, A.L. Simon, to praise the exceptionalism of those protesting while simultaneously pointing to the alleged ignorance of their listeners. Simon's claim that radio is a "boon" for women not so "culturally fortunate"[54] was a theme that would be repeated throughout the "I Won't Listen" campaign. A contemporary study found that, on average, the more education a woman of that era had, the less likely she was to listen to serials, and this correlation between education level and serial listening held true across all age groups and income levels, according to a series of surveys conducted by Herta Hertzog in the 1940s. Hertzog's study found that 48 percent of women surveyed in Iowa listened regularly to serials, with approximately half (23.5 percent) listing serials as among their five favorite types of programs. Hertzog's surveys of women nationwide demonstrated an inverse relationship between education level and serial listening, with those women who completed only grade school more likely to listen than those who completed high school or college. This relationship held up when controlled for factors such as age and income.[55]

The Filth of Soap

Broadcasters were aware of this, and they understood that their business depended on appealing to the masses—and therefore less-educated—female listeners than other forms of media, including literary novels or high-end magazines. These attitudes allowed daytime radio to become what Hilmes describes as "the venue for a debased kind of commercialized, feminized mass culture."[56] With limited exceptions, broadcasters had made a clear delineation between nighttime and daytime programming. At night, listeners (assumed to be men home from work) experienced more "sophisticated, respectable, and masculine" programming,[57] leaving women with programs which male broadcasting executives deemed unworthy of or of no interest to male listeners. This was somewhat ironic, of course, since the serial began at night, with such programs as *The Rise of the Goldbergs*; *Clara, Lu, and 'Em*; *Myrt and Marge*; and *Just Plain Bill*. These programs had large and dedicated audiences of men as well as women, but once the serial transitioned profitably to daytime the engaging, commercial traits that had made the format popular with both men and women became the source of disrespect.

The "I Won't Listen" committee members weren't the only ones condemning daytime serials. Vehement opposition came from a number of sources, including psychiatrist Dr. Louis Berg, who described the ill-effects soap operas could have upon the listeners. He based his findings upon his listening to just two soap operas, *The Right to Happiness* and *Woman in White*, for three weeks in the first months of 1942:

> Pandering to perversity and playing out destructive conflicts, these serials furnish the same release for the emotionally distorted that is supplied to those who desire satisfaction from a lynching bee, lick their lips at the salacious scandals of the *crime passionnel*, who in the unregretted past cry out in ecstasy at a witch burning.[58]

In a speech to the Buffalo Advertising Club that March, Berg said that soap operas caused his patients to become addicted to their perversity, causing them to relapse into neuroticism, and issued a warning that the same could happen to those who listened to soaps:

> The cumulative effect of a diet of corrupting melodrama could not fail to produce an 'anxiety state.' Even those patients who were cautioned of the baleful effects of listening to these serials

found it harder to resist.... The hairline that divides the normal from the neurotic ... can disappear from such influence as the unwitting sadism of suppurating serials.[59]

Radio pioneer Lee de Forest was equally unkind to the genre, claiming that soap operas "could be ordered off the air very easily without much of a cultural loss to the American people."[60]

Dr. Berg's attack was only one shot fired from the ivory tower against the serial. The sheer volume of soap operas, and the loyalty of their mass audiences, had caught the attention of more serious academic researchers, who marveled at the soap-opera phenomenon. Predominantly male researchers and intellectuals began to focus on soap operas as an abnormal form of media consumption, studying whether their audience was in some way different from that for other types of programming. The only significant difference they found was gender: Soap-opera audiences were primarily female. Nevertheless, the amount of research and attention given to studying soap-opera demographics marked the genre as problematic, and left its audience stigmatized as mentally unbalanced, easily persuaded, and weak—the same characteristics that many male researchers had historically applied to women in general.[61]

Yet what academic researchers often failed to see was that the audiences for daytime soap operas felt they offered several positive benefits, and could help listeners face challenges in their own lives.[62] One rare positive report from academia, a 1948 study by Drs. W. Lloyd Warner and William E. Henry of the Committee on Human Development of the University of Chicago, said that radio serials could serve as "old-time morality plays" and can "help to hold families together" by illustrating the hopes and fears of a housewife and the standards of good and evil in an easy-to-understand manner.[63] The study, which focused on the drama *Big Sister*, went so far as to claim that the programs provided casual but important entertainment that helps the women listening to "preserve American family life as we know it."[64]

Radio gave American women the ability to go beyond their environments and experience, albeit vicariously. This was particularly true in regard to occupations. While working-class families were not excluded from the daytime drama, they were certainly outnumbered by an array of professionals, including role models for women.[65] Women in serials, in particular, held positions of skill and prestige. They were attorneys, such as Portia Blake in *Portia Face Life*, Terry Regan in *Terry Regan: Attorney at Law*, and *Her Honor, Nancy James*. They were represented in the medical field as both nurses and physicians: *Woman in White*; *Kate Hopkins, Angel of Mercy*; *Girl Intern*; *Dr. Joyce Jordan*; and *The Lives and Loves of Dr. Susan*. *The Story of Bess Johnson* and *Hilltop House* depicted women as social workers, while *We, the Abbotts* and *Against the Storm* presented women in the role of educators. Women were also represented in the United States Senate by Mary Marlin, who filled her husband's seat when he went missing in her eponymously titled show.[66] There were also entrepreneurs like Ma Perkins, who ran a lumber yard; Jenny Peabody, who ran a hotel and owned a general store; and the merchant heroine of *Caroline's Golden Store*.[67] In some instances, such as *The Career of Alice Blair*, the heroine was able to engage in multiple careers, ranging from a personal secretary to actress, among others, all within the program's one-year run. Of course, not every program depicted women in glamorous and successful positions. In *Arnold Grimm's Daughter*, the character of Connie Tremaine opened a lingerie store following the death of her husband. Shortly thereafter, when her father became sick she replaced him in his factory job.[68] Another serial, *My Son and I*, depicted the widow of a vaudeville star trying to support her son any way that she could. Nevertheless, these programs showed women taking an active role in the working world.

Of equal importance were positive depictions of the housewife by women like Lorenzo Jones's devoted wife, Belle; Julie Palmer, wife of Dr. Dan Palmer in *The Doctor's Wife*; the matriarch of *Pepper Young's Family*; and Mary Young, who helped to ground the family as it made its way through difficult times. Sade Gook offered what may have been the most accurate portrayal of a housewife, and, thus, the most relatable for audiences. Sade rarely encountered a drama greater than a disagreement with a neighbor. Her work was real, and it was "never ending"—whether washing up after dinner, dusting the house, ironing, darning socks, Sade was almost perpetually in motion. On those rare instances when she was able to take a few minutes to sit on the porch swing and enjoy a brief respite, listeners were happy for her. Sade may have been uninterested in politics and the affairs of the world, but, as Paul Rhymer explained, in "her own kitchen she's as deft, wise and capable as any human being could be."[69] While later generations might look upon such a description as patronizing, in this era Sade demonstrated that a radio personality could attract audiences by presenting a sensitive, heartfelt portrayal of her audience as they were, not just through the glamorous lives they wished they could lead.

For the Masses

The attack on soap operas did not come only from the realm of sociology. Artistic considerations played a part as well. The sheer quantity of daytime serial programs inundating the airwaves caused many to question their overall quality. Few programs were spared the ravages of radio critics, including *Vic and Sade*, which had been described as "the most literate of all daytime serials" and "one of the few radio shows that is always consistently mature in conception and writing."[70]

As will be discussed in depth in Chapter Four, radio was a popular target of critics, who objected to its low-brow programming and contributions to fostering a mass culture. These critics believed that appealing to the public's base impulses was a threat to society as a whole. Despite the hyperbole, the critics had a valid point. As we've seen, serials were frequently sensationalistic and intended to appeal not to the intellect of their listeners, but rather to thrill and excite them.

Adorno and Horkheimer wrote of the modern "culture industry" in which a sterile, factory-like environment yielded "standard products to meet the same needs at countless locations."[71] Perhaps nothing reflects this notion more than the assembly-line–like production of the Hummerts, whose studio was routinely called a "mill," a "plant," or a "factory," and which churned out more than six *million* words in 1943 *alone*. While the Hummerts themselves prepared the general scenarios, a staff of writers and editors created the actual scripts.[72] Or consider the output of Irna Phillips, who by herself, each week in 1940, produced six serials (*Woman in White, Guiding Light, Road of Life, Right to Happiness, Springtime and Harvest, Tomorrow's Children*).[73] Surely, under such conditions quality would be variable.

Vic and Sade *as Serial and Anti-Serial*

> Well sir, it's about ten-thirty o'clock in the morning as our scene opens here now in the kitchen of the small house halfway up in the next block, we find Mrs. Victor Gook busily ironing clothes. She's a day late getting around to this business because Monday she cleaned wallpaper and yesterday she entertained the ladies. And there's Victor Gook approaching the doorway. Listen.
> Opening narration, *Vic and Sade*, May 6, 1936[74]

With openings like that it's easy to distinguish *Vic and Sade* from many of its peers. Few serials titillated with ironing and wallpaper cleaning since, after all, those were precisely the sorts of menial chores from which listeners were tuning in to escape, and yet *Vic and Sade* embraced these and many other facets of daily life. While Mary Noble fought off obsessed followers and Stella Dallas did battle in the Suez Canal, Sade Gook was more than likely darning socks or planning a night of 500 with her neighbors, the Stembottoms. While Lorenzo Jones was concocting outlandish inventions, Vic Gook was busy serving as an accountant for a kitchenware manufacturer. There were clear differences between *Vic and Sade* and other daytime soap operas, not the least of which was the fact that *Vic and Sade* was a comedy. Unlike other soap operas, its intention was not move listeners to tears or to the edge of their seat, but rather to laughter through the depiction of day-to-day domestic life of its recurring characters.

But the Gooks weren't entirely different from other daytime programs; along with the differences there were similarities. Perhaps one way to examine these similarities and differences is to recall James Thurber's description of soap operas. Thurber, as we have seen, identified seven, albeit facetious, ingredients which he believed to be consistent in every soap opera: (1) thick slices of advertising, (2) twelve minutes of dialog, (3) predicament, (4) villainy, (5) female suffering, (6) rich announcer sauce, and (7) served five times a week. Perhaps, in applying these terms to *Vic and Sade* we would be well served by beginning with Mr. Thurber's seventh criteria: *Vic and Sade* was a daily serial, airing Monday through Friday. Like its peers, it had time to develop its characters and ensure that its audience was fully acquainted with them. *Vic and Sade*, also like its peers, was contained between "thick slices of advertising." These "slices" were provided by Procter & Gamble and came in such varieties as "Crisco" and "Ivory Flakes." Such advertisements were presented by maternal figures or by the program's narrator, who provided a familiar and trusted voice, the same voice that set the scene at the Gooks' house each week and invited listeners to "smile again."

In most instances, the product was directly linked to the program and its characters: "Crisco's *Vic and Sade*." This let listeners know that there was a direct relationship between the program and the sponsor and made it clear that if you liked one, you would like the other. The advertisements, like the programs they were sponsoring, had a homey, welcoming feeling. In a typical advertisement from June 13, 1940, announcer Melvin Allen informs listeners of the "wonderful things good food can do" for them, including keeping the whole family happy. Of course, only Crisco can bring these good foods—and family happiness—together. Lasting one-minute and fifty-four seconds, the advertisement was a thick slice indeed. Another, thinner slice of advertising was typically placed at the end of each program, reminding listeners of Crisco's (or another Procter & Gamble product) association with *Vic and Sade* and emphasizing that product's benefits. In the case of the June 13, 1940, episode, the sponsor's closing message ran for one-minute and nine seconds, most of which was spent emphasizing Crisco's versatility and its ability to produce better fish fries.

Later in the series, Procter & Gamble introduced spokeswomen like Zella Lane and the maternal Mrs. Isabella Beach, "your radio neighbor," who delivered "household hints," all of which happened to utilize P&G products. The following was originally heard in an episode broadcast on August 24, 1942.

> Well you know friends, taking advantage of these "Victory Food Specials" is a big contribution we can make in this war and it's such an easy thing to do, why our own good, domestic cheeses are the Victory Food Special right now and cheese is something we should serve more often anyway; it's one of the most nutritious foods there is. And there are so many ways of including

cheese in our meals, for instance have you ever tried a toasted cheese top on an apple pie? You just lay narrow strips of cheese across the top crust and then toast under the broiler until the cheese just begins to melt—my, it's good. The combination of that toasted cheese flavor and that tender, flakey Crisco pie crust is just about perfect, at least that's what my husband says, and like all men he's pretty fussy about pie. I know before Crisco's new pastry method came along I used to turn out a tough pie crust occasionally and he'd complain, but not anymore, because every pie I make this new Crisco way has a tender, flakey crust, in fact that's what the Crisco people guarantee you—tender flakey pie crust every time or your money back. Yes, they're so sure of this new Crisco pastry method they'll actually refund you the price of a whole pound of Crisco if you aren't satisfied with your pie crust. You see, Crisco's different from other shortening in your store; it's specially made just to give you tender, flakey pie crust, and that's why I'm so anxious for you all to try Crisco and the new Crisco pastry method; the method is right on the Crisco label, you know. So try it real soon, won't you? Try it for that toasted cheese apple pie I was talking about. And now, let's drop in for a visit with Vic and Sade.

Although a commercial spokeswoman, Mrs. Beach *sounded* sincere in her efforts to convince listeners to try Crisco's "new pastry method." Yet while her motherly tone seemed well suited to the product, not every listener appreciated her presence. In a *Billboard* magazine review of the program, Beach was cited as "the only weak spot" in the show, with the critic adding that she delivered segments in "in a voice that sounds as tho [*sic*] it had been incurably frightened by a mike."[75]

Let's turn to Thurber's second point (twelve minutes of dialog) and sixth (rich announcer sauce): Despite being rich in well-crafted dialog, *Vic and Sade* fails to live up to Thurber's twelve-minute standard, with each episode ranging in length from roughly nine minutes and thirty seconds (with the occasional shorter episode) to just under eleven minutes; however, this was comparable to the length of most other soap operas after commercial messages are removed. Moreover, Paul Rhymer did not have "rich announcer sauce" to rely on in padding out each episode. *Vic and Sade* did not include an announcer's recap of the previous day's adventure or a lengthy organ overture to cushion the episode. Each *Vic and Sade* installment was purely dialog between the characters, with no "artificial ingredients" added.

Predicament, villainy, and female suffering were the *sine qua non* of Thurber's soap operas. For example, on July 7, 1947, Lora Lawton, on the program that shared her name, found herself in a predicament. In addition to Lora's struggling with being the wife of one of the richest, most attractive men in the country, her husband, Peter, had woken from a coma in a hospital for the criminally insane, presumably guilty of murder. Should Lora encourage him to have the operation that will restore his sanity, even if that means reopening his case which would lead to a whole new investigation or allow him to accept his circumstances and remain in the hospital for the criminally insane?

During the December 10, 1932, episode, Sade learns that Rush's mother may want Rush to live with his aunt, who recently came into some money. The problem is compounded when Vic announces that he may lose his job. Yet this was an anomaly on the program. Most predicaments involved everyday situations that listeners would have faced themselves. For example, in the August 5, 1936, episode, the Gooks face a simple predicament when, while playing baseball, Vic and Rush break Mis' Fisher's basement window. As Rush is young and innocent, Vic wants him to take the blame so that repercussions will be less severe. However, as Rush notes, he is "hardly what you'd call the lisping lips of an innocent *child*." As the pair debates how best to handle the situation, Sade suggests fixing the window before Miss Fisher returns home. Of course, Sade's remedy leads to another predicament: how to accomplish this seemingly easy task.

Villainy, like predicament, can come in varying degrees. Ellen Brown, of *Young Widder Brown*, certainly encountered her share of villainy at the hands of the deranged Louise Simpson. Louise, not content to enjoy the wealth passed on to her by her murdered husband, was also determined to have Ellen's beau, Anthony. The ensuing madness left Ellen the victim of plots, conniving, and a near-fatal gunshot wound. Like the majority of the predicaments

The Merchandise Mart in Chicago was the world's largest building when it opened in 1930. NBC's Chicago radio studios were located here, and the cast of *Vic and Sade* would gather there to broadcast the day's episode for most of the series' run (Carol M. Highsmith Archive, Library of Congress, Prints and Photographs Division).

the Gooks encountered, the villainy they faced was in small and manageable doses and often exacerbated to some degree by Sade's imagination. It was not uncommon for Mis' Applerot, a member of Sade's Thimble Club, to be involved in the villainy that Sade encountered. Mis' Applerot was a busybody, and a pretentious one at that. While most of her schemes appeared to be aimed at bolstering her own image, some were worse, as was the case with the January 23, 1939, revelation that she had been coercing the Thimble Club ladies to purchase flowers even when they couldn't afford them because, unbeknownst to all, the flower man "amounts to bein' the nephew of Mis' Applerot."[76] Sade recounts to Vic the way in which poor Mrs. Atkins had to sacrifice buying butter in order to afford flowers, all because of Applerot's "rotten and deceitful" behavior. Sade heroically prepares to take to the phone to defeat this villainy by informing her fellow members of the truth.

Villainy was also found in a much more dramatic, though far less realistic, manner through the adventures of Rush and Russell's hero, Third Lieutenant Clinton Stanley, who faced villains and received romantic rewards comparable to the likes of *Stella Dallas*. But this was never presented as anything other than completely, unrealistically fictional, as Stanley battled everything from counterfeiters to twelve-foot boa constrictors while always defeating his enemy in time to receive one more kiss from his beloved, Lady Margaret Pinkerton.

This brings us to the last of Thurber's criteria for daytime soap operas: female suffering. Suffering, like villainy and predicament, is relative to one's circumstance. To the best of the radio audience's knowledge, Sade was never forced to endure the torture of seeing the love of her life married to another man in the way that Helen Trent and Nora Drake had, but she did engage in some self-inflicted suffering by making herself jealous of the women who worked with Vic at Consolidated Kitchenware Plant 14, particularly Pom Pom Cordova. Listeners were led to understand that Pom Pom was the antithesis of Sade: loose, wild, and carefree. She was frequently seen at the Butler House Hotel, entertaining guests and playing musical selections on exotic instruments like the tropical guitar and Caribbean dream flute. Much to Sade's chagrin, Pom Pom was the only female member (albeit honorary) of Vic's lodge, the Sacred Stars of the Milky Way. Sade also seethed when one of Vic's female co-workers suggested that Vic enter the "prettiest eyes" contest at Consolidated Kitchenware Plant 14, a contest that he actually won.[77]

On another occasion, Sade comes home from a Ladies' Thimble Club meeting and is excited to tell Vic that she has learned that another of his female co-workers, Lolita DeRienzi from the boxing department, is an actual Indian princess. However, Vic already knew this, causing Sade to have "the wind taken out of my sails." She is annoyed to learn that Vic had known this tidbit for ages, but never told her. "I just eat up details about Indian princesses," she says, recalling the soap opera's fascination with the exotic and the aristocratic. Worse, her jealousy is again piqued over Vic's familiarity with Lolita. She interrogates him until he gets flustered, at which point she leaves him to brood in the living room alone as she heads off to make dinner.[78] This sort of "suffering," however, paled in comparison with the life-threatening melodrama of *Vic and Sade*'s daytime competitors.

But if *Vic and Sade* was both serial and anti-serial, it was nevertheless a pawn in a broader struggle to define culture, one that went beyond the "I Won't Listen" movement to interest some of America's most elite culture critics.

Four. The "ins and outs of modern life": Mass Culture and Its Critics

Since the development of modern media, critics have found cause to complain about its supposed effects on the audience, particularly its ability to breed passivity and conformity and its negative impact on morality. The German poet Goethe was already disenchanted with the theater at the end of the eighteenth century, complaining that audiences were trained to demand immediate gratification and base emotions. Theater critics of the era similarly bemoaned the appearance of the supernatural on the stage, charging that works like Matthew Lewis's *Castle Spectre* promoted superstition among the uneducated. At the end of the nineteenth century, Nietzsche wrote of the "barbarism" of contemporary mass culture and the way the mass media were debasing language and destroying appreciation for the arts. In England, the literary critic Harry Quilter raged against the "Gospel of Intensity," a push toward extreme sensationalism in the media that he attributed to the triumph of financial motives over morality—all at the cost of the morality of the mass audience, which needed protection from temptation and sin.[1]

"The various ins and outs of modern life": Defining Culture

The theme that the public at large was the tool of more powerful forces directed by a media and financial elite carried over into twentieth century media criticism, particularly regarding the rise of movies and radio. As Rush said to Sade, "The trouble with you, Mom, is that you refuse to understand the various ins and outs of modern life." For culture critics, modern life could be summed up as the gradual triumph of mass culture. Their critique had three important areas of emphasis: the role of mass culture in leisure activities; the effects of mass culture on education; and the power of mass culture to challenge traditional notions of individual and community.

The definitions of popular culture, mass culture, and media culture have varied significantly over time and among researchers. Herbert J. Gans provides a useful, though somewhat broad, definition of mass culture as "the symbolic products used by the 'uncultured' majority."[2] A more useful definition of mass culture, I believe, would be that of symbolic expressions and products for the non-cultured (that is, those not participating in high culture, defined below) transmitted through mass media, whereas popular culture would be any symbolic expressions and products with widespread appeal, regardless of their source.[3] This type of

Culture critics viewed scenes like this one, of audiences flocking to a Chicago movie theater in April 1941, as proof of a culture in decline. Movies, William Orton said, were canned entertainment that encouraged a passive, intellectually hobbled audience (Library of Congress).

mass culture overlaps with, but is not synonymous with, popular culture, which can include non-commercialized aspects and activities enjoyed by the masses, in addition to the elements of mass culture they have adopted and adapted for their own use. Under this definition, folk songs like "Oh! Susanna" are a part of popular culture, but not mass culture. Therefore, for our purposes, I am using mass culture to refer to the commercialized culture mass produced for mass consumption by media and corporate entities. By contrast, high culture refers to the symbolic products and expressions that the social and economic elite produce and consume in the belief that they are the highest expression of aesthetics and culture.[4] This is the "official" culture of the economic and social elite, often characterized by its exclusivity and restricted access by non-elite members of society.

One of the important debates over the definition of mass culture is the degree to which the term implies the origin of culture with the masses rather than those in the media who create cultural products for their consumption. Therefore, some theorists prefer to use the term *media culture* to emphasize the role of the media in creating the cultural elements mass audiences consume. However, mass production and mass consumption occur not just within the media but across a spectrum of cultural activities that individuals select from in developing their own personal consumption patterns; therefore, since the individual is not a passive recipient of media messages but a participant in the culture, I prefer the term *mass culture*.

Worse Than Fruit Salad: Critiquing Mass Culture

As historian Bruce Lenthall has outlined, public intellectuals of the 1930s had two primary critiques of mass culture in general, and of radio in particular. The first, advocated primarily by the conservatives and classical liberals, emphasized the threat which mass culture posed to the cultural standards of America, and to high culture in particular. The second, advocated primarily by the political left, emphasized the threat posed by the concentration of power and influence in the hands of the corporate owners who produced the products of mass culture.[5] Lenthall described the two camps through the work of the classical liberal economist William Orton, representing the first position, and the Marxist journalist James Rorty, representing the second. They were, of course, far from the only two cultural critics, but their work is representative of the arguments occurring in the era. However, as Lenthall notes, their critiques occurred from the position of high-culture participants who neither considered nor engaged the audience for radio programs; instead, they spoke primarily to other intellectuals and members of the cultural elite. Lower down on the critical spectrum, the *New York Tribune* launched the first radio criticism column, "Last Night on Radio," in 1924, though it was less a reflection on mass culture than a somewhat snarky review of the previous night's offerings.

On the political right, cultural conservatives developed a mass culture critique that excoriated mass-produced cultural products as bland and homogenous, a threat to traditional forms of leisure, the transformative power of education, and the relationship of individual and community. For them, the primary fear was that mass culture would cheapen the value of high culture and lead to a decline in creativity and intellectual rigor. In order to be popular, radio needed to be bland and unchallenging; but in creating a broad audience for a single cultural expression, it also put at risk the ideas of individualism and self-reliance. A concept as old as Alexis de Tocqueville, this is a theme we will return to in discussing individualism and individuality in *Vic and Sade* in Chapter Nine. A mass audience was, by definition, one that descended to the common denominator, and for critics like William Orton, America was a community of individuals united in pursuit of a common high culture. Orton laid out the foundations of his mass-culture critique in his 1933 book *America in Search of Culture*, published the year after *Vic and Sade* hit the air. There he discussed the iron triangle formed by the screen, the radio, and the stage in creating a celebrity culture for the masses to absorb and on which to spend money.

Orton was concerned with the threat that mass culture posed to the traditional values of individualism, as well as traditional creativity and human connection. He likened mass culture to canned vegetables, something that lacked the freshness of the garden and which had been boiled, diced, and packaged for quick and easy consumption. In the case of motion pictures, Orton found the comparison especially apt given the cans in which nitrate film was shipped and stored: "Mass production and world-wide distribution of American canned foods we take for granted. Canned entertainment (literally canned) on a similar scale seems still a little startling."[6] Orton felt that movies lacked the human touch of the theater, and worse, they encouraged the audience to become a passive consumer of a production created thousands of miles away by people they would never meet. Audiences for films sit in darkened rooms, silent, consuming a fantasy crafted from makeup, marketing, and lighting. Orton situated this in economic terms, discussing the way mass culture required audiences, in turn forcing studio executives to create films that exploited audiences' desires and biases without challenging them in the manner of true art. Worse, the drive for profit led studios to produce more than six hundred films per year, a rate far greater than could sustain the high quality of true art. Regrettably, Orton blamed the Jews in Hollywood for this, claiming that the Jews patronized the fine arts for themselves while the Jewish "race" was "compensating for the failure to organize its own collective life by exploiting that of other people."[7] He implied that the U.S. should join Soviet Russia, Fascist Italy, Nazi Germany, and Imperial Japan in regulating artistic output for the greater good. Even the Hays Code was not enough; its prohibitions merely ensured that audiences would never face the true challenge of good art. However, unbeknownst to Orton, the Hollywood studios had entered into collaboration with the Weimar and then Nazi German governments to censor American movies worldwide and rewrite them to meet German government standards in order to ensure distribution in Germany. As a direct result, negative depictions of Nazi Germany all but vanished, and Jews found their names removed from production credits to appease Hitler's censors.[8] This was not precisely the type of governmental intervention Orton had in mind.

Despite the unfortunate use of anti–Semitic stereotypes, the refrain that mass culture was somehow driven by an outside elite, exploiting the masses for financial gain, would recur in many versions of the mass-culture critique, perhaps never more so than in discussions of radio.

The advent of radio marked an important shift in the way individuals and families consumed media, and it also marked a shift in how public intellectuals began to discuss popular culture. Increasingly, they looked at radio and saw a medium that was creating a mass culture, and many critics were disturbed by what they saw. When *Vic and Sade* premiered in 1932, 60 percent of American homes had a radio, and when it left the air in 1945, that figure had risen to nearly 90 percent.[9] The economics of mass communication required broadcasters to program for a mass audience—that is, programs needed to appeal to the widest possible demographic in order to be attractive to advertisers, who were overwhelmingly corporations and businesses looking to reach wide, general audiences. In 1933, the president of NBC affirmed as much, noting that radio was a medium of "mass distribution, and the message delivered must be suitable for mass consumption."[10] Among those advertisers were an assortment of national food brands, cleaning products, toiletry manufacturers, gasoline companies, and the makers of other necessities of daily middle- and working-class life. Local advertisers included restaurants, department stores, and other businesses.

As Minneapolis radio station KSTP put it in a 1936 guide for the station's advertisers, "Over 90 percent of the 'Twin Cities' families own radios. An advertiser, therefore, is assured that his message will reach the greatest number of sales potentialities in the quickest possible time and at the lowest cost, in using the facilities of KSTP."[11] As a direct result of such appeals, major advertisers began shifting resources from newspapers to radio. In 1930, advertisers reduced their newspaper ad buys by $22 million while adding $8.5 million in radio spending. Advertisers followed audiences, and radio had the largest audience going. Some newspaper publishers threatened to retaliate by refusing to publish radio listings or program reviews, claiming they were free advertising for companies that refused to buy ads in their papers.[12]

Radio's audience was large and broad, and programming followed suit; there was no room for niche markets or niche programming in a broadcast landscape dominated by a handful of stations and limited broadcast licenses. And it worked. As one home furnishing store wrote to KSTP in 1936, "As a result of our broadcast we sold five dozen electric irons before ten o'clock. [The store had opened at 9:00 a.m.] ... enthusiastic responses have made us decide to continue indefinitely our morning program."[13] No other medium had been so

Radio executives, advertisers, and business leaders, like those seen here with the cast of *Vic and Sade*, believed that as a mass medium, radio must cater to a mass audience with a message "suitable" for mass consumption. Critics complained that this led to homogenized, generic programming (courtesy Mark C. Lancaster, reproduced by permission of NBC/NBC Universal PhotoBank).

effective in reaching and motivating listeners, which advertisers and executives alike had already decided were synonymous with "consumers."

But for culture critics, the commercialized nature of radio (even more so than movies), which existed to convince listeners to buy electric irons, vegetable shortening, and all manner of other products, produced a decided unease. Could art and commerce exist together? Would either truly benefit the individual or society at large?

In fact, for Orton, the most important concern was that the radio was beholden to no one but the financial interests of the salesman, that radio's programming "is dictated, not by the public, nor by persons responsible to the public, nor by persons charged with the interests of the public, but by persons concerned solely with making money out of the public."[14] At least movies were primarily selling themselves; radio was different—it advertised for others.

In those years, programming existed for two purposes: to encourage people to buy radio sets and to encourage people to buy sponsors' products. Therefore, Orton saw sustaining programs—those without sponsors, like *Vic and Sade* for its first months—as little more than public relations moves designed to lure listeners to more profitable programming, even though they were almost the only programs of value; commercial shows were so much pabulum. Worse, while the airwaves had the capability to broadcast as many as forty different programs at once, to meet the needs of many audiences, Orton noted that the government and radio companies have acted in concert to ensure that "the same material comes every night" from most stations, limiting choice.[15] This programming, Orton stressed, all originates in the same commercial concerns—drawing the maximum audience—and thus results in no "real variation in the type of programme coming over." It was, in short, a monotonous slog through undifferentiated, low-quality entertainment. Those who studied radio at the time agreed, and Orton was correct that radio executives and advertisers commissioned research to help them create homogenized programs that would overcome regional, local, and interpersonal differences and appeal to a large demographic with a uniform product—one size fits all. The effects, Orton feared, would be innumerable unserved and underserved audiences and the creation of a "mass-mind" that overwhelmed cultural diversity and made the individual into part of a single, uniform bloc.

Orton, however, imagined that he spoke for the public in calling upon the government to impose, by force, standards of worth and merit upon radio programming. The public, he wrote, "is far more sick of the situation than the profiteers realize."[16] Isolated in the upper-class world of his alma mater of Cambridge University and his teaching position at Smith College, Orton seemed oblivious to the real way individuals of the working class and the middle class encountered and utilized the radio. Orton, for example, called upon the great cities like New York and Chicago to "maintain opera and music on par with their fine municipal art enterprises,"[17] and demanded more opera on the radio. (He had been a concert pianist in his youth.) Everyday Americans, however, disagreed with Orton's elitist perspective. A national survey taken around the same time Orton wrote, for example, found that 81 percent of Americans listened to the radio every day, often for four hours or more, and 94 percent of them listened to more than one station daily. Another study, this one involving Philadelphia listeners from the same period, found that people in Orton's income bracket shared his elite tastes, favoring classical music and educational programming; however, those in lower income brackets favored exactly the type of drama, comedy, and children's programming that Orton found so objectionable. In yet another survey, rural residents in particular were the least likely to share Orton's enthusiasm for classical music and opera. In fact, even among urban listeners, dance music outranked classical and opera by wide margins.[18] (About 20 percent of broadcast music was dance, to less than 1 percent symphony orchestra.[19]) In short, even as Orton was committing to paper his assumptions about what the public believed, radio station owners were receiving the results of surveys telling them that Orton's position was a considerable minority.

Orton could, however, take comfort in the fact that the chairman of the Federal Radio Commission, Charles McKinley Saltzman, agreed that advertising was "excessive and nauseating."[20] In fact, it was widely reported in the media of the early 1930s that audiences were in open revolt against advertising on radio.[21] But was it effective? A Gallup poll survey found only 38 percent of listeners could remember what product a show advertised.[22] Nevertheless, despite government and media concerns, American listeners told pollsters of the early 1930s that they were generally okay with radio advertising—certainly Saltzman noted, more than a British-style tax to fund broadcasting, as filled the coffers of the BBC. While half of the listeners surveyed felt there was too much advertising, only 13 percent agreed with Orton that it was monotonous. A full 81 percent said they liked the programs sponsors put on and wouldn't give them up. However, in analyzing the results shortly before his mysterious disappearance while hiking at Glacier National Park in 1934, Frederick H. Lumley, a professor at Ohio State University, noted that complaints about advertising were directly correlated to income, with the wealthiest listeners complaining loudest. Among less wealthy listeners, the majority said they found advertising useful.[23] Unsurprisingly, elite journalists and their middle- and upper-class sources and readers created a media landscape opposed to radio advertising in its present form. The less wealthy were less likely to be represented in media discussions.

When Orton complained about the sins of radio, he spoke not for America but for the wealthy in America, whose interests—by definition a minority of Americans—radio's mass audience appeal would not and could not consistently serve. Yes, Orton's position was shared by many other denizens of America's high culture, including the novelist Irving Fineman, music critic B. H. Haggin and the *New Yorker*'s Ring Lardner, who compared the vulgarity of radio and its crudity to his least favorite food, fruit salad, as the only two things that really angered him outrageously.[24] After World War II, intellectuals like Dwight MacDonald, Bernard Rosenberg, C. Wright Mills, and others resurrected the idea of mass culture and the critique of it as homogenizing and stultifying. Where Orton's critique extended to the media of his day—movies, radio, music—the postwar intellectuals added to their repertoire comic books and television, two more mediums producing generations of intellectually enfeebled mass audiences.

"Acquisitive, emulative, neurotic": Educating the Masses

Against the criticisms leveled at radio, educators and media executives held out the educational potential of the new medium, particularly the power of the medium to bring education and basic cultural awareness to the remote parts of America, where few teachers and fewer books ever passed. Federal law, after all, required since 1927 that radio serve the public interest, and, to that end, the radio stations and the two major networks trumpeted their news and information programs, as well as their educational programming.

In 1931, CBS broadcast a series of lectures on topics ranging from women in politics to the relationship between science and religion. Local stations and radio networks alike offered on-air classrooms, and in the New York metropolitan area, listeners of WOR in the 1920s could be found standing before their easels learning to draw from lessons transmitted over the air. French lessons could be found each Friday at 3:45 p.m. in 1931. Schools like the University of Iowa offered correspondence courses by radio in the 1920s, with Iowa's studies giving students twelve twenty-minute lectures for ten dollars, along with a pamphlet explaining how to complete written work. Obviously, people who did not pay also listened in to the broadcasts. However, critics were quick to charge that such lessons encouraged passive behavior, discouraged critical engagement with material, and standardized and homogenized the material it taught to the most basic level so all could understand it.[25] Audiences, Orton said, became mere consumers of education and entertainment alike, not producers of knowledge or art. Worse, and most obvious, listeners could, at any time, simply turn the dial to find something more fun. And they did; federal regulators forced Iowa's radio station to change frequencies six times in the four years between 1925 and 1929, each time to accommodate for-profit commercial broadcasters with bigger audiences.[26]

As later critics would note, the public was not the passive recipient of radio waves, and they actively made choices about what to consume. For example, David Manning White would note in the 1950s that once the inexpensive paperback book was introduced in the

Before the daytime serial, radio stations often broadcast educational programming. In this 1924 photograph, Harold Shaver of New Jersey learns to draw from lessons broadcast on WOR (Morris Rosenfield/Library of Congress).

1939 Pocket edition, sales of classic novels soared, reaching two billion copies in over twenty years' time. Further, twenty million copies of Toscanini's recordings were sold in the three decades after 1920, and Mozart alone sold around a million copies each year, from 1903 to the 1950s.[27] This suggested a substantial audience for the products of high culture, and early radio executives had high hopes that radio could serve as a positive force for culture.

In a radio address from the White House in 1931, President Herbert Hoover announced that the National Advisory Council on Education was meeting in the auditorium of the New School for Social Research in Manhattan. He introduced Dr. Robert Andrews Millikan, of the California Institute of Technology, to speak to the educational potential of radio. Said Dr. Millikan:

> The radio is obviously one of the great new unifying and educational forces.... If you do not believe in it because you fear its use by the demagogue and the propagandist, then you despair of the ultimate success of widespread ballot governments as such, and you can logically join one of the two world groups, the Soviets, and in somewhat lesser degree the Fascisti, which [attempt] to push the world back ... to the time when the Pharaoh under the strategy of his Prime Minister, Joseph, became an absolute despot.... Any talk of loss of liberty through the monopolistic control of the ether ... is too grotesque to need to be given more than a line in an address like this.[28]

The secretary of the interior, Ray Lyman Wilbur, confidently proclaimed that, in time, radio would lose its crassness and soon become substantive and cultured. Therefore, of course, there was no need for government action; the market would provide moral uplift.

That, too, had been the attitude of some of radio's earliest pioneers. Lee de Forest, who operated one of the first experimental stations, entered the 1920s confident that broadcasting would serve the cause of education and uplift, but in 1932, he begged Canada's regulators to avoid the mistakes of America, particularly those involved in allowing advertising to support broadcasting. Here in America, he claimed, broadcasting had become "so debased by commercial advertising" that the entire medium was one long sales pitch, radio sets a "drug on the market." Programming, he proclaimed, was a "vulgar, cheapjack show designed to coax dollars out of the pockets of the public."[29] There was some irony there since de Forest had broadcast the world's first radio commercial in 1916, for products he himself sold.

This intimate connection between radio and commerce was at the heart of leftist critics' complaints about radio, which focused less on the problems of mass culture and more on the power of the owners of radio stations to centralize control in the hands of a wealthy few. As a tool of big business, radio was destined to subvert democracy and undermine culture in pursuit of business interests, which were, inevitably, more profits and more power. The National Committee on Education by Radio, a radical reform group, believed radio had the power to educate the masses, but its members despaired that it could never reach this potential so long as it remained in the hands of large corporations. Self-described liberal radio commentator H. V. Kaltenborn was famous as a foreign correspondent for CBS and an anchor for NBC. But in 1931 he was in trouble with the networks because his politically charged commentaries clashed with the networks' need to curry favor with business and political leaders. As he wrote in the committee's journal, network educational programs "usually sound far more important in published announcements than they ever become on the air"—a cynical exercise in appearing to operate for the public good while actually working to serve only the interests of money and power.[30] The committee also prominently featured in its publication the words of *Christian Century* managing editor Paul Hutchinson, calling for a public broadcasting for educational purposes, for, as imperfect as they were, programs "for radio education represent the only considerable part of the radio fare which is not yet fully under commercial auspices."[31]

The Marxist journalist James Rorty, formerly an advertising copywriter and P.R. agent, supported the goals of the National Committee on Education by Radio, but he went still further than the committee in assailing the capitalist underpinnings of radio. In his acid exposé of the advertising industry, *Our Master's Voice*, Rorty described the way radio companies and advertisers collaborate to foist "vulgarity and commercial irresponsibility" upon the public in the name of profit. It was not, he wrote, a system for broadcasting culture to the masses but rather of delivering an advertising-based "pseudoculture"—"acquisitive, emulative, neurotic and disintegrating."[32] Rorty wrote passionately about the squandered potential of radio as a force for education and cultural uplift, bemoaning the de facto censorship that the corporate masters of radio used to keep radical views off the air (sometimes cutting speakers off in mid-speech) in order to keep radio safe, palatable, and unthreatening—both to audiences and to the political and business elite that gave them the ability to turn broadcasting licenses into profits.

Rorty feared that President Franklin Delano Roosevelt, so skilled at radio communication, might turn the medium into an instrument of government control. He cited the 1933 words of federal radio commissioner Harold A. LaFount, who advocated for government-produced educational programming: "The whole nation would be taught by one teacher instead of hundreds, and would be thinking together on one subject of national importance."[33] The same concept that so thrilled William Orton—government control and quality guarantees—worried Rorty, who saw the potential for even greater abuses of power. Across the sea, Hitler had turned the radio into an instrument of government propaganda, and leftist critics worried that America might similarly face a period where centralized offices delivered mass messages to create compliance in the public.

That such a thing was possible was proved with the coming of World War II and the American broadcast networks' acquiescence to and embrace of the Roosevelt administration's efforts to add propaganda messages to radio dramas and comedies, including *Vic and Sade* (see Chapter Nine), promoting the virtues of recycling, war bonds, and other wartime homefront measures. As Rorty and other left-wing critics feared, the networks fully embraced government restrictions on broadcasting when it seemed advantageous from a business perspective—right down to control over weather reports—and eventually became so enthusiastic that they went above and beyond government requirements, producing such a volume of propaganda messages that the Office of War Information was forced to make changes to its program to avoid public backlash at the flood of war messages.[34]

Such was the debate over radio and mass culture in the years when *Vic and Sade* first came to the air. It is not surprising that Paul Rhymer's program would show a relationship to the currents swirling around radio at the time of the show's creation. Although not intended as a direct rebuttal to the critics of radio, *Vic and Sade* would offer a far more developed and nuanced portrait of American engagement with mass culture than either of the major camps of culture critics, both of which privileged the views of the elite over those of the masses in whose name they criticized mass culture. Rhymer's *Vic and Sade* would, over its run, deal with many of the major cultural issues explored by the culture critics: changes in leisure activities, the expanding reach of centralized education, and the changing relationship of the individual to the community. If the circumstances and subject matter of *Vic and Sade* did not specifically address radio, either in content or its business model (which, of course, provided Rhymer the income he used to support his family), the show itself served as a rejoinder to the oft-heard claim of culture critics that little that was relevant or artistic crossed the airwaves.

It is to *Vic and Sade*'s depiction of the social and cultural contexts that culture critics identified as suffering under the transformative power of mass culture—leisure activities (including interactive activities, movies, and reading), education, and the relationship of the individual and community—that we now turn.

PART II: SOCIAL AND CULTURAL CONTEXTS

Five. Leisure:
"It represents quite a problem"

"Doing what we don't have to do"

The economic hardship of the Great Depression is the prism through which we tend to view the decade of the 1930s, and much of the popular impression of the period focuses on unemployment, disaster, and despair. However, even in these conditions, life had to go on, and that included leisure and recreation. Around this time, the "shortening industrial work week and new labor-saving devices in the home" along with factory efficiency specialization produced not only additional time for leisure, but also a new way of life.[1] As one scholar explained, "The new leisure of our era simply must be bringing its own specific culture, its own mutation of human values."[2] As the Depression wore on, both those who were working or in school and those who found themselves with significantly more free time due to the loss of work engaged in a variety of leisure activities.

Leisure can, of course, come in many different forms, some of which may be unexpected. Kenneth R. Cunningham noted that popular leisure activities of the period included talking, radio, arts, reading, music, car travel, and other passive activities.[3] In addition, dancing, participation in or viewing sports, and club and lodge activities were also popular. Commercialized forms of leisure will be examined in future chapters dealing with two of the Gooks' favorite pastimes, reading and attending motion picture shows. This chapter will focus on non-commercialized activities, including conversation, writing and reading correspondence, travel, card playing and other games, shopping, participation in organizations, and low-brow recreation.

Defining Leisure

Before considering the role of leisure in *Vic and Sade* it may be useful to gain some perspective into *what* leisure is. To many of us leisure is simply "free time"[4]; however, more formal definitions may be useful in providing insight into the nature of leisure and how it is used. In an attempt to get at the essence of leisure, in the early 1930s Lundberg, Komarovskya, and McInerny studied suburban leisure-time behavior. To do so, they separated all observed behavior into two categories: leisure and non-leisure. As one might expect, non-leisure were those activities that are highly necessary or those that we are obligated to perform. By contrast, leisure was "defined residually and operationalized to include the following activities: eating, visiting, reading, public entertainment, sports, radio, motoring, clubs, and miscellaneous; of course, these activities are not necessarily mutually exclusive."[5] Such activities are commonly regarded as "left over" activity carried out when all other essential functions have been completed. However, researchers have found that leisure is, in fact, a "process" rather than a mere "state" or "fixed posture" occurring when not at work. Robert N. Wilson notes that "even when a person at leisure appears passive or immobile, he is engaged in a process of events."[6]

In other words, rather than a simple rest position between bouts of work, leisure is something "that must be earned and re-earned," as Margaret Mead noted—an active choice to engage in "nonessential, optional," recreational activities in order to experience joy.[7] To Mead, the word *recreation* "epitomizes the whole attitude of conditional joy" that exists between the need to work and the need to play.[8] Leisure, then, is a matter of lifestyles and leisure choices: "chosenness, discretion, or freedom."[9] For our purposes, the simplest and most potentially illuminating definition of leisure is "doing what we don't have to do." Freedom of choice is an important facet of leisure in *Vic and Sade* and will provide us with a prism through with to view Vic, Sade, Rush, Russell, and Uncle Fletcher as they choose and engage in leisure activities.

Leisure Choices: "Give me simple things every time"

As was true for many families, the youngest member of the clan is often the one advocating for leisure. Children, it seems, choose leisure over work as often as possible. The Gook family was no exception. On August 3, 1932, Vic, Sade, and Rush were cleaning strawberries when a spontaneous game of catch broke out at the insistence of Rush, who wanted a break from chores.

> RUSH: Aw c'mon ... just for a little while. Well [*sic*] play three-handed catch.
> SADE: No, Rush ... Mom's not a ball-player. You and gov ...
> [...]
> VIC: (*CALLS*) Catch, somebody!
> RUSH: Here it comes, Mom. You get it! Oh, no ... (*CATCHES IT*) ... (*LAUGHS WITH DELIGHT*).... Well, I *did* catch it.
> RUSH: Sure you did. Swell stab, too.[10]

Buoyed by her success, Sade enthusiastically joins the impromptu game, and the three play until they accidentally break Mis' Fisher's bay window. The exchange has a light, joyful quality that emphasizes the beneficial qualities of stolen moments of fun, of the choice to experience joy. Although, as we will see, depictions of leisure on *Vic and Sade* were often positive and emphasizing qualities of "freedom, intrinsic reward, happiness, pleasure, humor, and playfulness," leisure was just as frequently seen as a source of tension between the individual and the group.[11] Because of the specific nature of leisure, the individual rarely exercises concern for social interests.[12]

On Labor Day weekend in 1934, the Gooks faced a choice between the private and the public as they prepared to spend the day at Kickaroo Creek, where they would enjoy the "parade of lofty oak trees" and enjoy the company of the "citizens of the forest ... like rabbits, the squirrels, and the birds."[13] The woodland retreat offers the "tranquility" of being "away from the crowds"[14]; however, Vic's plans present little appeal to Sade, who would prefer to

In this photograph from Art Van Harvey's personal collection we see Art Van Harvey, Bernadine Flynn, and Billy Idelson roller skating, a popular leisure activity in the 1930s (Mark C. Lancaster/The Art Van Harvey Collection).

attend the parade in town and watch the American Legion Band and the spectacle that will accompany them. It is only when Vic is given the opportunity to participate in the Labor Day parade and become a source of attention that he agrees to change his plans.

The need to fill individual leisure needs at the expense of others is seen regularly throughout *Vic and Sade*. Vic, in particular, is often found putting his leisure needs above those of the family group. His sense of priority could be attributed to the fact that, because of work and other obligations, Vic's "play" is "interruptible regardless of how valuable a direction his play may be leading him in" and thus must be had whenever he was able to insist upon time for recreation.[15] With this potential motive in mind, it becomes understandable that Vic would, on occasion, resort to deception in order to achieve his recreational goals. An example occurred on April 30, 1936, when Vic falsely tells Sade there was pressing lodge business so he could get out of an obligation at Rush's school in order to play indoor horseshoes with Hank Gutstop. Similarly, on June 15, 1936, he falsely informs Sade that there are problems with the lawnmower so he can go to a "bowling grudge match" with Rush.[16] In these instances, Vic is able to free his time and achieve his leisure goals—but at the cost of dishonesty, which Vic sees as a necessity for shirking his family's and society's overbearing obligations.

Rush, too, finds himself in situations in which his quest for leisure is dependent upon others and his ability to compromise. In one particular instance, Rush is presented with a hammock by Uncle Fletcher. Rush's only chance for finding a location to hang his leisure device depends on compromising with his nemesis, Nicer Scott, who has two trees ideally suited for hanging a hammock. The situation presents Rush with "numerous complexities," beginning with that fact that, in his own words, "I don't like Nicer and never will like Nicer."[17] Yet the opportunity for Rush to satisfy his leisure needs holds the potential for him to overcome his contempt, demonstrating the intense value placed upon leisure, even above enmity. Vic suggests a decidedly non-leisure approach to resolving the situation, claiming that a "cold blooded down to the bone business undiluted by the milk of human kindness" may provide the means for overcoming the antipathy between the boys—as well as between Sade and Mis' Scott, who are not "arms around the neck chums"—by allowing both parties to benefit and share in the leisure.[18] But such attempts smack of work and become the antithesis of the leisure they were meant to attain. Ultimately, Rush, aware of the needs and interests of others, forgoes his leisure needs and determines that the stresses related to the situation outweigh the potential leisure.

Travel as Leisure

By contrast, the Gooks' neighbors, the Donahues, represent a vastly different view of the role of leisure, one that sees leisure not as a break from routine or an end in itself but as an obligation. They were "miserable" at the prospect of a vacation. Mr. Donahue worked for the railroad and vacation time forced him to alter his sleep patterns. According to Mis' Donahue, vacations were "horrible, wretched days of fighting and struggling and working and straining to stay awake."[19] Similarly, Uncle Fletcher holds that there are limits to the amount of leisure an individual could partake in before it becomes either overwhelming or drudgery. Just as the Donahues hate vacations, Fletcher feels himself forced to take a short respite from his own vacation to recharge and recoup. For Fletcher and the Donahues, planned leisure activities such as vacations represent too great of a break from the normal routine of obligation to serve their intended purpose, becoming instead just another obligation foisted upon the individual, with all the intended stress and difficulty.

The idea of recreational leisure emerged in the 1920s with the promotion of paid vacations to white-collar union employees. In 1920, 40 percent of white-collar, union employees were entitled to paid vacations—a figure that would double by 1930.[20] Despite the growing number of individuals eligible for vacations, the concept was still a novel one; individuals and families who vacationed were the source of curiosity, and interest in their travels were frequently covered in the newspaper social pages. In 1937, Vic and Sade began planning for a trip to Hawaii in 1940 for the Sacred Stars of the Milky Way Convention. The proposed trip illustrated the wonder of air travel and its ability to make the exotic possible. The trip was presented both from the perspective of a glamorous adventure, one that would shrink the Atlantic and expand their boundaries. The proposed trip would place Vic and Sade in a land that, while a U.S. territory, was both foreign and exotic. The islands are, as Vic described them, "Out amidst the blowing swells of the oceans angels have dropped little bits of heaven."[21] Yet despite Vic's glowing description, Sade remains ignorant of their travel plans and asks if they will be passing by Cincinnati en route to their destination. Despite all of the excitement surrounding their plans, Paul Rhymer presents a dark side to the trip by presenting envious friends and neighbors who endeavor to throw cold water on their happiness. While the Donahues found vacations burdensome, the Gooks' friends and neighbors found another way to transform leisure into a source of unpleasantness through envy, which was a price paid by those who sought to enjoy conspicuous—and conspicuously costly—leisure.

But long-distance vacations were only one way travel appeared as a source of leisure in *Vic and Sade*—and in 1930s America. By 1933, more than half the volume over U.S. highways and 60 percent of all American cars were for the purpose of recreational travel,[22] and the

The automobile was adopted quickly, and within just a few years it was already seen as a source of leisure and fun. These people from Bethlehem, New Hampshire, took their car to the Old Man of the Mountain in New Hampshire. Unfortunately, within a few years the car would destroy the city's thriving hotel industry when patrons could travel on day trips rather than weeks-long grand excursions (Library of Congress).

automobile had become the chief symbol of recreation and freedom across America. Since the first automobile had been manufactured in 1899, Americans had taken to cars like no other people. When Henry Ford began mass producing the Model T in 1908 and famously paid his workers a sufficient wage so they could aspire to own one themselves, the car became associated with status and success. While the automobile helped to transform America by shortening the social distance between communities, contributing to the growth of distant suburbs far from crowded city centers, and promoting mobility in society, it also had the immediate effect of helping to change the culture of leisure. Ford recognized that the repetitive tasks of his assembly line—modeled on a butcher's animal disassembly line—were hard on workers, so he reduced the workday from twelve hours to eight. This change, which spread to other industries in the 1920s with the eight-hour workday movement, created more free time for workers, which they chose to spend in new and unprecedented ways. Thanks to the automobile, those new ways included vacations, travel, and local recreational drives. At the same time, however, "car culture" had begun to break individuals away from traditional communities by giving them the freedom to associate in new ways, at greater distance, and with communities defined by interests rather than geographic proximity. These trends would come to fruition in the post-war period, but in the 1930s, they were already beginning to manifest. The car was, in short, the American Dream.

In 1938, Vic, Sade, and Rush waited, as Vic described it, in their "glad rags," for the Stembottoms to pick them up and take them for a ride in their automobile. By the end of the 1920s, the automobile had become a common part of American society, with four out of five families owning one.[23] As the Depression wore on, though, auto sales fell and used car sales outnumbered new car sales. Nevertheless, the automobile remained the symbol of the American dream, and in its factory assembly line, also the model for how culture critics imagined cultural products were being produced. However, that did not mean that there wasn't an air of novelty about the automobile, particularly for those who, like the Gooks, did not own one. The automobile proved itself a valuable leisure tool as it also allowed for the individual to extend the reach of their leisure, sharing it with those they might not otherwise have been able to. Sade, for example, was able to extend her leisure to her sister Bess's in Carberry through the use of an automobile. Even during the height of the Depression, families prioritized their car, so much had it infiltrated American life in the preceding twenty years, leading to new patterns of consumption, new social relationships, and a transformation of American cities through the creation of suburbs. In a survey of the 1930s, Americans said they valued their car above such seeming essentials as indoor plumbing, electric lighting, and even homeownership.[24]

For Sade, leisure is derived from the novelty of car, its role as a class symbol which she tries to live up to, and the ride itself. Going out with Fred and Ruthie for a spin in their car, Sade scolded Vic in response to his complaints about dressing up: "For decency's sake it's up to us to dress half-way civilized."[25] Rush and Vic have grown tired of the route that Fred travels and the stops he makes; the car is merely a commonplace means of transportation. Sade, though, views this as a novel means of relaxing and enjoying the companionship of her friends. A similar scenario is played out when the Stembottoms invite Vic and Sade to a double feature in Hopewood. The trip is unnecessarily long, but gives Fred a chance to show off during what he views as a leisurely trip for his neighbors. Neither Vic nor Sade is enthusiastic about the trip, particularly Vic, who was taken away from a game of indoor horseshoes (a much less pricy form of leisure); however, they accept the invitation out of concern for their social interests—once again underscoring the importance of social relationships and community in the performance of leisure.[26] Automobiles, though, were not always necessary to facilitate a leisure activity. In 1940, when Vic and Sade's neighbor Mr. Sludge wanted to spend time at his parents, it was not in an automobile or train that he traveled, but Mr. Gumpox's garbage wagon. The simple approach allowed not only for Sludge to reach his vacation destination, but also reinforce the bond of friendship with Gumpox and strengthen social relationships and community through shared travel.

"A person can always use washrags": Shopping

Major trips, however, were, by definition, rare occurrences and certainly not an everyday form of leisure. Even automobile travel was comparatively rare for those who did not own a car. By contrast, everyday excursions, such as shopping trips, could and did become a source of leisure, serving almost like miniature vacations from home life and an opportunity to see new things and socialize with friends—friends who could approve in-town excursions without the jealousy that accompanied more formal vacations.

The November 2, 1933, episode of *Vic and Sade* opened outside of the small house in the "heart of the shopping district" on Washington Street, across from the courthouse. Vic and Sade are off to purchase a new winter coat for Rush, who tags along. As they make their way to Yamilton's, they watch acquaintances and greet a number of friends. Vic and Sade stop to chat with Mr. Freestul about his wife and take time to admire the Christmas display at Foster's. Rush proudly observes that Vic knows "everyone," to which Vic replies, "Fancy I am not unknown about town."[27] The Gooks' excursion is taken at so leisurely a pace and without concern for time that they do not arrive at Yamilton's until after it has closed. On the surface it would seem that the shopping trip was an exercise in futility, not having achieved its goal. However, the excursion accomplished another, unintentional, goal: socializing and re-establishing the Gooks as part of the larger community. After a day of veritable isolation at home, the opportunity to socialize with friends, neighbors, and acquaintances provides a means of escapism for Sade in much the same way that listening to the radio did for women. Similarly, though to a lesser degree, Vic is provided with a sense of escapism after having spent the day at work. Though Vic has the opportunity to socialize with colleagues and co-workers, the shopping experience allows him to socialize with individuals that he *chooses* to interact with outside the realm of work.

Throughout the show's run, there is often a sense of excitement or joy associated with shopping and encountering those whom one may not otherwise have encountered. Even when Sade attends "the biggest and most successful sale Yamilton's ever had" with washrags two for a nickel, it is the social aspect of shopping that is pre-eminent in Sade's mind, as she declares that "everybody and their brother was there"—"squillions" of people were there.[28] Sade recounts meeting old friends that she hadn't seen and catching up on the events of their lives. The expedition also exposes her to other sides of her close friend Ruthie Stembottom, who, Sade observed, is a "comedian where there's crowds and excitement." So great were the opportunities to socialize that Sade refrained from purchasing anything, despite the many bargains.

During the first half of the twentieth century, shopping became no longer simply an obligation and chore conducted to satisfy material needs. Instead

> it was transformed from a functional activity of women into a form of leisure. Like attending a matinee, eating at a restaurant, or going to the beauty parlor—all new activities for women—

The era of the grand department stores, like Wanamaker's Department Store in Philadelphia, built in 1910 and featuring a dramatic atrium and pipe organ, made shopping into an entertaining experience and an escape from domestic reality (Carol M. Highsmith's America, Library of Congress, Prints and Photographs Division).

shopping took place in a semi-public, commercial, and safe realm, an important consideration for women concerned about their respectability.[29]

As Rhymer recognized, shopping was still a commercialized form of leisure and, as such, could not be free of flaws. Shopping relied upon mass-produced, commercialized products and sales and advertising techniques geared to appeal to consumers' base instincts. Even seemingly innocuous products such as washrags could cause consumers to behave lowly. *Vic and Sade* depicts instances of shopping-related physical violence not dissimilar to today's Black Friday frenzies. On November 16, 1941, Sade returns from a washrag sale at Yamilton's that was a "regular riot."[30] In the midst of washrag-inspired mêlée, a lady was knocked over and stepped on, and Ruthie Stembottom was kicked. In another episode, Sade reports on a child who collapsed after being dragged around by his mother for hours.

"Gifts galore": Commercializing Christmas

As such incidents make clear, not all shopping was leisure, especially with regard to the most important shopping season of all: Christmas. A leisure-free variety of shopping was brought home to the Gooks when, in the heat of summer, they were bombarded with opportunities to purchase Christmas cards from friends, neighbors, and relatives. Months before Christmas arrived, Vic and Sade were confronted with pressure, coercion, and, at times, emotional blackmail by those attempting to peddle their wares, illustrating the commercialization of the holiday and its effects. While Vic might quip in jest, "Maybe this heartbreaking problem will work out without a heart being broken or a drop of blood spilled,"[31] as he and Sade deal with conflicting offers from Hank Gutstop, Mis' Harris, and Sade's sister Bess. It's likely that Sade reveals their true sentiments when she refers to the situation as a nightmare. It is a situation that the Gooks would be confronted with on many occasions, including in 1942 when Sade's niece "tricked" her into purchasing cards by sending a package of them C.O.D.

The stress associated with the cards was furthered by the cards themselves, in which Rhymer parodies the trite, standardized verse associated with greeting cards:

> Wash off the dirty neck of your and get rid of your sneer,
> I'm wishing you Happy New Year
> And give me a kiss while it's snowin' and sleetin'
> And accept this heartfelt holiday greetin'
> And give me a hug for Christmastime's sake.
> If I don't receive presents I'll jump in the lake.[32]

The garish verses represent an exaggerated appeal to greeting card audiences' base instincts. The low-brow nature of the product serves to not only devalue consumers, but also the holiday itself, which is treated as a commercialized event instead of a sacred religious holiday. While the Gooks reject the cards based upon their content, they often succumbed to purchasing them due to social pressure and a desire to avoid being on the "outs" with those selling them.

The materialism of Christmas was a common theme of *Vic and Sade*. The program depicted a holiday that had been diminished by mass culture and whose only meaning was that of gifts. Vic, in particular, was preoccupied with gift giving as a means of impressing even the least-significant acquaintance to preserve the "bond of friendship." In some cases these bonds rested on something as little as a candy bar. Ignoring the costs of an ever-growing gift list, Vic explained to Sade, "You are a housewife. I am a businessman. Naturally, a business man has many more obligations."

On February 25, 1937—exactly ten months prior to Christmas—Vic and Sade return home to find an array of wrapped gifts, all Christmas "remembrances" prepared by Rush for various friends. "Suppose somebody gave *you* a Christmas gift almost a year ahead of time?" he asks Vic. "You'd have a warm rush of blood to the heart. You'd say to yourself, 'My *my* how much this person must care for me.'"[33] Rush has wrapped pieces of brick and wood along with notes imploring them to not open until December 25. He anticipates that the recipients will spend the year conjecturing about the contents of the packages and, by the time Christmas arrives, will want to reward Rush with a magnificent gift equivalent to what they've imagined he has given them. Nevertheless, Rush was not entirely or even predominantly selfish; indeed, he was often a selfless and loyal friend, as seen in another scenario involving materialism and gift-giving, albeit in the context of a birthday. When fourteen-year-old Smelly Clark breaks what will be his twenty-first birthday present, a pocket watch he had taken out of storage to impress a girl, Rush tells Vic and Sade that he wants to withdrawal money from his bank account to help "a dear friend who is in terrible trouble" and needs nine dollars to repair the damage (an amount Smelly won't ask his father for as a "matter of honor"). Vic and Sade have forbidden Rush from touching his savings until he is twenty-one, but they agree to "loan" Smelly the cash since Rush has been so selfless and is clearly in despair over his friend's upcoming humiliation when he is found out.[34]

Rush's occasional machinations and greed could be written off to childish impulses; however, there was no shortage of adults in *Vic and Sade* exhibiting the same tendencies. The Stembottoms evaluated the success of Christmas by the fact that they received "gifts galore."[35] Fred Stembottom contrived to get the Gooks to give him five tires for his car for Christmas. According to Sade, he explained that "in the past you girls have been made miserable and sick because one family gives a present that costs more than the other family's present.... You tell me how much money you spent on the automobile tire and Ruthie and I, knowing to the penny what you spent, can go and duplicate that sum, buying whatever we select for you."[36]

It's likely that Fred is speaking the truth when he claims that the "girls" have "been miserable and sick" over their choice of gifts for one another, as we see the commercialism of Christmas expunging the joy of the occasion and replacing it with the need to maintain status on a material level through the offering of appropriate presents representing a web of social obligation and socioeconomic status. Giving a gift as a gesture of friendship or love is not sufficient in the commercialized environment of a *Vic and Sade* Christmas; the gift giver must ensure that his or her gift is equivalent in cost and status to that which they expect to receive in order not to appear beneath the socioeconomic status of the gift's recipient. And woe unto anyone who gives a gift that fails to match the recipient's.

Rhymer provides a counterview of a holiday tarnished by the ills of commercialism in Sade's description of Ruthie, who "loves Christmas so; loves the fun and surprises and tinsel and gay little nonsense and all this and that that we have at Christmastime."[37] A similar idea can be found in Uncle Fletcher's insistence on providing non-commercial gifts from materials he obtained through means other than consumerism. Uncle Fletcher stands out as one of the most creative gift givers that we encounter. His gifts, almost without exception, are notable for being unique offerings and reflections of Fletcher himself. On November 12, 1937, the Gooks received their first package of the Christmas season, from Uncle Fletcher. Before it is even opened, the package is greeted with a collective and doleful, "Oh my" from Vic and Sade, who anticipate with some dread its contents. As Vic explains, "Sometimes I wake up in the middle of the night drenched in cold sweat because I've dreamt Uncle Fletcher's sent me a rattlesnake all gold an' blue with his forked tongue."[38]

With some trepidation they open the package that has "little Santy Clauses" pasted all over it and find a verse: "Smoke a cigar on Christmas day while, while organs yuletide carols play; puff, puff, sweetheart, the strong black smoke; good will to men, but do not choke."[39] Inside they find a box marked "horse and cattle cure" containing fifty cigars that Fletcher had gathered piecemeal over the years, each tagged with an explanation of its history. Initially, Sade believes that this is a very thoughtful gesture on Fletcher's part, as he knows that Vic enjoys cigars; however, her attitude changes once Vic explains that cigars have a limited shelf-life unless they are sealed, and they begin looking through the relics. Among the cigars is a "souvenir of the Kentucky Tobacco Growers' Exposition ... St. Louis World's Fair" of what they suspect was 1895 (in real life, it was actually held in 1904). Another cigar was credited to the Wilson Creek dedication ceremonies. Sade recalls that Wilson Creek was a town before she was born and realizes that the cigar would have been from the time Fletcher was a child. Still another reads: "Handed to me by Elrod Y. Scrouch." Vic suspects that Scrouch sailed with Columbus. Other cigars include a chocolate cigar from the House-wives'

Cooking Exhibit at the 1911 Illinois State Fair and a cigar butt, with teeth marks, labeled "memento of the Great Chicago fire."[40]

Fletcher's gifts weren't restricted to Christmas. In the summer of 1941, he had the notion of giving the Gooks, the Stembottoms, the Donahues, and Mis' Keller four-foot sections of railroad track, each weighing 440 pounds, to use as door stops. According to Rush, Fletcher's logic was sound: "Four hundred and forty pounds of solid steel can be depended upon to hold a door open or hold a door shut."[41] While Fletcher's reasoning might have been difficult to dispute, Sade knew that none of his intended benefactors wanted such a "contraption" on their front porch and was certain it would result in "embarrassment all around."[42]

Fletcher wasn't content with merely providing stretches of railroad track for his friends' daily door-stopping needs; he also wanted to ensure that his offerings were aesthetically pleasing. To that end, he planned to have Mis' Keller cover them in velvet and embroider them with lettering, an act that Vic believed was a reflection of modern society: "Velvet-covered railroad tracks! It's an effete civilization. Pretty soon the human race will get so soft it'll place melted marshmallows on its wienie-worst."[43]

Fletcher's sense of style and generosity extended to four-legged friends as well. Days after Christmas of 1940, Sade noticed that Mr. Gumpox's horse, Howard, was "all decked out" in a fancy, expensive-looking new harness with "brass doo-dahs on the bridle an' trash" and "grand thing-a-ma-doodles way up and down his back, and the do-funny in his mouth ... looks like silver." He looked like a "circus horse," thanks to the gifts of "an anonymous donor" that Sade believes was her uncle.[44] In contrast, Howard was also the recipient of one of most practical Christmas gifts given by Fletcher in 1941: a red woolen blanket.

We can see in Fletcher's eccentric yet kindhearted gifts an exaggerated illustration of something that everyone has encountered: the gift givers who place their needs to be sincere or creative above the needs of the recipients, leaving them feeling awkward, embarrassed, and often in mental torment and anguish, all of which could have been avoided with a proper present. Despite, or perhaps because of, the presumably good intentions of the sender, there are inherent risks for the recipient of gifts that had been lovingly made rather than purchased at the local department store. However commercialized such a gift might have been, the recipient could have had reasonable expectations for a minimum level of quality; not so for the creative, individualized gift which was, ultimately, the sum of its creator's skills and talents in the realm of gift production. Still, one could count on a homemade gift being far more creative than a mass-produced, commercialized item that everyone in the neighborhood would be receiving from their less imaginative friends. Then again, in many instances, creativity was one of the most notable drawbacks of the homemade gift.

In these depictions, Rhymer provides an alternative to the individual corrupted by the greed purportedly generated by mass culture. In this view, it is the simpler things, especially family and togetherness, that make the holiday special. In this way, Christmas can be seen as a celebration of the types of interpersonal interactions between friends and family that occur in everyday life and form the most common and persistent forms of daily leisure.

"Nice family gossip": Conversation

Interpersonal social relationships between family and friends are an important source of leisure because they provide an outlet for sharing and bonding. Such relationships are achieved through interactions defined by conversation. Conversation is abundantly important to the Gook family and to the program. It is through the dialog exchanged by Vic, Sade, Rush, Russell, and Uncle Fletcher that listeners learn of their activities and come to know the goings-on throughout their town. Through their conversations, we learn about and come to know their neighbors and friends without those characters ever appearing on mic during the more than ten years of the serial's run. These conversations, to which we listeners are privy, are for both the audience and the Gooks a source of recreation and leisure. In a real sense, the pleasure the audience experiences from sharing the gossip and stories via the radio approximates the recreational pleasure the characters' experience in sharing these same stories and tales.

For example, we learn that across the alley from the Gooks, on University Street, lives Mis' Florence Harris. Mis' Harris owns a boarding house whose tenants includes Mr. Harry Sludge, a forty-three-year-old who cries with little provocation and who needs to sleep at the Vic and Sade's when his landlady is away so that he won't be alone. The man-child was the object of Vic's scorn: "Brother Sludge, I'm afraid, is in for a lot of heartbreak before he shuffles off this mortal coil."[45] Despite Sade's protestations that Sludge has been spoiled his whole life by his mother and his brother, Vic maintains that the man is a "half-wit." It's this very attitude that allowed Vic and Russell to deface Sludge with an ink moustache while the man was napping on the Gooks' davenport.

Charlie Razorscum and his wife also live across the alley from Vic and Sade, their fence being alongside Mis' Harris's garden. Like Vic, Charlie works at Consolidated Kitchenware Plant 14. As Sade shows Rush and Vic his family's photo album, we learn that that the forty-four-year-old Charlie was married in Harriet, Wisconsin, in 1922, wearing a $75 tailored suit. His car is twenty years old and in a state of perpetual disrepair, so much so that he wants to tie his car onto Fred Stembottom's on a trip to Chenoa for the express purpose of retrieving the parts to fix. Listeners, as well as the Gooks, are made privy to the fact that Razorscum's family has a long tradition of oblong heads.

The Hushers were also neighbors of the Gooks. Mis' Husher was a fellow member of the ladies' Thimble Club, of which Sade was a member, as well as a gardener who specialized in in sweet peas. Like Mr. Sludge, Mr. Husher was perhaps overly reliant on his mother and, in a practice that would almost certainly have created a riff in most marriages, mailed his shirts home to be washed and ironed by her.

The Kneesuffers, Ike and Ida, live across the alley to the south of Vic and Sade. Like Vic, Ike works for the Consolidated Kitchenware Company at Plant 14, and frequently partakes of indoor horseshoes with Vic.

The listener takes in such facts, learned secondhand from the Gooks' conversations, much the same way one experiences similar stories from family and friends. But the Gooks' conversations were assisted by Rhymer's carefully constructed dialog. *New Yorker* writer Jean Shepherd observed that it was the fact that "Rhymer wrote real *dialogue* that distinguished *Vic and Sade* from other comedy programs that parlayed a string of one-liners and sought what could best be described as cheap laughs."[46] Rhymer's dialogue was natural and unaffected. His characters spoke the way real people spoke—the way that listeners spoke. Conversations were not always neat and orderly, but sometimes, just as in life, messy and disorderly, as in this excerpt from May 11, 1938, in which Vic and Sade discuss a vacation to Hawaii that they are planning for 1940. As Vic tries to explain where Hawaii is located, the telephone rings:

> VIC: All right, let's let this piece of paper represent the United States an' also the Pacific...
> (*TELEPHONE RINGS*)

SADE: Telephone, sonny.
RUSH: I imagine it's Blue-tooth Johnson. Blue-tooth *threatened* to call.
VIC: Kiddo, I'm drawin' in Illinois an' Iowa an' Wisconsin to demonstrate ...
SADE: Let's see who this is.
RUSH: *(INTO PHONE)* Hello? Yes. Oh, hello, Mis' Stembottom. Just fine. No, I been readin' a book an'—
SADE: *(BRISKLY)* Give me that.
RUSH: *(INTO PHONE)* Year, she's right here. I think she—
SADE: *Give* me that.[47]

The conversation is *real*. In life, people vie for attention; they have competing interests, they talk over and ignore one another, confident that what they have to say is more interesting and important than what anyone else has to offer. Young Rush and Russell were most often steamrolled in the course of such conversations, typically by Sade, who believed that her maternal status afforded priority in any family discussion. Sade's domineering approach to conversation is illustrated in a January 27, 1944, episode. A rather bored Sade asks Vic and Russell for some "nice family gossip," in which "each party gets an equal chance" to speak:

> RUSS: Well, Mom, *here's* something you're interested in: Miss Monroe was telling us in algebra class this morning that most people have trouble remembering—
> SADE: *(TO VIC, CANDIDLY)* No, but all jokes off to one side, lots and lots of time I do have stuff to tell you about and try to keep it in my head, but by the time you get home of an afternoon I've completely forgot as many as half a dozen times.[48]

Russell and Vic's attempts to speak are foiled by Sade's virtual soliloquy, one that transformed what should have been a period of group leisure into a self-serving event. In this instance, the radio audience has gained more leisure from the conversation than any character except Sade herself.

The Gooks' conversations also reveal fully developed, multi-faceted characters not only within the Gook family, but throughout their community. Partly, this is due to Rhymer's goal of creating entertaining characters, but it also represents the way real conversations build upon the characteristics and traits of those discussed. Such conversations grow richer, more intimate, and more satisfying when they become connected to fully realized individuals.

One example of this is Mr. Gumpox, the Gooks' trash man. Although (almost) never heard, listeners were well acquainted with him. The Gooks knew his horse, Howard, and even knew Howard's sister, Bernice. Listeners were introduced to Gumpox's bride when she arrived in town and made her inaugural ride in his trash wagon. On August 2, 1938, Sade and Rush engage in a revelatory conversation with Gumpox in their alleyway as he was collecting trash. Sade is on the back porch drying her hair while Rush is taping his baseball. Later that evening, as Vic sits in his easy-chair reading the newspaper, Sade sews, and Rush plays solitaire, they decide to share the story with Vic. Laughingly, they tell Vic that Gumpox is considering "pullin' up stakes and leavin' town," feeling that he's done all he can do for the town and now he "wants new fields to conquer."[49] Though they assure Vic that they are not making fun of Gumpox, they do admit they had difficulty keeping a straight face during their talk with him. Vic says, "You folks are havin' a jolly time for yourselves. Let me in on the joke an' I'll join in with my tinklin' laughter."[50]

Although there is an air of sarcasm to Vic's remark, Sade and Rush do share with him their garbage man's plight. He has been giving some thought to cities like New York and Paris, which are "every garbage man's dream," but he's conscious of the fact that it is easy to "lose his identity" in such metropolises. According to Rush, Gumpox emphasizes his point by quoting (somewhat accurately) from Longfellow's "Courtship of Miles Standish": "Better first in a little Iberian Village, quoth Caesar, Than second in Rome."⁵¹ Vic notes that he must be educated to have made such a reference and is surprised to learn that Gumpox never had any formal education, but rather has gained his knowledge by spending his evenings reading in the public library. The Gooks, and their audience, also learn how it was that Gumpox came to be a garbage man. He recalled that when he was eleven years old he saw a garbage man in action and was impressed by the man's "easy skill and flashy technique."

The Gooks didn't *need* to know the information Gumpox provided, and Gumpox was under no obligation to provide it to them. However, the conversation allows all parties to share and, though a serious matter to Gumpox, his comments brought a sense of delight to Vic and Sade (and likely the radio audience) and "fascinating information" on an "absorbing subject" to Vic in a relaxing evening setting, demonstrating the leisure potential of conversation.

At the same time, *Vic and Sade* recognized that conversation in the 1930s was no longer limited to face-to-face interactions. The growing prominence and changing nature of the telephone in the American home was a frequent topic on *Vic and Sade*. The first telephone exchange opened in New Haven, Connecticut, in 1878, and was just sixty years old when *Vic and Sade* premiered. In 1880, fewer than 50,000 people had telephones, while just twenty years later 2.3 million were connected and the *New York Times* declared the device irreplaceable, an "annihilation of time and space which would belong in the realm of magic if it was not a commonplace of daily experience."⁵²

The Depression caused many families to give up their telephones in the early 1930s, but this trend reversed as the Depression conditions abated somewhat in the mid–1930s. By the late 1930s, 15 percent of American households had a telephone, up from 13 per-

The stereotype of the housewife who gossips on the phone was already established in 1919, when Norman Rockwell painted this cover image for *Leslie's* magazine (Library of Congress).

cent five years earlier. By 1946, more than one out of every five American homes had a telephone.[53]

During the first half of the twentieth century, women were increasingly using the telephone. "Conversation, even so-called 'gossip,'" became an important part of the social process.[54] Because fewer women were in the paid workforce, they were more isolated than their husbands and the telephone played an important role in maintaining social contacts.[55] Part of women's affinity for the telephone, then, results from the duties they have: their sociability is in service to the household, the extended family, the friendship circle, and the community.[56] This did not escape the notice of the (male) executives of telephone companies, which attempted in various locales to impose surcharges on long calls to discourage women from gossiping on party lines.[57]

On the January 28, 1943, episode, listeners were treated to what can best be described as a *tour de force* from Sade. The entirety of the episode featured Sade speaking on the telephone, first to neighbor Mis' Trogel, then to Mr. Croucher the grocer, and, finally, to good friend and neighbor Ruthie Stembottom. Although Sade did utilize the telephone as a means to manage her household in speaking with Mr. Croucher, the primary function was conversation or, more accurately, gossip:

> SADE: Oh nothing much. Mis' Trogel just called. *Yes*—she *did*. We're going to meet in at Yamilton's underwear Saturday afternoon two o'clock. Uh-huh. They're all fine—Margaret's been bothered with a chest-cold but is back in school now. Yeah. Oh? Where'd you see *her*? (surprised and delighted) *Really*? In *June*? Why, goodness, the *other* baby is only ... no, wait a minute I guess I'm thinking of Mrs. Graham. Yes, I *am*. Well, *say*, in *June*, huh? Oh that's grand. Well is she ... does she look.... Uh-huh. Well, *June's* not so far away. I must call her up.[58]

The conversation provides Sade a respite from the tasks of the day and allows her to escape the isolation that was often a part of the housewife's life. By connecting with another housewife she was claiming her role as part of a broader community.

Not everyone, though, shared equally in the benefits of the telephone. For Uncle Fletcher, the device was still something confusing and akin to magic, and a device that drove people apart as much as it brought them together. In a typical example of his lack of understanding of the mysterious device, he tries to call Joe Walters at Mis' Keller's from Vic and Sade's house to invite him for dinner. Mis' Keller answers, and Fletcher is oblivious to her talking while he tells a story to Vic, Sade, and Rush. Then, he's weirdly pleased that Mis' Keller recognizes his voice, since he has trouble understanding phone calls due to the hearing problem he refuses to acknowledge and, in fact, attributes to others. As Vic says, "She's a *wizard*."[59] For Fletcher, the telephone fails to adequately substitute in-person conversation.

"Dear Sister an' All ...": The Joy of Letters

Of course, since only 15 percent of American households had a telephone, this new technology could not be relied upon as the sole way to share conversations across space. Additionally, since answering machines had yet to be invented, telephones were useful only when the intended receiver and the sender were present simultaneously. Thus, telephones were also unable to allow individuals to share conversations across time. Therefore, the most traditional form of long-distance communication, letters, remained an important means of communication and, in some instances, leisure. For example, the Providence-based American horror writer H. P. Lovecraft composed an estimated 80,000 letters during his lifetime

(1890–1937). They served as his primary social outlet and kept him connected to his circle of far-flung friends from New York to California.[60]

Until the middle twentieth century, letters served as an important form of entertainment and were typically meant to be read aloud to family and friends to share stories, triumphs, tragedies, and above all else news, both local and national. At one end of the spectrum were published collections of letters written by the rich and famous; at the other, letters shared between family members; all, however, were meant to be read and enjoyed. By 1922, in the first edition of *Etiquette*, Emily Post already noted that such letters were in precipitous decline. Scarcely 10 percent of U.S. mail was made up of personal letters, she wrote, since the telegram and newspaper had replaced them as a source of important news.[61] The letter continued on, though in diminished form, as a way for friends and relatives to share details of their lives and remain in communion in the absence of a telephone.

This correspondence was found frequently in *Vic and Sade*, most often, though not exclusively, between Sade and her sister, Bess. Like a phone call, a letter could allow the recipient to be part of a larger community. The reader could learn of people and events beyond her or his own surroundings. Letters represented the sort of "self-generated" entertainment that culture critics favored over commercial entertainment, such as movies and professional sports.[62] Unlike conversations, though, letters could be read at the leisure of the recipient, and they could be shared with others. It was, then, the *choice* of the reader to make receiving a letter a leisure activity by choosing to share it with a broader social circle. However, while correspondence was an escape from the commercial leisure so often condemned by culture critics for its monotony, they were not immune from similar criticism from their recipients, especially in an age when the art of letter writing, as Post noted in 1922, was in inexorable decline: "The difference though, between letter-writers of the past and of the present, is that in other days they all tried to write, and to express themselves the very best they knew how—to-day people don't care a bit whether they write well or ill."[63] Throughout the run of *Vic and Sade*, Paul Rhymer illustrates the potential strengths of letters as leisure while simultaneously providing a criticism of them.

On February 9, 1944, Sade complains to Vic about a letter that she has received from an acquaintance named Stella Klank, who wants to strike up a "big" correspondence. Stella has sent Sade an extremely lengthy dispatch and will, in turn, expect a similarly long letter from her. The letter, according to Sade, consists of "little inconsequential trash," such as the tale of Stella's lost gloves, and miscellaneous jokes that Sade does not understand.[64] Despite the fact that Vic points out that this is precisely the type of content that Sade and Bess include in their letters, Sade is not swayed and decides to ignore Stella's letter.

Rhymer addressed the burden of responding to or composing letters—the type of obligatory, long-distance correspondence Post specifically cited as "gradually dwindling" in 1922—in several episodes, including one in which Sade's niece Eunice seeks retaliation for the overzealous way in which her mother and Sade forced she and Rush to correspond with one another. Eunice's "plot" is to write to Sade incessantly, compelling Sade to do the same. As Rush explains to Vic, "She never realized before what a burden me and Eunice were carrying. Holy smoke, there for a while we were writing as often as there were times in a week."[65] Compare Post two decades earlier: "As for the letter which younger relatives dutifully used to write—it has gone already with old-fashioned grace of speech and deportment."[66] That duty had become an obligation and then a burden, as Rush well knows.

Rhymer also frequently contrasted personal correspondence as a means of leisure and entertainment with mass media. One common approach was to have the two forms of leisure compete with one another. For example, on March 19, 1940, a letter from Bess was read alongside a Third Lieutenant Stanley novel, Rush's favorite genre of fiction. As Rush reads from *Third Lieutenant Clinton Stanley and the United States, or Outwitting the New York Stock Market Plungers*, Sade attempts to read the letter she's received from her sister. Each narrative is markedly different—Stanley's swaggering adventure stands in stark contrast to the mundane details of Bess's life in her home of Carberry. While Third Lieutenant Clinton Stanley "gives his sweetheart an evening gown made out of fifty dollar bills," Bess writes of "dandy" weather and mundane news about friends and neighbors in her community. The letter is meaningless to Vic and Rush, both of whom would rather find escape in Rush's novel.

Although there were dramatic differences, Bess's letter and Rush's novel share significant similarities. Both follow a predictable format, so much so that Rush and Vic are able to read the introduction to Bess's letter in unison with Sade, "Dear sister and all, Thought I would write and see how you are feeling. Walter's kneecap has let up considerable on the twinges,"[67] as it was an introduction they had heard countless times before. By the end of Bess's "lovely long letter," even Sade has grown weary of this form of leisure and says, "Wasn't that a lovely, long, interesting letter?" She then yawns loudly and says, "Let's go to the picture show."

"The loser's a dirty ol' banana with all the insides scooped out": Fun and Games

Conversations and letters were forms of entertainment that occurred in the home, while much mass leisure occurred outside the home. During the Depression, the home remained an essential focus for entertainment due to the necessities of economic hardship. Such leisure activities included listening to the radio, playing cards and other games, as well as reading and gardening. These activities emphasized "family togetherness" during an economically uncertain time and, as Gary Dean Best notes, were not dissimilar to the practices of the 1890s.[68] Throughout *Vic and Sade*, we find these types of at-home entertainments represented, along with that hallmark of early home entertainment, the jigsaw puzzle.

"A REGULAR CIRCUS": MUSIC

For most radio listeners, music was a source of relaxation—indeed, it was one of the key elements of radio programming. But, within the world of *Vic and Sade*, listening to music was not an entirely leisurely—or joyous—pursuit, as Vic discovered on April 18, 1934. On that particular evening he returns home with a phonograph that he has borrowed from one of the Sisters of the Shining Sea, a sorority group who meet in the room next to the Sacred Stars of the Milky Way. Vic excitedly explains to Sade and Rush that he's been permitted to borrow the phonograph for one hour and is looking forward to playing all of the old records that he and Sade once enjoyed:

> VIC: Sade, we're gonna have a real treat this evening. We haven't heard the records in the attic for ten years! [...] Won't it be a regular circus to hear 'em again?[69]

Sade is markedly less enthusiastic about Vic's plans for a spontaneous musical evening, grumbling because the records are stored in a trunk in her recently organized attic. Undeterred, Vic is certain that they will have a "big time." Eager to listen to the old records and to appease Sade, Vic suggests that they take the phonograph to the attic and listen there. Vic's suggestion is greeted with astonishment from Sade, who counters that only "heathen in Africa" would listen to music in the attic in the middle of the night; however, she ultimately relents and she and Rush accompany Vic to the attic for his stroll down musical memory lane.

As they begin looking for records, Vic recalls favorites such as the Rufus Rustus Johnson Brown tune "What You Gonna Do When the Rent Comes 'Round?" "Gives Us a Kiss, Minnie," "Down in the Land Where the Black-Eyed Susans Grow."[70] Beyond Sade "pourin' on cold water,"[71] Vic encounters one stumbling block after another from cracked records, to a missing phonograph needle to, the final straw, a missing phonograph crank. In the end, Vic and Sade agree that the whole plan had been a silly idea.

Comparatively, pretending to play music is a far more leisurely endeavor. Although he does not know how to play the cornet, Vic readily agrees to fill in for L.W. Sloan during a band concert at Rush's high school. Vic explains, "I'm just gonna pretend to play, hold it up to my mouth and work the plungers up and down."[72] Although he maintains that it is his duty as a "good citizen" to help out the community project, there's little doubt that he is taking delight at the thought of his moment on stage, replete with a "gold-braided suit." (Interestingly, the "whole smear of high-class tunes" that the evening's program consists of served as the inspiration for Jan Bach's aptly titled "Vic and Sade's Band Concert: A Whole Smear of High Class Tunes." The piece, which premiered in November 2010 at the Merit School of Music in Chicago, was performed by the Gaudete Brass Quintet and featured the selections referred to by Vic, including "Green Dragon March," "Hunkelman Suite," "Three Little Girls Skippin' to School," "Bright Birds in the Forest," "Rhapsody in F# Major," and "Clark Street Stomp.")

Actually learning to play cornet held considerably less appeal to Vic. Indeed, when Alf Musherton, a cornetist for the Sewage Disposal Band, insists on giving Vic lessons to thank him for coaching him in preparation for joining the Sacred Stars of the Milky Way, Vic is anxious to find someone else to take the lessons. Rush is "not in the least" interested, explaining that "if I was to learn to yip on a horn, I'd learn to yip on a big horn."[73] Even attempting to entice Rush by claiming he would "enchant the pretty girls" fails to impress him. Rush counters, "I expect I enchant some of 'em."[74] Perhaps years of hearing tales of Sade's niece Eunice and her piano lessons, which once resulted in a bruised and swollen foot and a broken thumb,[75] soured the family on the appeal of attempting to master a musical instrument.

"A SISSY THING": JIGSAW PUZZLES

By 1932, mass-produced, die-cut jigsaw puzzles had "swept the country like wild fire,"[76] appealing to adults as well as children. Puzzles became ubiquitous and were given away as premiums for products, including Listerine and Pepsodent as well as department stores, such as Woolworth's. Their popularity was so great that it was estimated that the more than 2.5 million sold each week were preventing the nation from working[77]; by 1933, sales had increased to an astounding ten million per week. Consumers were treated to new puzzles each week, and puzzle clubs sprang up throughout the county.[78]

A jigsaw puzzle was used as a source of leisure and a means of promoting family togetherness in at least one episode of *Vic and Sade*, but the amusement, which was new to Rush, was not greeted with enthusiasm. In fact, after Vic explained the purpose of the puzzle to him, Rush described it as being "kind of a sissy thing" and asked for a nickel for working on the "baby game."[79] However, left with few other choices, Rush began working on and appre-

Along with jigsaw puzzles, board games were another popular family leisure activity. Rush (left) wins against Vic in a game of checkers, as Sade looks on (courtesy Mark C. Lancaster, reproduced by permission of NBC/NBC Universal PhotoBank).

ciating the puzzle. Soon, Rush's enthusiasm piques Vic's curiosity, and the two begin working on the puzzle together, attempting to guess what the picture will be.

"It's awful dull and tedious": Card Playing

In the 1930s, more than forty million decks of playing cards were sold each year. The numbers, however, belie the true popularity of card games in these years. People were simply replacing their old decks less often to save money. Card games, being inexpensive, gained popularity in the Depression, especially contract bridge, a game that encouraged social interaction, and boasted more than twenty million players in 1931.[80] The legalization of poker and other forms of card-based gambling in the casinos of Nevada during the 1930s also helped make card games more socially acceptable.

"I can certainly understand," Sade confessed during a July 4, 1944, game of rummy, "why Wild West fellas shoot each other over card games. Cards make people feverish and funny."[81] Sade's observation came as Vic and Russell waited impatiently for her to make her next move during a casual evening game. As was typically the case, interpersonal "animosity and hostility" was the result "not from the innate qualities of the game, but from the lack of skill of some players."[82] Yet, despite Sade's observation, cards played a pivotal role in the Gooks' leisure life. While rummy was the favored game between Rush (or Russell) and Vic, it was 500 (a form of euchre) that occupied many of Vic and Sade's evenings, along with Fred and Ruthie Stembottom. The game 500 was copyrighted in 1904 by the U.S. Card Playing Company, who also promoted it. Teams are dealt ten cards and, as the name of the game suggests, each team attempts to earn 500 points. The first successful team wins.

The couples partook in card games on numerous evenings as a means of relaxation and an opportunity to share in each other's lives; card playing provided them with a reason to meet when there was no other.[83] Card games are frequently seen as a social conduit in *Vic and Sade*, and, in some instances, cards made for strange bedfellows. For example, Vic and Sade entertained the "classy" Mr. Buller and his wife for a game of 500 along with the Stembottoms on December 4, 1934. The Stembottoms were also present for a round of 500 with Rush's friend Rotten and his girlfriend after Rotten discovered that he could not afford to take her to a motion picture at the Bijou—a clear instance where cards are depicted as a low-cost substitute for pricier mass leisure. Despite the fact that Rotten is eccentric, Vic and Sade decide that they will enjoy the evening—and take pleasure in the fact that it will annoy Fred Stembottom.[84]

Card games offered many opportunities for sharing among family and friends that might not have been afforded by other forms of mass or commercialized leisure or recreation. As Crespi explains, when watching mass entertainment, even as part of a group, the individual is still isolated[85]; similarly, the competitive nature of card playing and the "intense concentration on a common but highly personal activity"[86] also frequently interfered with socialization, as illustrated by Sade's exclamation regarding "the Wild West." There were also social pressures attendant with good friends that they saw frequently; Sade frequently lectured Vic on the need to "primp," despite the fact that the Stembottoms were close friends and were aware of their everyday appearance.[87]

"Brotherly love is a fine thing": Gendered Organizations

"In Hoc Signe Vince": Community Organizations

Socialization, however, also took on a more formal aspect for Victor Gook. In his world, the Sacred Stars of the Milky Way was his third love, behind only Sade and Consolidated Kitchenware. The fraternal organization provided him with fellowship and validation beyond his job; it was through the organization that Vic found a means for socialization, recognition, and creativity. It also provided him with a sense of elitism, of being something and someone special, someone who was part of an organization to which others could only aspire.

> VIC: (*SINGING*) I am a happy, happy man. I love my brotherhood. I help the poor and feeble and I am always kind and good. The Sacred Stars of the Milky Way is the lodge I like to serve. Its regulations are mighty fine, from them I will not swerve. So, come, my brothers, let us dance. Let's clap our hands with glee for the Sacred Stars of the Milky Way we'll always ...
>
> Later ...
>
> VIC: Jolly lads, quick, come to me, a story I will tell; about the Sacred Stars of the Milky Way, the organization we love so well. 'Twas founded in 1833 by six wise men so true.[88]

So protective was he of his lodge that Vic was livid when he learned that his neighbor Fred Stembottom was considering joining it—despite the fact that the Stembottoms were close friends of the Gooks. Vic clearly disliked the encroachment on what was, for him, a separate social circle. Vic feels that Fred is also patronizing regarding the possibility of being "talked into" joining the "club."

> VIC: Sade, do you realize that a man has to be sponsored and vouched for and everything else to become a Sky Brother in the Sacred Stars of the Milky Way?
>
> Later, reading from Volume 7:
>
> VIC: Membership in the Sacred Stars of the Milky Way is a precious amulet to be worn gloriously through life.[89]

For Vic, the Sacred Stars of the Milky Way is both a source of respect and a status symbol. On February 18, 1935, he is elected Exalted Big Dipper, a high honor and a high rank in the organization. The lodge separates him from Fred and establishes a separate identity (though, interestingly, in a 1935 episode, Fred is referred to as a member of the lodge).

Approximately 425 fraternal and sororal organizations were formed in the United States between 1700 and 1972, with 265 founded in the heyday between 1865 and 1899.[90] Such well-known organizations as the Freemasons, the Elks, the Moose, and the Lions flourished in these years. While twentieth-century competitors based membership on occupation, early fraternal organizations did not base either membership or hierarchy within the order on occupation, which explains how an often-unemployed and sometimes homeless individual like Hank Gutstop could rise to the position of the Exalted Little Dipper within the Sacred Stars of the Milky Way despite the fact that there "don't seem to be anything outstanding about Hank" and he "lacks distinction" though he could "sleep ten hours at a stretch on the Illinois Central Depot platform."[91] This lack of discrimination promoted fellowship between lodge members. As Willard C. Sutherland explains, "Persons enjoy their fellowship with others in objective enjoyment of the common activity."[92] It is then the individual's performance within the environment of the lodge, their commitment to the lodge, their status within the lodge, and the work and effort that they put forth toward the lodge that determined their position within the fraternal order. The sense of fellowship was heightened by participation in groups within the lodge. For, Vic this entailed being a member of the Sacred Stars of the Milky Way marching band. Despite the fact that the members of this unit were scattered throughout the country and unable to practice together (leading to absurd scenes of Vic marching alone), their participation and interest in the unit produced a community in that the members possessed shared interests, assumptions, and a sense of common good.[93] While Rhymer depicted a thriving fraternal organization (as later would the *Honeymooners* with the Raccoon Lodge and the *Flintstones* with the Loyal Order of Water Buffalos), it is not clear that this was the case in the world beyond radio and TV. In the 1920s and '30s, the Lynds discovered, while interviewing lodge participants, that despite the fact that membership was up, many found their lodges "cold" and "impersonal," a means for making business contacts instead of a place for fellowship.[94] The Lynds quoted one local lodge member as saying that lodges had been "shot to hell by the Depression," and the researchers predicted that lodges were "doomed," except among the working classes, whose lodges had social welfare functions.[95] These would be the lodges of *The Honeymooners* and *The Flintstones*.

Nevertheless, there were clear psychic benefits to lodge membership in the Depression years. Lodges, for example, provided their members a means of escaping the daily grind by exchanging the day-to-day clothing for colorful robes, providing a safe place to transgress social boundaries, and even gender-based sartorial restrictions. "It enabled them to wear, within the sanctuary of the lodge hall, outfits which on the street would likely have occasioned their arrest."[96] Indeed, the flamboyant nature and cost of Vic's robes was subject of more than one episode. His 1935 robe was covered in more stars than Sade had ever seen in her life, while on February 1, 1936, Rush and Sade decide to play a prank on Vic regarding his newly arrived robe, which is described as being pink with fur trim and real silver bullets. The robe is, according to Sade, "simply beautiful."[97] On other occasions Sade was less than enthusiastic, such as in 1939 when Vic paid $48.75 for the latest fashion.

Although lodges may have had different foci depending upon whether they were

Single-gender lodges allowed members the freedom to act in ways social pressures would have prevented in public. Here, Freemasons wear costumes and robes for enacting rituals, just as Vic's lodge gave him the freedom to wear flamboyant robes (Library of Congress).

founded prior to or after the Civil War, they did share certain traits, including "material indicators of an initiate's status," such as baubles and badges.[98] Rhymer seized upon this universal concept and depicted a lodge obsessed with materialism, one operated as much for profit as for fellowship. The Chicago headquarters of the Sacred Stars of the Milky Way put forth a perpetual string of merchandise guaranteed to exploit members' needs to be seen as dedicated Sky Brothers. The "baubles" ranged from swords to encyclopedias to telescopes to dinnerware. It was a marketing strategy that was effective, at least with Vic, who, having made his commitment to the lodge, wished to remain in its good graces and show his support through its merchandizing. In doing so, he was receptive to every lodge request, without regard for its practicality. The offers from lodge headquarters came frequently, and they made little effort to conceal the fact that, in Sade's estimation, they "just lay awake nights figurin' up stuff to grab a person's money."[99] In this 1943 episode, Sade braces for the new lodge catalog:

> SADE: (*WEARILY*) *I* don't want any electrical shoe trees; *I* don't want any statues of R. J. Konk with just his undershirt on for out in the front yard; I don't want any plumed hats or tasselled boots or framed pictures of...
> [...]
> VIC: The dinner-plates we are about to examine quite naturally are decorated with emblems and insignia relative to esoteric matters pertaining to the Sacred Stars of the Milky Way—
> SADE: Pictures of R. J. Konk in just his underwear plastered on 'em?
> VIC: (*AFTER A BRIEF PAUSE, FROSTILY*) You are *blunt*, Sadie.[100]

As it happened, Sade's hyperbole was justified as she was presented with dinner plates featuring, among other things, a "man in full dress suit and his tongue lolling out fierce and all his teeth showing and *pointing* at you."[101] The plate also featured the sentiment, "You are rotten guilty and you know it, you dog," as well as one of the Sacred Stars of the Milky Way's founders, R. J. Konk, sporting bright "carroty" hair; in others, he was featured with green or scarlet hair. Other lodge offerings included an electric portrait of R.J. Konk in which, once electricity is turned on, his lips part and "he smiles a beautiful white-toothed smile," and a "Manual for Wives of the Sacred Stars of the Milky Way."[102]

The lodge's manual mirrored the "outpouring of advice literature" that began in the Victorian era with titles such as *Handbook for the Use of a Lady in Polite Society* (1860), which maintained that "every part of your person and dress should be in perfect order" and further instructed users to "avoid all such tricks smoothing your hair with your hand, arranging your curls, pulling the waist of your dress down."[103] These manuals covered such topics as "How Not to Cough" and "How to Dress Tastefully with Rules for Courtship, Marriage, etc."[104] Racier manuals, especially from the 1920s onward, offered sexual advice to married couples, while the most famous of all, Emily Post's *Etiquette* (1922) took a comprehensive view of all forms of polite behavior. The "Manual for Wives of the Sacred Stars of the Milky Way" was in this latter tradition. Wives are, for example, instructed to keep their hands and faces clean at all times. More specifically:

> To be a true and loyal wife of a Sky Brother in the Sacred Stars of the Milky Way, Madame will take pains with the neatness of her person. She will never appear in her husband's presence with soiled hands or dirty face. [...] Madame will refrain from stealing property belonging to others, using coarse language, and engaging in street brawls.[105]

The manual, albeit satirical, is indicative of the attitudes of fraternal organizations that men and women inhabited separate spheres, with men at work, while women were either at home

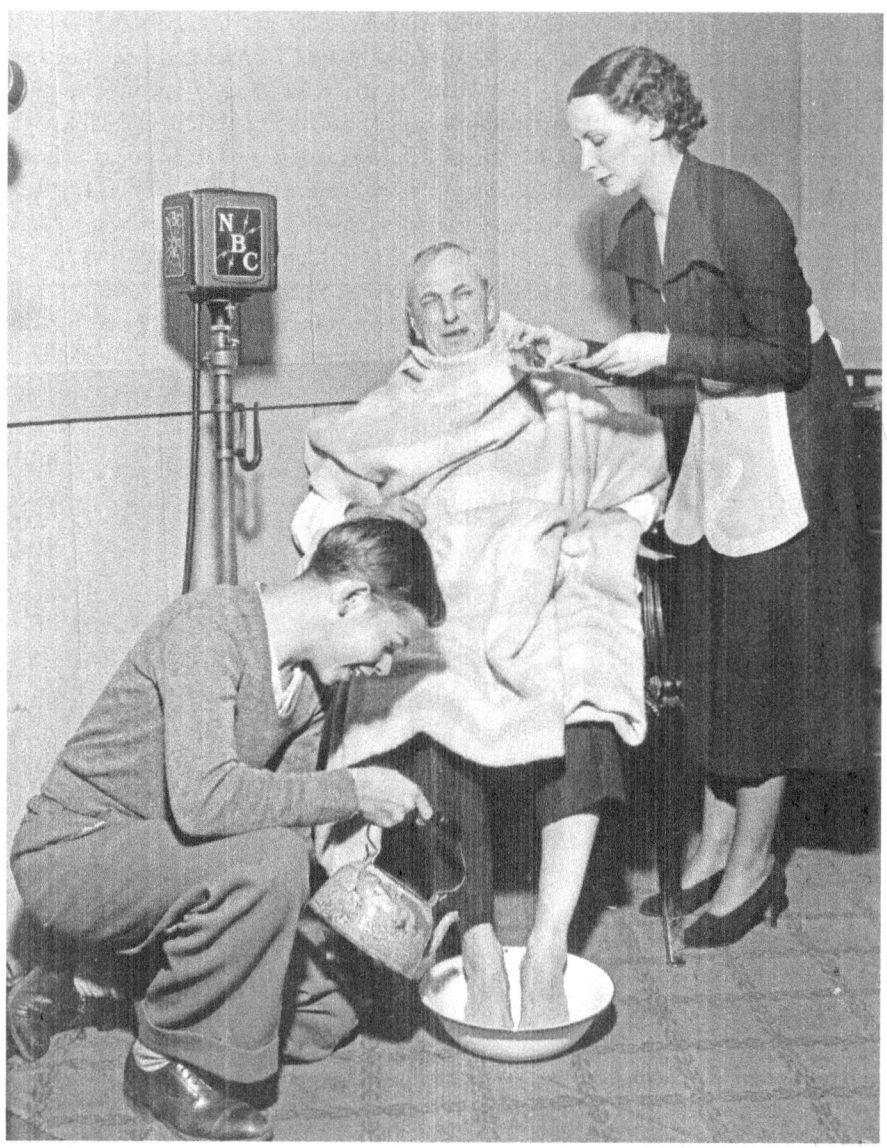

The Sacred Stars of the Milky Way tried to enforce rigid ideas about men's and women's places in the family. The Sky Brothers would have been pleased to see this scene of Sade and Rush providing barber services to Vic, the man of the house (courtesy Mark C. Lancaster, reproduced by permission of NBC/NBC Universal PhotoBank).

or in church; men were "rough and aggressive," while women were expected to be "ministering angels" from whom men could catch a "glimpse of the divine."[106] Given such unrealistic expectations, it is no wonder that the Sacred Stars of the Milky Way would feel compelled to remind wives of their "duties." This attitude, and the inherent patriarchal worldview associated with it, is further illustrated during the ritualistic Big Dipper Day, on which Big Dippers throughout the nation must be served their dinner following the prescripts of the lodge. According to the ritual, Big Dippers must sit alone at a small table and be served their meal precisely at 11:00 p.m. by their wives. The wife, rules state, must be free of makeup, and barefoot; she must bow twice upon serving the man.[107] The best that can be said of such patriarchal, male-dominant "rules" is that spelling them out implied a recognition that, even in the satirical world of radio, the ideal of the submissive wife was honored more in the breach, suggesting that the lodge's ritual was recreating a gender power balance that no longer existed.

"Sew an' chat an' gossip": The Thimble Club

Men were not the only ones who found companionship in a group setting. Sade's Thimble Club was, at once, a world apart from the Sacred Stars of the Milky Way and, at the same time, very similar. Unlike the Sacred Stars of the Milky Way, the Thimble Club lacked the preoccupation with materialism that was so integral to Vic's lodge. Instead, the group was centered on fellowship, leisure, and education. Sade neatly summarized the mission of the Thimble Club as "sewin' an' chattin' an' gossip." The club appears to have gotten its start in 1933 by Mis' Henry, with Sade filling out her application for membership on May 26 of that year. Sade would go on to become president of the club, rising to the top of her organization just as Vic did in his.

Like Vic, Sade took considerable pride in her role in the club. Though likely not as exclusive as The Sacred Stars of the Milky Way, the Thimble Club was still a tight-knit organization, one that Sade was as protective of as Vic was his lodge. Sade was as indignant when, on January 3, 1941, Mis' Applerot proposed allowing new members as Vic was at the prospect of Fred Stembottom joining his lodge. Similarly, we learn that the other ladies in the club are equally shocked at the prospect, as audible gasps are heard, one of the ladies drops her purse, and tears stream down Ruthie Stembottom's face. Sade is, however, quick to point out that members are always welcome to bring guests at any time, but membership is exclusive. Thus, members can show off their unique group to others, who will remain outsiders.

Even within the group not all members are created equal; there is an unspoken social hierarchy that frequently results in friction. This dynamic is often best displayed by Mis' Applerot. On several occasions, Sade's "friend" disturbs the club's peace by doing such things as proposing that the club admit new members, threatening its mission by insisting that it petition for the demolition of the Bright Kentucky Hotel, and forcing the ladies to send flowers from her niece's husband, who runs a flower store on Center Street.[108] It is also not uncommon for Thimble Club members to judge one another, as Sade does upon learning that Mis' Kisser has not done any spring cleaning, "No civilized lady," Sade insists, "don't do her spring cleaning."[109] The revelation caused Sade to question Kisser's nature: "You just can't tell about people. On the surface they're sayin' and doin' one thing. Inside they're something else."[110] Such interpersonal rivalries and jockeying for social position contrast with Vic's lodge, which makes a great show of avoiding hierarchy and emphasizing fraternity. Instead, the Thimble Club seems to recreate and enforce social hierarchies as a way of creating order. In both cases, the social interactions within the group are differentiated from social interactions outside the group, reversing the typical social situations of the members: the men, who in their work lives are in rigid hierarchy, seek egalitarian fraternity; the sorority of housewives struggle to create (fictive) elite status.

In addition to their other activities, the Thimble Club participates in casual educational activities. In the fall of 1933, for example, the ladies were inspecting different place each week in a "very educational program."[111] Among the sites on the ladies' itinerary was a news-

Women's clubs could be found at every level of society, including the Gridiron Women's Club, made up of female reporters and officials and the wives of Washington politicians. In this 1938 photograph, the club is performing a skit (Library of Congress).

paper plant, where they saw how the presses operated; the roundhouse; and a machine factory. Other activities included listening to one another's reports on everything from birds to "Human Souls versus the Beautiful Blue Danube," and poetry reviews. However, just as the Lynds noted in their discussion of women's study groups in Middletown, the ladies shied away from "talk of a continuous sort" as "there is no tradition of facile talk for its own sake for cleverness in that such things tend to be confusing and therefore annoying."[112] Education served as a form of status and display as much or more than a form of actual improvement; it was enough to seem to be interested in culture, not to participate in it.

"Watchin' fat men play handball": The Not-So-Guilty Pleasures of Non-Commercialized Low-Brow Leisure

Even the appearance of an interest in high culture was frequently a social mask meant to provide status and a cultured façade over those who were frequently more interested in what culture critics would decry as base, low-brow forms of leisure, some of which took the form of what an outside observer might term a kind of *Schadenfreude* or sadism. In 1932, not long after coming to live with the Gooks, young Rush Meadows woke in the middle of the night with a stomachache. Unable to sleep, Rush asks his adoptive parents to tell him a story—one that he orchestrates. The story centers upon boxers Jack Dempsey and Gene Tunney meeting in a cigar shop and proceeding to engage in a fight. Amidst the tale of boxers scrapping, Rush finally drifts off to sleep.

Several years earlier, in 1927, Dempsey and Tunney had been participants in what became known as "The Long Count Fight." New rules allowed a fallen boxer ten seconds to rise, but only *after* his opponent reached a neutral corner, something that took Tunney at least four seconds to do, giving rise to the phrase "long count." The Dempsey-Tunney bout, which pitted the two boxers in a rematch of their 1926 fight, took place at Soldier Field in Chicago before a crowd of 104,943,[113] where it simultaneously became both the sport's first $1 million gate and $2 million dollar gate. The Dempsey-Tunney fight was carried by seventy-four radio stations and broadcast to an audience of forty-five million.

With one bedtime story, the Gooks managed to illustrate everything that intellectuals despised about mass culture. The story featured icons whose notoriety was derived through actions derived for the masses, actions predicated on the enjoyment of violence and suffering. The Dempsey-Tunney fight didn't just spontaneously occur—that would have been bad enough—it was promoted to and seen by the masses in the arena and over the air. It was also, in the eyes of culture critics, a vile display of violence intended to appeal to the lowest common denominator. Even among the sport's supporters, advocates cast Dempsey as "primitive" and "exciting," while Tunney was seen as "intellectual" and "dull." *The Nation* wrote that the national good and the cause of high culture would be served if "mind were to triumph over matter."[114] The fight became a litmus test for how one chose to read American culture in the 1920s.

The Dempsey-Tunney fight was well known enough even five years after it occurred that each member of the Gook family was aware of the players and their part—even Rush would have been four at the time of "The Long Count." However, were they familiar with aspects of high culture? Could Rush or Sade have hummed even part of a symphony or an opera?

The Gooks didn't restrain their enjoyment of a good brawl to relaxing nighttime fare; a good round of fisticuffs could be appreciated at breakfast time as well. This was the case on December 9, 1935, when two cars collided outside of the Gook house, prompting Rush to hope for a "good accident. I mean I hope this is a high-class head-on collision."[115] Vic, Sade, and Rush watch from the window, anticipating a fight between the drivers and speculating on the cause of the accident. As they watch, Vic amuses himself by playing the role of the antagonist, mouthing words in the hope of provoking a fight. The Gooks' fun is temporarily interrupted by a telephone call from Mis' Call, who is also watching the outdoor proceedings and wants to bet on a fight. Unfortunately, all are disappointed as the drivers move on without fanfare and Monday morning continues on as per usual.

Vic and Sade frequently depicted what culture critics would deem "low-brow" recreation as self-generated recreation. This depiction provided Paul Rhymer with not only a source of irreverent humor, but also a means of illustrating the potential deficits of self-generated recreation, particularly in comparison to commercialized recreation. As Rush once announced, "Smelly Clark and myself are going to the YMCA after a bit and watch the fat men play handball."[116] This is a regular activity, one that the boys look forward to; it is not mere happenstance.

One could easily recoil at the fact that they are taking delight in what they perceive as the misfortune of others; however, while the young men's recreational pursuits seem cruel, they are not without precedent. P.T. Barnum, for example, made a career parading "human curiosities" and "freaks" before an American public that was more than willing to indulge its morbid curiosity. On the upper floors of Barnum's museum, patrons "could gawk at some of the most popular and controversial exhibits ... such as bearded ladies, legless individuals, albinos, giants and midgets."[117]

Barnum was not the only one profiting from "curiosities." At Coney Island, Samuel Gumpertz had assembled a wide assortment of unusual people, including three hundred midgets to inhabit "Lilliputia," and 212 "friendly non–head-hunting Bantocs" from the United States' new and most remote colony, a fact that intrigued the public. Gumpertz also created "The Dreamland Circus Sideshow," including acts that ranged from a dog-faced boy, an armless woman, an 804-pound man, and men who were more than eight feet tall.[118] The fascination with such oddities reached a sort of apex in Tod Browning's 1932 film *Freaks*, which used actual freak show performers (many of whom suffered from what we would classify as genetic disorders) and cast them as objects of horror.

LeRoy Ashby suggests that "freak shows" did more than merely titillate audiences who viewed the human oddities with a combination of "fear, inquisitiveness, and feelings of supe-

Taking pleasure in the suffering of others, whether real or perceived, plays a major role in leisure. P. T. Barnum capitalized on this with freak shows, which remained popular in the Depression and were immortalized in Tod Browning's horror movie *Freaks* (1932) (Library of Congress).

riority."[119] Shows like Barnum's also provided a means for assisting audiences in understanding an industrializing and urbanizing society by providing them with something to "measure and define themselves against those strange Others whose presence helped distinguish the normal from the deviant."[120] The "freak show," then, provided audiences with reassurance and insight into themselves, though these mitigating factors hardly make the exhibitions any less exploitative. In a minor way, watching fat men play handball recreated the experience of the freak show, involuntarily turning the out-of-shape men attempting to exercise into surrogate freaks. Rush and his young, thin friends could compare themselves and feel superior.

Similarly, in July 1937, Smelly Clark lay in the hospital, waiting to have his tonsils removed. For Rush and his friends, Smelly's surgery was an opportunity for gruesome, sensationalized entertainment. Rush was truly aggrieved to learn that his plans would not be acceptable to Smelly's doctors: "You mean to sit there with a calm face an' tell me that a guy that's gonna have his throat slashed from ear to ear can't give his personal friends permission to *watch?*"[121] Had he lived one hundred years earlier, Rush's desire to see the gruesome may well have been fulfilled. Displays of human curiosities may have been tasteful when compared to public autopsies offered by Barnum and others. One of his earlier (1835) and more noteworthy curiosities was Joice Heth, who, Barnum claimed, was the 161-year-old nurse of George Washington. Heth, an elderly black woman, barely able to move, demonstrated considerable theatrical ability in her exhibitions in which she told stories about her young ward, and sang hymns. Upon Heth's death, Barnum ensured one final show by giving her a public autopsy, in which her true age would be determined. Heth, according to the doctor performing her autopsy, could not have been more than eighty years old.[122] As with the case of the fat men playing handball, Rush's seemingly outrageous request is actually a watered-down form of amusement that had once been commonplace in a less-civilized era. In a real sense, the shock and humor of Rush's amusements testifies to the changing morals and standards of twentieth-century America. If it is true that the defining trait of the state is a monopoly on violence, the growing Hollywood monopoly on displays of violence reflect the growing power of mass culture in the face of traditional leisure outlets.

The appeal of violent, sadistic entertainment could and did best other forms of leisure whenever it was on offer. On several occasions, a more wholesome, self-generated form of amusement was forced to compete with sensationalized amusement. This was the case on May 10, 1938, when homespun recreation threatened to interrupt Vic and Rush's plans to see notorious bank robber Bill Meekins at the Illinois central depot. As the pair excited planned to head off to see the "big bank robber" in person,[123] Sade announced that they would first need to settle in and be treated to snapshots of Mis' Scott's trip to Burlington, Iowa.

The choice, then, is between the illicit thrill of encountering a "famous bad man" and sharing the quaint experiences of a member of the community. It would seem that viewing Mis' Scott's snapshots would offer benefits that far exceed the sensationalized experience of viewing a notorious criminal; however, in being forced to stay for Mis' Scott's photos, Rush and Vic are put in a position in which they resent the situation and derive no enjoyment whatever. There is no intimacy gained from the experience as Mis' Scott does not join the Gooks, but merely watches from her window. As such, Rush and Vic are "treated" to a series of seemingly meaningless photos, such as a balcony, miscellaneous relatives, and a one-legged man.

Rhymer took a similar approach in July of 1940, when Sade required Rush and Vic to

People-watching was a source of leisure, but could also be tiring work. In this 1933 photograph from Art Van Harvey's personal collection, the cast of *Vic and Sade* pauses to rest their feet after a long day of being out and about among the masses at the Chicago World's Fair (Mark C. Lancaster/The Art Van Harvey Collection).

spend an evening at home looking at Charlie Razorscum's family photo album, which Sade, once again, forces them to view, claiming it is the "civilized thing." "The civilized thing," Vic says sarcastically, "is to wear my eyes to the bone looking at Razorscum's relations, huh?"[124] While an evening with the Razorscums illustrates deficits in traditional leisure activities, it also reveals the relationship between such activities and low-brow or commercialized events. The weaknesses in traditional activities are seen in direct relation to the more titillating low-brow recreation. Through this lens, traditional, non-commercialized recreation, void of sensationalism, pales in comparison. It was this preference gap that mass culture would use in creating alternative forms of leisure, such as movies that would, in many cases, win out over less sensational forms of leisure. The Gooks, of course, were able to create their own sensationalism in such seemingly self-generated forms of leisure as people-watching. The railroad yards and depots were generally depicted as seamy places where one might find the likes of Hank Gutstop, or some other individual of questionable repute, napping at any given point in the day. Rush, however, saw something different in the train station: romance. Perhaps showing the influence of so many dime novels, Rush paints a vivid picture of the "feverish excitement"[125] to be found there as he and Vic wait at the Union Railway Station for Sade to return from a trip. To Vic, the train station seems fairly empty; however, Rush, under the influence of romantic imagery and expectations of sensationalism, maintains that it will soon swell with excitement. "It's the *romance* I got reference to. Gives me a thrill to watch the many weary travelers."[126] While the station might seem deserted, he is sure that not long ago it was "humming with life" as "little children trustingly holdin' the hand of their mother" and "guys givin' their girl one last kiss."[127]

There is, for Rush, an intriguing angle to the commonplace elements of his surroundings.

> VIC: There's a copper over there by the magazine stand.
> RUSH: Yeah—keepin' a sharp an' vigilant eye out for evil-doers.
> VIC: Aw shucks, bet he ain't arrested anybody in ten years.[128]

The intrigue continues as they watch a man approach the window to purchase a ticket. Rush speculates as to where he might be going, but believes that if they asked him he would "probably turn us over to the policeman as a couple of suspicious characters." Vic, who is gradually succumbing to Rush's view on their location, notes that the man was "whippin' out quite a bundle of money" and was probably headed for someplace like California.[129]

While Rush sees an environment of "romance" and "feverish excitement" as one might encounter in a Third Lieutenant Clinton Stanley novel, Vic's take on things becomes increasingly sensationalistic as well. He gets into the spirit of entertainment and notes, for example, that it would be "darn mean" of the policeman to "turn around an' shoot us in cold blood." He also wonders what the policeman would do if "I walked over to the magazine stand and kicked him in the stomach." Vic is disappointed to learn that, despite fact that Rush and the officer "barely come close to gettin' over the edge of enjoyin' a feeble nodding acquaintance," his son would be unable to save him from immediate arrest.[130] Despite Vic's sensational speculations, the influence we see exerted by Rush's reading selections is, in fact, inherently positive. He is thinking creatively and imagining scenarios that, though perhaps more compelling than reality, are positive and life-affirming.

There are other instances in which *Vic and Sade* depicts instances of recreation that was both self-generated and sensationalized. Vic and Rush, for example, found spontaneous recreation and took considerable delight in the effects of electricity. One source of this "recreation" was derived from Sade's washing machine, a perpetual source of household trouble. In June of 1936, listeners would learn of Sade's home remedies, which included everything from elastic braces to newspapers to molasses. Prior to this, in 1934, Vic and Rush investigated the machine after Sade reported that it had been emitting shocks directly into the water. It's not long before Vic receives a shock and unexpectedly takes delight in it. Soon, Vic and Rush are taking turns shocking one another and plotting ways to increase the shock. Vic suggests that public restrooms should be fitted with a device to provide users with a "good healthy shock" when drying their hands.[131] Their fun continues until Mr. Drummond arrives to repair the washing machine, at which time they prepare to shock him. Sadomasochistic behavior is now being extended to other characters. According to Sade, Fred Stembottom plays a game at work in which the loser must sit still while everyone hits him with a sledgehammer[132]—a game not far removed from a classic Victorian party game, "Hot Cockles," in which partygoers took turns hitting a guest positioned upside-down over another's lap, with his or her eyes covered. The unfortunate victim "wins" by correctly identifying each person hitting during that person's blows, and the "fun" derived from how hard each guest chooses to hit the victim.[133] As odd as it may seem, striking one's friends was once considered a standard form of leisure activity and can be found in many early party games.

Leisure's Threat

Of course, it is important to remember that no individual consumes exclusively low culture or high culture. Most participate in a variety of leisure activities, at many levels. At the same time that the antics of *Vic and Sade* depicted a middle-class family's relationship to the many forms of leisure available to them, culture critics of the 1930s expressed concern regarding these activities. Many feared that the working class would be unable to use their surplus time wisely, unlike "artists and philosophers and authors."[134] Moreover, leisure had become "standardized and automated," with most involving passive activities, like listening or watching.[135] As was discussed in Chapter Four, culture critics believed that the masses would blindly follow whichever trend presented itself to them.

Perhaps most troubling to the elitists was the fact that, in an "environment of downward mobility and heterogeneous leisure"[136] it became difficult to maintain class boundaries. More traditional form of leisure, such as folk art, was favored for the masses by the elite because it was clearly symbolic of the masses.[137] Writing in 1926, George Barton Cutten compared the meaningful uses of leisure time with leisure activities pursued by steelworkers:

> When the steel mills had their hours shortened by one-third, did they dash wildly to libraries, schools, oratorios, art museums, grassy banks, and murmuring brooks? Not so noticeably as to obstruct the traffic. It is probable that the attendance at pool halls, dime movies, and other places of loafing would have shown a sudden increase.[138]

Cutten, like other mass-culture critics, ignores the increasing availability high culture available to the masses. Radio, whose content had been almost uniformly condemned by intellectuals, had exposed audiences to a wide range of literature and music that it would likely not otherwise have encountered. By 1926, NBC was airing New York Symphony concerts; this was followed in 1927 by the Boston Symphony, and the Philadelphia Orchestra in 1929. CBS began airing Sunday afternoon concerts from the New York Philharmonic, and the following year NBC devoted Saturday afternoons to the Metropolitan Opera.[139]

Having been exposed to classical music and able to exercise their own will regarding what they do and do not enjoy, many not only embraced a form of high-brow art, they acted on it by purchasing classical records and participating in or attending symphony orchestras, which increased in number from seventeen in 1915 to 270 in 1939.[140] Similarly, school bands and orchestras, which had heretofore been a rarity, increased to 20,000 bands and 30,000 orchestras by 1940.[141] Radio, however, led the music scene. While record sales for the largest manufacturers increased 600 percent between 1933 and 1938 for all music, since records of the era could hold only about five minutes of music, there was a limit to the number of classical pieces they could present.[142] Thus, for most listeners, Americans radio was the source for classical music.

Cutten's elitism is not surprising. Although culture critics claimed to be working to protect the masses they did little to engage them, and even less to understand their chosen forms of leisure. As noted, *Vic and Sade*'s commentary on mass culture was unique by the very fact that it was part of mass culture and reached the very masses critics purported to represent.

The masses had, Cutten maintained, lost "the art of self-expression and the ability to amuse ourselves," yet Cutten and other intellectuals were resolute in *how* the masses should amuse themselves, and failed to recognize the variations in valid leisure. From participation in community organizations, participation in sports, enjoying conversation, and writing and reading correspondence, non-elite masses did find ways to amuse themselves outside of commercialized leisure. Commercialized recreation provided an alternative to these forms of leisure—a respite *from* entertaining yourself. The masses didn't flock to Coney Island or other amusement parks, buy dime novels, or listen to jazz because they had to, but because they chose to.

Throughout the run of *Vic and Sade*, Paul Rhymer depicts non-elitists using a variety of forms of leisure, including some that could be labeled "low-brow." However, contrary to the claims of intellectuals, the majority of those found on the show *used* the available forms of leisure—it did not use them. Rhymer depicts individuals with individual tastes and individuals who seek out recreation for a variety of purposes; however, that is not to say that these individuals are not influenced by others. The leisure that they select is commercialized and non-commercialized, public and private. There is both success and failure in the depiction of each type of leisure; each has strengths and weaknesses. The Gooks, like most Americans of their era, had access to a variety of leisure activities and utilized those that worked for them in their lives. Their choices are not "wrong," but exactly that—*choices*.

Six. "Let's go to the picture show": Movies

One of the most common forms of entertainment and leisure depicted in *Vic and Sade* is the motion picture. The Bijou (pronounced Buy-Joe) motion picture theater was a staple in the Gooks' lives. It was at the Bijou that they escaped from chores, homework, and the banalities of the non-commercialized forms of leisure discussed in the previous chapter. There they were entertained by the likes of Gloria Golden, Four-Fisted Frank Fuddleman, Annabelle Ainsworth, and Donna Dreamerson; and engaged in social interaction with friends and neighbors.

Movies in the Early Twentieth Century

Early efforts to produce motion picture pictures emphasized just that—*motion*—with no sound, story, or plot. These shorts, as epitomized by the early efforts of the Lumiére brothers in France, consisted of fifteen- to thirty-second shots of such things as a train arriving at the station or a man working in his garden; at the same time in America, Thomas Edison began making short films, including shots of Niagara Falls. This all changed in 1903. With Edwin S. Porter's *The Great Train Robbery*, the transition to the narrative style of film began. *The Great Train Robbery* utilized a number of innovative techniques to further its narrative, including "parallel editing, minor camera movement, location shooting and less stage-bound camera placement"[1] as well as new editing techniques, like cross-cuts and jump-cuts.

D. W. Griffith further demonstrated the viability of film as a medium with *The Birth of a Nation*, a 1915 Civil War feature that cost a reported $100,000 to make and which earned a staggering $18 million. The three-hour epic introduced movies to middle-class audiences while simultaneously helping the medium to gain an "upper-class status."[2]

Hollywood's Golden Age

The 1930s witnessed major developments in motion pictures, most notably the introduction of sound and, later, color. Between 1926 and 1931 theaters began being fitted for sound, with the overwhelming majority being wired by 1930. By 1934, silent theaters had virtually disappeared.[3] However, while the introduction of "talkies" is remembered as being heralded with much acclaim, Richard Butsch explains that audience reaction was, in fact, mixed, noting that while some audiences found them to be a great improvement and enjoyed being able to actually hear what actors were saying rather than having to rely upon subtitles, other missed the "soothing characteristics" and "unique dramatic quality" that silent films offered.[4] Talkies also changed the social nature of film going, effectively silencing audiences that were once lively and boisterous. As Robert Sklar phrased it, "The talking audience for silent pictures became a silent audience for talking pictures."[5]

Sound wasn't the only thing introduced to movie audiences in the 1930s. Audiences were greeted with a variety of "firsts," including Donald Duck's first appearance in 1934's *The Wise Little Hen*, an eight-minute Walt Disney short. The decade also saw the introduction of such icons as everyone's favorite sailor man, Popeye, and Max Fleischer's Betty Boop. One year earlier, America's curly-topped sweetheart, Shirley Temple, made her big-screen debut in *Baby Burlesks*. Meanwhile, 1936 saw the release of Hollywood's longest talkie, MGM's *The Great Ziegfeld*, which ran two hours and fifty-six minutes, while the following year marked the release of the first full-length animated motion picture, Walt Disney's *Snow White and the Seven Dwarfs*.

Taking in a Show in Bloomington

In most regards, the ascent of motion pictures as a source of entertainment, leisure, and popular culture in Paul Rhymer's Bloomington paralleled that of other American cities. The first motion picture projector to appear in McLean County was in neighboring Normal, at the First Christian Church, in 1911. The first theater in either town built specifically for the showing of motion pictures was the Irvin Theater, situated on East Jefferson Street in Bloomington, a "first-class" establishment, located in the heart of the city.[6] The Irvin was significant in that it was intended specifically for the showing of motion pictures, whereas most other theaters of the period shared their duties and housed other types of performances, including vaudeville acts.

The local paper, the *Pantagraph*, described the Irvin as having an "attractive exterior" and an interior consisting of 1,000 seats and a scooped floor that prevented obscured views. Further, it boasted a new pipe organ, air conditioning to remove "foul odors," and ten exits allowing patrons to leave the theater without delay.[7] According to the *Pantagraph*, the Irvin Theater's exterior was "terra cotta," with "elaborate trimming." As was the case with many theaters of the era, the Irvin was modeled after "respected civics" buildings," allowing it to appear "formidable and impressive."[8] The grandeur of such theaters reflected the change from a work-based to a leisure-based society. The movie-going experience of the period emphasized the exotic; interiors of theaters often featured Egyptian or Oriental themes. Also, many theaters utilized electricity to provide moviegoers with a "splash of glamour." The sense of grandeur was likely enhanced by the location of theaters which, in the case of Bloomington, was in the town's wealthier areas, including Washington, Front, Madison, and Market Streets.[9] These locations helped to ensure that theaters were in well-lit, family-friendly locations that discouraged unwanted activity.

While the Great Depression provided Americans with more leisure time, it also limited their financial resources and the ways in which they could use this time. The impact of the Great Depression brought changes to the motion picture industry, including their means of exhibition. New theaters began to shift their décor to the still exotic, but less-expensive Art Deco style. Theaters nonetheless provided patrons with a comfortable setting, as was the case with the Normal Theater, which utilized both refrigeration and air conditioning. The Normal Theater also featured "plush coral and leather seats," along with state-of-the-art RCA sound equipment to enhance the appreciation of films' soundtracks. The theatergoing experience was further enhanced by "modernistic" walls and ceilings, a tastefully decorated powder room for the ladies, and a lounge for men. Outside, the theater was adorned with stucco Vitrolite glass, while red, blue, green, and white neon lights comprised the marquee.[10] But, by 1933, nearly one-third of movie theaters had closed down,[11] and attendance had fallen by 40 percent.[12] Those that remained needed to find ways to draw moviegoers back into the

Built in 1935, this Alabama movie theater embodies the Art Deco style of the era, which was still luxurious but more budget-friendly than the exotic and ornate movie palaces of the 1920s (Carol M. Highsmith's America, Library of Congress, Prints and Photographs Division).

In Elkins, West Virginia, in 1939, this movie theater offered games of chance three nights a week, as seen on the marquee, to generate revenue on slow business nights (John Vachon/Library of Congress).

theater, which for many included promotional activities. One of the most popular events was known as Bank Night, in which patrons wrote their names alongside a number in a large book at the beginning of the evening. Later that evening numbers were drawn, typically by a child, and prizes that normally began at $150 value were awarded. Prize winners would have three minutes to claim their prizes before another number was drawn, thus encouraging patrons to remain in the theater and perhaps take in a second show. More than one-third of all American movie theaters participated in Bank Night, and by the end of 1937 more than 100 million moviegoers had participated in the game.[13] Other promotions included "Scenario," a game similar to Bingo; premieres, in which theaters used searchlights and glamour to provide patrons with the sense of a Hollywood opening; and double features. Special features and local performers were also introduced to provide patrons with a longer theatrical experience. Boegen describes an account from the *Daily Pantagraph* of a performance by "Mickey, the Singing Mouse" at a Bloomington theater's amateur night.[14]

In the January 1, 1935, episode of *Vic and Sade*, the feature *True Hearts and Red Balloons*, starring Donna Dreamerson and Conway Clinton, is accompanied by the added attractions of Fatty Frisco and Dimples Duffy in *Look Out Below*. Further incentives to the town's moviegoers came in the form of displays of pictures of points of local interest and talks by local leaders. In the script it is suggested that these added features provided the impetus for Vic and Sade to venture to the Bijou that day. Additionally, a double-feature plays a prominent role in the October 6, 1939, episode, in which Vic is forced to endure an interminable trip to Hopewood with the Stembottoms in order to be "treated" to two Gloria Golden films he had already seen.

"One more kiss, Esther, then I'll put on my first baseman's mitt and go to my position at first base for the third inning"

Throughout the Depression years, Hollywood sought to achieve a delicate balance between fantasy and reality, reflecting the realism of the era while also providing audiences with a means to escape it. Warner Bros., for example, produced a series of films in the gangster genre that highlighted the social ills of the period. Films like *Little Caesar* (1930), *Scarface* (1932), *I Am a Fugitive from a Chain Gang* (1932), and *Angels with Dirty Faces* (1938) reflected the nation's "shaken confidence in authority and the country's social traditions."[15] Even the escapist fare of choreographer Busby Berkeley, like *Gold Diggers of 1933*, was set amidst the backdrop of the Great Depression, and films about the horrors of the First World War, like *All Quiet on the Western Front* (1930), and even the Depression itself, like *Our Daily Bread* (1934) and *Wild Boys of the Road* (1933), reminded audiences of the struggles of daily life. Understandably, these films were in the distinct minority compared to escapist fare.

Films provided moviegoers with a "pseudo environment" that helped them to manage in a real world that had grown too big to fully understand.[16] Hence, Jay Haley suggested in the 1950s, fans sought *help* from films rather than escape by seeking the comparative safety of "a more orderly world."[17] Filmgoers understood that, in the movie world, problems would be resolved by the end of the film, and the film's story would proceed mostly logically from beginning to end. Movies provided audiences with some degree of certainty in a world in which social conflict and change was constant and in which family and friends "lose their cohesiveness and their stabilizing influence."[18]

That is not to say that audiences did not seek refuge from their worries at their local motion picture theaters; this is clearly suggested by the increase in attendance at the start of both the Great Depression and World War II:

> The stock market crashed in the autumn of 1929 and movie attendance reached 110 million admissions per week through the following year (an increase from 48 millions in 1925). Attendance declined and then rose again with the war years, to 97 million admissions per week in 1944. Movie attendance could be said to act as a thermometer of the tensions in society.[19]

By some accounts, eight out of every ten Americans saw a movie each week in 1930,[20] though this figure would fluctuate through the Depression. Perhaps the role of motion pictures as a means of escape from daily life was summed up most succinctly by a "professional woman" coping with the hectic nature of home renovations when, according to *The New Yorker*, she left a note for the carpenter reading, "Must take a movie in, otherwise go batty."[21] Movies provided audiences with the opportunity to not only escape from the overwhelming burden of the Great Depression, but also from life's daily annoyances and upsets. Comedic acts like W.C. Fields, the Marx Brothers, and Laurel and Hardy provided moviegoers with an opportunity to laugh, thus taking their minds off the daily stresses that they encountered.

Similarly, screwball comedies such as 1938's *Bringing Up Baby* and 1940's *His Girl Friday* (both starring Cary Grant and Rosalind Russell) provided an irreverent take on the battle of the sexes. These comedies, along with the likes of 1936's *My Man Godfrey* and *Theodora Goes Wild*, 1933's *Design for Living*, *The Front Page* from 1931, and 1938's *Holiday*, among other madcap farces, brought a "frenetic pace, physical slapstick humor, and quick one-liners" (Dirks, *The Golden Age of Hollywood*) distracting the minds of moviegoers. Science-fiction fare, such as the children's serials *Flash Gordon* in 1936, 1938's *Flash Gordon's Trip to Mars*, and 1939's *Buck Rogers*, sought to transport moviegoers to other, often more troubled, worlds, putting the problems of earth in some perspective. The 1930s also saw the rise of the horror films, largely from Universal studios, including the classic *Dracula* and *Frankenstein* (both released in 1931), through which the troubles of the Depression found a Gothic, mythologized reflection.

Escape is one of several uses of the motion picture as depicted in *Vic and Sade*. In some instances, such as the June 4, 1941, episode, movies provide a form of escape in a very literal sense. Upon learning the Sacred Stars of the Milky Way have named her the "Grand Old Lady" of the lodge without her consent, Sade confronts Vic, who, after unsuccessfully attempting to defend the lodge's honor, announces, "I'm going to the show ... now, by myself."[22] Movies, then, could provide a means for fleeing an undesirable situation, an approach Vic also uses on August 9, 1944, when he "plays hooky" from work to enjoy the air-conditioned comfort of the Bijou with Russell.

Motion pictures also provided potential audiences with an opportunity to escape other forms of leisure, including reading. In a March 1933 episode, young Rush complains to Vic that he is tired of reading a "darn old book" which happens to be *Principles of Electrical Engineering*.[23] Vic proposes that they look at a picture album, but that, too, bores them. Ultimately, the two decide to escape the tedium of less-scintillating fare and head for the movies. Similarly, even a "lovely long an' interesting letter" from Sade's beloved sister, Bess, compels Sade to admit that an evening at the Bijou was more entertaining.[24] On November 8, 1943, Russell sat at the library table and struggled to write an essay about birds. Despite his effort, he found himself with little more than "Birds fly overhead" and Sade's confidence that he would certainly think of "interesting trash to fill out his required two pages of composition paper on both sides."[25] As he struggles to identify interesting facts about birds, Russell is spared further work by an invitation from his friend Arthur to see *One More Kiss, Esther, Then I'll Put On My First Baseman's Mitt and Go to My Position at First Base for the Third Inning*. Confident that he could complete the essay in the morning before class, Russell heads off to the Bijou for an opportunity to escape further thought about birds, as well as his parents' discussion of Pom Pom Cordova.

On another occasion, Vic and Sade are en route to visit Vic's boss, Mr. Ruebush, at the hospital as Rush heads to the Bijou. Vic and Sade carry with them presents for Ruebush, including light reading material in the form of *Death-bed Scenes of United States Presidents* and *Ivanhoe*, which Sade felt "seemed fitting for an important fella" as it was "too deep" for her.[26] Vic, however, questions the tact in giving a sick man a book of death scenes, and it isn't long before they drop the bag of pecans that they had brought for Ruebish and then discover that they had brought with them the Spanish version of *Ivanhoe*, given to them by Uncle Fletcher. Their best intentions in ruins, Vic and Sade decide to escape with Rush to the movies. Interestingly, throughout this, Rush considers going with his parents to the hospital as an escape from the routine of movie-going, noting, "I kinda like the *smell* they got."[27]

Motion pictures provided the Gooks with less of an escape from life's major hardships and unrest than from its frequent moments of tedium and boredom. The opportunity to see Gloria Golden and Four-Fisted Frank Fuddleman cavorting on the big screen was merely something else to do—something better to do than the task at hand. Sade *could* have written a reply to her sister, Bess, just as Russell *could* have buckled down and forced himself to write two double-sided pages about birds, but, fortunately, they had the Bijou to escape to, allowing them to forestall their tasks just a little bit longer.

"A mighty, mighty punk show"

Eric Johnston, president of the Motion Picture Association of America, defended the ability of the motion picture to divert audiences' attention from the "complex, wearing, worrisome world,"[28] yet to critics of mass culture, the escapist nature of films was merely more evidence of the negative role of mass entertainment and the industrialized society responsible for producing it. To these critics, the overwhelming majority of motion pictures were little more than a means of providing temporary relief to the worker from his "semi-robotic status," while simultaneous reinforcing his "passivity and boredom."[29] While critics of mass culture would contend that entering a movie theater is like a "neutral womb," a place in which audiences escape their frayed selves and, in essences "cease to exist,"[30] Vic, Sade, Rush, and Russell's movie consumption suggest otherwise. The Gooks recognize the often-escapist nature of the movies that they consume, just as they appreciate their formulaic construction.

Motion pictures were not regarded indiscriminately by the Gooks. There were those films that contained "a real high-class performance,"[31] while others were deemed "a mighty, mighty punk show."[32] Contrary to the concerns of culture critics, the masses were not always clamoring for the next mass-produced treat that would be fed to them.

Vic and Sade finds the Gooks, at least to some extent representative of others in their class, evaluating their entertainment choices prior to going to a film. Eager to see the latest Gloria Golden romance, *Smoldering Teardrops*, Sade makes her case to Vic by reading from a review of the film:

> Once again Gloria Golden reaches the dizzy heights of sheer emotion. Pittsburgh, Pennsylvania, cried when it witnessed her heartbreaking performance in this, her latest drama of soul-searing light. *Smoldering Teardrops* is the story of how one woman faced the agonizing problem of loving two men. Never before in American moving picture history...[33]

Sade is ultimate interrupted by Vic, who says the description of *Smoldering Teardrops* makes him "sad, sick, and melancholy." Vic and Sade have clearly divergent opinions not only on whether to attend the film, but also regarding its star, who, Sade informs us, is regarded as "the curly-haired darling of the civilized world." This makes Vic's flesh crawl. As Vic and Sade debate the merits of the motion picture, Russell informs them that, according Smelly Clark, it is "rotten." Smelly issued "just about as bad an insult as a picture show can get," by leaving the theater before *Smoldering Teardrops* was over. Vic and Sade do not automatically attend the film, hungry for the latest mass-produced entertainment being offered to them. Instead, they consider a number of factors: their personal attitudes toward Gloria Golden; the opinions of a newspaper critic; and the views of an acquaintance. When Vic and Sade finally *do* decide to take in *Smoldering Teardrops*, it is an informed decision.

Newspaper critics play a role again when, in 1938, Sade suggests seeing *Broken Hearts Versus Mother Love*, which has been described as "an extra-special good picture."[34] The praise is enough to prompt a reluctant Vic not only to see the film, but also to treat Sade to soda and ice cream. The film parallels Rush's dealing with his friend Mildred, who has been evoking melodrama, claiming that "I am a sweet, fragile child" who is "like a pale blue candle flame."[35] According to Rush, his young friend wants to be like Joan of Arc and Elaine the "lily maid of Astolat" from Tennyson's *Idylls of the King*.[36] Like the finest starlet from a Hollywood melodrama, Mildred wants "everyone in the United States crying bitter tears over the delicate little girl in Central Illinois that's got a heart as big as a scrub bucket."[37]

The Gooks also evaluate the potential entertainment value of attending a movie and other, often non-commercial, forms of entertainment. In one episode, from April 4, 1940, they clearly view going to the motion pictures as a last resort when they are unable to play cards with the Stembottoms. That "fat-headed Gloria Golden"[38] was pale competition for the "highly diverting and exciting"[39] interaction offered by a game of cards. Throughout the episode, Vic and Sade hope that it is an invitation to partake in something other than moviegoing. On another occasion Rush invites Sade to accompany him to the Bijou to see a double feature *I Place My Heart in Thy Rosy Hands* and *Part-Time Freight Agent Lewis*, while Vic is away on business. Although Sade gladly accepts, she quickly cancels these plans when given the opportunity to visit with members of her ladies' Thimble Club. Rush agrees with his mother's decision, noting, "We can take in the half-wit Bijou any ol' time."[40] Rush's comment could be viewed as a judgment on the merits of any one film in the overall movie-going experience.

The contemporary humorist, scholar, and director of the Motion Picture Research Project, Leo C. Rosten, suggested in a 1939 study that movie-going can become a habit in which the specific movie is of little or no consequence to potential audiences. Such audiences, he contends, are interested only in seeing "a" movie rather than a specific title.[41] As we have seen, characters in *Vic and Sade* do periodically attend movies when there are no other entertainment options. For example, we learn that Rush attends movies "twice a week, regular as clockwork."[42] Rush also informs Vic that several residents of the Bright Kentucky Hotel, including Mr. Gumpox, Mr. Jeffrey, and Mr. Cunningham, all attend the opening of each new film at the Bijou. There is, therefore, a clear division between those who view movie-going as a regular activity in and of itself, regardless of the movie and circumstances, and

"Movies are your best entertainment," proclaims a sign on this North Platte, Nebraska, movie theater in 1938. A Saturday morning movie crowd is seen gathering at a theater playing a Marx Brothers movie. Such comedies served as an escape from the burdens of the Depression and gave audiences of both children and adults the opportunity to come out and be seen (John Vachon/Library of Congress).

those who evaluate movie-going based on the quality of the film and the other options available.

"Watching the various passer-bys go past"

Perhaps the most significant role of movie-going as depicted in *Vic and Sade* is its ability to promote social interaction. While the films exhibited at the Bijou are undeniably the mass-produced fare that culture critics have so vocally expressed concerns over with their appeals to the lowest common denominator and inherent threat to high culture. However, the Bijou has a life independent of these films, a life in which neighbors are brought together and stories are born. Vic and Sade might attend a movie with the Stembottoms, or Sade with Ruthie of the Thimble Club. Rush, most certainly, utilizes the social function of the Bijou, with his many friends.

On March 25, 1940, a Monday night, Rush returns home from the Bijou with a "very exciting piece of news": "Smelly Clark's got a girl." Smelly's new "lady friend" marked a milestone in the lives of Smelly and his friends, one that was worthy of exciting discussion afterward with Vic and Sade. The scene that Rush describes in which he and his friend Rooster Davis are presented to Smelly's girlfriend illustrates the role of the Bijou as a social hub, a venue that not only exhibits films, but also serves as a place where neighbors can meet or observe one another. As Rush describes it: "Rooster and myself arrived at the Bijou early, see, we like to do that so we can stand out in front and watch the innocent passerbys go past."[43] The pair, Rush explains, uses the opportunity to greet their various acquaintances before the show. Given the social nature of the events leading up to it, the screening of the film becomes almost a secondary event.

On July 4, 1935, Sade argued that motion pictures could be used to promote family unity. Vic, on the other hand, favored watching the single and married Chicago and Acton Railroad guys playing baseball against each other. Sade, not wanting to attend the game, suggested that they take in Annabelle Ainsworth in *Madness Beneath the Moon*, contending that it was the one activity that the entire family could enjoy together. Rush, however, countered that Annabelle Ainsworth was "always hopping around with no back on her dress." Disgusted, Vic insists that he "wouldn't walk across the street to see her turn a flip flop."[44] In the end, the Gooks find unity in an activity more lowbrow than a motion picture: watching the commotion surrounding Hank Gutstop, who had collapsed following a bout of heat stroke.

While the act of watching a motion picture itself may not promote the same level of face-to-face interaction as card playing,[45] the act of visiting the motion picture theater does provide the opportunity for social activity. Visiting the Bijou afforded Vic and Sade with the opportunity to, among other things, hear lectures from community leaders and interact with members of their community. Moreover, the movies can serve as a "justification for meeting"[46] when one might otherwise not exist, as is the case when Vic reluctantly agrees to accompany the Stembottoms to Hopewood for a double feature of Gloria Golden films, *You Are My Own Wonderful Husband, Subaltern Gleek* and *Yours Is a Magnificent Love, Petty Officer Griswold*, that he had already seen. Movie-going does, then, have the ability to impose social obligation. This imposition is seen in many instances in *Vic and Sade*, ranging from casual arrangements, such as Sade planning to have ice cream with the Thimble Club ladies after taking in a film on September 29, 1944, to more grandiose plans, such as the time Rooster

Davis acquired a block of movie tickets. By highlighting the social role of motion pictures, we see an intertwining of "the trends of the culture industry"[47] with the social process and are able to see that, although the masses are attending motion pictures, they are not being manipulated; rather, they are engaged in a mutually beneficial relationship, one in which motion pictures can be used for entertainment, an impetus for social interaction, or both.

According to Rush, Rooster plans to "shock" the audience by being ushered in and escorted to the center of a block of seats of seats with a sign reading, "Reserved for Mr. Davis."[48] According to Rush, members of the audience like to arrive at the theater early so they can "stare at each other an' see who's with who."[49] Wearing his long overcoat with a fur collar, Rooster is certain to create a spectacle as he ascends to his block of seats and "waves condescendingly to some acquaintance he spots in the gallery."[50] After hearing Rush's description of the anticipated events, Vic and Sade decide to join him so that they, too, can take in the "spectacle." In this scenario, entrance into the theater becomes a performance in itself, as artificial and entertaining as the one on the screen. The audience and the movie blend together, becoming, in effect, a single performance in which the seer and the seen become one.

You Are My Own Wonderful Husband, Subaltern Gleek *and* Yours Is a Magnificent Love, Petty Officer Griswold: *Romances and Other Genres in* Vic and Sade

The 1930s saw the development of a number of new film genres, ranging from sensationalist gangster films to the uplifting movie musical, replete with often over-the-top production numbers; from the zany screwball comedy to the horror films popularized by Universal Studios. Such genres grew into clichés so quickly that *Vic and Sade* was able to appropriate their stilted, generic qualities to craft simulacra of Hollywood productions whose titles were simultaneously hyper-specific and yet stood for the entirety of familiar genres.

Although there were examples of gangster films prior to 1930s, including 1927's *Underworld*, directed by Josef von Sternberg and, the following year, Lewis Milestone's *The Racket*, it was the introduction of sound films and the events of the Prohibition era that made the genre a viable box-office attraction.

The Prohibition era introduced Americans to the likes of Al Capone and other real-life gangsters as well as bootlegging, organized crime, and increased urban violence. Through stars like Edward G. Robinson, James Cagney, and Humphrey Bogart, audiences "vicariously participated in the gangster's rise to power and wealth on the big screen. They vicariously experienced the gangster's satisfaction with flaunting the system and feeling the thrill of violence."[51] While the gangster genre may have reflected a nation's insecurity in authority and social traditions, they were also evidence of the premium that Hollywood placed on action and violence at the expense of the "thoughtful and contemplative."[52]

Gangsters were not the only deviants being cast in a favorable light in 1930s films. Horror films of the era celebrated the monstrous and the macabre. Like other genres, the horror film benefitted immeasurably from the introduction of sound. As Karina Wilson explains, sound added "an extra dimension of terror, whether it be the music used to build suspense or signal the presence of a threat or magnified footsteps echoing down a corridor."[53] Unlike the realism of the era's gangster films, horror films were, in essence, what Wilson calls "exotic fairy tales," period pieces that were far removed from the reality of the day. Films were set in comparatively exotic locations, often in an imaginary version of Europe, and populated by characters speaking in foreign accents. Audiences of the 1930s were drawn to horror films, taking in such pictures as 1931's *Dracula* and *Frankenstein* followed in 1932 by *The Mummy* and Tod Browning's *Freaks*, which featured an array of real-life freak show performers, many suffering from rare medical conditions, and the terrifying story of an attractive blonde woman transformed into a circus freak. King Kong climbed the Empire State Building with Fay Wray in 1933, and, in doing so, helped to save financially troubled RKO. Sequels, including *The Bride of Frankenstein* (1935) and *Dracula's Daughter* (1936), helped assure that moviegoers were sufficiently horrified throughout the decade.

The introduction of sound to motion pictures also spawned the movie musical; however, while the 1930s are regarded as the Golden Age of the movie musical, the genre got off to a bumpy start. Because "screen musicals inherently require a substantial investment of time, talent and money,"[54] keeping the genre alive was not to be taken for granted. Hollywood studios were quick to produce lavish musical production numbers following the success of *The Love Parade* and *The Broadway Melody* in 1929; however, for the most part these films were ill-conceived and poorly executed. John Kenrick notes that these early efforts caused the movie-going public to soon become disenchanted with the often-bizarre movie musical.

Life was breathed into the movie musical by director Busby Berkeley with films like *42nd Street* (1933) and *Gold Diggers of 1933, '35, and '37*. Berkeley demonstrated an understanding of screen choreography, using the placement and movement of both the dancers and the camera for maximum effect. Unlike his predecessors, Berkeley kept the camera in motion on booms around the dancers. The result of his efforts was "fantasy numbers on a grand scale."[55] One of Berkeley's most well-known routines was the sight of uniformly outfitted dancers moving in unison and seen from above to form the illusion of a kaleidoscope. Among Berkeley's most successful work were those films in which he directed Judy Garland and Mickey Rooney, with titles such as 1939's *Babes in Arms*, a screen adaptation of the Rodgers and Hart stage musical. The film centered around Mickey and Judy's attempts to save their vaudevillian families by putting on a show. Capturing the warmth of Mickey's and Judy's relationship and Mickey Rooney's effervescent personality, *Babes in Arms* grossed millions for MGM. MGM featured the dynamic duo in other musicals, including 1940's *Strike Up the Band* and *Babes on Broadway* (1941), as well as 1943's *Girl Crazy*.

Although they may have been the best, Mickey Rooney and Judy Garland were not the only stars to make the musical film genre a successful one. In 1933, Fred Astaire, a veteran of Broadway, was offered a role in *Flying Down to Rio* as a band leader. Given the choice of a dance partner Astaire chose Ginger Rogers, who had choreographed the stage production of *Girl Crazy*. Although their roles were secondary, their on-screen chemistry and unforgettable dancing was enough for them to be noticed by moviegoers and moguls alike. The pair was starring in *The Gay Divorcee* the following year, and *Top Hat* and *Roberta* in 1935. *Follow the Fleet* was released in 1936, with *Swing Time* the following year.

Meanwhile, Bing Crosby was being featured in movie musicals produced by Paramount, following his success as a radio personality and recording artist. Crosby starred alongside Marion Davies in MGM's *Going Hollywood* (1933), in which he plays a radio personality. Crosby would go on to appear in such movie musicals as *The Big Broadcast* (1932) and *College Humor* (1933), in which he plays a college professor. In 1935, Crosby played the role of Tom Grayson in *Mississippi*, which featured a Rodgers and Hart score, while in 1936 he tackled Cole Porter's *Anything Goes*, followed by *Pennies from Heaven*. Crosby also starred

Genre films were a big part of the 1930s box office, including horror, romance, Westerns, and period pieces. In this photograph from Art Van Harvey's personal collection, Van Harvey and Bernadine Flynn pose in period costume, poking a bit of fun at period drama (Mark C. Lancaster/The Art Van Harvey Collection).

in the immensely popular *Road* series with Bob Hope, as well as in classic titles such as 1942's *Holiday Inn* and 1946's *Blue Skies*, both of which exclusively featured the songs of Irving Berlin.

Although the movie musical played a major role in movie-going throughout the 1930s, it is difficult to discern this from *Vic and Sade*. Only *My Baby of Brilliant Broadway*, first mentioned on January 1, 1935, and starring Gloria Golden with Skinny Skinner and Darwin Drake, hints at being a musical.

Typically, *Vic and Sade* provides scant details of the fictional movies referred to in the scripts. There are, as has been mentioned, the periodic references to reviews of films, but such reviews are often brief and pertain more to the performance of Gloria Golden, Donna Dreamerson, or another bogus celebrity. This ambiguity leaves the listener to interpret the nature of the film based largely upon its title. The overwhelming majority of films referenced in *Vic and Sade* are clearly romantic in nature and are depicted as having the greatest appeal to Sade. The pictures themselves represent Hollywood's often mass-produced fare, in which "the spectator must need no thoughts of his own: the product prescribes each reaction."[56] *Vic and Sade* romance feature heroines—be they Donna Dreamerson, Annabelle Ainsworth, or the ubiquitous Gloria Golden—are depicted as being both strong and vulnerable to the men in their lives. Gloria Golden was the head of a gang of jewel thieves in *Smoldering Teardrops*, able to have "swell clothes and jewelry,"[57] yet her position is threatened by her love of a preacher. In *My Baby of Brilliant Broadway*, Golden once again faces heartbreaking love, this time on the Great White Way.

The films also provide audiences with some level of titillation, if not redundancy, as Rush observed of Annabelle Ainsworth, who was always "hopping around with no back on her dress."[58] Sultry undertones are also suggested by the titles of films such as *Smoldering Teardrops*, and *One More Kiss, Esther, Then I'll Put On My First Baseman's Mitt and Go to My Position at First Base for the Third Inning*, the latter of which is indicative of Paul Rhymer's pairing of the potentially salacious with the completely mundane, creating an absurd effect.

"The last ten picture shows I've been to have all been the same"

Moreover, the films depicted in *Vic and Sade* suggest most frequently variations of one another, a fact observed by Russell when he noted that "the last ten picture shows I've been to have all been the same."[59] The majority of the movies exhibited at the Bijou star Gloria Golden and her leading man of choice, Four-Fisted Frank Fuddleman. Their titles are formulaic, often combining the romantic with the mundane such as *My Heart in Your Hands, Part-Time Freight Agent, Lewis* or *You Are My Own Wonderful Husband, Subaltern Gleek*. As such, they perfectly represented the lesser output of the major Hollywood studios, which released on average one new movie almost every single day from 1930 until America's entry into World War II.[60] With such mass output, not all of these films could be works of genius, and the vast majority certainly were not.

Throughout the 1930s the American film industry was dominated by five major studios: 20th Century–Fox, Paramount, Metro-Goldwyn-Mayer (MGM), Warner Bros., and RKO, with Columbia, United Artists, and Universal nipping at their heels. Throughout the 1930s and 1940s these studios maintained control over the bulk of Hollywood's output, exerting their influence over choice of films, budgets, the selection of personnel and scripts, actors, writers, and directors, editing, scoring, and publicity.[61] The rise of the studio system brought with it further claims of homogenized, mass-produced fare that sought only to cater to the lowest common denominator. However, as Eric Johnston noted at the time, the motion picture was designed to be primarily "an instrument of 'mass entertainment.'"[62] Contrary to the protestation of culture critics who believed that motion pictures should cater only to highbrow tastes, in order to be a viable form of entertainment and allow for highbrow tastes to be addressed, the motion picture required "mass market, mass audience, mass appeal."[63] Averaging 353 films per year, there was no other profitable way for the major studios to engage in filmmaking.

We can see, albeit implicitly, the studio system at work in *Vic and Sade* with manufactured titles and scenarios intended to appeal, if not to the lowest common denominator, then certainly to the masses. From what is described, the motion pictures are neither substantive nor do they in any way evoke "art"; rather, they provide light entertainment for those who elect to see them. Assuming the voice of the industry's critics, the president of the Motion Picture Association of America Eric Johnston asked in 1947 why "are so many 'cheap, trashy' pictures made? Why, we are challenged, do we cater to the 'lower tastes?'"[64] It is, he said, easy to condemn that which is not pleasing to the critic as "trashy" without weighing its relative merits. Johnston compared mass-produced films to comic strips, which have been relegated to a form of entertainment solely for children, who are not yet able to recognize their lowbrow nature. Even then they have been considered inappropriate for children's development. Yet this value judgment, Johnston claimed, fails to take into account the significant number of adults with "recognized intellectual capacity" who regularly read comic strips.[65]

The Curly-Haired Darling of the World

But Johnston must also have recognized that the film industry had become a vehicle for developing relationships between producers and their audiences through the medium of celebrity—relationships commercial interests meant to foster and exploit. Samantha Barbas explains that, by the 1920s, a solid relationship between movie fan magazines, the movie industry, and corporations had formed. The movie industry joined with the increasingly present advertising industry to promote the sale of everything from automobiles to appliances, from cosmetics to clothing. This relationship served to increase the sale of movie tickets by enhancing the visibility of Hollywood. Further, Hollywood's role in advertising encouraged moviegoers to "use the movies," as one fan magazine put it, to "learn about the newest fads and trends."[66]

In their desire to embrace celebrity gossip and advertising, the movie fan magazine promoted images of the "frivolous female fan magazine reader."[67] Subsequently, by the end of the 1920s men were no longer viewed as acceptable movie fans, although they still attended movies—celebrity culture was a female activity. The feminine nature of the movie fan is depicted in *Vic and Sade* through both Sade's general enthusiasm for films and the likes of Gloria Golden and Annabelle Ainsworth, and Vic's overall disdain for the medium and its stars. To Vic, these celebrities are "half regarded as little more than a half-wit," whose work can be concisely described as "bunk."[68] It is only the Gooks' oft-crying neighbor Mr. Sludge, who is viewed as effete, who is depicted as part of the fan culture, so much so that he receives a sunburn because "he spent his whole noon hour today standin' on the sidewalk in front of the ten cent store lookin' at the window displays" that featured "framed pictures of Gloria Golden."[69]

Whether it was Donna Dreamerson, Annabelle Ainsworth, Skinny Skinner, Arwin Drake, Conway Clayton, or the ubiquitous Gloria Golden and Four-Fisted Frank Fuddleman, it was clear that motion pictures were vehicles for the stars that appeared in them. It was Gloria Golden who inspired Sade's determination to see *Smoldering Teardrops* while simultaneously acting as a deterrent to Vic. *Vic and Sade*'s depiction of the movie star was representative of the "star system" spawned by Hollywood's studio publicity departments.

Of all of the major Hollywood studios, it was MGM that boasted the largest number of stars, with more than sixty under contract by 1934. Among MGM's properties were the likes of Mickey Rooney, Judy Garland, Clark Gable, William Powell, Greta Garbo, Joan Crawford, James Stewart, Spencer Tracy, and Katharine Hepburn. The studio would become known as the "Home of the Stars" with "more stars than there are in heaven."[70] In marked contrast to Hollywood's earliest days, in which films did not release the names of actors for fear of making them stars and subsequently raising their salaries, movie actors were now "the demigods and goddesses of the screen," Rosten asserted, and could become of "libidinal importance" to the "average movie addict."[71]

Though not of "libidinal importance," celebrities and motion pictures did influence the Gooks and their community in a variety of mundane ways. In one episode, for example, Sade wears a hat like one Gloria Golden wore when she "told a guy she'd rather jump in a volcano than go back to her husband."[72] The influence of motion pictures on the imaginations of both Rush and Russell is often noted. When Russell learns that Sade has accidentally opened the Rev. V. Cook's mail, Sade insists that she cannot give the letter, which is a bill, to Kleesburgers to give to the reverend because she would be too embarrassed having him know that she knows about his debt. Russell, however, sees a more ominous scenario than the potential for embarrassment:

> RUSSELL: Here's the big danger: The incident will throw him off base. When he discovers you're on to his trick of gypping the clothing store ... well, anyway he's jumpin' the gun when it comes to payin' his honest debts.... Reverend Cook realizes you know about the money he owes Kleesburgers, all right, along comes Sunday, y'all go to church. Reverend Cook climbs into the pulpit, he sees your white nervous face in the congregation. He goes shaky all over, his finger clicks, he can't think of his sermon, suddenly he can't stand the strain any longer and pitches over on his face. Thrown into confusion ...

Sade's response is to curtail the influence on Russell's imagination:

> SADE: Guess I'll just have to keep you away from the Bijou for a while. Too many motion picture shows makes boys' imaginations all wild.[73]

"You an' your movie talk"

Motion pictures served a variety of purposes within *Vic and Sade*, and while the quality of the films exhibited at the Bijou was often questionable, the Gooks and others used discretion in choosing which films to see and for what purpose. While the motion picture could, as Eric Johnston suggested, be a means of coping with a "complex, wearing, worrisome world,"[74] it could just as easily be used as an impetus for socialization or, in a rare instance, what Rhymer's characters call "a real high-class performance."[75] Whatever the case, Rhymer depicted audiences as being aware of the flaws of what were often contrived, repurposed and even "mighty mighty punk" motion pictures rather than as the "semi-robotic"[76] and driven to act because their feeble minds are unable to resist the machinations of Hollywood. Rhymer instead depicts moviegoers who are using motion pictures for their own purposes. In our next chapter, we will examine another source of leisure: reading.

Seven. "Seated on the davenport reading": The Role of Reading

One of the most frequently heard introductions to *Vic and Sade* finds the narrator describing one or more members of the Gook family seated either on the davenport or at the library table, reading something, whether it's Rush immersed in one of the adventures of Third-Lieutenant Clinton Stanley, Sade with her romance story, or Vic contemplating the newspaper, lodge magazine, or, if the time of year was right, possibly *The Kitchenware Dealer's Quarterly*. Like other families in the early twentieth century, reading provided the Gooks with a source of entertainment, a means of escape, and a source of information about the world in which they lived and the way that they interacted with it. Through reading, Rush and, to a lesser extent, Vic and Sade, could experience the far-flung adventures of the heroic Third-Lieutenant Clinton Stanley (whom Rhymer named for NBC director J. Clinton Stanley) while also vicariously partaking in his romantic escapades with Lady Margaret. Sade (sometimes) enjoyed the romantic stories printed in the daily newspaper, despite their sometimes-repetitive nature.

This chapter will examine the different roles and purposes of reading within the Gook household and within the broader context of the Depression era, in which the general public was in need of both information and entertainment.

Literacy and the American Reader During the Great Depression

Throughout the eighteenth and nineteenth centuries, illiteracy was fairly commonplace in America, with a full 20 percent of the nation's adult population being illiterate in 1870. By 1930, however, with the increased availability of public schools and education across social and economic classes, the rate of illiteracy had been markedly reduced, to 4.3 percent.[1] The United States' high rate of literacy would prove beneficial to its citizens as they sought to cope with the mounting toll of the economic crisis. Purchasing books, magazines, and newspapers may not have been a priority for those struggling to make ends meet, for as Douglas Waples noted in his treatise on reading in the Great Depression: "Though man cannot live on bread alone, Americans normally buy 'bread' and many luxuries before buying print."[2] However, while the Depression saw a reduction in more expensive publications, it "also supplied many incentives toward reading which doubtless increased the number of readers."[3] These incentives, it can be reasoned, helped to lead to the success of public libraries, whose circulation peaked in 1933, while also causing the more economically depressed to

In this photograph from Art Van Harvey's personal collection we see Vic and Sade seated on the davenport while Rush reads to them, a typical scene in the Gook household (Mark C. Lancaster/The Art Van Harvey Collection).

borrow magazines and other print materials from friends. It also resulted in multiple persons sharing the same copy of books, magazines, or newspapers. Overall, readership for all publications increased in the 1930s, including the fluorescence of pulp magazines.[4]

A cursory examination of the period's best-selling novels finds readers favoring a wide range of genres and literary styles. *God's Little Acre* (1933), by Erskine Caldwell, was a "steamy" novel that dramatized a South Carolina family obsessed with sex and wealth. The novel contained scenes that were, for the period, considered so sexually explicit that there were calls to censor it by groups like the New York Society for the Suppression of Vice. Despite the controversy—or perhaps because of it—*God's Little Acre* would become one of America's all-time best-sellers.[5] Other titles, such as Faith Baldwin's *White Collar Girl*, fit into what Maureen Corrigan describes as the "chick lit" genre. The "chick lit" of the 1930s was similar to what readers encounter today, with one significant difference: the majority of the Depression era plots "featured plucky young women whose family fortunes had taken a nose dive."[6] This was the case with *White Collar Girl*, in which college student Linda Anthony is forced to cut her studies short and "seek work in a five and ten cent store owing to financial reverses suffered by her banker father, now dead."[7] For men struggling with economic adversity there was no shortage of books that detailed "hard-luck male extreme adventure tales"[8] that included such novels as *Anthony Adverse*, *Mutiny on the Bounty*, and *Rabble in Arms*. These titles, and others like them, provided comfort to those struggling through the period.

The Depression era also provided readers with weightier fiction, including Pearl S. Buck's *The Good Earth*, the story of life in a Chinese village prior to the start of World War I. The novel, which follows the life of Wang Lung and the rise and fall of his fortunes, won a Pulitzer Prize in 1932 and played a significant role in the decision to award Buck the Nobel Prize for literature in 1938. Set in an exotic, escapist setting, Buck's novel clearly appealed to readers, making it the best-selling work of fiction in both 1931 and 1932. A.J. Cronin's *The Citadel*, the story of a young physician treating Welsh coal miners in the 1920s, credited by some with laying the foundation for the eventual introduction of Britain's National Healthcare System, was 1937's third-biggest seller, and the second-biggest selling title of 1938. Welsh mining was the subject of another best-seller, Richard Llewellyn's *How Green Was My Valley*, released in 1939 and topping the best-seller list in 1940. Other now-classic novels proved to be commercially viable during this period, including Margaret Mitchell's 1936 *Gone with the Wind*. Ranking as the best-selling novel of both 1936 and 1937, it spawned not only the 1939 film adaptation, but also "an outpouring of historical fiction."[9] That same year, 1939, also saw the release of John Steinbeck's tale of farmers dispossessed by the Dustbowl, *The Grapes of Wrath*. Unlike many other best-selling works of fiction that offered readers at least some amount of escape from the economic adversity in which they found themselves ensconced, Steinbeck's novel dealt unflinchingly with the hardships facing rural America directly.

Readers were drawn to an equally—if not more so—diverse list of non-fiction titles throughout the 1930s, including Will Durant's *The Story of Philosophy*, in which the author demonstrates the relationships between Western philosophers such as Nietzsche, Plato, and others. In contrast, in 1931, the nation's ongoing enthusiasm for contract bridge was represented in two best-sellers by Ely Culbertson. Thought by many to be the most "colorful and flamboyant figure in the history of bridge," Culbertson's success at bridge and his best-selling volumes on the subject made him "fabulously wealthy even at the height of the depression" as well as a credible source of expertise for readers.[10] Culbertson would be among the best-selling authors of 1933 as well, with the *Contract Bridge Blue Book of 1933*.

Not surprisingly, self-help books also proved popular throughout the decade. Psychologist Walter Pirkin asserted the "revolutionary outcome" for a "new era" that *Life Begins at Forty*. Although the book made the phrase popular in America, Pirkin did not coin it. "Life begins at forty" had, in fact, been used in print numerous times since 1932 and had been the title of a 1937 Sophie Tucker song. In 1937, Dale Carnegie released a book that would top the best-sellers list for two years and spawn a veritable cottage industry of courses and seminars. *How to Win Friends and Influence People* offered readers a positive message during bleak times and insight into the "Fundamental Techniques of Handling People," the "Six Ways to Make People Like You," the keys to winning people to your way of thinking, and the ways of becoming a leader without creating resentment. Following an initial pressing of only five thousand copies, *How to Win Friends and Influence People* would go on to motivate readers to buy more than fifteen million copies since its release.

An "innovation in bookselling": The Three "Brows"

Before the 1950s, critics divided American culture into three "brows"—high, middle, and low—corresponding to the tastes of the upper class, middle class, and working class.

Later, Herbert Gans revised this into five "cultures" (high, upper-middle, lower-middle, low, and quasi-folk low) on the argument that post–1960s culture had altered the class structure of America.[11] For our purposes and our period, the recognition of the differences between highbrow, middlebrow, and lowbrow as corresponding to the cultural preferences of the wealthy, the middle class, and the working class, is sufficient.

Clearly not all best-sellers were—or are—created equal, yet to proponents of highbrow literature they are united by their regrettable appeal to the masses, an appeal that, they reason, can only reflect negatively on their literary value. Peter Swirski summarizes the elitist view of literature as: "Popular Literature = Bad Literature (if it were good, it would not be popular in the first place), and Popular literature = Genre Literature (it appeals to many by being simplistic, schematic, and repetitive—in other words, by amply betraying its heritage)."[12] While one can say with a high degree of certainty that not all popular fiction is "quality" fiction and that some "goes in one eye and out the other," it is equally safe to assert that popular fiction can be ambitious and, by virtue of its ubiquitous nature, serves to comment upon modern life and the many facets that comprise it and, in the process, can transform or, in some instances, form values and beliefs.[13]

Culture critics, as Gans notes, offer four charges against popular fiction—and indeed against all of popular culture's offerings. These critics contend that popular fiction, rather than being an artistic endeavor that challenges and stimulates its readers is, instead, merely an attempt to produce reformulated works designed for the express purpose of attracting large audiences and even larger financial gains for the author. However, as Swirski notes, authors of highbrow fiction must also be concerned with such seemingly base matters as profit, especially in lieu of sponsors and subsidies.

Culture critics also argue that the need to appeal to a mass audience leads popular fiction to be homogenized. However, one could easily reason that highbrow authors who are persistently writing for a small niche audience, are often far more homogenous. Swirski also points to the fact that, despite the claims that popular fiction is formulaic, highbrow writers often turn to formulaic solutions. To illustrate his point, Swirski uses Norman Mailer's *The Naked and the Dead*, which, he claims, borrows its structure from Erich Maria Remarque's *All Quiet on the Western Front* and Henri Barbusse's *Under Fire* and its narrative technique from John Dos Passos's *U.S.A.* trilogy.[14] Gans pointed out that other highbrow authors of the middle-twentieth century frequently employed the theme of the artist as a young man, a concept utilized by James Joyce and D.H. Lawrence.[15]

There is also, on the part of the cultural elite, a fear that popular fiction draws talented writers away from writing serious literature that challenges his or her limited audience. This, Swirski acknowledges, is likely true; however, there is no reason to believe that if popular fiction were abolished today, highbrow writers would be prepared to come forward and take the place of their counterparts. Moreover, in this charge critics ignore the fact that writers of popular literature often "try their hand at more ambitious projects ... lured by the cultural prestige attached to highbrow fiction."[16] Within culture critics' claim that popular fiction is deleterious to society, Swirski identifies three claims. First is the notion that popular fiction, in effect, bombards its readers with a steady diet of gratuitous sex and violence. By feeding these "spurious gratifications" these works of fiction leave their audience emotionally debilitated. Second, critics argue that popular fiction is escapist in nature, thus rendering its readers incapable of coping with the onerous burden of reality. However, there is no reason to believe that consumers of popular fiction are left so enfeebled that they are unable to successfully cope in society. As Swirski notes, those "most at risk," such as the lower-middle class and middle class, are, on the whole, not isolated "brutes living out escapist and violent fantasies," but rather members of families and other social groups.[17] Those typical readers of popular literature appreciate it as a form of entertainment or diversion and would scarcely consider adopting that which he or she reads as a blueprint for life.

It is not only the individual at risk from the debilitating effects of popular fiction, according to culture critics. Society is threatened by popular fiction because it prevents readers from reading more serious and challenging material. This was just one of the criticisms leveled against the Book-of-the-Month Club after its 1926 founding, when critics worried that such clubs would standardize reading tastes, encourage passive consumption of middlebrow literature, and lower the overall taste of the American public. "The reader who takes advantage of this innovation in bookselling," Ernest Boyd wrote in 1927, "will be adding to the process of standardization which has invaded every department of American life."[18] However, in making such claims, critics often contrasted the greatest works of past literature with the most mundane of contemporary literature. Moreover, critics failed to recognize that the reader made a choice to participate in popular culture, including the selection of popular reading materials, to form their own "taste culture," as both Swirski and Gans noted.

Reading and Radio

In considering the role of reading on *Vic and Sade* and the context in which its depiction occurred, one must first consider the impact of radio on reading as both a leisure activity and a means for obtaining information. Radio provided its listeners with the opportunity to be entertained and informed without the effort involved in securing reading materials and actually reading them. NBC's *University of the Air*, a program through which listeners could enroll with participating schools to earn college credit, offered listeners the opportunity to hear serialized adaptations of classic literature including works by Faulkner, Huxley, Steinbeck, and Hemingway, among others. *American Novels*, a *University of the Air* offering, focused, much as its title would suggest, on presenting great American novels like *Moby Dick*, *Tom Sawyer*, and *Little Women*. *The World's Great Novels*, another product of *University of the Air*, produced even more serialized adaptations of classic novels, broadcast over two to six episodes. Paul Rhymer, who had failed to break into the world of highbrow literature with his short fiction, satirized such adaptations of the classics in his *Busyman Program*, which suggested, in its extremely sped-up way, that listening to a book on the radio was not quite as satisfying as reading it.

Listeners also found no shortage of informational programming. Each of the networks broadcast regularly scheduled news programming. A variety of other informational programs, dealing with everything from cooking and childcare to travel and entertainment, were also radio fixtures in the Depression years.

Cognizant of the competition posed to print communication by radio, Paul Lazarsfeld, along with associates from the Princeton Radio Project, endeavored to discover the factors behind choosing one medium over the other, the results of which were printed in *Radio and the Printed Page* (1940). According to Lazarsfeld's findings, the difference was largely due to cultural factors. For example, when asked "Where do you like to get your news?" those from lower cultural groups responded "radio," markedly more than those from other cultural groups.[19] Similarly, when housewives were asked whether they would prefer to read serialized stories in magazines or listen to them on the radio, 69 percent of those who had attended high school indicated that they preferred magazines while 55 percent of those who did not attend high school said that they preferred radio.[20] An additional study of adults in the Midwest found that 73 percent of those with less than a high school education preferred listening to the radio when they wanted to learn about something, while only 37 percent of those with at least a high school education selected radio as their preference.[21]

According to Lazarsfeld, radio's role was far more significant to those at a lower educational level, something attributed to the fact that these individuals are not skilled readers. While the skilled reader might find listening to a radio program a less efficient means of gathering information than reading, a less efficient reader might feel that it "takes a lot more energy to read" or that they can't put the "necessary" effort into reading.[22] To a "less-skilled reader," radio may also have seemed more accessible because content was presented in "plain English" and "explained better."[23] Radio also played a directive role in that it followed a set schedule with limited programs offered at limited times as opposed to reading, which offered great flexibility—perhaps too much flexibility for the less-skilled reader.[24]

The U.S. government recognized the power of the written word and during World War II produced propaganda posters encouraging reading by raising the specter of Nazi book burnings (Library of Congress).

"You kids read too many of them dime novels": Dime Novels, Pulp Fiction, and Cheap Stories in Vic and Sade

The most frequently read literature in the Gook household came in the form of the adventures of Third-Lieutenant Clinton Stanley, a book series directly descended from the dime novel. In addition to its specific meaning it would also come to be applied to a variety of forms of popular literature in the late nineteenth and early twentieth century, particularly that which was sensationalistic and quickly written. Given Paul Rhymer's lack of success in breaking into the highbrow fiction market, it is perhaps not surprising that this form of literature would be featured on *Vic and Sade*.

The first true dime novel appeared in 1860, when the Beadle and Adams Company published *Maleaska, the Indian Wife of the White Hunter*, written by Ann

Stephens. The book was a "thin little volume" that measured approximately six inches high and four wide inches, allowing it to be easily carried in one's pocket.[25] Of course, the origins of the dime novel can be traced back to the first half of the nineteenth century, when authors like James Fenimore Cooper published volumes that "dramatized tensions between the wild, untamed frontier and rapidly encroaching civilization."[26] Beadle and Adams became the first publishing company to develop a successful formula for bringing inexpensive fiction to the masses. While other publishers had previously attempted this, Beadle and Adams's success lay in reducing the cost of their titles to only ten cents, a feat accomplished through such budget-cutting steps as relying upon a standardized publishing format and making each book the same size. The firm also used the least-expensive paper available, along with cheap bindings and cover illustrations. Another of the publishing house's cost-cutting measures was to frequently use previously printed material; this allowed Beadle and Adams to save money by paying the author only a relatively small fee to reprint the work.[27]

Between 1860 and 1874 a new Beadle Dime Novel was produced every two weeks; ultimately, there would be a total of 321 titles. These volumes were stand-alone titles until the 1880s, when series began to appear. The stories often featured melodramatic or sensationalistic plots with cliffhanger endings intended to ensure that the reader would purchase the subsequent entry. Beadle Dime Novels were, as Edmund Pearson describes, novels of romance, love, and warfare that maintained "surprisingly strict moral standards"; however, "in their pages, during the next four decades, tons of gunpowder were to be burned; human blood was to flow in the rivers, and the list of dead men was to mount to the sky. They dealt in violent action; in sudden death and its terrors."[28] In his study of dime novels, Pearson contends that *Maleaska*, which had previously been published in *Ladies Companion* in 1839, contrary to preconceived notions of the dime novel, was neither cheap nor gory. He offers glowing praise of author Ann Stephens, referring to her as "a writer so eminently worthy, so assured of her own dignified position in American letters, that I have been unable to think of a novelist of to-day with whom to compare her."[29]

In the summer of 1860 the Beadles followed *Maleaska* with *Seth Jones; or, Captives of the Frontier*. The title was launched with a "massive advertising campaign" in newspapers, billboards, and handbills, all of which posed the question: "Who is Seth Jones?" The "tantalizing question" was answered by a lithograph of a man in a coonskin coat, declaring, "I am Seth Jones."[30] The response was overwhelming; *Seth Jones* sold more than 600,000 copies, was translated into several languages, and is said to have been one of Abraham Lincoln's favorite books.[31] The book's success established the tradition that a dime novel should have a subtitle preceded by the conjunction "or."[32] For the next half-century, readers would be treated to titles like *The Great Spy System; or, Nick Carter's Promise to Be President*; *Fred Fearnot's Revenge; or, Defeating a Congressman*; *Frank Merriwell's Finish; or, Blue Against Crimson*; and *Dashing Diamond Dick; or, Tigers of Tombstone*. Although they may not have been dime novels in the strictest sense, this formula would extend to Rush's Third-Lieutenant Clinton Stanley novels. Although there were instances when books were issued without subtitles, like *Third-Lieutenant Clinton Stanley's Big Affair* and *Third-Lieutenant Clinton Stanley, President of the South Sea*, it was Rhymer's usual practice to employ the device, as the following titles illustrate: *Third-Lieutenant Clinton Stanley on the Campus; or, Winning Laurels for the Old Alma Mater*; *Third-Lieutenant Clinton Stanley and the United States; or, Outwitting the New York Stock Market Plungers*; *Third-Lieutenant Clinton Stanley Amid the Frozen Alps; or, the Mystery of the Poisoned Moccasin*; and (somewhat repetitively) *Third-Lieutenant Stanley on the Campus; or, the Thrilling Capture of the Bank-robbing Professors of Yale College*.

In retrospect, the presence of Third-Lieutenant Stanley was a bit of an anomaly. By the late 1920s, the era of the dime novel had passed. The types of thrilling adventures Stanley experienced moved to the cheap pages of pulp magazines, named for the wood pulp paper used to print them, a process that had been slowly building since the launch of the first pulp, *Argosy*, in 1896. These magazines presented short stories, serial novels, and other fiction, in

Dime novels often featured Western themes and other tales of frontier adventure. In this photograph, from Art Van Harvey's personal collection, we see Vic enacting the part of a dime novel cowboy for the amusement of Russell (Mark C. Lancaster/The Art Van Harvey Collection).

genres ranging from railroad and cowboy stories to science fiction, mystery, horror, and romance. There seemed to be something for every reader: *Astounding, Weird Tales, Dime Detective, Love Story Magazine,* and *Ranch Romances,* to name a few. They continued, however, the literary traditions and conventions of the dime novel and were their lineal successors, as were, in juvenile literature, such series as the Hardy Boys and Nancy Drew. In fact, publishers like Street & Smith collected and linked together serials and stories from their pulps and published them as "thick-books," much like dime novels, into the 1930s. Thus, when Paul Rhymer wrote of Third-Lieutenant Stanley, he was looking backward affectionately at a recent but fading era of "vigorous" fiction that would soon give way to comic books.

Dime novels, like the later pulps and, still later, comics, treated their readers, most often boys, to tales of love and adventure that "were not for persons of consequence to be read in their libraries."[33] The volumes were "light and easily carried" and made it relatively easy for schoolboys to take them to school and hide them from their teachers; however, it was not only schoolboys who enjoyed the dime novel, but rather a broad cross-section of readers, with the exception of "a very small class of persons."[34] Indeed, the dime novel counted among its fans the likes of Lincoln, Secretary of State William Seward, and Vice-President Henry Wilson. The cross-generational appeal of the dime novel is witnessed on a number of occasions in *Vic and Sade*. While the Gooks didn't approve of the novels and their characters, with Vic frequently denouncing Stanley as being a "fathead" as well as "feeble-minded," or claiming that he is "too gay" and maintaining that he "doesn't give a darn" about the fictional hero's latest adventure.[35] Sade, too, is quite vocal in her disdain for Stanley and his inamorata, Lady Margaret, claiming that they "both make me a little sick; they act so silly."[36] Sade has also expressed concerns about the potential detrimental effects that such adventures can have on a young mind. She bases her fears on anecdotal evidence, recalling a girl from Dixon, who "read too many of them dime novels [and] went out of her head from doin' that."[37] The young lady in question, Bertha Joiner supposedly "ate up cheap story books by the dozen an' finally turned up dotty one day." So extensive were Bertha's dime-novel–related problems that she "required six months to cure her. An' even after she was *cured* she behaved kinda simple. Only wore one shoe."[38]

Yet despite their criticisms and concerns regarding Third-Lieutenant Clinton Stanley's novels, Vic and Sade sometimes found themselves drawn into his and Lady Margaret's latest adventures. In a 1940 episode, Rush refuses to lend Vic his copy of *Third-Lieutenant Clinton Stanley and the United States; or, Outwitting the New York Stock Market Plungers,* contending, "You'd start reading it and get interested and I wouldn't get it back for an hour."[39] As it happens, Rush's concerns are well founded. Two years earlier, while Rush was thought to be at the Bijou, Vic became engrossed in *Third-Lieutenant Clinton Stanley amid the Frozen Alps; or, the Mystery of the Poisoned Moccasin.* Looking up from the book for the first time in half an hour, Vic explains to Sade that the Lieutenant is in a "tight jam," only to learn that Sade herself had already devoured the vigorous volume of fiction. In her defense, she explains that, though she is not a "devotee" of the books, it "was on the bathroom floor."[40] In another episode that same year, Sade laments the fact that Rush has returned *Third-Lieutenant Clinton Stanley's Big Affair* to Blue-Tooth while she was in the middle of reading it, while, at the same time, questioning whether the books were good for boys.[41]

Dime novels routinely offered entertaining and exciting adventures with wild animals that were not indigenous to most readers' areas.[42] To be sure, wild animals were a standard peril that Stanley and Lady Margaret encountered in each adventure. In January 1940, for example, Rush reports that Stanley "fights four lions blind-folded"; however, even though he ends up in a "mighty tight place" as "the handsome young officer, bleeding in forty places, grew weaker by the second," Rush reports that, in the end, "He licks all four of them." Stanley surveys the carnage and observes that "the carcasses of the mighty kings of beasts lay in grotesque positions."[43] In some instances, Stanley was not only able to defeat his wild foes, but to use them to advance his own purposes, as was demonstrated in February 1938 when he tied snakes together to make a rope.

One 1940 episode offers good examples of both adventure and romance while also maintaining the role of menacing animals. As Sade attempts to tell Vic about Mis' Applerot's attempts to have the Bright Kentucky Hotel condemned, Rush repeatedly interjects with updates on the latest Stanley novel, in which the hero attempts to foil counterfeiters.

> RUSH: (*DRAMATICALLY*) The counterfeiting smugglers try to murder Third Lieutenant Stanley by tying him to a tree an' smearing melted marshmallow all over his clothes an' releasing two grizzly bears from a cage. Grizzly bears are very fond of melted marshmallow so it looks like curtains for Third Lieutenant Clinton Stanley.[44]

However, as the counterfeiting smugglers would soon realize, not even marshmallow-loving grizzly bears could stop Third-Lieutenant Clinton Stanley:

> RUSH: (*READS*) The handsome young officer faced death valiantly. "You fellows can go jump in the creek, I'm not scared," he growled to the leader of the counterfeiting smugglers. But for Margaret he had a sweet smile an' eyes that twinkled merrily. "Give me one more kiss an' one more hug before I kick the bucket, sweetheart" he gloated. The beautiful woman simpered and coquettishly pretended that the mother-of-pearl buttons on her fashionable French spats had come unbuttoned. Finally, blushing furiously, she lifted her veil an' thrust forward her lovely head. "Just *one* hug an' *one* kiss now," she warned an' Third Lieutenant Stanley howled loudly his satisfaction an' approval.[45]

It is interesting to note that, even in the most dire of circumstances, Third-Lieutenant Stanley, inasmuch as we are able to ascertain from Rush's reports, remains civil, even when addressing his captors. Pearson observed this trait in his examination of *The Privateer's Cruise*, a "story of ocean adventure," set at the start of the Revolution. Shortly after leaving harbor, the ship encounters a storm and a brig that is in danger. The privateer rescues the brig's passengers and crew who, within moments of being rescued, engage in polite conversation with the privateer's crew.[46]

Romance was another constant in the dime novel, so much so that, in 1867, Robert M. DeWitt began publishing *DeWitt's Ten Cent Romances*, which focused primarily upon Western- and frontier-themed stories, modeled closely after Beadle's publications. The Third-Lieutenant Stanley novels were not without their share of romance and salaciousness. Stanley and Lady Margaret engaged in frequent and torrid clinches—even during the most precarious of moments:

> RUSH: (*READING*) Third-Lieutenant Clinton Stanley showed no trace of fear as he watched the slow approach of the counterfeiting South Sea Islanders. Lady Margaret, on the other hand, was frantic with apprehension. "We shall be assassinated, sweetheart," she quavered. "Perhaps so," rejoined the handsome young officer, "but not without a fight. Shall we enjoy a hug and kiss before we are attacked by these rascals?" The beautiful woman gazed down at her fashionable French spats. "As you please," she murmured, and Third Lieutenant Stanley's face glowed readily with hungry anticipation.[47]

The relationship between Third-Lieutenant Stanley and Lady Margaret also revealed strong sexual dynamics, as in this excerpt:

RUSH: "That was a delicious kiss," crowed the handsome young officer, carefully wiping his mouth with his sleeve, "I will require another directly." "You shan't have any more kisses until Tuesday," coyly replied Lady Margaret as she playfully tapped the mother-of-pearl button on her fashionable French spat with the handle of her dainty pink parasol. Third-lieutenant Clinton Stanely [sic] broke into a loud guffaw. "Either you give me another kiss or I'll wrench your arm," he laughed. The beautiful woman, aware he spoke in jest, giggled a tinkling little giggle for all the world like the jingle of tiny Chinese bells. Soft baby cloudlets hovered in the clear blue sky and old Mister Sun beamed down brightly on the...[48]

Though not afraid to physically commandeer his love, Stanley repeatedly proves that he is a generous lover by lavishing Lady Margaret with such tokens of his affection as an evening gown made out of fifty-dollar bills and a bicycle made out of solid gold. Vic's sarcastic assessment: "Third-Lieutenant Stanley is a man of perfect taste. No one could ever accuse him of being vulgar." This sarcasm is lost on Rush, who feels that his hero has "style in his actions."[49]

The details of Third Lieutenant Stanley and Lady Margaret's grand and, at times, ostentatious, romance, frequently serve as a means of contrasting the mundane, day-to-day events in the lives of the Gooks. For example, on July 20, 1944, Stanley exchanges a "delicious kiss" with Lady Margaret and is immediately thereafter bitten by a twelve-foot boa constrictor. Not to be deterred, Stanley promptly informs Margaret that she is his "little cup-cake."[50] Meanwhile, at the same time, Uncle Fletcher offers details of his not-so salacious or exciting plans for the day, which include visiting the Interurban Station, the Royal Throne Twenty-Five-Cent Barbershop, and the Butler House Hotel. In other episodes, their exotic love scenes serve as a parallel for other storylines. In December 1940, for instance, when Stanley's devotion to Lady Margaret provided an interesting parallel to Gumpox's devotion to his horse, Howard.

The introduction of every Third Lieutenant Stanley novel proclaims that the book's hero is a "shining example for every American boy to follow,"[51] a statement that some might have found questionable, given the violent nature of Stanley's adventures and his rather bawdy relationship with Lady Margaret. Stanley did, however, possess strength, ingenuity, and an undeniable sense of chivalry, exceptional manners, and an implacable sense of honor—all excellent traits by any measure. Yet, as we've seen, despite their own periodic enjoyment of the books, Vic and Sade remain skeptical of their worth and even, at times, consider them a detriment. Dime novels faced similar skepticism due in large part to their very popularity, as Pearson notes, for they were "regarded with suspicion by many stern moralists and to be sneered at by the supercilious type of critic."[52]

In addition to condemning their literary value (or lack thereof) and formulaic stories, critics of dime novels suggested that they were immoral and lurid and would eventually lead readers—especially their young readers—into a lifetime of vice and crime. This was not, however, a view held by every critic. Writing in *Lend a Hand*, William McCormick chronicled what he describes as "The Dime Novel Nuisance." In reviewing an array of Beadle titles, McCormick pondered whether "runaway schoolboys, house breakers, and baby bandits" could possibly be attributed to the content of the reviled dime novel. He explains that, although their perusal of dime novels had led to "many a rough and ready street lad" having his mind corrupted (and perhaps, in some cases "may have even led to a life of crime"), a more serious threat can be found in the "cant phrases" and "pious talk" in the "average Sunday school book." This, McCormick reasons, far more than dime novels, has the potential to "stimulate the acute boyish mind to prefer a life of crime to one of virtue."[53] McCormick also contrasts the "novel-heated lad" and his "Philistine brother" who does not enjoy reading regardless of the book, and makes a case for the former, stating that the book-loving boy possesses "docility and ductility" that boys who do not enjoy reading lack.[54]

The adventures of Third Lieutenant Clinton Stanley may have provided a degree of nostalgia to *Vic and Sade*'s adult audience, but it also reflected, to some extent, the type of reading material that was of interest to children of the Depression and World War II. Studies conducted between 1929 and 1945, in a variety of locations in the United States, offered similar results regarding the reading preferences of adolescents. Although there were variations, children and adolescents were, overall, interested in what Ruth Strang described as "the perennial three": mystery, adventure, and love.[55] Third-Lieutenant Stanley represented a moment when the old dime novel format was ending but its eventual replacement, the comic book, had not yet ascended to prominence. Surveys of adolescents of the era capture this slow transition.

Young readers' selections for their favorite books over the course of this period seem to confirm the status of the "perennial three" genres as favorites. Jennings's 1929 study listed *Tom Swift*, *The Adventures of Tom Sawyer*, *Nick Carter*, *Little Women*, the River Boys series, the Tom Slade books, *Treasure Island*, *Rebecca of Sunnybrook Farm*, and Edgar Rice Burrows's Tarzan books.[56] Conducted a decade later, Brinks's study found adolescents surveyed offered similar responses, with students overwhelmingly favoring fiction to non-fiction, and boys preferring adventure and detective stories. A survey of 46,000 New York City students found that their most-read selections were, in order of popularity, *The Call of the Wild*, *The Adventures of Tom Sawyer*, *Alice Adams*, *David Copperfield*, *Seventeen*, *The Three Musketeers*, *The Count of Monte Cristo*, *The Adventures of Huckleberry Finn*, *The Good Earth*, and the adventures of Sherlock Holmes.[57] What is most striking about the results of this survey is, of course, its emphasis on the classics.

Despite the popularity of the classics with adolescents, it is hardly surprising that White's 1942 study determined that students in all grades preferred those books classified as "recreation" the most.[58] The recreational, or leisure, aspect of reading was further reinforced by a 1945 study of junior-high students in Eau Claire, Wisconsin, when the rise of comic books as replacements for dime novels and pulps becomes obvious. Here, a study by Witty and Kopel found that boys' first reading preference was comics, followed by fiction. Among boys' favorite books were *The Adventures of Tom Sawyer*; *Huckleberry Finn*, *Thirty Seconds over Tokyo*, and *Thunderhead*. Girls, too, the study found, enjoyed comics, but preferred reading books.[59] Among girls' favorite titles were *Lassie, Come Home*, *Heidi*, *My Friend Flicka*, and the Nancy Drew Mysteries.[60] Overall, of the 886 students surveyed, 88.9 percent admitted that they liked reading, putting them in good company with Rush and Russell.

"The paper comes out with the strangest things": The Role of Newspapers in Vic and Sade

Although they were not depicted as extensively or their content discussed as fully as the Third-Lieutenant Stanley novels, reading the newspaper was a common activity for both Vic and Sade, though often for very different purposes. In early representations the newspaper, which coincidentally bore the same name of Bloomington's *Pantagraph*, was a barrier in communication between the husband and wife. Beginning with the June 26, 1932, audition episode, Vic is ignoring Sade in favor of reading the paper. However, even at this very early stage of the program, the depiction of a newspaper's content provides a commentary on the press. Sade, for example, laments that newspapers are always "misleading." To make her point, she relates an item involving a woman marrying an "excavation engineer" when she might, in fact, be marrying a ditch digger.[61] She goes on to tell Vic the absurd story of a man who shot his sweetheart with his own glass eye and a boy's slingshot, an indictment of the sensationalistic nature of a press determined to turn the mundane into the melodramatic.

At the start of the twentieth century there were more than 2,200 daily newspapers published in the United States. By 1929, at the start of the Great Depression, this number had fallen to 1,944 and would continue to drop until 1933, when only 1,911 dailies were published in the U.S.—the smallest number of English-language daily newspapers published in the preceding century,[62] this following an increase in newspaper publications and an approximately 43 percent increase in newspaper circulation between 1920 and 1930.[63] Although circulation fell between 1930 and 1933, newspapers overall decreased far less compared to other publications, a fact that may be attributable to its relatively low cost.

The circulation of newspapers was also bolstered by the fact that the Great Depression supplied, as Waples notes, many "incentives to read," providing the news, information, and opinions that facilitated life in larger cities, and playing a role in shaping public opinion.[64] Beyond these formal functions, as Robert E. Park suggested in 1923, the newspaper and its writers have a responsibility to "produce, in the city, as far as possible, the conditions of life in the village," where "everyone called everyone by his first name."[65] According to Park, newspapers must serve as a "printed diary of the home community," one that is a chronicle of "marriages and divorce, crime and politics."[66]

Due to the low cost of newspapers, they were among the publications least affected by the Great Depression and remained an essential component of many people's daily routines, like this man seen reading the paper at Fountain Square in Cincinnati in 1938 (John Vachon/Library of Congress).

The concept of the newspaper as a community diary is one that was frequently depicted in *Vic and Sade*. As one would expect from a comedic program, the articles discussed did not address particularly serious topics, although they did offer the Gooks news of their neighbors and their comings and goings. The local stories described by the Gooks are examples of what Park terms a "provincial newspaper." That is, a record of community events and happenings, such as weddings, births, funerals, lodge meetings, and other community occurrences. On October 9, 1933, for example, the newspaper reports that Eleanor Sweeting is going to be marrying a "Chicago fella" named Carter Dubois Chubam the fourth. Elsewhere, the newspaper reports that "Harry Cowler of East Washington Street has returned after three-months' absence," though Vic and Sade remain clueless as to where he had gone or that he ever left in the first place.[67] The "Hospital Notes" section of the newspaper provides the Gooks with news and information on the health of their neighbors. An item appearing in the October 19, 1933, edition of the paper reported, "Mrs. R.T. Legthorne's condition is satisfactory after an appendectomy operation on Tuesday."[68]

Given Paul Rhymer's predilection for physical injuries and abnormalities in his early fiction-writing efforts, it is interesting to note the prominence of the "Hospital Notes" in *Vic and Sade*'s early years. Even though the injuries were not grotesque in nature, they are specific, e.g.: "Mrs. R. K. Wheeler of 1912 West Market Street reports that the leg of her daughter, who is vacationing at home from a year in Chicago, is knitting nicely."[69] Although such news does not appear to be of much consequence, they do promote a sense of community. Park suggests that "a newspaper cannot do for a city of 1,000,000 what a village spontaneously did for itself through gossip and contact,"[70] yet, in many regards, this is precisely the role in which the newspaper is depicted on *Vic and Sade*.

In addition to providing the Gooks with a diary of their community, the newspaper also served to promote sometimes important family discussion. In the same "Hospital Notes" that reported on Mrs. Legthorne's appendectomy was news of "Harold and William McVeigh, young sons of Mr. and Mrs. Eustance McVeigh of 910 North Mason Street, underwent tonsil operations early this morning. The boys are doing nicely."[71] This brief dispatch leads Vic and Sade to discuss the apparent need for Rush to undergo a tonsillectomy.

Based on the stories discussed by the Gooks, offering readers local gossip may well have been one of the primary functions of the *Pantagraph*. In addition to this, "news" stories concerning the comings and goings of community members also offered an impetus for them to speak to one another, as when Sade approaches Mrs. Copperman to say that she had seen in the newspaper that she and her husband had returned from Dayton. By helping to instigate such conversations, the newspaper indirectly strengthened community ties.

Private events, like Mabel Corner's Christmas Eve 1934 recital, were also given a public airing in the newspaper. Allowing readers to know that Mabel performed "Red Bird Dying" and "Why Is Life So Short and Sweet" prompts Vic to assess the gathering as a "real jolly party."[72] In some cases, the news pertained to the Gook's themselves—if only indirectly. For example, a piece about a party held by Pom Pom Cordova from Vic's office at the Purple Room of the Butler House Hotel triggers a negative response from Sade, who has long been jealous of the woman. On another occasion, Vic believes himself to be the subject of a story about "Distinguished Local Luminaries" doing some last-minute shopping, and sets out to convince everyone else of that fact.[73]

Not all of the news pertains to specific members of the community. Instead, the paper also offers news of general interest, ranging from construction on West Emerson Street in 1941 to the city's plan to purchase a gorilla for its park zoo. Such pieces increased readers' awareness of what was actually taking place in their community so they could, if they so chose, become more actively involved. It also meant that readers had the opportunity to form an opinion, and the newspaper itself to shape public opinion.

In many regards, the *Pantagraph* is a throwback to earlier days, when "most newspapers operated under the premise that the best news that they could print is a death notice or a marriage announcement."[74] It does not, as Hearst's *New Evening Journal* so successfully did, attempt to "find news material that would thrill the crudest intelligence,"[75] though there are exceptions to this, as when Vic relays a story about a man who is "astonished" when his horse decides to crawl instead of walk.[76]

Despite the services provided by the *Pantagraph*, either Vic or Sade would bemoan the substance of their newspaper:

> VIC: (*YAWNS*) This doggone paper gets worse every night.
> RUSH: No news in it?
> VIC: No nothin'.[77]

Twelve years later, the assessment was much the same:

> SADE: Not a single darn thing in the newspaper. 'Cept for the little daily love story, it's just so much piffle.
> VIC: Did you read the front page?
> SADE: Nah.
> VIC: There are one or two items of interest to be found there.[78]

Complaints about the paper's substance—or lack thereof—may have been the most frequently voiced, but they were not the issues the Gooks had with it. On various occasions either Vic or Sade deemed the paper "misleading" or questioned its editorial decisions and the writing style of its reporters who, in Sade's opinion, said "the strangest things. *Worded* so funny, ya know."[79]

Perhaps the most astute criticism of not only her own newspaper, but newspapers in general, came from Sade when she complains that the weatherman never wrote about Illinois, lamenting, "What do *we* care about New York an' outlandish places?"[80] Without realizing it, Sade had pointed to a source of growing dissatisfaction many readers were finding in their local newspapers, due to the growth of syndication. As William and Nancy Young explain, in the 1930s "news became less regional and more national and international, only far-flung syndicates could file regular stories to their growing lists of subscribers."[81] As a result of syndication, newspapers became increasingly standardized; what appeared in one paper was likely to appear in another paper in another city. While the Youngs contend that this level of standardization meant that "the insularity of a small town American daily lessened and it came more into the mainstream of American life,"[82] it also meant that the paper lost some of its individuality and ability to address the unique needs of its specific readers.

"I still have my little newspaper daily love story to read": Newspapers as Entertainment

Although listeners were rarely treated to any details about them, Sade was frequently found engrossed in or complaining about the love stories that appeared in their newspaper. In reading her "little daily love story," on December 22, 1937, she mistakes the suitor's cheesy line to a girl he just met—"Where you been all my life?"—for a joke.[83] These stories, based on Sade's scant comments, offered little substance, but they did serve as a diversion. As Waples notes, "Entertainment and recreation function of the newspaper increased as other diversions became too expensive."[84] During a period when a family's resources were sorely limited, most newspapers offered a viable diversion in the form of short fiction, comic strips, and other entertaining features for substantially less money than attending a movie or play, for instance. Thus, newspapers of the era sought to appeal to a wide variety of audiences, with something for everyone. In the case of Sade, the romance stories were her version of the Third-Lieutenant Stanley novels.

The economics of the Depression, which had closed newspapers and magazines and constricted markets, pushed many fiction writers out of the book and glossy magazine market. A disproportionate amount of the short fiction found in newspapers throughout the Depression was produced by women and minority writers, while white male writers retained control over the declining high-culture fiction market. The female Polish-American writer Melania Nesterowicz, for example, serialized her novels for publication in a Buffalo newspaper throughout the 1920s and 1930s.[85] According to Bill V. Mullen, during the Depression era, short stories published in community and ethnic newspapers were often written by minorities "because their writers had fewer options for breaking into the major New York literary magazines."[86] One such literary magazine, *The Forum*, had rejected Paul Rhymer and then folded, contributing to his move away from literature and toward radio, where more opportunities lay. Carl Murphy, president of Afro-American Newspapers, explained the important role of fiction in his Depression-era newspapers in Chicago:

> Everybody has his own daily problems, and the newspaper which must carry the news can, through means of fiction, turn its readers' minds away from the real to the imaginative. The writer of a clean, well-written "boy meets girl" short story is one of the most important contributors to any newspaper. He probably has cured more indigestion than all the stomach specialists combined.[87]

In 1927, Wright Patterson, then the editor-in-chief of the Western Newspaper Union, maintained the fiction played an important role in small town newspapers as well, claiming that "fiction is in very great demand, whether in the form of short stories, novelettes, or serials. It's a little surprising how much fiction the American farmer and his family will read."[88] Yet Patterson's claims were not supported by newspaper readers. A study of rural newspapers in New York and South Dakota in 1920 suggested that fiction features were typically the least read, whereas they had been among the most read fifty years earlier. The decline could be attributed to increased access to major metropolitan newspapers and magazines (both literary and pulp) as a result of improvements in roads and transportation networks in the 1890s. Fiction readership declined slowly but steadily in small-town newspapers from the 1890s through the 1930s.[89] In the bigger cities, where magazines and other options were readily available, fiction had lost its prominent place in many newspapers, which increasingly focused on news reporting. Indeed, a 1936 study of more than 22,000 women in New York City found fiction was rather far down on their list of favored newspaper features, with news, comics, and the woman's page taking precedence. The study also suggested that fiction had become less prominent in New York City papers, since only five out of twenty papers were listed as having a fiction section.[90]

By the start of the twentieth century, the three largest suppliers of newspaper fiction had vanished as big-city magazines sought to undermine the reputation of newspaper fiction while also securing talent and content for their publications. However, syndicates were still able to present major authors to more readers than any of the literary magazines of the period,[91] if only due to the fact that newspaper circulation dwarfed that of any given magazine. For a while, the syndicates were able to bring to newspapers and their readers such distinguished authors as Henry James and Steven Crane, whose *Red Badge of Courage* was syndicated in newspapers. But both Arthur Conan Doyle and Jack London disdained the syndicates, and the gradual flight of popular authors to more prestigious literary magazine and book markets left only lower-quality fiction, including women's romances, of the type which Sade read, for small-town newspapers to run.

In many ways, Paul Rhymer's use of newspaper fiction seems to imply that Sade is traditional and somewhat backward, since this harks back to 1890s–1910s newspaper practices that were falling out of favor in the 1930s, as magazines and books replaced newspapers as the source for fiction, just as radio was replacing newspapers as a source for news.

A more popular source of the type of romantic fiction Sade favored would have been found in the pulps. Originally, as noted above, a term used to refer to a specific type of cheap publication printed on a poor quality paper made directly from wood pulp, pulp magazines eventually came to refer to any cheap, hardboiled fiction, particularly genre fiction. By 1920, romance, detective stories, and westerns constituted the three-biggest genres of pulp magazines. The romance genre, as seen in the pulps, reflects the type of romantic love stories Sade read, in perhaps less-sensational form, in her small-town paper.

The romance pulps presented a world that often revolved around marriage. From the advice columns to the advertisements, from the short stories to the poems, marriage was not just idealized as the culmination of a relationship; it was presented as the life object of the modern woman. But perhaps surprisingly, the audience for such magazines was not restricted to women. Advertisements in the magazines are targeted to men, especially out-of-work men, and the lonely hearts pen pal column in *Street & Smith's Love Story Magazine* (a dime novel successor) featured more than a few young men—presumably readers—seeking pen pals, primarily male. The magazines included a mixture of novellas, short stories, poems, and serials, and they tended to follow a fairly similar pattern. A female protagonist, often attempting to live or work independently, encounters an attractive, more powerful man and falls deeply in love. Complications ensue that keep the lovers apart, but eventually the woman realizes that she is not complete without him. The story ends either with marriage or with the promise of marriage (explicit or implied), through which the woman can finally achieve fulfillment.

In Mary Anne de Forest's "Thrill Chaser" (1934), the female protagonist, Linda, seems empowered by her penchant for performing stunts, but her activities lead only to trouble, trouble that only a man can solve. She cries to Denny, her love interest, "I know it was foolish of me to come and that I told you to wash your hands of me. But now I'm asking you to forget that and help me out of this mess. Surely there must be some way!"[92] Denny, of course, rescues her, but not before she throws a tantrum and he reminds her that she behaves like a child. Eventually, under the powerful but paternal protection of Denny, Linda learns that love—and marriage—are the greatest thrill of all.

Many stories seem to rely on the audience's stereotypical preconceptions of men and women for their effect. Marie McGookey's "Office Scandal" (1934) teaches its heroine an important lesson: that a solid marriage requires commitment, trust, and fidelity. Elsa Barker's "A Song on the Trail" (1933) revolves around the heroine's concern that she is too dainty and feminine to make a good wife to the rough and manly sheriff of a Western town. Bernice

Although seen in this photograph reading a book with Vic and Rush, Sade was much more likely to be found reading the love story in the newspaper, a genre marketed specifically for housewives (Mark C. Lancaster/The Art Van Harvey Collection).

deVore's "Beloved Enemy" (1942) makes use of not one but two stereotypes—the bickering pair destined for love, and the meddling mother who sets them up. Such stories were not far removed from Paul Rhymer's presentation of a newspaper's daily love story on April 8, 1940: "Sylvia Starbrooke was tired of being a rich man's pampered daughter..."—a line that could easily have been found in a real romance pulp of the time.[93]

A similar approach can be found in "Heritage of Conflict," a story that appeared in the September 1933 issue of *Ranch Romance*. Declaring itself "Love Stories of the Real West," *Ranch Romance* proved to be one of the most successful and longest-running pulps ever, being published continuously from 1924 until 1971. In L. P. Holmes's "Heritage of Conflict," readers were introduced to Lorna, a strong woman, running "a glorious bit of rangeland." Despite her fierce independence, she is "too lovely a thing" to be left in the hands of "traitorous, thieving riders" and is sent a "stalwart young ranger to protect and cherish her."[94] In the same vein—and in the same issue—"Fire Frenzy" offers a depiction of yet another strong female ranch owner who, despite her strength and savvy, needs to be rescued from rivals desperate to buy her ranch by a former arsonist. The magazine also maintains the romance pulp's traditional focus on marriage, with features like the "Whom Shall I Marry?" horoscope, written by "Professor" Marcus Mari.

Newspaper love stories, like Sade's "Daily Love Story," fulfilled many of the same functions as their pulp-magazine competitors, though at reduced length, and served as one of the sections of the newspaper designated for women's interests, in contrast to the tacit assumption that news, business, and sports were, by default, areas of interest for men. Many papers of the time had a dedicated "women's page" devoted to issues presumed to be of interest only to women. By presenting Sade as someone who turns toward the "Daily Love Story" for entertainment, Rhymer is suggesting that she has interests typical of a woman of her time. Perhaps the best illustration of the utility of the love story—and the fantasy escape it provides—occurred in the April 8, 1940, episode. Sade and Vic are seated across from each other, diffidently playing solitaire (together), when Sade becomes bored and tells Vic to go play with someone else so she can escape to the romantic fantasy of the "Daily Love Story." Sadly, though, the story is a rerun. Sade complains loudly that she has no intention of rereading the tale, but does so anyway.

The Kitchenware Dealer's *(More Than)* Quarterly

Although the newspaper may have been a steady companion to Vic, *The Kitchenware Dealer's Quarterly*, the publication issued by his employer, Consolidated Kitchenware, with a much greater frequency than four times a year, proved to be a regular source of reading pleasure—and displeasure. For Vic, *The Kitchenware Dealers' Quarterly* was a way to feel more connected with and, indeed, more integral to his company. The publication kept him up to date with the goings-ons of his colleagues at other plants and, in doing so, could either instill in him a sense of self-worth or fuel his insecurities. *The Kitchenware Dealers' Quarterly* is, then, more than a mere employee publication for Vic; it represents an important context for living and even a source of "excitement" that parallels that which Rush reaps from the Third Lieutenant Stanley novels.[95]

As it is described, *The Kitchenware Dealers' Quarterly* provides an opportunity for the employees of Consolidated Kitchenware to learn about their company's history, learn about one another and, on occasion, promote fun and socialization between employees. The publication regularly offers news items and biographies about employees, as well their photographs. In fact, Sade once commented on the number of photos that the editors requested, quipping, "They want one every two minutes, sixty-nine times a month."[96] In June 1944, Vic announces that he has tied with Lolita DeRienzi in a contest that the employees at Plant 14 held to determine who had the "prettiest eyes." To mark the occasion, Vic and Lolita are planning to have a picture taken of them to submit to *The Kitchenware Dealers' Quarterly*. As Vic explains, "I know it's childish and silly, but it's innocent fun and it's good for the morale of a big outfit like Con-situated Kitchenware Collar—Consolidated Kitchenware Company—if the boys and girls take time out now and then for a laugh."[97]

The premise, as Vic states it, behind the "prettiest eyes" contest, and of much of what listeners hear of *The Kitchenware Dealers' Quarterly*, is indicative of the shift in management—and organizational communication—away from a scientific-management approach to the human-relations approach in this era. As first set forth by Frederick Taylor, the scientific-management approach to organizations was often "referred to as the machine metaphor because of how employees were viewed as interchangeable parts."[98] Managers exerted a great deal of control over employees, and communication followed a top-down model, focusing on efficiency and on avoiding costly misunderstandings when conveying information. The 1930s saw a significant shift with the prominence of the human-relations approach. In many ways a response to the rigid structure of the scientific approach, human relations placed an emphasis on the needs of employees rather than their tasks. Simply stated, the human-relations approach to management views "the organization as a *cooperative* enterprise wherein worker morale is a primary contributor to productivity."[99]

With that description in mind, it is easy to see how *The Kitchenware Dealers' Quarterly* is indicative of the human-relations approach to management and organizational communication. Rather than a top-down model of communication, in which management issues directives to employees with the express purpose of facilitating a task, the publication provides a forum for employees to be represented in a casual manner. When, for example, the editors are seeking a biographical sketch of H.K. Sleeber, they ask a co-worker—Vic—to write it, and they specifically indicate that the piece be a "breezy, informal, and colorful sketch."[100] Such an approach, one that emphasizes the use of a combination of both formal and informal communication, is more likely to make employees feel connected and comfortable with one another and, subsequently, more a part of the Consolidated Kitchenware team.

It's ironic, then, that, while *The Kitchenware Dealers' Quarterly* may have proven a valuable tool in promoting cooperation and solid human relations' modeled work practices at Consolidated Kitchenware, Vic was able to use the publication just as effectively as a means of eluding work in an episode dated May 8, 1933. In that episode, Vic continually dodges Sade's attempts to draw him into helping her and Rush with housecleaning, in part through reading from *The Kitchenware Dealers' Quarterly*—just as Sade used the "Daily Love Story" to get a break from Vic, and Rush escaped from schoolwork with Third Lieutenant Stanley.

Thus, in *Vic and Sade*, Rhymer portrays reading as a source of entertainment and of escape, as a break from daily life and a window into the world beyond the small house. When the Gooks choose to use reading as a form of leisure, they can be transported to exotic locations, more romantic situations, or projections of business success. The Gooks see in their reading material reflections of the way they imagine themselves to be. But reading has another aspect, which we will explore in our next chapter. Therefore, we will look next at depictions of education and the educated in *Vic and Sade*.

Eight: "Where'd you copy that from?": Education

"Edwards school is the springboard from which we leap into the icy waters of success"

As a program about family life in Middle America, *Vic and Sade* would, of course, have to deal with the topic of education on some level. It did, after all, feature a main character (first Rush, then Russell) who, along with his friends, was making his way through middle school and on to high school. Although an increasing number of children were attending high school throughout the years of the Great Depression, this level of education was not to be taken for granted—a fact reinforced by Sade, who had never attended high school herself, and those of Rush's friends who were forced to leave school in order to find work. But beyond Rush's and Russell's experiences in school (which seemed to be dominated by algebra), *Vic and Sade* also pondered the nature of learning, and of being learned, in its depictions of Vic's and Sade's very different educational backgrounds and intellects. While Sade was quick to dismiss all things intellectual as "talky-talk" irrelevant to her life, she also demonstrated that a lack of education was not equivalent to a deficit of intelligence. Vic, on the other hand, countered the misconception furthered by public intellectuals that being educated was synonymous with being pretentious.

Although education and the nature of learning did not play a dominant role in *Vic and Sade*, its use within selected episodes offers insight into its relationship to social and economic status. The depiction of attitudes toward intelligence and intellectualism, or more accurately anti-intellectualism, also served to poke a finger in the collective eye of public intellectuals' and culture critics' pompous attitudes.

"Getting in line, single file": The Foundations of Modern Education

In order to evaluate the state of education on *Vic and Sade*, we must first look at how the elements of education available at that time—public schools, vocational education, etc.— had developed over the previous century. It was not until 1840, and the efforts of reformers such as Massachusetts' Horace Mann and Henry Barnard of Connecticut, that statewide education systems began to emerge, replacing highly localized community education, instruction in religious schools, or none at all. "The Common School Movement," as it became known, originated in the Northern states and was driven largely by several factors, including the perceived need to bring about social order during an influx of immigrants. Common schools would, in part, serve to Americanize immigrants while also producing a more educated and, in turn, more productive, population.[1] Moreover, supporters of the Common School Movement believed that, through universal education and the promotion of common values, they could also "secure social stability."[2]

There was also, during this period a general mistrust of parents, perhaps another factor related to feelings toward immigrants at the time. As *The Massachusetts Teacher* noted in 1851:

> In too many instances the parents are unfit guardians of their own children, left to their direction the young will be brought up in idle, dissolute vagrant habitats, which will make them worse members of society than their parents are; instead of filling our public schools they will find their way into prisons, houses of correction, and almshouses ... the children must be gathered up and forced into school and those who resist or impede this plan, whether parents or *priests*, must be held accountable and punished.[3]

Overall, however, Mann and other reformers sought to develop statewide systems that would, ideally, increase opportunities for all children while also establishing bonds among an increasingly diverse population. The Common School Movement espoused that public funds should be used to make free education available for all children, and that attendance for these children be compulsory.

By 1918, free, state-controlled public education had become a reality. Compulsory education, which had been spearheaded by the National Child Labor Committee and its campaign against sweatshops, expanded the role of education in the United States, necessitating the construction of new schools and school programs. By 1910, kindergartens were in the majority of schools, helping students to prepare for elementary education. Junior-high schools, first introduced in California in 1909, would assist in preparing students for a high school education, which would become more readily attainable.[4] With the increasingly formalized nature of public education, combined with its availability, schools gained in prestige as they came to be considered pillars of civic organization and a means through which a middle-class lifestyle could be made available to a working-class child.[5] The accessibility of education was further enhanced by the proliferation of the automobile during the 1920s, something we've already seen reflected in *Vic and Sade*, in terms of recreation and freedom. Its rapid growth allowed for school districts to consolidate into larger districts. Also, the introduction of the school bus, initially horse-drawn, allowed for rural children to be transported in larger numbers.

Education in McLean County, Illinois, was in the midst of considerable change during Paul Rhymer's time in school, in the second decade of the twentieth century. Much of the country, which was then home to more than four hundred separate school districts, still relied upon a large number of one-room school houses, particularly in rural areas.[6] While students in rural regions of the county would continue attending classes in these primitive structures through 1947, those in cities like Bloomington and Normal found themselves in somewhat grander settings. Edwards School, which would serve as the namesake and template for Rush's place of learning, was constructed in 1903 at the corner of Market and Allin Streets, where it would serve students until 1967. The school is an impressive building, markedly different than those used by rural school children. Built in a neoclassical style, Edwards School features Romanesque arches and pilasters. Perhaps more significantly, the school was home to what the PTA's *Child-Welfare Magazine* deemed "the best playground in the city," as well as a home-economics room and "costly" pictures.[7] As we learn from Rush,

Eight. "Where'd you copy that from?" 143

Paul Rhymer attended the Edwards School in Bloomington and used its name for Rush's school. The Edwards School is seen in this 1908 postcard, as it appeared in Paul Rhymer's youth.

Vic and Sade's fictional counterpart to the Edwards School even had a "new jigger" in the basement restrooms that dried one's hands with warm air.[8] Elsewhere in McLean County, progress was being made in transporting students to school. Approximately six miles southwest of Bloomington, in Shirley, Illinois, the Ben Funk Consolidated School began the county's first school bus program in 1917, using horse-drawn buses to transport students who had previously been forced to attend classes in either Normal or Bloomington.[9]

One of the most important changes of the era was the increasing availability of high school education to working-class children. Originating in the 1800s, public high schools served as an alternative to private academies and featured a curriculum that was practical in nature, along with college-preparatory courses. They generally catered to the socioeconomic and academic elite and imposed strict admissions requirements. The first decades of the 1900s also saw enrollment in high schools increase as they began to gradually relax their standards to allow more students to attend. Such changes in admission standards would likely have allowed students like Rush and his compatriots, none of whom came from upper-class families or were depicted as students of the highest caliber, to attend high school.

As education became more readily available to students from all social classes, middle-class parents became concerned that the credentials their children earned "maintain prestige."[10] Comprehensive high schools offered a compromise by providing students with both academic and vocational courses. The intertwining of the academic and vocational realms is illustrated by the course in commercial geography Rush took, taught by Mis' Adams. Commercial geography—a real course offered in schools of the time—examined commodities, their places of origin, and their routes of transportation, as in the 1903 text *Commercial Geography: A Book for High Schools, Commercial Courses and Business Colleges* by Jacques W. Redway. This volume covered the role of commerce in civilizing mankind, topographic control of commerce to the transportation of specific goods, including grains, cereals, textiles, and plants, as well as the geographical data of various regions and their influence on trade. A similarly practical and somewhat rote approach to learning is illustrated by Russell's physical geography course in 1943. Wishing to go the Bijou on the eve of a "great big enormous *examination*" that he's "been shrieking and hollering about,"[11] Russell agrees to allow Vic to ask him questions that are likely to appear on his exam. A few of their exchanges follow:

> VIC: (*PROFESSORIALLY*) Name the states bordering on the....
> RUSSELL: (*PROMPTLY*) Washington, Oregon, and California.
> VIC: (*RATHER SHARPLY*) I didn't even finish posing the problem.
> RUSSELL: I'm familiar with the first three or four.
> VIC: Still and all though, I am not inclined to be shoved, hurried, or pushed around.[12]
> VIC: What are the geographical features of Iowa?
> RUSSELL: Flat as a pancake. Wonderful farming country. It is surrounded by the Mississippi on the East, the Missouri River on the West, and its great cities of Des Moines, Keokuk, Fort Madison, Burlington...[13]
> VIC: (*TO RUSSELL, RATHER SHARPLY*) Well, *bound* your native state of Illinois.
> RUSSELL: (*PROMPTLY*) Wisconsin on the North, Iowa and Missouri on the West, Lake Michigan and Indiana on the East, and Kentucky on the South.[14]
> RUSSELL: (*LOW TONES, IMPLORINGLY*) Next question, gov, *please*.
> VIC: How would you travel by water from Detroit, Michigan to Buffalo, New York?
> RUSSELL: (*PROMPTLY*) Lake Erie.[15]

Vic is incredulous at Russell's (correct) response and only accepts an answer when the boy solemnly, if somewhat impatiently, pledges "*You're* not being gulled and misguided. I cross my heart and hope to die, eat a banana and holler Hi if a person don't travel on Lake Erie when they want to travel from Detroit, Michigan to Buffalo, New York by water."[16] Nevertheless, Russell makes it clear that his education in the subject does not go much beyond memorizing the answers, since he was able to provide standardized answers after only a few words of standardized questions. Russell is interested in proving to himself that he has memorized the required material for the sake of passing the test; Vic, by contrast, shows interest in the actual content of the questions—even asking Russell to get a map from the bookshelf to help him locate Detroit, Michigan, to see the water route to Buffalo.

"Wheels within wheels"

This is not to say that the students or their parents particularly appreciated the finer theories of education or its benefits. As with students everywhere, Rush rarely saw beyond the particular educative problem of the day, though, on occasion, the broader purpose of learning makes itself known to him. In a script dated September 21, 1933, Rush is given the task of writing a four-page composition on a topic such as "Our Friend, the Dog" or "The Indian of Today." Having selected the former, Rush struggles to fill the required space before finally producing a composition that begins:

> Among the multifarious adjuncts to a well-rounded civilization, none is so felicitous and necessary to man's social existence as the dog. It is said of the poet Burns, immortal bard of simple people, that the dog...[17]

This recitation is cut short by Sade's simple and astute question: "Rush, where'd you copy that from?" The highfalutin vocabulary and complex grammar immediately marked the lines as something more than the work of a junior-high student, as did the reference to Robert Burns, the famed Scottish poet whose work was a bit more advanced than that found in the books featuring Third-Lieutenant Clinton Stanley.

Rush concedes that his text was taken from a book in the family bookcase, an act immediately condemned by Sade as cheating. The paper is torn up, despite Rush's protestations that "lotsa kids go the library" and copy their essays from other sources.[18] To support his claims of widespread corruption, Rush points to his friend Skinny Forbes, who paid his sister fifty cents to write his composition for him, and Bill Benjamin, who copied his composition from a student who had been in the class the year before. Later, after reflecting on his actions, Rush begins to understand how what he had done could be interpreted as cheating and is devastated by the label. "It's a ... pretty mean word, Mom."[19] At this point, Rush has moved beyond viewing education as a series of tasks to be completed, like the examination answers memorized in advance, and has instead grasped something of the moral dimension of learning and its relationship to one's own integrity and character—a true teachable moment. Ultimately, Rush decides to write his own composition about dogs, this time focusing on his own dog, Mr. Johnson, and their trip to Lake Bloomington together.

School, as depicted in *Vic and Sade*, then, was a dynamic and fluid process riddled with complexities, or, as Rush's friend Leeland Richards described it, "High school is a hotbed of politics. Wheels within wheels, crossed. High school is a seething river of human emotions."[20] The seething river, more often than not, ran directly between social and academic pursuits. Education is often depicted less as the process of acquiring knowledge than an obstacle course that students, teachers, and school administrators are required to navigate. Assignments are, for the most part, hurdles that need to be overcome in order for the student to proceed to addressing the social aspects of school life. Although school sets the stage for social activities, its own agenda must be overcome in order for the social aspect to occur. For example, on Rush's first day in the eighth grade he excitedly tells Vic and Sade that his friend Rooster Davis has transferred to his school; however, in order to exploit this fortunate occurrence he and Rooster have been forced to develop a series of hand signals that allow them to communicate, undetected by the teacher.

Some occasions would find Rush attempting to juggle the academic and social aspects of high school, with varying degrees of success. It was not uncommon for him, as in an episode from January 9, 1935, to enlist the help of his father. It was in this episode that Rush faced dueling demands: the need to complete a composition on brotherly love and the conflicting need to prepare for a snowball fight with Bulldog Drummond. Rush asks Vic to "help" him by writing the essay while he prepares snowballs with a bucket of snow he's brought into the kitchen. Clearly, his revelation of 1933 on academic honesty did not outlast the growing social demands of youth. "Let us [...] never lift the hand of force to harm our fellow creatures," Vic begins as Rush's excitedly plans for what he anticipates will be a "terrible fight."[21] Oblivious to the marked contrast in his tasks, Rush assesses his snowball arsenal and reports, "Well—guess I got enough good ol' snow-balls to put that low-down *Bulldog* in the hospital for six weeks. Gov, give me my composition on Brotherly Love."[22] Here, and with the complicity of his parents, Rush has sidestepped the purpose of education: not only has he cheated by having Vic write his essay for him, he has also failed to absorb any of his lessons. Rhymer is taking aim at the failures of institutionalized education, echoing Plato's famous line from the *Republic*: "Bodily exercise, when compulsory, does no harm to the body; but knowledge which is acquired under compulsion obtains no hold on the mind."[23] Here, however, Rush's exercise threatens his moral development, rendering his compulsory education worse than futile.

When Rush needs to create a motto for the graduating class—a task that should have involved reflecting on the educational and learning process—he once again enlists Vic to assist him. Previous mottos had been indictments of graduating classes' experience, such as "Give me liberty or give me death,"[24] used by the classes of 1919, 1923, and 1934—a recognition of the priorities of that year's graduates and their strong desire to escape from what must have seemed a repressive educational system. A similar indictment was issued by the graduating class of 1930: "Edwards School, blessed alma mater, thy teachings sleep within my brain." Suggesting a more optimistic view of education, Vic offers an allegory in the form of a Latin motto from the lodge, which he wrongly translates as, "Let us pick raspberries from the top of the tree."[25]

Finally, Vic suggests, "Edwards School is the springboard from which I leap into the icy waters of success." Not one to allow others to do his work for him (at least until the snowball fight the following week), Rush revises the motto, transforming it into "Edwards School, *you* are the springboard from which I leap into the icy waters of success" and modifying it one final time, changing "you" to "thou art," at Vic's suggestion.[26] The humorously inappropriate (though arguably accurate) use of the adjective "icy" contrasts with the increasingly pompous phraseology Vic and Rush employ, from the plainspoken to the archaic and near–Biblical phrasing "thou art," a nod to the traditions of education, which, with its neo–Gothic buildings and neo-medieval robes, hark back to a more aristocratic culture.

In other instances, the social realm of education was sacrificed in an attempt to manipulate the academic realm, something drawn from Paul Rhymer's own experiences. During his time at Bloomington High School, Rhymer took part in numerous school clubs and extra-curricular activities. These included serving as president of the Short Story Club; working on the staff of the *Aepix*, the school's yearbook; and taking part in the Roosevelt Debate Club, the Latin Club, and other groups. Like their creator, both Rush and Russell participated in extracurricular activities, including the Sophomore Pathetical Society, The Boys' Nitroglycerine Pep Club, the Shakespeare Dramatic Union, Deep Sea Fancy Diving League, Better English Club, Enthusiastic Order of Football Fanatics, and High School Choral Group, Fellowship of Auditorium Watchers. Although these club names poke gentle fun at the nature of academic clubs, they do reflect the broad educational interests high schools were meant to inculcate.

A script written originally for Rush (c. 1939) and later reused with Russell (c. 1943–44) offers another example of the way in which obstacles are navigated in order for the student to achieve his goals. The activities in which Rush and Russell participate, with few exceptions, offer more social opportunities than academic advancement. Rush, however, contrives what Vic deems a "low-cunning" scheme in which he "resigns" from his activities and organizations in order to make a "red-hot impression on the teachers." Reasoning that his teachers will be impressed by his dedication to his subjects, Rush drafts formal letters of resignation to the faculty representative of each group, explaining that he must give all of his attention to his studies.[27] But here, too, Rhymer humorously implies that even a superficial dedication to book learning is just another form of social advancement, the true purpose of education.

Of course, there are times in which the academic and the social come together in mutually advantageous situations. For example, in 1934, while in eighth grade, Rush served on a

Paul Rhymer did astonishing work putting together a complete radio script five times a week, but on rare occasions he reused scripts from Billy Idelson's time on the show (seen here performing with Bernadine Flynn and Art Van Harvey) during David Whitehouse's run, substituting "Russell" for "Rush" (courtesy Mark C. Lancaster, reproduced by permission of NBC/NBC Universal PhotoBank).

class course committee that allowed him to work with fellow students and teachers on an academic matter. Additionally, in 1940, Rush was given the opportunity to spend more time with his friend Mildred while serving as her algebra tutor. Rush's new role was not only an opportunity to wed the academic and the social, it also served as, in Vic's words "a *feather* in your cap."[28] Having suddenly become a self-proclaimed "professor," the perception of Rush's intelligence was enhanced via his low estimation of his pupil, in to whose skull he plans to "pound information." Rush also see his earning potential increase immediately, noting that "professors don't work for *nothing*, ya know."[29] It is only after Vic reminds him of Mildred's father's "circumstances" that Rush agrees to a "rock-bottom price," but only if Mildred agrees to call him "professor." Even with such a drastic reduction, Rush is beginning to discover some of the more tangible benefits of education, particularly its role in increasing earning potential and social standing.

The practical application of Rush and Russell's learning was not always so readily apparent—or potentially lucrative. In some instances, academic exercises, such as memorizing definitions, appeared only to "clutter up an individual's brain."[30] Rush's attitude toward the memorization of definitions was shared by Russell, who, on July 11, 1944, declared, "No sense to memorizing definitions,"[31] especially in the summer, when no real kid would be caught *studying*, least of all algebra definitions—this despite the fact that he was doing exactly that under the guise of settling a dispute with a friend. He appears to have made his point when Sade, who learned algebra definitions when she was in school, concedes that the only one she remembers is that of a "mixed number." Despite this, however, education in *Vic and Sade* appears as a universal good, a benefit that will carry the student forward into a successful life. However, during the run of the show, the fate of Rush's counterparts in the real world did not look so bright.

"Beat it" Back to School: Education During the Great Depression

In McLean County, where things had been flush during Paul Rhymer's time as a student, the picture for public education had grown rather bleak by the time he was writing *Vic and Sade*. Fiscal troubles had forced budgets to be cut.[32] The county's plans to build larger, more modern schools had been scrapped, and, in 1940, there were fewer than ten students in fifty-four of the county's schools.[33] Across the country, by the 1929-1930 academic year, slightly more than twenty-eight million children and adolescents nationwide were attending public or private schools.[34] While the financial crisis did not, initially, have an adverse effect on most schools, by the fall of 1931 this would change as lower incomes resulted in lower tax rates, placing significant financial strain on many institutions. As schools faced their own financial crises, opponents of universal public education questioned its viability. Others, however, believed that public education should focus solely on the development of trade skills.[35] Many institutions of learning were forced to shorten their school year, eliminate or reduce programs, especially those that fell in the extracurricular category.

The financial burden encountered by many schools was made worse by the increased enrollment in school systems across the country. High school attendance in particular rose dramatically, with working-class children making up the majority of the new students, a 28.9 percent increase nationally between 1930 and 1934. By 1940, working-class children comprised the overwhelming majority of high school students in urban areas.[36] These figures suggest that individuals who would otherwise have likely left school after completing the minimum requirements "remained in high school because of the dismal employment situation."[37] However, attaining this level of education was still a new achievement and not one to be taken for granted. Rush is often reminded that he has been given a privilege not given to everyone. Sade, for example, takes to referring to Rush as a "monstrous big high school boy" whenever she deemed his behavior unacceptable or immature. She also frequently reminds Rush that not everyone—including herself—was fortunate enough to attend high school.

In more than one instance we learn of the Great Depression's adverse effect on the educational pursuits of Rush's friends. On June 15, 1933, Sade plans to visit Mis' McCain's house, a fancy dwelling described by Rush as "swell."[38] Rush believes that, given her surroundings, Sade should wear a silver gown so that she is suitably attired. In order to help, Rush decides to surprise his mother by presenting her with a pair of eight-dollar pink pearl earrings that he had intended to give her for her birthday. Rush's opulent, if not tasteful, gift and Sade's plans to visit Mis' McCain's house are juxtaposed with her discussion with Vic regarding layoffs at Consolidated Kitchenware, a concern that continues to trouble him. While Rush is able to save enough of his allowance to buy Sade birthday presents, we learn that his friend Skinny Martin's father has been laid off, forcing Skinny to quit school and look for a job.

He would not be the last, as Rhymer's scripts continued to reflect the experiences of American teenagers coming of age in the Depression.

While the "dismal employment situation" may have been cause for some students to continue their education through high school, for others the harsh realities of the Great Depression necessitated that they forgo additional studies. In 1935, Rush began his high school career amid considerable and justifiable excitement. For Rush, high school was not a means of avoiding unemployment but, rather, a pathway to college and further opportunities. The excitement of the first day of school is so great that he decides to cut his lunch break short and "beat it" back to school because he has "*plenty* of business" back there.[39] However, while Mildred is in Rush's Latin class and Rooster Davis has been assigned to all of Rush's classes, we learn that two more students, Horace Chatman and Wally Wilson, have been forced to find jobs instead.

"Chickens for tuition": College Education During the Great Depression

For the wealthiest students, as well as those of exceptional academic merit, college was the culmination of the high school experience. For those few who graduated from college or a university, a degree conveyed status and allotted them a place in the community. A college degree, it was widely assumed, was a marker of intelligence, one that set the graduate apart from others. This belief was reinforced by what some considered the discriminatory admission practices of these institutions, which aimed at creating an intellectual and socioeconomic elite.[40] David O. Levine contends that, throughout the 1920s and 1930s, a college education was less an intellectual endeavor than one directed toward networking and improving one's social status. One could reasonably argue that this was true for Paul Rhymer and the connections he made during his three years at Illinois Wesleyan University.

However, colleges were not entirely closed to those from less-privileged backgrounds. College education was transformed during the Great Depression. During this period, blue-collar workers suffered far more than their white-collar counterparts. Subsequently, a college degree provided both the means for a better life as well as proof that the degree holder was more intelligent and prestigious than those without one. Recognizing this, students from rural or blue-collar backgrounds increasingly worked toward white-collar professions and the status that accompanied them.[41] The Lynds observe, in their second study of Middletown, that in the early years of the Great Depression, the financial crisis was something to read about happening elsewhere as its effects had yet to be felt in Middletown, and there was "a strong tradition that one's 'future' (i.e., one's wealth and happiness) is in one's own hands." During this relatively unscathed period, pursuing a college degree was "the logical thing to do in the absence of jobs." However, the "rising tide of college graduates" had caused many in Middletown to feel that the prestige of a degree had "sagged."[42]

However logical the pursuit of a college degree may have been, given the dearth of employment opportunities, such a pursuit would remain elusive for many. Whereas, in 1924, the Lynds found that 34 percent of high school graduates went on to college, in the first years of the Depression college applications rose by 40 percent, as those without jobs sought educational alternatives; that figure fell back to 1920s levels as the Depression sapped financial resources.[43] At the University of Illinois, for example, students paid $35 a semester, the equivalent of $540 today. With room and board, the average student could have spent up to $1,000 a year at a time when the average worker might have earned $20 a week. After

Paul Rhymer's alma mater, Illinois Wesleyan University, allowed students to pay tuition with livestock, like these cows and pigs photographed near Aledo, Illinois, in 1936, in order to keep young people in school during a bleak economic period (Russell Lee/Library of Congress).

reaching an all-time high in 1930, enrollment at the school crashed by 25 percent in 1934, to 10,675 students.[44]

At Paul Rhymer's alma mater, Illinois Wesleyan, an innovative plan was introduced to allow struggling students hit hard by the economic downfall to continue their studies. "Produce for Tuition" allowed for students to pay their tuition with crops and livestock. According to the *Argus* at the time, "All kinds of farm products were on hand. There were cows, pigs, sheep, chickens, a truck of oats, a truck full of cream cans." According to the university's president, Harry McPherson, "Illinois Wesleyan adopted this plan ... not for publicity sake nor because we had a dearth of students, but because we wanted to encourage worthy young men and young women to continue their educations."[45]

Charting the Future to the Year 2000

Although *Vic and Sade* did, on occasion, recognize the obstacles that the Great Depression placed in the path of education, such hindrances were neither experienced nor expected by the Gooks. As has been mentioned, Rush was a "monstrous big high school boy" who would almost certainly pursue a college education and achieve a successful career and a privileged social status. Such confidence in Rush's future academic endeavors may have seemed misplaced at times given his sometimes less-than-stellar academic performance—a quick review of one eighth-grade report card finds him earning an "excellent" in math, a "fair" in composition, and "low" in deportment, spelling, and geography.[46]

The certainly of Rush's trajectory was outlined in 1935 when, on the prompting of Superintendent Chinbunny, he developed a chart of his future through to the year 2000. Chinbunny, we learn, had determined that every child "girl or boy—when they reach the age of thirteen years should start workin' on a plan for their future life."[47] Rush has made "just an ordinary plan." Like most adolescents, he believes that anything is possible, and his chart reflects this sense of confidence. His plans also illustrate the belief that education can provide an individual with a level of prestige and social status he might not otherwise possess. According to his master plan, following the completion of his high school education at Edwards School, Rush would proceed to college, graduating in 1943 at the age of twenty-one, at which time he would attend medical school until 1949. Rush's decision to pursue medicine—a decision made the morning that he completed his chart—was not one born of deep contemplation. Indeed, as he explained to his parents, "A guy's got to be *somethin'*. I might as well be a doctor. What the heck."[48]

Rush's plans depict a series of successes—a multi-year-long trip to Europe to recover from his extensive education, a successful medical practice and marriage at thirty-three ("Oughta be *plenty* of ladies around willin' to marry a rich *doctor*"[49]). By the time he is sixty-five Rush plans to retire from medicine and enter politics, with an eye to being elected governor. Earlier in the series, he had anticipated one day being able to introduce himself as "Rush Gook, United States senator from Illinois.[50]

As depicted by Paul Rhymer, education was still seen, even in the heart of the Depression, as a ticket toward a better life, a credential marking a person as socially privileged, and a way to secure the future against the ravages of a changing economy. If Rush's working-class friends were forced to drop out to seek work, Rush, by contrast, could benefit from the relative security of his family's middle-class status and look forward to parlaying it into a still-higher socioeconomic status of his own.

"Let us pick raspberries from the top of the tree"

However, education did not stop at the schoolhouse door, and throughout *Vic and Sade* and indeed elsewhere in the period's radio programming, the impact and effects of education were frequently depicted and, indeed, celebrated. While the majority of public intellectuals and culture critics decried radio programming en mass for its appeal to the lowest-common denominator, programming throughout the 1930s and 1940s did, in fact, reveal contradictory attitudes toward education and intellectuals. Listeners were at once offered programming that celebrated the benefits of education and lauded the intellectual as one to admire and aspire to be, while also offering programs that depicted the intellectual as effete or a buffoon lacking in all practical skills. The anti-intellectual was, on the other hand, celebrated as the common man, one whose savvy and street smarts were superior to anything a school could offer. Both of these trends were depicted on *Vic and Sade*, though, to understand this, we must first explore how the dichotomy is illustrated by the popular quiz programs of the era.

The most famous of these programs was *Information, Please* (see below), but perhaps the most interesting was *Quiz Kids*, which first aired on June 28, 1940, on NBC. The program featured a panel of five "genius" children between the ages of five and sixteen, answering listener-submitted questions on everything from ornithology and mythology to music and mathematics and more. The genius label was not merely hype, with the kids' IQ typically ranging between 135 and 180, a few at 200, and some even higher.[51] But rather than seeming pretentious or threatening, they "sounded exactly like the kids next door."[52] The kids also fared favorably against *Information, Please* in the ratings, earning an 11.6 in the Crossley ratings, compared to an 11.9 for their adult contemporaries.[53]

Following the program's debut, *Variety* expressed doubts that it had been unrehearsed, due to the scope of the children's knowledge. Indeed, *Variety* was not alone in harboring such doubts. Gerard Darrow, one of the program's first panelists, displayed "such a deep and mature grasp of mythology that the network received angry letters charging that the show was a fake."[54] The questions posed to the kids were definitely not soft balls. It was not uncommon for a question to require them to possess knowledge of more than one subject to answer it correctly, as was the case of this opening question from the March 20, 1949, episode:

> Name the atomic numbers of sulfur, helium, and hydrogen and you will have a once-famous political slogan. What is this slogan? Question submitted by Mary Lewis from South Bend, IN.[55]

The answer was provided by twelve-year-old Joel Kupperman, who offered the atomic numbers of 16, 2, and 1, and eleven-year-old Patrick Owen Conlon (last name unintelligible), identifying the slogan as "16 to 1, the famous political slogan of William Jennings Bryan."

To further flex their intellectual muscles, the kids periodically took on challenges from the adult world—with excellent results. In 1941, for example, they challenged professors from the University of Chicago and "trounced" them, with the Quiz Kids scoring 275 to the professors' meager 140. It should be noted, however, that in a rematch one year later, the University of Chicago faculty members came out on top, with a score of 110 to 105, a defeat the kids attributed to having stayed up late to watch a lunar eclipse.[56] In 1942, the kids took another adult challenge in the form of the Army aviation cadet screening test. Passing score for the test was 80, a feat easily surpassed by the kids, whose scores averaged 101. Fifteen-year-old Van Dyke Tiers, who earned a score of 131—only twelve points behind the highest score ever recorded on the test at the recruiting office in Chicago—explained, "Some of the math and physics problems I recognized from school before I was halfway through them."[57]

Despite some criticism from adults who, *Radio Life* suggested, were "too limited in intelligence to enjoy the show,"[58] it was huge success. The kids appeared on Jack Benny's program, welcomed Milton Berle as a guest host, and appeared in several movie shorts; there were *Quiz Kids* board games, novels, and even a *Quiz Kids* edition of Webster's Dictionary. Local *Quiz Kids* competitions were held throughout the country.

Perhaps one factor that was crucial in the appeal of *Quiz Kids* was that of the "quizmaster himself," Joe Kelly. In contrast to his panel of young prodigies, Kelly, the emcee of WLS's *National Barn Dance*, seemed an unlikely choice for such a cerebral affair. Kelly had left school following the third grade to pursue a career in show business. Billed as the "Irish Nightingale from Crawfordville, IN," he performed until his voice began to crack. Kelly reportedly received the role as quizmaster because he genuinely liked children, a sentiment that was reciprocated by the children in his on-air "classroom." Rather than being an impediment, Kelly's lack of formal education proved an asset on the program. Although "each new broadcast was ripe with potential humiliation,"[59] Kelly's good humor and willingness to concede that he was no match for the children made him "their perfect foil." Kelly recognized that the children knew more than he did, and was genuinely impressed. He was "just folks, like the audience."[60]

Similarly, *Information, Please* was created by Dan Golenpaul as an alternative to other radio quiz programs that he found to be "inane and ultimately embarrassing."[61] Unlike conventional quiz contests which, Golenpaul believed, involved "putting some ignorant contestant onstage and highlighting his ignorance," the series featured a panel of experts, including newspaper columnists Franklin P. Adams and John Keran and writer, actor, and pianist Oscar Levant. In addition to panelists, each episode featured a guest panelist drawn from the world of politics, the arts, or sports. *Information, Please* offered listeners the occasion to hear a unique range of personalities. Over the course of the series' run, guests included such luminaries as Alfred Hitchcock; radio's Sherlock Holmes, Basil Rathbone; renowned prizefighter Gene Tunney, who "surprised the nation with his knowledge of Shakespeare"[62]; actor Boris Karloff; journalist and broadcaster Dorothy Thompson, who, in 1939, was named the second-most influential woman in America (the first being Eleanor Roosevelt); and writers Dorothy Parker and Carl Sandburg, among many others. The *New Yorker*'s literary critic, Clifton Fadiman, served as the moderator each week.

While *Quiz Kids*' panelists dazzled audiences with their presentation of facts and ability to answer often-obscure questions correctly, on *Information, Please* a correct answer came second to the lively exchange of dialog between panelists. As panelist John Kieran explained, "An uproarious error or a brilliant bit of irreverence was rated far above any dull delivery of truth" the resulting program had "the entire country by its mental ears."[63] A question about Shakespearean speeches illustrates the program's less-structured format, while also highlighting the playful interaction between regulars John Kieran and Franklin P. Adams, with guest, actor John Carradine:

> CLIFTON FADIMAN: I'm going to give you situations from three Shakespearean plays. You are to quote from the famous speech made in each case. I'll explain each case. Now this is Act III, scene iv of *Hamlet*. Hamlet is showing his mother the picture of two kings, and he's comparing them. What does he say? Mr. Carradine?
> JOHN CARRADINE: "See what a grace was seated on this brow..."
> FADIMAN: Yes.
> CARRADINE: "Hyperion's curls; the front of Jove himself..."
> FADIMAN: That's very good.
> CARRADINE: "An eye like Mars, to threaten and command...." Shall I go on?
> FADIMAN: Very, very good. Amazing repertory, Mr. Carradine. I hope Hollywood's listening in. What were you going to say, Mr. Adams?
> FRANKLIN P. ADAMS: Same thing.
> FADIMAN: Same thing, yes. (*LAUGHTER*)
> ADAMS: Less well!
> FADIMAN: (*LAUGHTER*) Mr. Kieran?
> JOHN KIERAN: I can go on from there for a couple of lines.
> FADIMAN: All right.
> KIERAN: "A station like the herald Mercury, New-lighted on a heaven-kissing hill...." Is that all right?
> FADIMAN: A dandy. How's that, Mr. Carradine?
> CARRADINE: Oh, it's fine.
> FADIMAN: OK.
> CARRADINE: "A combination and a form indeed." "Where every god did seem to set his seal..."
> FADIMAN: (*LAUGHTER*)
> CARRADINE: Shall we just go on with the play?
> FADIMAN: Uh, we better get off Shakespeare sooner or later.[64]

A quick check of *Hamlet* reveals that, rather impressively, the panelists were each correct in their quotations. Unfortunately, while the question does display an impressive knowledge of Shakespeare and recall abilities by three of the four panelists that evening, the fourth panelist, Boris Karloff, remained silent during the exchange.

The Value of Knowledge

Audiences of *Information, Please* and *Quiz Kids* were shown both the tangible and esoteric benefits of possessing a vast body of knowledge and being able to readily draw from it. On a purely material level, both programs awarded prizes to listeners whose questions had been selected for use. Audience members whose questions were selected for use on *Quiz Kids* were awarded a portable Zenith trans-oceanic radio, if the kids answered the question correctly, and a radio-phonographic combination, on those rare instances when a question was answered incorrectly. Similarly, *Information, Please* initially awarded two dollars to listeners whose questions were selected to be posed to the panel, and five dollars for those which the panel failed to answer correctly. In time, a set of the *Encyclopædia Britannica* was added. Later, when it transitioned from a sustaining program to being sponsored by Canada Dry, prizes increased to a more respectable five and ten dollars, respectively. Prizes were again increased, this time to ten and twenty-five dollars, when Lucky Strike took over as sponsor. The tangible offerings were only part of the rewards that these programs offered listeners. There was also the satisfaction of answering a question correctly—especially if it was one answered incorrectly by a panelist. Moreover, each program provided listeners with a chance to "stump the experts" with the questions that they submitted. The ability to pose questions to the panelists allowed listeners to demonstrate their own expertise on a given topic, or their ability to craft clever questions intended to baffle individuals who were, in theory, their intellectual superiors.

Quiz Kids and *Information, Please* also heard the intellectual take center stage. The panelists on both shows were congenial, likable, and easy to welcome into listeners' homes. Even the Quiz Kids, who in some ways were regarded as curiosities, showed that the possession of a high IQ could make someone the source of esteem. Panelists also introduced the nature of "the expert." *Quiz Kids'* Joel Kupperman was dubbed "the midget Euclid" by *Time* magazine[65] because of his prowess in mathematics; quiz kid Gerard Darrow and John Kieran both possessed high level of expertise in nature, so much so that Darrow was often referred to as "a little John Kieran"[66]; Lonnie Lunde and Joan Bishop were two of *Quiz Kids'* musical prodigies; meanwhile, poetry and the works of Gilbert and Sullivan were among the areas of specialization for Franklin P. Adams on *Information, Please*.

Such programs demonstrate the value that the public placed on knowledge and education, and it is no coincidence that *Vic and Sade* reflected this, though in its characteristically absurd way. Vic frequently assumes the role of the intellectual, at times in an attempt to gain a little prestige. We know that he "enjoyed reading" and likely read "all of the books in school"[67] and that he possesses a certain level of curiosity that draws him still to volumes on "every war since the beginning of mankind"[68] and *Facts and Figures of the Civilized World*.[69] What is not clear, however, is whether he actually possesses the education or deep knowledge to support him in his assumed role.

One of Vic's most touted areas of expertise is the field of literature and poetry, from which he frequently draws (often questionable) references. A 1932 episode finds the first of numerous references to the (real) nineteenth-century poet John Greenleaf Whittier, when

Vic cites him as having said, "Be leisurely in your eating always, but be *most* leisurely when eating *peaches*"[70] to justify the slow pace at which he was eating. The second half of the sentence, pertaining to peaches, was clearly added by Vic to fit the situation and add credibility to his stance with Sade, but what of the first half? In examining 482 of Whittier's poems, one of the few references to eating can be found in "Mogg Megone": "The wolves are eating the Norridgewock." However, Whittier fails to mention the pace at which the wolves were eating. Eating is again mentioned, this time in "The Haschish," in conjunction with the strange plant of the Orient. To be fair to Vic, the topic of leisure does appear somewhat more frequently, but, again, not in the context in which he presents it.

In a 1937 episode, Vic again references Whittier. As Sade chides Rush for a mess that he has left in the library, Vic interjects that the "poet Whittier says a boy's thoughts are long, long thoughts an'...."[71] In this particular case, Vic seems to be referring not to Whittier, but to Henry Wadsworth Longfellow who, in "My Lost Youth," wrote, "And the thoughts of youth are long, long thoughts." Again, however, the use of poetry punctuated the situation and gave Vic an opportunity to appear somewhat lofty in his thinking, especially when compared with Sade's more confrontational approach to conflict resolution.

Another of Vic's frequent forays in to the world of poetry involves the poets Keats and Browning. According to the lore perpetuated by Vic on several occasions, he attributes the poetry of Keats to a curious origin: "Well, as the poet Keats said as he held the dandelion beneath the chin of the poet Browning to determine whether or not he liked butter, 'Life, life, life, life, life, life, life, life, life....'"[72] There are variations of this tale. For example, on June 4, 1944, Vic reported that as Keats held the dandelion beneath Browning's chin, "'Browning' muttered Keats with a smirk, 'I have always considered you a fat-head.'"[73] Inaccuracies and discrepancies such as these were not limited to literature and poetry, but indeed made their way into Vic's discussions on a variety of topics, as we have seen in his inaccurate Latin translations.

One could reasonably suggest that Vic was lacking a fully developed knowledge of the topics he was addressing; however, while this could be true, it is equally possible that his misstatements were examples of his showing off by deliberately mangling references through malapropisms, parody, and "Spoonerisms." The latter were named for Archibald Spooner (1844–1930), a British clergyman who was known for mixing up his words. F. Chase Taylor, otherwise known as "Colonel" Stoopnagle of *Stoopnagle and Budd* was prone to Spoonerisms which, along with the malapropisms, were popular comedic techniques in 1930s radio. Malapropisms, the misuse of similar-sounding words, were often encountered on *Easy Aces*, in the dialog of Jane Ace, who was prone to utterances such as, "You're so obsolete," when she meant obstinate, or "international" flu when she actually means "intestinal."[74] While there is no question that Vic's errors were a deliberate ploy on Paul Rhymer's part, particularly given the popularity of such wordplay during this period, Rhymer never definitively clarified whether listeners were intended to interpret Vic's errors as intentional or accidental—that is, whether Vic was a man attempting but failing to appropriate the aura of an intellectual, or one who enjoyed using his knowledge for humorous intent.

"What do I care about human ingenuity and trash": Knowledge and Intellectualism in Vic and Sade

At the same time that intelligence and the intellectual were being celebrated in both low- and highbrow programming, including Norman Corwin's *Columbia Presents* and *26 by Corwin*, along with other programs that lauded fine drama, literature, and classical music, there was also a concurrent and contradictory air of anti-intellectualism present in radio programming—as in much of American life, according to Richard Hofstadter. As Hofstadter explains, the anti-intellectual "has a resentment and suspicion of the life of the mind and of those who are considered to represent it; and a disposition constantly to minimize the value of that life."[75] Or, more tactfully, as Donald Clark Hodges described it, a "populist resentment by know-nothings for the sophistication that only comes with higher education."[76] Anti-intellectualism, it has been charged, reaches "into every corner of life," including interpersonal relationships, academic, business, and mass communication, as well as social and physical sciences.[77] While this has always been a facet of American life, it was particularly noticeable in the Depression, when traditional elitists seemed powerless and discredited in the face of seemingly irrational economic forces. Thus, a great deal of American anti-intellectualism was directed toward intellectuals in government. Such distrust is understandable given the nature and role of government and the public's relationship to it. This was particularly true in the era following the Great Depression, when the weaknesses of the U.S. government—and the intellectuals at its helm—had been made so readily apparent.

On radio, characters like Fibber McGee and *Lum and Abner*'s Lum epitomized the anti-intellectual. Both men had limited educations and appeared to distrust those more learned. McGee and Lum offer comedic representations of the common man struggling to prove his worth. McGee is "a comic everyman"[78] who perpetually boasts and exaggerates his escapades in an effort to outdo those he perceives as his betters, such as the town doctor and mayor. Both McGee and Lum frequently undertake ventures for which they lack both the education and intellect to accomplish; in Lum's case, this even included opening his own dental practice, despite never having been to dental school.

However, neither McGee nor Lum—or any other character on radio—was quite as opposed to the very notion of the intellectual as was Sade Gook. To Sade, any discussion not directly related to the practical purposes of her daily life was dismissed summarily as "talky talk," something meant for intellectuals and professionals, not down-home normal folk. Rather than concern herself with worldly affairs, Sade focused on those things that most affected her and her family's daily existence, whether that be home maintenance, sales and shopping, or the comings and goings of her neighbors. As Paul Rhymer explained to *Radio Stars* magazine in 1935, she "was in the dark about most things that go on in the world." However, this was not meant as a slight; Rhymer pointed out that "in her own kitchen she's as deft, wise and capable as any human being could be."[79] Yet things outside of the home failed to interest Sade, as she demonstrated in an episode first broadcast on November 28, 1937:

> SADE: Says here about the Supreme Court doing somethin' or other, what is that Supreme Court business?
> VIC: You're asking me rather an involved question. To answer it I'd ...
> SADE: Part of the United States President, ain't it?
> VIC: I wouldn't say that it was part of him. It might be part of his trusted ...
> SADE: Mis' Applerot and Mis' Brighton was talkin' about the Supreme Courts and things other day. They're such know-it-alls. They'll sit around and tell about Constitution and Congress and all like that.[80]

Such discourse, Sade believes, has no place at a ladies' Thimble Meeting, where the rest of the ladies just "stand and gawp" at the intrusion.

SADE: Supreme Court, Ulysses S. Grant, none of their bee's wax.
RUSH: Knowledge of our national government and how it functions is every American's bee's wax.

But, to Sade, discussion of such matters amounted to little more than "monstrous, big important talky-talkin,'" intended to inflate the ladies' egos. In her mind, other, more salient matters took precedence:

SADE: No, but ain't it ridiculous.... Mis' Applerot's a grown-up woman with a family and a house to keep clean. What on earth does she care about the Congress?

Sade's refusal to learn about the U.S. government and its structure, despite Vic and Rush's best efforts, is not the result of a lack of intelligence on Sade's part, but rather a stubborn conviction that she maintains her focus only on those things that relate to her family and home. At the same time, she is able to recognize her potential to appear ignorant or dull, a fact she noted early in the series when Vic was bringing Mr. Ruebush home for dinner. She expressed her concerns about appearing "stupid and silly,"[81] as she often did on occasions when she was to entertain someone she considered more educated or successful than herself.

The fact that Sade refused Rush and Vic's attempt to educate her about the United States' government was not uncommon; she often dismissed any attempt to inform or educate her. Although this may have been done under the premise of maintaining a tunnel-vision focus on those things most relevant to her home and family, it also had the effect of making her appear ignorant. For example, in one instance she returned home from Yamilton's with a "monstrous big" light bulb that she estimates has "a million volts" in it.[82] When Vic decides to scrape off some contact points Sade is worried that he will scrape off the "good whits."[83] Sade's confusion with "watts" and "whits" is reminiscent of her belief that a "gavel"—"those little hammers that you pound on the table when you conduct a Thimble Club meeting"—is a "gravel," despite repeated admonitions from Russell, who offers her dictionary definitions which she flatly ignores.[84] Sade believes that these "whits" (or "whats," as she also calls them) are a "chunk of electricity" and that they were now smeared all over the new light bulb. Concerned by his mother's ignorance, Russell attempted to explain just what a watt is.

RUSSELL: A watt is one-seven hundred an' sixty-fourth of a horse-power. In simple language that means seven-hundred an' sixty-four watts would be required to shove a full-grown horse one foot past...[85]

Not surprisingly, Sade ignores him.

Later, in a last-ditch effort to provide some insight into the nature of electricity, Russell proposes a simple experiment: Vic holds the light bulb with one hand and places his other hand on Russell's knee, while Russell places his hand on the library table. He then asks Sade to place her hand on his algebra textbook, which is sitting on the table. Sade refuses to do so, certain that she will be shocked by the light bulb. Teased about her ignorance concerning electricity, Sade dismissively says, "I'm just as satisfied" to, in Russell's words, not "know shucks about electricity."[86]

There is a marked contrast in the level of intellectual curiosity between Vic and Sade. While Vic is regularly seen as being interested—and at times almost obsessed—with how everyday items, such as alarm clocks and doorbells, function, Sade is decidedly uninterested. Even in those relatively rare instances in which she *is* interested in knowing something, she very rarely takes the initiative to seek out the information. As the Gooks prepared for their trip to Hawaii in 1938, Sade had numerous misconceptions, some of which were the fault of friends, regarding the islands and their travel requirements. Eager to hear of her plans, the Thimble Club ladies posed a number of questions to Sade. Mis' Applerot, for example, was wondering what the latitude of her destination was, to which Sade informed her, "Mr. Gook hasn't decided yet."[87] Meanwhile, other ladies have inquired whether she would be passing through Cincinnati en route to Hawaii, and how close she would be to China. She is also curious as to how far they will be riding on the Pacific Ocean. Predictably, despite her need to have information in her "noodle," Sade steadfastly ignores Rush's attempt to explain the relation of latitude and longitude to the equator, as well as Vic's suggestion that she visit the library to do some research on her own. Sade's rationale for not visiting the library, or reading books that Vic brings home, is that she can't be reading because "I've got my *eyes* to think of." They are strained enough already from up-close sewing work, an excuse highlighting her practical nature and devotion to home.[88]

What becomes apparent, then, is not only that Sade is suspicious of the role of experts and learning in broad areas that may not directly affect her, but that she eschews efforts to educate and inform her, even when such efforts would clearly prove beneficial to her. In this, she reflects the strain in American life that extolled the inherent virtues of the common person and looked with suspicion upon the sophisticates who would trade valuable home truths and traditional folk knowledge about everyday experiences for abstract and impractical information.

There are, of course, exceptions. In those cases in which being ignorant on a given topic has the potential to cause her embarrassment, Sade will make an effort to educate herself, though often by consulting only Vic and/or Rush, rather than pursuing the topic independently. When she needed the names of five wildflowers and an interesting fact about each one for a Thimble Club meeting, she asks Vic, despite having had all week to go to the public library. Although she believes that he is an expert on the topic because he was brought up on a farm, Sade soon finds that neither Vic nor Rush is especially knowledgeable on the topic. The result of this consultation is a haphazard compilation of flowers with, for the most part, fabricated facts such as, "Sweet Williams were discovered by Balboa when he explored the Pacific coast."[89] Though not strictly true, Rush rationalized that Balboa must have encountered the flower at *some* point in his explorations. Peer pressure also proved to be the driving motive behind Sade's decision to read *Bridges of St. Louis Bay*.[90] While the book, lamentably, had no pictures, the fact that it had been lent to Sade by Mis' Fisher, with the expectation that she would read it, compelled her to do so — although, as we have seen, she was eventually driven to seek respite from all those words by going to the movies.

In a script apparently written to be performed in conjunction with the 1936 annual meeting of the National Education Association in St. Louis, Missouri,[91] Mis' Brighton's brother Willard's book of poetry offered Sade another opportunity to expand her horizons when Mis' Brighton asked her to review the book at a Thimble Club meeting. Given the public nature of the commitment, Sade had little choice but to read what is shown to be a collection of pretentious nonsense (typical for Rhymer's jabs at all forms of pretention) that included titles such as "My Feet Are in My Shoes, So Stand Back, Sweetheart, While I Dream," "Oh Wind, Whistle, Whistle," and "Tiny Autumn Leaflets Scurry Past My Couch." Ironically, Sade's sincere effort to glean meaning from poetry is wasted on material that she could, for once, have justifiably deemed "talky talk." In the volume's first poem the author intones: "Oh Snow-capped elbow of yawning chasm. I see my lady's face beneath the sands. The world is but a storm that knows no quilting. So whistle Wind, Whistle. Whistle."[92]

Rush very astutely, if literally, translates the author's sentiments as simply meaning "there's a great big ditch with a *hill* beside it. There's *snow* on that hill ... his wife is *in* the ditch."[93] Throughout this episode Sade uncharacteristically *listens* to Rush who, having recently written a review of Sir Walter Scott's *The Lady of the Lake*, possessed some degree of intellectual authority in literary interpretation.

Ultimately, Sade asks Rush to return the book to Mis' Brighton, her review incomplete. What might have been a positive learning experience for Sade instead reaffirmed her predilections regarding the intellectual and artistic. As it happens, it also reinforced Rush's assessment of poetry:

> Rush: (*WHO KNOWS ALL ABOUT IT*) This is *poetry*, Mom. You hafta take poetry like it comes.... Poetry is different. You can't *expect* it to be like a piece outta the newspaper.[94]

It's telling that the collection of poems Sade was to review were pretentious and, overall, meaningless. Throughout *Vic and Sade*, education, intelligence, and intellect are portrayed as important; however, Paul Rhymer also illustrated that one could easily feign intellectualism through something like a faux-highbrow poem. Had Sade a more literary bent, she might have condemned so much of intellectual life as "full of sound and fury, signifying nothing." Rhymer, who was first and foremost a writer, but a populist one, positioned his art carefully along the line that divided the intellectual from the common man, elite culture from mass culture. His gentle mockery of intellectual pretention could apply not just to philosophy, history, and the arts but also to his own work. *Vic and Sade* was a conversational show meant to mimic the tone and tenor of everyday life. Rhymer looked for the wisdom and grace of quotidian conversation and made quiet fun of those who tried to subvert this homey ideal with abstraction, elitism, and appeal to some distant and unknowing authority. It was not that the anti-intellectuals were right and that intellectuals were suspect and vaguely dangerous; it was that the professors and pundits were in a college separate from the masses, a world of their own, and one unwelcome in the small house halfway up in the next block.

Nine: "Doing exactly the same thing": The Individual and the Community

We have heard the Gooks and their friends engaging with various aspects of the culture they inhabit, from leisure to career, from civil organizations to education. In so doing, we have been privy to each member of the family and their many friends and neighbors selecting numerous alternatives their culture offered. In making the choice of what literature to read, what forms of leisure to pursue, and what path to take toward a future career, the various individuals asserted individuality, making and remaking their world through a combination of standardized parts drawn from the mass culture that surrounds them. *Vic and Sade* provided its listeners with a critique, albeit a humorous one, of mass cultures that was markedly different than that advanced by public intellectuals and culture critics of the period. Paul Rhymer's critique took place within the context of popular culture, which recognized the public's ability to think critically and make choices, even if these choices are sometimes flawed. Therefore, in our final chapter we will look at the broader ways the Gooks formulated personal identity and individuality within and against an increasingly standardized and homogenized mass culture, whose products we have already reviewed.

Critics of mass culture long maintained that its products, in their desire to meet the needs of the masses, promoted homogeneity and conformity among audiences. The individual, it has been said, was lost amid the need to appeal to the largest possible audience. These claims were certainly renewed with added vigor as radio's popularity grew. As Lenthall notes, public intellectuals believed that radio programming, in its attempt to appeal to base impulses, devalued the individual through programs which disregarded diversity.[1] Radio programs like *Vic and Sade* were undoubtedly aimed at a specific audience. Stations at the time kept careful track of their listeners, as shown in a 1936 marketing manual assembled for advertisers on KSTP, the Minneapolis NBC affiliate. While praising *Vic and Sade* as a show that drew listeners to the station, it also provided advertisers with a breakdown of everything from household income to the number of automobiles and optometrists in a given city to better target the more than 90 percent of households with radios.[2]

The upshot of trying to maintain the attention of an audience comprising most of the country was that programs had to appeal to everyone, not just a specific niche. Nevertheless, even though the characters of *Vic and Sade* represent the "universalizing" tendency of mass broadcasting, within their own world, they demonstrate how the ordinary person could assert his individuality within the broader context of mass culture. We've already seen the way in which the program distinguished itself from other serials in the daytime schedule with its irreverent and often-absurd comedy that dealt with the small, sometimes seemingly insignificant matters of day-to-day life. The characters, whether they be the Gooks or their friends and relatives, were not wealthy, did not face heartbreaking misfortune, rare and death-defying medical maladies, or encounter peril from villainous foes. Rather, they lived their lives in a manner similar to the majority of their listeners. The program took place largely, though not exclusively, in the Gook home, with listeners hearing about such decidedly non-exotic locations such as the Bijou, Vic's office, or Yamilton's department store. In so doing, *Vic and Sade* offered a realistic platform to explore the ways in which individuals navigated the intersection of culture and identity in Depression-era America. In order to see this process at work, we must first say a few words about individualism in American life.

Standing Apart from the Crowd

"Individualism," Alexis de Tocqueville wrote, "is a mature and calm feeling, which disposes each member of the community to sever himself from the mass of his fellow-creatures; and to draw apart with his family and his friends; so that, after he has thus formed a little circle of his own, he willingly leaves society at large to itself."[3] Tocqueville is careful to differentiate the concept of individualism from that of egotism, which he describes as "passionate and exaggerated love of self, which leads a man to connect everything with his own person, and to prefer himself to everything in the world."[4] Individualism, which implies self-reliance and independence, sets the individual apart from society in a physical sense. But individualism itself, as a doctrine and driving force in American life, also runs up against individuality, which requires a larger society as a stage and an audience for the performance of identity. In that sense, individuality, as a reaction against conformity, overlaps with, but is not the same as, individualism. In the middle-twentieth century, Roger J. Williams explained that "every human individual (even in the case of identical twins) is distinctive and different," and noted that it is how he or she exhibits distinctiveness that provides insight into the individual.[5] Although a simple observation, considering the ways in which characters on *Vic and Sade* exhibit the distinctive characteristics and behaviors that separate them from others provides us with a means of assessing the role of the individual and his or her relationship with the collective.

One of the attributes most commonly associated with *Vic and Sade* is the distinctive and unique names given to many of the characters. While it is true that there are families named Adams, Anderson, Baker, and Carter, there are also Applerots, Brainfeebles, Cheebawsters, Chinbunnys, Klunkfaucets, Sludges, and Stembottoms. Within a clique that includes nicknames like Rooster, Rotten, Smelly, Nicer, Blue-Tooth, and Oyster Kracker, Rush is occasionally referred to by the less-colorful moniker "Splash" by his friends in gym class simply because "they just do."[6] "Mush," a largely unused nickname, is one he claims to have been fighting his whole life, ever since his grade school companions tried to foist it upon him because it sounds sort of like Rush.[7] As we shall see momentarily, Vic also had a myriad of private nicknames for Rush, including such seemingly random handles as Egg Yolk and Coal Oil.

Surprisingly, perhaps, such a well-recognized facet of American life as the tendency to bestow nicknames on one another has received relatively little study among sociologists and other scholars. In early editions of his *American Language*, H. L. Mencken made reference to the American tendency to invent new names, and by the supplements he added in the 1940s, he found an increase in the use of nicknames. In 1937, George Earlie Shankle published a volume on nicknames, but these were primarily those of places and sports teams; his discussion of personal nicknames was restricted largely to those of the famous, who had sported well-known monikers since the early days of the Republic. So little did scholars of the time care for the practice that, in 1935, psychologists Samuel Z. Orgel and Jacob Tuckman concluded that nicknames were "of no value" and served only to cause fights among children. Interestingly, however, this same study found that more than 95 percent of children had a nickname. Among these, boys' nicknames fell into the following categories: one-third referred to physical abnormalities; one-third to prominent personality traits; and the rest divided among contractions or distortions of the child's name, ethnicity or birthplace, an animal name, and an affectionate pet name. A few were unclassifiable. For girls, one-third were affectionate pet names; one-third referred to physical abnormalities; and 15 percent were distortions or contractions of the child's name.[8] This study was limited by its researchers' use only of children in New York City foster homes, but its results were probably roughly analogous to children elsewhere. In that sense, Rush's friends like Blue-Tooth, Smelly, and Rooster were typical of the nicknames used by their real-life peers. Even Rush confirms, in an episode in 1936, that he got into "*plenty* of fights" over being called "Mush," just as the New York psychologists feared children in his age bracket were wont to do.[9] Similarly, Harper Scott's nickname of Nicer derives from his friends' uproarious glee and merciless teasing after seeing a love note Harper writes to Mildred that reads in its entirety "You are nice," to which his friends offer in rejoinder, "An' *you*, Harper, are *nicer*."[10] Rush and friends also subject him to "millions" of punishments, including prank phone calls to tell him he is nice. Rush predicts the nickname will stick for life.

Much later studies found that nicknames were more common among men than women, among children and teenagers than adults, and within families and circles of close friends than in broader social relationships. Late twentieth-century studies found that nicknames were tied to social status. Examples include "Chip," implying higher social status than "Bubba" or "Chico," nicknames associated with specific ethnic groups, regions, or social classes.[11] In this sense, the nicknames of Rush's friends were closer to the lower-middle-class appellations of the time.

Beyond their names, the characters on *Vic and Sade* were also distinct from many of their fictional peers found on the daytime schedule: neither Vic nor Sade conformed to the mold for the typical soap opera hero or heroine. Sade, being a steady and dependable housewife, never found time to engage in romantic dalliances with other men or to take part in the sort of dangerous sleuthing that would put the likes of Helen Trent in such precarious positions. Similarly, Vic was a hard-working husband and father who, despite Sade's jealousy concerning Lolita DeRienzi and Pom Pom Cordova, never became embroiled in a love triangle, or left Sade thinking he was dead for months as he roamed the country with amnesia.

Within the context of the show, Victor Gook possessed many characteristics that distinguished him from other characters, including an irreverent sense of humor fueled by such disparate sources as poetry and history. Though he often masked it with curmudgeonly behavior, there was an underlying silliness and playful spirit in Vic that one might not have readily associated with a chief bookkeeper. His irreverence could be found in the myriad private nicknames that he had for Rush and Russell that included the likes of Cigar Butt, Coal Oil, Bottleneck, Bullfrog, Cotterpin, Old Bear Track; Egg Yolk, Old Triphammer; Ironing Board, Melon Seed, Ice Pick, Adolph, Henrietta, Toad Stool, and Pocket Arch, along with dozens and dozens of others. These nicknames, for private use within the family, are different from the types of nicknames we've already examined, in that they are not tied to a specific trait or aspect of Rush or Russell's personality but are instead simply humorous, an expression and projection of Vic's personality.

Vic also possesses physical characteristics that allow him to stand apart as an individual, including his "heart-shaped face" as well as having the prettiest eyes in Plant No. 14 of Consolidated Kitchenware.[12] Of course, Vic was not unique in his individuality; Paul Rhymer's characters all had distinctive qualities, as well as distinctive ways of exhibiting those qualities. Consider, for example, Rush's dog, Mr. Albert R. Johnson, who, unable to bark, makes the occasional "swoosh" sounds. Despite being prone to extended periods of motionlessness, Mr. Johnson had the rather unique ability to raise his eyebrow like a human, leading Sade to note that he "looks as if he knew everything there was to know in the whole world."[13] Other characters also possess distinctive physical traits. Sade discovered in the July 1, 1940, episode that Ruthie Stembottom had been secretly wearing glasses and is now also wearing bigger shoes to hide her small feet. She does not confess this to Sade until March 4, 1941. Rush's friend, Harold "Rotten" Davis, chooses to express his individuality through unconventional and somewhat ostentatious dress that includes a fur coat, a chicken feather in his derby, and a different colored spat on each foot. He presents himself in what Sade describes as a "rude, noisy 'look at me everybody'" manner.[14]

Beyond the Gooks themselves, Paul Rhymer shows a society in which people are classified and defined by their physical traits. We see this through the mention of institutions like the Missourian State Home for the Tall, and the Ohio Home for Bald Headed Persons (later referred to as the Ohio State Home for the Bald), where an individual's most defining characteristics can be grounds for being ostracized, and where a single trait defines a person, apparently for life.

As Roger J. Williams notes, given that "brains are so different from one another, we should not be surprised that individuality in thinking is the rule rather than the exception."[15] There are numerous depictions distinguishing psychological characteristics in *Vic and Sade*, including the behavior of Mr. Sludge, the Gooks' neighbor who resides in Mis' Keller's boarding house. Sludge, we learn throughout the course of the series, is an emotionally fragile individual prone to outbursts of crying and driven by myriad fears. Although Vic regularly dismisses him as a "half-wit," Sade endeavors to be more sensitive to him, expressing the belief that, despite being forty-three years old, he is a spoiled "mama's boy" who longs to be back in Pontiac with his mother and sister. However, given Sludge's propensity for tears and his fear of everything from the dark to cars to trains, it would not be unreasonable to believe there are more complex reasons for his instability.

But perhaps no other character stands more apart from his peers and emerges as an individual than Sade's uncle, Fletcher Rush. Whether one regards Uncle Fletcher as irrepressible or indomitable, the character is almost always unyielding and unwilling to suppress any of his unique characteristics in order to better assimilate into a group. As we proceed through the remainder of this chapter, we will make frequent reference to Fletcher's distinctive brand of individuality—one that seems to reflect that of Paul Rhymer himself. The *Milwaukee Journal* declared Rhymer an "individualist" and, in a 1943 article, backed this up with some examples. He was said to have worn the same necktie every day for twenty days before using it to bind *Vic and Sade* scripts; he also once wrapped a telephone in a brown paper bag to see how fast he could get it out; and he had in his home a large statue of a muscular man in a boxing pose with a sign around his neck reading, "Hello, George."[16] Such individualized pursuits are mirrored in Fletcher's more outlandish schemes. However,

Even though, through much of the series run, listeners heard only the voices of Vic, Sade, and Rush (and later Uncle Fletcher), Paul Rhymer was able to make every off-mic character they encountered memorable by making each character a distinct individual (courtesy Mark C. Lancaster, reproduced by permission of NBC/NBC Universal PhotoBank).

before we examine these, we need to look at the other side of the coin of individuality: the community whose norms make individuality possible.

"Scream defiantly": Civic Engagement

As far back as Alexis de Tocqueville's *Democracy in America*, scholars have noted that civic engagement, often via voluntary participation in civic organizations, is an essential element in the functioning of a democratic state. As Tocqueville saw it, civic engagement leads to the creation of civic organizations, which, in turn, allow individuals the experience of participating directly in small-scale forms of self-governance, contributing directly to support for the democratic process on a larger scale. We have already examined Vic's participation in his lodge in terms of the social benefits Vic received from it; however, his lodge, like most fraternal organizations of the time, had a civic function as well, and this civic engagement helped to mediate between the individual as rugged individualist and as an integrated member of the larger community. It is through such organizations that people like Vic were able to express individuality within a framework that supported community and the broader society, but it also helped to provide platforms for individuals to use the broader community to define and project an identity, something possible only through the recognition of others.

Although Victor Gook gives the impression of being a community-minded individual, it is difficult to gauge precisely how civically engaged he was. It is true that Vic was dedicated to the fraternal organization to which he belonged, but it is not clear what, if any, role charity and volunteerism played in the lodge's activities. Based on Vic's descriptions of lodge functions, it would appear that the Sacred Stars of the Milky Way could be characterized as practicing "anti-progressive" Victorian fraternalism like that of the Masons. Like the Masons,

Vic's lodge, the Sacred Stars of the Milky Way, focused on ritual rather than charity, as did the Freemasons of the era, who placed great emphasis on ceremony and ritual spaces like this Masonic Lodge in New Bern, North Carolina, photographed in 1936 (Frances Benjamin Johnson/Library of Congress).

the Sacred Stars of the Milky Way placed an emphasis on ritualism, rather than charity. As Putney explains, "It was ritualism upon which lodge members concentrated, ritualism which provided their main source of activity."[17] Rather than presidents, leaders were "masters, monarchs, illustrious potentates, and grand illuminators"—and, presumably, big dippers, as well. This allowed members, including Vic, to exercise their desire to project self-importance and rank.

Indeed, the role of ritualism was so prevalent within the Sacred Stars of the Milky Way that the arrival of a visiting dignitary necessitated "an appropriate greeting." In the July 5, 1944, episode, for instance, Vic has Russell read to him as he hurries to meet Hunky J. Sponger:

> RUSSELL: Oh, yellow-colored messenger from celestial galaxies. Oh sweet-fingered zither player from the skies, let the hem of your garment touch my flesh. [...] Scream defiantly to the yellow stars and kick your heels in delight. Crush the crazy moon between your great white teeth and roll your eyes at the Milky Way. Stop, little brother, while the....[18]

Vic of course, could be civic-minded and had great concern for members of his community. In a 1937 episode, he takes charge of planning the town's Decoration Day parade, an event that the citizens are "looking forward to with pride and pleasure." He faces a "desperate crisis," however, when he learns that he must travel to Chicago and will not be back in time for the parade, lamenting that "when I'm gone the whole thing will be paralyzed." Of course, as much as Vic is genuinely concerned that the parade be held, he has a competing interest: the need for recognition. Despite Sade's statement, "I don't see how one measly little fella can hold up a whole city from enjoyin' their Decoration Day parade" because "all the people gotta do is line up and march to the cemetery," Vic is adamant that he is essential to the event's success. Ultimately, Vic's self-importance is dealt a savage blow when Mayor Simmons informs him that he won't be attending the parade himself, but will put a piece in the newspaper with parade instructions.[19]

Sade is decidedly less engaged in matters that do not directly impact her family and home. We've heard her dismiss talk of government as "monstrous, big talky-talk," and scoff at individuals who tried to make themselves seem intellectual by talking about such topics as the "Supreme Court," "Lincoln," "Gettysburg," and "Ulysses S. Grant."[20] While Sade may not want to converse with her friends on the Civil War, she actively refuses to take an interest in U.S. government and the law-making process.

Not surprisingly, Sade is equally resistant to Mis' Applerot's attempts to use the ladies' Thimble Club as an activist organization. When Mis' Applerot contrives the notion that the "Thimble Club ladies put on a monstrous campaign to have the city tear down the Bright Kentucky Hotel,"[21] Sade is irked, not because Mis' Applerot "button-holed" her into leading the petition drive, but also because the campaign goes against the tenants upon which the Thimble Club was founded. "Us ladies get together to sew an' chat an' have good *times*. Idea behind the organization never *was* to mix up in politics an' the government an' this, that an' the *other* thing."[22] Sade also rejects Mis' Applerot's notion that women need to be progressive, and she believes the women in the Thimble Club feel the same way: "*They* don't get together to change the world around an' stir up government an' all such axle-grease. Take ladies like Mis' Husher an' Mis' Tice. *They* don't even read the *news*paper. [...] All *they* want is a sociable afternoon."[23] Sade, like Tocqueville's individualist, places strict limits on her interactions with the broader community, selecting when and how to merge her interests with those of others.

These attitudes would soften as the 1930s gave way to the 1940s. The United States' entry into the Second World War brought about a new sense of civic responsibility, whether in the form of growing victory gardens, adhering to rationing, or buying war bonds. During the war years, citizens were encouraged to assume greater responsibility for community well-being, and the shared hardship of wartime shortages and sacrifices fostered greater community spirit. Radio played a key role in disseminating wartime propaganda, with programs being used to highlight important messages and deliver them in a palatable, easy-to-digest manner. Indeed, entertainment programming was an ideal venue for such messages to be dispersed because potential audiences would have their guard down and likely be more receptive to them. Moreover, using entertainment programs allowed audiences the opportunity to identify with favorite radio personalities and characters and, hopefully, to emulate their actions.

Fibber McGee and Molly was, perhaps, one of the most overt instruments for disseminating propaganda. The program regularly incorporated war messages into its episodes. From its first episode following the Japanese attack on Pearl Harbor, sponsor S.C. Johnson left little doubt as to their vision of the role the program would play and preceded the December 9, 1941, program with the following announcement:

> The United States is at war, we are all ready and eager to do our part. The makers of Johnson's Wax and GloCoat believe it is in the public's interest to continue programs as entertaining as *Fibber McGee and Molly*—They have a place in national morale.... We have asked the National Broadcasting Company to feel free at any time to cut into our program with important news flashes and announcements. Signed, H.S. Johnson Jr.[24]

Fibber McGee and Molly supported the war effort, but also showed the frustration the average American felt with issues like gasoline shortages and rationing, evening going so far as to have Fibber indulge in a black-market porterhouse steak during one 1943 episode, in which the McGees found themselves short of meat coupons. However, through Fibber's complaints and occasional skirting of the rules, the program was better able to convey to its listeners the reasons for wartime restrictions and the importance of complying with them.

Paul Rhymer felt that the war should not appear directly in *Vic and Sade*, and, in fact, had no role to play in the show's gentle comedy. But Richard Bellamy of the *Milwaukee Journal* reported that Rhymer "cheerfully makes room for government messages."[25] This was part of NBC's and Procter & Gamble's policy of working with the U.S. government to emphasize key themes and ideas during the war years, including the "need for all-out civilian participation." The Office of War Information asked broadcasters to emphasize such themes as "rationing, conservation, taxes, War bonds, and savings," as well as nutrition and health,[26] during the Network Allocation Plan's rotating schedule, whereby programs would produce war messages on a staggered schedule to improve domestic morale. Serials were originally expected to produce two war-related messages per month.[27] NBC employed a team of censors to ensure programs complied with wartime needs, and eventually exceeded the government's original allocation plan in the number of messages delivered. This prompted an increase in allocations after September 1942, doubling the monthly allocation for each serial.[28] The network encouraged writers to incorporate messages into programs organically, though when this wasn't possible, war messages were simply announced in mid-program in place of a commercial. For *Vic and Sade*, Procter & Gamble's OWI liaison would receive a printed sheet of required topics for the program from the OWI and would pass it along to Rhymer, who then had to incorporate the government message into his script sometime during the suggested broadcast dates.

But before the OWI even existed, radio was already coordinating with the government on an *ad hoc* basis. Prior to the U.S. entry into World War II, *Vic and Sade* began to make its contribution to the defense effort. September 9, 1941, for example, found Rush working on collecting debts from his friends so that he could purchase more defense-savings stamps, an act Sade heartily approved. "Everybody should buy as many defense-savings stamps as

Like all network programs, *Vic and Sade* supported the war efforts. During World War II, Bill Idelson (Rush), seen here in uniform in a photograph from Art Van Harvey's personal collection, served in the Navy, and Paul Rhymer added Russell (David Whitehouse, at left) to the cast (Mark C. Lancaster/The Art Van Harvey Collection).

they can," she says, adding that not only are "the Thimble ladies saving up for stamps" Sade herself is on the Defense Stamp Committee.[29] First offered in May 1941, these stamps, sold in denominations of ten cents, twenty-five cents, fifty cents, one dollar, and five dollars, were designed to be pasted into albums that could be traded in for a ten-year savings bond. This provided a way for the public to help finance the government's defense (and then the war) effort. Sade's role on the Defense Stamp Committee presented an excellent opportunity for listeners to identify with her and feel compelled to take similar action.

On June 29, 1944, we're made aware that a neighbor, Mis' Oglesby, is planning to stop by to sell war bonds. Sade explains to Vic, Russell, and Uncle Fletcher that Mis' Oglelsby is "determined to do the very best she can, but at the same time she's apprehensive she'll run into chilliness or people gettin' the notion she's prying into their private affairs."[30] Vic, however, reminds Sade that there's "some person on every block and in every city and town in the United States who's doing exactly the same thing." Mis' Oglesby's visit allows Sade to remind listeners of how daunting a task selling war bonds can be: "Mis' Oglesby has gotta visit every house on the block, friends, relations, acquaintances, and even strangers and none of them, of course, is her house, so she's at a disadvantage." The responsibility, Sade says, is not only that of the individual selling war bonds, it's "not anymore her job than it is the neighbors she visits."

The importance of the wartime recycling effort was highlighted by the unlikely alliance between Rush and Nicer Scott. In order to aid the war effort, Rush, Nicer, Vernon Pickles, and Blue-Tooth Johnson have "organized a big elaborate organization," a scrap salvage business that the boys christen the Virginia Avenue Area Sons of Patriotism Salvage Indemnity. Although Vic questions their use of the word *indemnity*, Rush feels that it has "a swing to it."[31] The episode exemplifies the effective use of radio as propaganda, for several reasons. First, it educates listeners on the particular problem, in this case the government's urgent need for scrap metal, paper, fabric, and other materials commonly found in the home. As Rush explains to his parents, "You'd be astonished at what the government is anxious to get ahold of—doorknobs, hinges, keys, locks, knives, scissors, ashtrays, roller skates, stove pokers, screwdrivers, faucets, sinks, pliers, hoses, pick axes—I could run along half an hour."[32] There was also an urgent need for paper, and for good reason. Rush impresses upon his parents and listeners just how much paper is needed for the war effort by offering memorable trivia, like

Americans from all walks of life collected scrap metal and other commodities for the war effort. These scrap parts were collected by Michigan farmers in 1942 as part of a scrap-metal drive (Ann Rosener/Library of Congress).

the fact that it takes one hundred pounds of scrap paper to make the containers for shells, or that two thousand pounds of scrap paper was needed to pack the cans of tomatoes that the Army purchased in 1941.

Rush explains that, since the government has no way to handle all of the material being collected, they will sell it to the junkman who will, in turn, sell it to manufacturers. He acknowledges that some in the neighborhood may want to take their items directly to the junkman; however, as the government has asked the public to only contact their junkman when they have a hundred or more pounds of recycling, this isn't necessarily feasible for everyone. As Rush explains, "Most everybody's got some little knickknack cluttering up their attic or cellar; trash they hate to throw away, yet trash they hate to give house room to. That kinda scrap they'll hand over quick as a wink. Glad to get rid of it and feelin' good because they know they're takin' part in something."[33] The episode also allows for a response to possible critics of those who, like Rush, are endeavoring to organize scrap drives in their neighborhood. Having listened to his son's plans, Vic ponders the fact the Virginia Avenue Area Sons of Patriotism Salvage Indemnity is going to be profiting from their efforts. He asks Rush, "Isn't that kind of mixing up financial gain with your patriotism?" Profit and patriotism do not need to be seen as mutually exclusive, as Rush suggests: "I don't know as it is, gov. Realizing a profit is somewhat of an incentive. 'Course patriotism is a great big incentive in itself, but makin' money on top of that just adds to the incentive."[34]

The fact that Rush is willing to set aside his long-standing feud with Nicer helps to bring home just how important the salvage operation is to the war effort; it also reinforces the need for listeners to do their part. In this manner, Rhymer used the long-running and established relationships of his characters to deliver more effective propaganda messages.

"Seems to me we are pretty sociable people": The Social Context of Individuality

Although the communitarian spirit of the war years found expression in *Vic and Sade*, the community was still defined by individuals and their relationship with the broader society in which they operated. While Paul Rhymer had given birth to a world in which diversity, in some form or another, and individuality thrived, there were still limits placed upon the extent to which an individual could express one's individuality. The individual on the program, just as in life, lived within a social context in which the citizens partake in collective activities that can challenge their individuality or, in some cases, serve to strengthen it.

The same year that *Vic and Sade* came on the air, these tensions between the merits of collectivism and individualism were highlighted in the 1932 presidential campaigns of President Herbert Hoover and then–New York governor, Franklin Delano Roosevelt. Throughout the campaign, Hoover emphasized the Republican belief in the importance of the American ideal of "rugged individualism," reflected in the stories Americans used to define themselves and their world. He had laid out the core of his philosophy four years earlier during his successful 1928 campaign:

> We were challenged with a peace-time choice between the American system of rugged individualism and a European philosophy of diametrically opposed doctrines—doctrines of paternalism and state socialism. The acceptance of these ideas would have meant the destruction of self-government through centralization of government. It would have meant the undermining

The contrast between the "rugged individualism" promoted by Herbert Hoover (left) and the centralization favored by Franklin Roosevelt (right), seen here riding to the Capitol for Roosevelt's inauguration, mirrored the conflict between individualism and collectivism in many aspects of American life (Library of Congress).

of individual initiative and enterprise through which our people have grown to unparalleled greatness.[35]

Hoover used his own personal story as a self-made millionaire to extoll the virtues of individualism, and, in 1928, he told a fabulous story of progress through the careful use of statistics, facts, and evidence. But as with most campaign rhetoric, the story he told America was something of an exaggeration, and the trials of the Depression had dented that image of confidence and progress. Political and cultural observers of the time related America's Jazz Age confidence to a history of storytelling and self-defining folklore "typified by Paul Bunyan-esque excess" and the wildly exaggerated humor of the American tall tale.[36] While postwar scholars would come to emphasize the role of conformity in American life, in the time of *Vic and Sade*, the ideology of individualism and its folkloric expressions, including the tall tale, still held sway.

The tradition of the tall tale was one carried on—with great prodigy—by Sade's uncle Fletcher Rush, who wove a never-ending series of tales about various individuals that he has encountered throughout his life, each peculiar in his own way. These stories demonstrate not just Uncle Fletcher's individuality, but also the non-conforming expressions among his many alleged friends and acquaintances. Rarely does the mention of a place not conjure another of Fletcher's tall tales. Vic and Sade discovered that, even though he was without a story about Monongahela River, he still has a story to tell:

> FLETCH: No, I wouldn't know anything about the Monongahela *river*, of course, but I *did* know Art and *Joe* Monongahela. They married the William J. Cunningham sisters that had the slack-wire bearded-woman bicycle act. Maybe you saw 'em in the circus?[37]

In that same episode, Fletcher claims to know Edith Susquehanna and Myrtle Susquehanna of Cedar Rapids, Iowa, prompting Vic to quip that he knows "Fred Mississippi and Ralph Rio Grande and Dorothy Swanee."[38] Later, when the White River is mentioned, Fletcher claims to know Ed and Flora White. In that same episode he tells the story of Roger Figstonker, who lived in a converted boxcar and played train, shouting "Whoo-whoo" from the roof until he thought up a scheme to break his leg and sue the city of Toledo.[39]

In January 1943, Fletcher turns up with a brown paper sack containing items that his landlady, Mis' Keller, has asked him to clear out of his room. The contents of the bag include a baby rattle, a pair of too-small socks, a handkerchief with one corner burnt, and a belt buckle from the vaudeville act the Hiwire Hayseeds with Nerves of Steel, all of which he expects Sade to return to various stores for him. After informing her that he has decided to exchange the items, he, for no discernible reason, tells the tragic yet inspiring tale of Hunter Hackfram:

> FLETCHER: Remember Hunter Hackfram there in Belvidere that was gonna eat his lunch in the dark and lighted a match and held it up close to an olive to see if it was green or ripe and went to swallow it and swallowed the match by mistake and sued the Pittsburgh, Scranton, and Southern Pennsylvania railroad for five hundred and eighteen dollars and [...] sixty cents and hired the smartest lawyer he could put his hands on to take the case and it wound up with the lawyer taking all his money and garnishing his salary and running away with his wife and....[40]

Not all of Fletcher's subjects fare quite so well. On August 13, 1943, while visiting with Sade, Fletcher is reminded of Herman McFlongalotch, who, Fletcher explains, lived in Culpepper, which "used to be in the state of Minnesota before the Mississippi changed its channel." McFlongalotch was killed when a "connection on his wife's side" drove over him with a horse and buggy. So tragic was McFlongalotch's death that "his wife cried for a week and so did the connection." This tragedy wasn't the end of Fletcher's tale; rather, it prompted him to recount his memories of the "connection," a fellow named George Chalk. According to Fletcher, Chalk "loved to tease the girls. 'If you can catch me, you can kiss me,' he'd holler."[41] Tragically for Chalk, no girl ever took him up on the challenge. George Chalk is now, Fletcher reported, dead.

Such characters were individuals—bravely or foolishly forging their own path in the face of society's demand for conformity. But the listener is asked to laugh at their foolish antics, and at Fletcher's celebration of them, as exaggerated, impractical, or bizarre. On the world stage, President Hoover had argued that the same spirit of rugged individualism that drove Americans to settle the West, not government interventionism, was needed for the nation to recover from the Great Depression. But the horrors of the Great Depression, combined with the sweeping reforms of the New Deal and an emphasis on collectivism, brought about a change in the collective American psyche. Once perceived as "outgoing, optimistic, and self-confident," the American character was transformed to one marked by "timidity, conformity, and uncertainty as to personal identity." In such a climate, it is no wonder that dramatic expressions of confident individuality, like those of Uncle Fletcher and his acquaintances, created a tension that Paul Rhymer could resolve through laughter. As figures of jest, the extremes of individualism could be safely contained.[42]

Don Martindale contends that, despite having experienced panics before, no prior crisis rivaled the intensity of the Great Depression, not just because of the scope of the hardships that it inflicted, but also because of its timing. America had not long since "lost its international innocence" in World War I, and had "set irreversibly on a course toward large-scale industrialization and urbanism that no longer provided the symbol and reality of escape to the frontier."[43] Moreover, for the many Americans who were willing to work, but unable to find any, the Depression was a devastating blow to their confidence; "even the most arrogant symbols of government-defying rugged individualism, the business entrepreneurs, were brought to heel."[44] The personal security of the once-rugged individual was increasingly intertwined with those of the collective due, in part, to the rise of government agencies and organizations, as well as unions and other groups.

Philosopher John Dewey painted a rather bleak portrait of American individualism in which Americans were lost amid a "vast complex of associations," devoid of harmony or coherent reflection of their importance.[45] Indeed, despite the fact that the Gooks do have genuine associations with friends and neighbors, the November 15, 1941, episode helps to illustrate the way in which one could find oneself part of the "vast complex of associations" and obligations of which Dewey speaks. Sade confronts Vic about the number of people for whom he is planning to purchase Christmas gifts. Although he claims to have a "firm bond of friendship" with each person on the list, Sade's interrogation reveals that he has never even met some of them and has only the most tenuous of associations with others. Among the twenty individuals included on Vic's list is L. Wiley Fap from Consolidated Kitchenware Plant No. 17 in Dubuque, Iowa, who once bought Vic a chocolate bar and sent him a necktie for Christmas. Also included on Vic's list is U. F. Beekly, Exalted Big Dipper of the Purple Prairie Puppenjay Chapter of the Sacred Stars of the Milky Way, who, according to Vic, also once sent him a necktie. Although Vic maintains that those on his list are friends, he also makes it clear that "a businessman has many more obligations,"[46] thus suggesting that his intentions may be motivated by more than friendship alone.

Perhaps an even clearer illustration of Dewey's "vast network of associations" can be found in a conversation that Rush recounts having had with Nicer Scott. Nicer, Rush informs Vic, has determined that he enjoys a "speaking acquaintance" with 655,921 people, a figure that Vic insists is more than "twenty times larger than the figure representing the whole population of this city" and the combined population of in Peoria, Rockford, Moline, Springfield, and Decatur.[47] Nicer would later claim that this figure had grown to 2,108,697,483. Yet while Nicer claims to have such an extensive line of acquaintances, the loss of genuine association is highlighted when Sade learns that her friends Ruthie Stembottom and Mis' Harris have never actually met or spoken with one another, despite both having been Sade's friends for many years. Individuals could now claim many friends and acquaintances, but much less community. Relationships occurred increasingly in isolation due to lives that were compartmentalized and organized by outside forces, such as work, school, and organizations.

The mediating effects of organized and centralized social organizations caught the attention of theorists of the era. According to Dewey, writing in the immediate aftermath of the 1929 market crash, American individualism was now marked by the absence of critical thinking and an overriding goal of homogeny, in which the individual is submerged in a corporate civilization where loyalties that once provided strength and support have disappeared, leaving the individual "confused and bewildered."[48] Sade expresses this type of confusion when considering that her friends are strangers to each other. Dewey argued that a new individualism had come to pass, one that was the result of "definite social relationships and publicly acknowledged functions,"[49] much as Vic defined friends not by those with whom he shared intimate connections but with those he shared financial and organizational ties. Dewey's "new" individualism is, to all intents and purposes, was a type of communitarianism in which organizations, particularly the government and corporations, mediated and defined the individual experience—something the New Deal would bring to flower.

The Individual and the Collective

"Modern life," R. F. Swift wrote in 1926, "has become a great experiment in carrying out Callicles' ideal of the free development of giant desires and the use of knowledge to gain power over nature in order to satisfy them."[50] Given such challenges, individuals must rely upon the community in order to achieve their goals. To Swift, the forces of individualism are at odds with the community's ability to help the individual achieve a happy life. Throughout *Vic and Sade*, we are able to witness the positive association that exists between the individual and the collective, those instances in which the individual gains through his or her associations with a role in the collective, or the way one's role in a group or organization serves to strengthen that person's individualism.

Life, of course, can be difficult, and every individual needs a means of making life's challenges more bearable. This is the role of the community, according to Swift. Claiming it to be the original unit of human community, Swift, like Aristotle and others before him, believes that people can only achieve a good life and find happiness through their participation in community functions. However, *Vic and Sade* also depicts the other side of the coin, highlighting the ways a community can hinder the individual, suppressing their distinctive characteristics and forcing them to conform to standards with which they are in conflict.

Vic's associations through both his employment and his membership in the Sacred Stars of the Milky Way offer good insight into the positive role that the collective can play. As we've previously discussed, Vic's work for Consolidated Kitchenware, and his membership in the Sacred Stars of the Milky Way, provide him with both camaraderie and the opportunity to distinguish himself from those within each group as well as outsiders. Both Consolidated Kitchenware and the Sacred Stars of the Milky Way provide Vic with a community to which he belongs. He is able, in each organization, to form meaningful associations with other individuals, working together and aiding one another in a communal purpose. Each community is extended through the use of, respectively, *Kitchenware Dealers' Quarterly* and the lodge newsletter. Through his work and his participation in the Sacred Stars of the Milky Way, Vic has gained friendships and participated in activities that have enriched his life and made it generally more tolerable—even if Rhymer gently satirizes this by emphasizing the transitory and partial community feeling such friendships generate.

Although the extensions of these communities threaten to create the sort of vast complexes of meaningless associations described by Dewey, they also offer the potential for solid relationships. On May 1, 1944, Vic received news from lodge headquarters that the Skybrothers would be "traveling all over the country," and that they hoped to stay with their fellow Skybrothers rather than paying for a hotel. Not surprisingly, Sade protests, saying, "I wouldn't want complete strangers dropping in on me unexpected"; however, Vic is quick to point out that, as they are part of the same community, "Lodge brothers of Sacred Stars of the Milky Way do not regard each other as complete strangers."[51] Although the motivation for this plan was to save the lodge members money, it does provide the opportunity for building meaningful associations.

Vic's position within Consolidated Kitchenware and his role a Big Dipper of the Drowsy Venus Chapter of the Sacred Stars of the Milky Way allow him status in both the fraternal organization and the community at large. Membership in the Sacred Stars of the Milky Way is selective, and one's interest in or application to the lodge does not guarantee membership. A potential Skybrother must be "sponsored and vouched for and everything else" to even be considered for membership. As Vic once explained, when he applied to join the lodge, "My character had to be investigated; my past life had to be studied, six substantial citizens of the community had to vouch for me."[52] We have seen that Vic is adorned with particular ceremonial ephemera unique to his position; he participates in the lodge marching band; and he is featured in the lodge publication, all of which help to enhance his sense of identity. But, as if in reaction to Swift's notion that the individual is isolated from a sense of true community, the seemingly communal task of belonging to the lodge marching teams, to cite but one example, becomes an exercise in isolation.

Victor Gook appears to have gotten his first taste of marching on Labor Day of 1934. On that particular occasion it was Sade who wanted to attend a parade while Vic argued in favor of a family fishing excursion to Kickapoo Creek, declaring, "What better parade than the parade of the lofty oak trees? What better people than the simple citizens of the forest ... the rabbits, the squirrels, and the birds?"[53] Even the fact that the legion band will be marching in new uniforms, with some members on horseback, fails to sway Vic, who counters, "Personally, I feel I've out-*grown* parades. For real, full-bodied, *adult* pleasure, give me *simple* things every time."[54] It is not until Vic receives a call, asking him to replace the marching band's drummer who has fallen ill, that he relents and not only attends, but participates in the parade.

The All-Star Marching Team of the Sacred Stars of the Milky Way is, as one might expect, unique in several respects, beginning with the fact that its members, or the majority of them, must practice marching solo. Because the ten members of the All-Star Team were "scattered all over the country, making it impracticable from a financial point of view for you to get together for practice sessions, we have devised the following plan: You will practice your marching separately."[55] Members of the marching team were required to train themselves to "march at the rate of one stride every three and four-sixteenths seconds."[56] The members were, then, part of a collective with strict rules, while at the same time working as individuals in a manner that would lead them to be singled out from the community as a whole. The group had the form of a community, but its members were isolated and not actually interacting.

On the other hand, Sade's ladies' Thimble Club met in person, thereby offering more opportunities for deeper levels of interaction. Although the Thimble Club appeared to promote conformity far more than it actually achieved, Sade's membership and role in the club still distinguished her from non-members. The exclusive nature of the club was on full display on January 1, 1941, when Mis' Applerot proposes admitting new members—a proposal so shocking that there were gasps—one Thimble Club lady even dropped her purse. Such proposals are shocking because the organization becomes a community, one which stands apart from the larger society. This concept had been suggested by Swift fifteen years earlier, when he described the way Americans withdrew from society in favor of small-scale organizations that could replicate what he imagined to be the "primitive" fellowship of ancient city-states.[57] Part of maintaining community within a community involved keeping outsiders out in order to define its membership. In turn, this placed limits on a member's ability to express individuality without risking his or her status in the group.

"A whole list of fellas like you": Obstacles to Individualism

For every opportunity the lodge provided that bolstered Vic's individualism, there were an equal number that, in some way, stifled it. Typically, these instances were predicated on Vic having received an honor or some form of recognition that he believed distinguished him from his fellow Skybrothers and the public at large, thus making matters all the worse for him when he inevitably came to the conclusion that he had been duped.

One such instance took place on October 4, 1937, when Vic receives a letter informing him that he been appointed Stationery Scribe and Contributing Editorial Factotum to the lodge's official publication, *The Sacred Star Searchlight*. While Vic perceives his new position as a "title of honor," Sade rather pragmatically notes that it is a job without a salary; however, Vic remains adamant about the significance of the appointment until Sade makes a disappointing discovery while examining the editorial staff listing in an issue of *Searchlight*: "Hey, there's a whole list of fellas like you."[58] Under the heading, "Registry of Stationery Scribe and Contributing Editorial Factotums," is indeed a sizable list, leaving Vic deflated. On another occasion, individual photographs of members of the all-star marching team were to be featured in the latest issue of the lodge magazine. Again, Vic is excited at being recognized as part of what he considers an elite group, and at the prospect of being distinguished from his peers. However, once again Vic is left devalued and disappointed as the photo spread fails to distinguish anyone. Instead, the magazine has published pictures that appear to have little or nothing to do with the All-Star Marching Team. Among the photos were pictures of a little boy, a bicycle, and an old lady.

The lodge did, of course, recognize its members' need to stand out and be recognized as individuals and sought, for a profit, to provide them with the means to do this, even if those members seeking recognition didn't deserve it. One rather disingenuous approach taken by the lodge was a scheme that gave members a "sort of intangible commodity" in the form of honorary titles for sale. For thirty-five cents one could distinguish himself by claiming the title "Member of the Board of Directors of the Salt Lake City, Southwestern Montana, and Pacific Deadline Railroad"; while, for an additional eighty-five cents, one could assume the title of "Ex-Monarch of Preshuna and Bascadrill," which are islands in the Caribbean.

For those more inclined see themselves ensconced in an ivory tower, $1.20 could buy the title "Lifetime Honorary President of the Tom Bashaw College for Young Women" in Dismal Seepage, Ohio.[59]

Given that the titles carried with them a certain "impressiveness" and "glamor" that could be an asset in "modern business and progressive civilization," it only stands to reason that the more contrived a title was, the more glamorous and impressive it could seem; thus, something like "Member of the High Board of Executive Inactive Preemptor, Two Crosses, a Flume, and a Garter Without Portfolio for Colitionary Interstate Trusteeship Between Main and Nebraska, Kentucky and Minnesota, Indiana, and Texas Without Recourse or Recall and Unconditionally Vetoed Notwithstanding" would seem a terrific bargain at only ten cents. Such titles did more than simply set apart the individual from the masses; they also appropriated for their bearers something of the authority of the academic, political, and social elitism to which purchasers aspired. Boards of directors and trustees are business professionals of high rank, while the president of a college held a special place, not just as a ranking executive but also a person of academic accomplishment. (This is akin to U.S. president Woodrow Wilson, who had been president of Princeton University before moving on

Public opinion of occupations granting high social prestige remained remarkably steady from 1925 to 1947. Here we see the holders of several prestigious positions in 1925, including (from left to right) Food Administration official T.F. Whitmarsh, AT&T vice-president Gen. J.J. Carty; Stanford University scientist C.L. Alsberg; and Secretary of Commerce Herbert Hoover. Business, government, and academic posts all ranked high in lists of occupational prestige (Library of Congress).

to the governor's mansion and, ultimately, the White House.) In fact, the titles the lodge sold its members correlate quite well with academic findings from surveys conducted between 1925 and 1947 about the occupations that individuals ranked as the most prestigious and, thus, the most desirable. Among these were government officials, members of boards of directors, and those involved in higher education—and this was despite the fact that, like the made-up titles of Vic's lodge, most members of the public were at a loss to actually describe the duties of many prestigious occupations, for prestige was associated with social rank and importance, not with the actual position. "Thus, it appears that respondents are willing to evaluate occupations without a clear and well-defined idea of the duties involved in their performance."[60] For Vic's lodge, such forces contribute to a market for fake titles, which many would be unable to differentiate from the real thing.

For most, there is a limit to which they can express their individuality before incurring some form of consequence that impacts their status within the broader community. Smelly Clark discovered this for himself during an incident that left Rush "impressed as a horse." While gathered at the curb of Kelsey Street with Nicer, Leeland, Blue-Tooth, Leroy, and Rush, Smelly delivered an unusual address to his peers. Standing bareheaded before his friends, he announced:

> Fellas, you all know me, I am Smelly Clark.... I have been checking up on myself and I wish to tell you I am deeply gratified with my discoveries. [...] I have become smarter, taller, nobler, richer and better lookin.' If I were to pass away in the next five minutes, I believe it could be truthfully said that the world was better for my having lived. [...] When people come up to me on the street and tell me I'm wonderful, I wave my hand carelessly and remark, "Let time tell the story." [...] Fellas, I am strong. I am smart. I am good lookin'. I am patriotic. I am brave. I am gentle. I am kind. I am generous....[61]

Rush is in awe of "how much courage" it took for Smelly to stand before an audience of "tough monkeys" and deliver such an address. Much to Rush's surprise, those gathered refrained from cutting Smelly "into small pieces" and, instead, listened attentively to his proclamation. As just stated, there are limitations on the degree to which one can defy social norms without alienating a given group and, as Rush correctly observed, Smelly's time "had to end sometime." For Smelly, the end came when Leeland Richards lunged at his legs and Rush and the others proceeded to take Smelly's shoes and throw them onto the roof of a house. Meanwhile, Blue-Tooth Johnson took a handful of mud and applied it to Smelly's face; and Nicer relieved him of his belt, hat, and necktie. With these actions, Smelly's friends terminated his exercise in individuality and restored his place in the group. Such a reaction echoes the then-dominant psychological views of Sigmund Freud, whose essay "On Narcissism" helped to popularize the concept, which Otto Rank had defined as excessive vanity in 1911. Just two years before Smelly's speech, philosopher Martin Buber's influential 1923 book, *Ich und Du*, was translated into English as *I and Thou*, and described ideal relationships in which the individual relates to others as equals, and less-than-ideal relationships where the narcissist treats others as objects serving to inflate his own ego. Smelly, being the latter, experiences rejection from his peer group, who do not see themselves as objects in the pageant of his life. In making his egocentric speech without consideration for his friends' feelings, Smelly defies the unspoken assumption that Americans are to think of themselves as equals, and this rupture of norms yields anger.

There are times when conforming is essential to one's ability to achieve one's own goals. As the principal of Rush's high school, Mr. Chinbunny, has discovered the peril of nonconformist behavior and has, subsequently, endeavored to conform to the expectations that others within the school administration have on an individual in his position. When his picture appeared in the newspaper, Mr. Chinbunny was "bawled out" by the board of education, who deemed that it was an "undignified thing for the principal of a high school to engage in cheap and frivolous newspaper stunts."[62] Chinbunny's scolding from the board came hot on the heels of Mis' Adams, the commercial geography teacher, being dismissed for wearing too much jewelry and failing to heed the board's warnings. As a principal, Mr. Chinbunny must conform, not only to the professional standards necessitated by his position, but also to the image associated with it. Despite holding a Ph.D., Chinbunny is "very, very young to be principal of a big high school." As such, he takes numerous steps to conform to the image of the stereotypical high school principal, including "wearing spectacles he don't need," shaving a bald spot in his head, maintaining a "stern expression on his face," and asking Vic to teach him how to smoke cigars.[63] At one point, Rush even offers the startling revelation that "Mr. Chinbunny is suspected of wearing artificial side-burns," another desperate act to conform to the board's image of what a principal should be.[64] Chinbunny's situation was not dissimilar to that faced by Smelly Clark, who, upon leaving school at fifteen, found it difficult to find substantive work. He then attempted to change his age to twenty-one in order to be eligible to obtain a barber's license. Social stigmas and stereotypes thus induced concomitant efforts to conform in external presentation in order to realize broader goals individuals sought within a social context.

The notion of conforming to the ideas and ideals of another was not limited to the lone individual seeking to find career success; there were also occasions in which groups, consisting of individuals conforming to that group's standards, would themselves need to conform to the expectations of others. The Sacred Stars of the Milky Way, for example, required their members have their robes altered to meet the 1944 trends in fraternal regalia-wear, including the requirement that robes be three inches shorter, and raising the waistline to give the Skybrother "the attractively demure peach-squeezer effect so much en vogue."[65] The sleeves needed to be fuller and could include rosettes at the wrists and peek-a-boo shoulder vents and, finally, fashion dictated balloon shoulders to follow 1944 fashion trends.

While conforming could give one an aesthetically pleasing and highly fashionable lodge robe, it could also lead one to feel as though they had abandoned their principles. This, in turn, could make one feel inferior and, perhaps worse still, an individual may feel as though he has denied who he really is. Sade experienced such feelings when she allowed herself to be pushed into rearranging her furniture in the "latest style living room for the year 1940" by Mis' Applerot. Sade confesses, "I acted like a silly, dumb sheep and followed crazy orders exactly like I was told," even though she didn't want her furniture moved.[66] The fact that Rush could see that Sade had been crying indicates just how deeply Sade resented giving into Mis' Applerot's orders, but also how powerful the urge is to fit in with the expectations of others.

Uncle Fletcher Rush: The Not-So-Rugged Individual

Perhaps more than any of Paul Rhymer's other characters, Sade's uncle Fletcher Rush best embodies the nonconformist spirit. In his sixty-five–plus years Fletcher Rush amassed a dizzying array of acquaintances, individuals with whom he is familiar to varying degrees, but with whom he shares no bond of friendship. Fletcher calls upon these individuals and their life experiences for anecdotal material, but did so without sentiment. Whether Fletcher's non-sequitur approach was the result of age, a deep underlying eccentricity, or a desire to avoid listening to those around him, his sense of recall is nothing short of remarkable. As heard in these frequent excursions into the irrelevant, Fletcher seems oblivious to social standards and expectations. Although he cares for his family and friends, he is often unaware of their feelings, or the way in which his actions impact them. When he decides to take a 6:40 a.m. train to Dixon, he thought nothing of dropping by the Gooks' house at 5:30 a.m., and was oblivious to the fact that he had disturbed their slumber:

> FLETCHER: Glorious day, Vic.
> VIC: [*WITHOUT WARMTH*] Yeah. [*SIGNIFICANTLY*] What *time* is it?
> FLETCHER: *Yes*. I look for the thermometer to hit around eighty or so by *noon*.
> VIC: [*WITHOUT WARMTH*] That's just dandy.[67]

As is illustrated by this exchange, Fletcher's impaired hearing enables him to ignore social norms—or at least their ramifications. He also knew how to use his eccentricities to achieve desired results. On December 21, 1942, Fletcher promised to accompany Sade and Ruthie Stembottom on their downtown shopping excursion. However, Uncle Fletcher became preoccupied with the act of switching his shoelaces from the left foot to the right, while the women waited with growing impatience. As one might imagine, the "trick" of switching shoelaces had its origins in a tall tale, this one about a man named Harry Williamson, a "Belvedere fella. He married Dorothy Ratsimple when she was twenty-nine years old, taught her to read and write, and got her a job in a feed store. Harry used to attract considerable attention around Belvedere because of his habit of walking a block and crawling a block."[68]

Fletcher's attempt to switch his shoelaces are hampered by a broken aglet and his need to regale Vic with the story of Harry Williamson's brother Herbert and his wedding to Stella Gushpop. After the ceremony, the groom's father attempted to borrow from the minister the five dollars he had just paid him to conduct the service. As Sade grows increasingly impatient, Fletcher continues with his tall tales until, finally, Ruthie calls to inform Sade that she can wait no longer and is heading downtown by herself. Not surprisingly, Fletcher is unfazed when Sade announces that she and Ruthie are leaving without him. As Vic observes with a chuckle, "Uncle Fletcher is avvery [*sic*] deliberate guy."[69] He has managed to get out of an onerous task without ever formally backing out of his promise.

But because he was often absorbed in his own individuality, Uncle Fletcher frequently failed to appreciate the way in which his rather unique behaviors affected those around him. On January 15, 1943, Uncle Fletcher appears with "another monstrous box of stuff," prompting Sade to astutely observe:

> SADE: (Giggles) No, but *you* know:—he demands your strict attention when he's trottin' out them souvenirs an' momentoes [*sic*] of his, an' he don't half listen to any question ya ask him an' he'll tell the same story over an' over till....[70]

It was an not-infrequent occurrence that Uncle Fletcher would monopolize conversations, hijack activities, or otherwise inconvenience those on the receiving end of his whims. On one occasion, he was brandishing mementoes collected from Mr. Gumpox's so-called "Christmas Harvest." Seeing her uncle's collection, Sade sheepishly confesses, "I got caught in my little wickedness of tryin' to escape."[71] Among the "treasures" Uncle Fletcher proudly displays, on behalf of his friend, are a tie with a portrait of Death Valley painted on it; a postcard of cows eating grass in Corning, Arkansas; suspenders with no elastic; a rock that Fletcher claims is fossilized candy; a fancy lady's comb; and a tea cup with the inscription,

"Doris, Doris, drink your milk."[72] While this was useless to society at large, to Fletcher these items held not just meaning but value; he chose to see the world in a unique way and to applied his individual perspective to the material objects others overlooked. Nevertheless, as far as Sade was concerned, this was a box of trash he had brought into her home.

Fletcher's rather eccentric behavior was not limited to his relationships with his family and immediate social network. Just as Vic was offered titles from his lodge designed to appropriate the prestige of high-status professions, Fletcher assumed for himself some of the borrowed authority of law enforcement. On August 13, 1943, Fletcher relates that Mayor Greetchum has given him a badge, which he keeps in his pocket so as to better surprise "your criminal, murderer, traffic violator, and thief."[73] Despite having been "deputized," Fletcher has neither a revolver nor handcuffs, and, when pressed, reveals that as "deputy" he has one duty, to tell people to stand back, to "give 'em air" when someone faints, gets into an argument, or can't pay a bill.

> FLETCHER: In fact, when Mayor Greetchum appointed me Special Deputy this morning he told me that was my one and only duty, and as far as he knew I was the only man in the United States that *had* that one and only duty.[74]

With the above statement, Fletcher is quite literally marking himself as an individual, as separate from others. He is also essentially play-acting, using a very minor position to imply a connection with a broader organization that he does not actually serve in a significant way. In this, he is not really very different from the lodge members buying fictional academic titles.

Among his many attributes, Fletcher displays a strong entrepreneurial spirit and an apparent belief in capitalism, one that was indicative of America before the Great Depression. He has, for instance, a financial interest in the peanut machine at the Interurban Railroads station. He also works with Roy Dejectedly and Pete Upbleat on Hyena Grease, the "finest preparation for smearing on your shoes that there is in the entire civilized world."[75] This highly touted product is a combination of lamp black, turpentine, creosol, and tractor oil. Fletcher had plans to begin selling stingerberry jam, which "churns and writhes and crawls and breathes," for B.B. Baugh, within three to five years.[76] Fletcher is, however, sorely lacking in one of the traits essential to the pre–Depression Hoover-style rugged individualism: self-sufficiency. Although he believes that he can do anything and often does whatever he pleases, he is, in fact, highly reliant upon others. His choice of vacation destinations, for example, reflects his reliance upon his family. After staying at Hank Gutstop's and feeding his fish and puppy dog while he is away, Fletcher decides to take a respite at the Gooks' house. As he explains to Vic, occupying Hank Gutstop's hotel room for two weeks had taken a toll on him: "A man can't turn himself into no machine. Flesh and blood, you know, flesh and blood, flesh and blood." He now plans to give "body and brain a chance to mend."[77] As always, oblivious to the feelings of others (or pretending to be so), and enjoying the recuperative powers of vacationing three blocks from his own home, he decides to extend his stay with Vic and Sade, much to their dismay.

Fletcher's dependence and lack of self-reliance is a fact of which his landlady, Mis' Keller, is sorely aware. When she is planning to be away for five days she lays out his breakfast and dinner for each of the days that she will be away, and leaves instructions to eat his supper each day at a diner so that he can have a hot meal. Fletcher is offended by the act and plans to move in with Vic and Sade, exclaiming, "Mis' Keller treats me like I'm a *child*. I can fix my own meals; I don't have to have my meals scattered all over the premises like anthracite coal."[78] Sade, however, explains that Mis' Keller was apprehensive that he might get into trouble with sharp knives, gas from the stove, or possibly leaving the icebox open. Ultimately, Fletcher relents and agrees to stay at Mis' Keller's. Before taking his leave, he insists on kicking down the Gooks' front porch, which he believes needs to come down, so that Mr. Erickson can replace it. He also makes sure to do this in front of Mis' Keller, so that she can see that he is a violent man. In such actions, Fletcher reveals that his individuality is as much a performance as a genuine trait, a covering that masks his own anxiety about his reliance on others as he grows older and more dependent. Eccentricity allows Fletcher to project emotionally and socially a type of power to control his environment.

In the world of Vic and Sade, the tensions between individual and community, between personal expression and conformity, and between freedom and status, are never fully resolved. Instead, each character tries to navigate between the Scylla of individuality and the Charybdis of conformity, seeking to develop identity and autonomy within a world where mass culture and social pressures had created powerful challenges to traditional ideas of the role of the individual and the community. Paul Rhymer expertly employed humor to highlight some of these tensions, using laughter to explore the way ordinary people lived in the United States during a time of intense challenge, crisis, and change.

Conclusion: Saying Goodbye

On September 24, 1944, Vic, Sade, Russell, and Uncle Fletcher all prepared to depart from the small house halfway up in the next block, each for different locations. Everyone was dressed in in their good clothes and looked "bright eyed and eager" as they prepared to depart for their respective locations. Russell is off for an "invigorating evening watching the fat men play handball," while Vic prepares for a "jolly" lodge meeting, and Sade is off for a movie and ice cream with Mis' Kilgour and Mis' Trogel. Fletcher, meanwhile, is headed off to the railway station to spend some time with the peanut machine before proceeding to the Butler House Hotel to listen to the drummers talk politics.

This was to be the last time that the Gooks would be assembled together on daytime radio. With little fanfare, *Vic and Sade* had been canceled after twelve years. In what was expected to be the final episode, Paul Rhymer offered a rather transparent, albeit pleasant, metaphor.

SADE: We're all goin' in different directions.
FLETCHER: Is that a fact?
RUSSELL: Mom's goin' north, I'm goin' east, Gov's south and you're goin' west.
FLETCHER: All different directions, by George.
SADE: Uh-huh. We're all going downtown. We're all going to the same place.
FLETCHER: Yes, we're all going to the same place, and we'll see each other again.
SADE: Sure, we'll see each other again.
VIC: No doubt about it.
RUSSELL: Well, let's go.
SADE: Yes, let's go.
VIC: Goodbye.
SADE: Goodbye.
RUSSELL: Goodbye.
FLETCHER: Goodbye.[1]

As it happens, it wasn't really time for goodbyes—at least not quite yet. On August 21, 1945, it returned to the air, this time as part of the CBS evening lineup. The new airtime, however, was the least of the changes listeners discovered when *Vic and Sade* returned. The voices of characters whom audiences had once only heard about could now be heard. Yet, while these formerly off-mic characters had been brought so vividly to life in the conversations of Vic, Sade, Rush, Russell, and Uncle Fletcher, their on-air presence seemed, for the most part, oddly listless and often forced. Rhymer himself described the changes as having the program "needled up and revised somewhat," but "basically the same."² The addition of Mis' Harris, Mr. Sprawl, Vernon and Edith Korkle, Orville Wheenie, and the gimmicky Dwight Twentysixler (who spoke with his mouth full of shingle nails), as well as an array of others, detracted from the subtle humor that had been prevalent throughout the show's run. Once startlingly original, *Vic and Sade* now began to sound like a 15-minute impersonation of *Fibber McGee and Molly*, with the Gooks serving as host to a parade of improbable characters and situations.

By December 7, 1945, *Vic and Sade* had left the air once again, only to return six months later, on June 27, 1946, this time airing as a thirty-minute summer replacement for *Fibber McGee and Molly*, complete with a live studio audience. The expanded format, combined with the need to play for a live audience, seemed only to further detract from the program's original whimsy and wonder. Despite the proclamation of Ben Gross of the *New York Daily News* that *Vic and Sade*'s return was "out of this world,"³ the myriad voices, audience reactions, musical punctuations, and drawn-out stories somehow managed to dwarf the magic that had been *Vic and Sade*, shifting the emphasis from humorous storytelling to outlandish antics. Following the stint as *Fibber McGee and Molly*'s summer replacement the program had one last radio revival, again airing once weekly for thirty minutes, this time lasting until June 30, 1947, one day after *Vic and Sade*'s fifteenth anniversary.

Given that a number of radio favorites, including *One Man's Family*, *The Guiding Light*, *The Goldbergs*, and *Gunsmoke* were, with varying degrees of success, finding new life on television, so it is hardly surprising that there was also an effort to reintroduce audience to the Gooks via the dominant new medium. The first of these attempts took place in July 1949, with three episodes of *Vic and Sade* appearing in Monday evening's time slot of NBC's *Colgate Comedy Hour*, where the sponsor had been experimenting with various TV pilots under the series' umbrella.⁴ For the new production, only Bernadine Flynn reprised her role. Dick Conan assumed the role of Rush, and Frank Dane took over the part of Vic, as Art Van Harvey's health issues did not permit him to take the role.⁵ Produced by Norman Felton and written by Paul Rhymer, the three episodes found the family taking on three boarders, Mrs. Call and Mr. and Mrs. Starbright, new characters created for the television adaptation, and pitted Vic against friendly rival Ike Kneesuffer. Although there had been hope for a fall run for *Vic and Sade*, Colgate and NBC elected not to move forward with the show after reviewers called the program a "disappointment" and complained that Paul Rhymer, forgetting television is a visual medium, didn't "have much comical action." The commercials delivered by Sade, however, were apparently very entertaining.⁶ Studs Terkel attended a broadcast, and he poached one of the show's supporting actresses, Beverly Younger, for his own show, *Studs' Place*.⁷

Almost a decade later, Bernadine Flynn and Art Van Harvey were reunited for a new TV adaptation called *The Humor of Vic and Sade*, in which they appeared with Eddie Gillian in the role of Rush. These fifteen-minute episodes, broadcast in color on Thursday nights in early 1957, but only locally on Chicago station WNBQ,⁸ hark back to simpler times, before a cavalcade of additional voices dominated the series and emphasized the dynamics between the three characters and the humor of Paul Rhymer's writing. However, as refreshing as this sparse approach may have been to fans, the staging, which simply featured the three actors seated, reading from their scripts, was perhaps too sparse for a medium that emphasized visual excitement and interest. The program ended after seven weeks, closing out the last *Vic and Sade* adaptation, just shy of the show's twenty-fifth anniversary.

"We're all goin' in different directions"

In the end, as one would expect, Vic, Sade, Rush, Russell, Fletcher, and Paul Rhymer did each go their own way. Paul Rhymer continued writing freelance magazine articles and book reviews. He also penned *The Public Life of Cliff Norton*, a series of five-minute comedy sketches for "deadpan satirist and song and dance man" Cliff Norton, which aired as part of the *Dave Garraway at Large* program on NBC. The sketches typically consisted of the "inexpert expert" demonstrating his incompetence in a variety of areas.[9] In a treatment of the May 11, 1950, episode, Rhymer describes the scene:

> Here, with rod and reel, Cliff will expertize about the wonderful sport of fishing. He will remark the limberness of the rod, the nice sound of the reel, the importance of the bait and he'll show a gigantic hook and the habits of the fish (they like water). A cast of two will get the reel tangled. He untangles the reel and makes a last cast. As he reels in, the camera closes in on him. He notices this strange fact. Now he unreels a few feet and the camera backs away. Last of all, with a rather grim expression on his face, he reels in the line. The camera goes all the way in on him. His face registers pleasure. He's caught a big one: us.[10]

Other sketches found Norton teaching viewers how to place a telephone call, how to plan a delightful train outing, and demonstrating a breakfast-in-bed machine. This Rube Goldberg–like contraption delivered orange juice, eggs, coffee, and oatmeal with a tug on various ropes and pulleys, ending with each item dumped on Norton.

On October 26, 1964, Paul Rhymer was scheduled to appear on NBC's *Today* show but was instead taken to Chicago's Pleasantville Hospital, where he telephoned Clarence Hartzell and asked him to fill in for him on the program. It is said that Rhymer watched Hartzell's appearance from his hospital room. He died later that day.

In addition to appearing in the televised adaptations of *Vic and Sade*, Bernadine Flynn also took to the stage, including a touring production of Walter Huston's *Apple of His Eye* as the "shrewish neighbor."[11] *Apple of His Eye* marked a return to the stage for Flynn, who had appeared in several successful Broadway productions prior to joining *Vic and Sade*, including *Seven Year Love*, *Strictly Dishonorable*, and *Strange Interlude*.[12]

Flynn was also reunited, once again, with Art Van Harvey in the 1950s television serial *Hawkins Falls, Population 6,200*. The series, considered to be one of the first successful television soap operas, depicted life in small-town U.S.A. as it took place in Hawkins Falls, a small Midwestern town. Flynn's character, Lona Drewer Carey, was often at the center of activity. The series began in the summer of 1950 as an unusual mixture of comedy, drama, and music, narrated by the town newspaper editor. It was later retooled as a straight daytime soap opera when it returned in 1951, remaining on the air until 1955.[13] Bernadine Flynn retired from acting in 1957 following the second attempt at bringing *Vic and Sade* to television. She died on March 10, 1977, in her mother's home town of Clay City, Illinois.

In addition to appearing in *Hawkins Falls* as the town pharmacist, Calvin Sperry, Art Van Harvey played the role of Father Maguire in the 1950 motion picture *The Golden Gloves Story*. He spent some of his last months working with co-star Bernadine Flynn on the final *Vic and Sade* revival. Noticeably ill during the run of the show, he died only a few months after the final telecast, passing away on July 7, 1957.

Despite the image one might have of him based upon his performance as Uncle Fletcher, Clarence Hartzell was only thirty-seven years old when *Vic and Sade* finally ended. Hartzell went on to perform in a number radio and television series, including a stint as cousin Jediah

X. Barbour on *One Man's Family*. Due to negative audience reaction, show creator Carlton E. Morse wrote him out of the show.[14] He began working on radio's *Those Websters* not long after *Vic and Sade*'s first cancellation, in 1944. Beginning in November 1946, he assumed the role of absent-minded veterinarian Dr. Benjamin Franklin Withers on the popular *Lum 'n' Abner* series. Withers, who has been described as "a half-deaf, slightly senile old duffer who delighted in repeated stories about a seemingly endless parade of old cronies," bore more than a passing resemblance to Fletcher Rush.[15] Shortly after being introduced to the series, Withers's character was rewritten as a constable in order to appease the objections of sponsor Miles Laboratories, makers of One-A-Day vitamins and Alka-Seltzer, who were at the time attempting to launch a veterinary supply business and objected to Hartzell's portrayal of the incompetent vet.[16]

Hartzell's other credits included the 1952 NBC summer replacement series *Those Endearing Young Charms* about a "cheerful family" who ran its own mail-order business. The show's pilot was broadcast live a mere six days after NBC created the show and ordered its script.[17] Until 1951, he had also played the title role of *Cactus Jim*, host of a children's series in which he played an "old desert rat" who told stories about life in the Old West and introduced westerns.[18] In the 1950s, Clarence Hartzell appeared in a number of promotional films for automobile companies, including Ford and Chevrolet. At this time he also operated as an antique dealer and prop specialist in the Chicago area, catering to local television studios. Later in life, he moved to Belle Vista, Arkansas, where he was active in the Belle Vista Television Association, and wrote music, poetry, and a newspaper column on wildflowers.[19] Clarence Hartzell died of a heart attack at his Belle Vista home on March 10, 1988. He was seventy-seven years old.

Vic and Sade's youngest stars, Bill Idelson and David Whitehouse, both went on to achieve considerable success in very different areas. Idelson continued in radio following *Vic and Sade*, starring in the title role of *Cousin Willy*, the 1953 summer replacement series for *Fibber McGee and Molly*. Idelson played Willard O'Knotts, who leaves his home in Milwaukee to visit his cousin in California, and then refuses to leave. He also assumed the role of Henry Barbour's grandson (and Pinky Barbour's brother) Hank Barbour on *One Man's Family*, following a brief appearance as a boy that Hank's sister Margaret had a crush on the previous year. He would go on to play Cliff Barbour in the 1949 NBC television adaptation of the series.

Television was where Bill Idelson's career truly flourished. Although he appeared in a number of series, including *The Odd Couple*, *Perry Mason*, *The Twilight Zone*, *My Favorite Martian*, *Happy Days*, and *Will and Grace*, he is probably best remembered as Sally Rogers's milquetoast boyfriend, Herman Glimscher, a role that he made memorable in five episodes of *The Dick Van Dyke Show*. Glimscher was, in fact, so popular that the character was resurrected for the 2004 special *The Dick Van Dyke Show Revisited*, in which he and Sally Rogers are depicted as a long-married couple. He achieved even greater success as a television writer and producer, working for such series as *The Andy Griffith Show*; *Gomer Pyle, U.S.M.C.*; *Get Smart*; *M*A*S*H*; *Happy Days*; *The Twilight Zone*; *The Odd Couple*; *Dragnet*; and *The Bob Newhart Show*. He was twice presented with a Writer's Guild Award for episodic comedy for scripts that he wrote for *The Andy Griffith Show* and *Get Smart*. In 1971, he shared an Emmy nomination for Best Comedy for *Love, American Style*. In addition to writing, Idelson served as producer for episodes of *The Bob Newhart Show*, *Anna and the King*, *The McLean Stevenson Show*, and *Love, American Style*.

Bill Idelson died in Los Angeles on New Year's Eve 2007, of complications from a hip injury. He was eighty-eight years old. Shortly before his death, he released *The Vic and Sade Story*, published by BearManor Media.

David Whitehouse also assumed additional roles in radio following *Vic and Sade*, including his tour de force performance in *The Author's Playhouse* episode "Mysterious Stranger" and an *American Novels* adaptation of *Tom Sawyer*, as well as roles in *The Baxters*, *Turning the Pages*, and *The Guiding Light*. However, upon graduating from high school, Whitehouse decided that a career in entertainment was not for him and, instead, headed to Northwestern University, where he received a B.S. in Engineering. This was followed by a Ph.D. in Electrical Engineering from M.I.T., where he remained as a faculty member for ten years after earning his doctorate. Whitehouse then joined Raytheon, where he worked in research and development on high-power lasers. He later started and ran several small laser companies. Before retiring, David Whitehouse also became involved in the development of residential real estate.[20]

"By George, civilization has sunk pretty low..."

In a society in which everything is seemingly transitory it is difficult to imagine an entertainment program running for fifteen years, let alone one that, for the bulk of its existence, relied upon only the voices of a sparsely populated cast. Today, television programs come and go quickly, even those series that are considered bona fide successes rarely last for more than a few seasons before being replaced. With a seemingly endless array of television networks, each catering to a different niche, how could an old radio show possibly matter anymore? Surely, there's plenty to entertain us in the present—and lots more on the way—so what possible value could there be in looking back and *listening* to a show that celebrated some of life's more mundane moments? The answer is: great value.

Vic and Sade is simply magical. No, it didn't have big-budget special effects, stars who were embroiled in scintillating scandals, or ridiculously contrived plots that insulted the audience's intelligence. Instead, it had remarkable writing that could mix the mundane with the absurd in a way that everyone from the average housewife to the president of the United States could appreciate, writing that made the small things in life seem remarkable, writing that brought characters into their living rooms without ever actually hearing them speak. It also had exceptional acting from performers who, using only their voices, brought Paul Rhymer's scripts to life, often only minutes after receiving them—performers who made not only their characters real, but, also, the people and places they discussed.

At a time when culture critics were keen to disparage the new medium of radio and its influence upon the masses, *Vic and Sade* offered its audiences its own critique of mass culture. Unlike, however, the culture critics who stood apart and judged mass culture from a distance, *Vic and Sade* was part of it. Throughout the program's long run, Paul Rhymer depicted mass culture in a way that was often consistent with the concerns voiced by culture critics. The Gooks and their friends consume commercialized media that is devoid of any apparent artistic merit. Sade's love stories, the exploits of Third Lieutenant Clinton Stanley, and the sensational adventures of Four-Fisted Frank Fuddleman and Gloria Golden all followed the same standardized formats that had been so readily accepted by the characters' "real world" counterparts, formats that had been deliberately chosen to appeal to the largest audience possible.

These characters, for the most part, recognize the flaws and shortcomings of mass cul-

Vic and Sade **remains one of radio's greatest triumphs and continues to be celebrated by devoted fans. Paul Rhymer (second from right), seen here celebrating the show along with the cast and other guests, created an entire world of individuals who engaged with and experienced mass culture in a way that still speaks to us today (courtesy Mark C. Lancaster, reproduced by permission of NBC/NBC Universal PhotoBank).**

ture and they determined how best, if at all, to partake of it. Paul Rhymer's characters are, as Gans wrote of real-world people, not "isolated individuals hungering for and therefore slavishly accepting what the media offer them, but families, couples, and peer groups who use the media when and if the content is relevant to group goals and needs."[21] They may, at times, seem passive in their consumption of mass entertainment, but this might be indicative of the level of importance that they place upon it. Contrary to the view held by many culture critics, mass entertainment and other forms of commercialized leisure represented only small elements of well-rounded lives that were filled with work, friendships, civic engagement, education, and a variety of distinctly non-commercialized, self-generated forms of leisure.

Oh, and there again we see the folly of public intellectuals and culture critics who failed to recognize that spontaneous leisure and entertainment can be wrought with pitfalls and be every bit as base and vulgar as any commercialized form of leisure. Just ask Fred Stembottom, who engaged in a game at work in which "the loser must sit still while everyone hits him hard as they can over the head with a sledgehammer,"[22] or anyone who has spent an afternoon looking at Mis' Scott's photos when they would rather be entertaining themselves by watching a famous bank robber change trains. Is watching fat men play handball *really* preferable to watching a motion picture produced for a mass audience? William Orton worried that mass culture told people what to enjoy. James Rorty worried that government might do the same. *Vic and Sade* suggested that individuals made the decision about what and when to consume from a buffet of options to mediate their involvement in the culture and the community.

Vic and Sade's audience was made up of people like themselves: people who lived within a rapidly changing world dominated by mass culture, and who used the products of that culture for their own purposes—whether to relax, escape from homework or an irate wife, or as a means for spending time with friends and family. True, they are occasionally used by these same products, but there is every indication that they learn from these experiences and, again, make deliberate choices as to whether to engage with them.

Perhaps what *Vic and Sade* best illustrates is that a work can be produced for a commercial purpose and created for a mass audience and still be, not only meritorious, but brilliant and extraordinary as well. This was a lesson that Paul Rhymer delivered more than 3,500 times during the course of *Vic and Sade*'s run, and it is a lesson that can still be learned today by anyone who takes the time to listen to the goings-on in the small house halfway up in the next block.

Chapter Notes

Introduction

1. Mary Frances Rhymer, "Introduction," in *The Small House Halfway up in the Next Block: Paul Rhymer's Vic and Sade* by Paul Rhymer (New York: McGraw-Hill, 1972), p. xx.
2. Michelle Hilmes, *Only Connect: A Cultural History of Broadcasting in the United States* (Belmont, CA: Wadsworth, 2002), p. 79.
3. March 28, 1932, p. 4; Paul Rhymer Papers (hereafter PRP), Box 2, Folder 2, Wisconsin Historical Society, Library-Archives Division, University of Wisconsin–Madison, Madison, Wisconsin.
4. Jack Foster (producer), *A Tribute to Vic and Sade*, radio documentary, June 24, 1973, available from http://vicandsade.net/interviews.cgi.
5. Mary Frances Rhymer, "Introduction," in *The Small House Halfway up in the Next Block: Paul Rhymer's Vic and Sade*, p. xix.
6. Ibid.
7. William Aylott Orton, *America in Search of Culture* (Boston: Little, Brown, 1933), p. 221.
8. Mary Frances Rhymer, "Introduction," p. xix.
9. M. Denison, "Soap Opera," *Harper's Monthly*, April 1940, reprinted in *Friends of Vic and Sade* no. 43 (n. d.), 502–503 (available from The Friends of Vic and Sade, 7232 N. Keystone Avenue, Lincolnwood, Illinois, 60646).
10. *A Tribute to Vic and Sade*, radio documentary.
11. Ray Bradbury, "Remembrance of Things Present," in *The Small House Halfway up in the Next Block: Paul Rhymer's Vic and Sade* by Paul Rhymer (New York: McGraw-Hill, 1972), p. ix.
12. Michelle Hilmes, "Rethinking Radio," *Radio Reader: Essays in the Cultural History of Radio*, eds. Michelle Hilmes and Jason Loviglio (New York: Routledge, 2002), pp. 1–19.

Chapter One

1. "Wesleyan Contributes to New Microphone Playwright School," *Argus*, November 13, 1929, p. 1.
2. Frank Wright Tuttle, "This is the Way the Story Goes," *Vanity Fair*, December 1922, p. 124.
3. Mary Frances Rhymer, "Introduction," p. xx.
4. Ibid.
5. Paul Rhymer, "Reflection Marvelous," *Aepix* (Bloomington High School, 1924), pp. 52–53.
6. Rhymer, "Reflection Marvelous," pp. 52–53.
7. Ibid.
8. Ibid., p. 54.
9. Paul Rhymer, "Crilotte and the Engineer," *Aepix* (Bloomington High School, 1925), p. 24.
10. Ibid., p. 26.
11. Ibid., p. 29.
12. Time-Life Books, *This Fabulous Century: 1920–1930* (New York: Time-Life, 1988), p. 39.
13. Paul Rhymer, "Hen," *College Humor*, September 1928, p. 41.
14. Ibid.
15. Ibid., p. 120.
16. Ibid.
17. Ibid.
18. Ibid.
19. Ibid.
20. Ibid., p. 41.
21. Ibid.
22. Paul Rhymer, "Yella," p. 2; PRP, Box 40, Folder 4.
23. Ibid., p. 3.
24. Ibid.
25. Editors of the Forum, undated letter to Paul Rhymer, PRP, Box 40, Folder 4.
26. Paul Rhymer, "Adjustment," *College Life*, October 1931, p. 41.
27. Ibid., p. 40.
28. Ibid., p. 80.
29. "Wesleyan Contributes to New Microphone Playwright School," p. 1.
30. *Keystone Chronicle,* December 14, 1929, pp. 6–7; PRP, Box 1, Folder 1.
31. *Keystone Chronicle,* January 18, 1930, p. 8; PRP, Box 1, Folder 2.
32. Arthur Frank Wertheim, *Radio Comedy* (New York: Oxford University Press, 1979), p. 242.
33. *Keystone Chronicle*, February 1, 1930, p. 8; PRP, Box 1, Folder 2.
34. *Keystone Chronicle,* February 1, 1930, p. 9.
35. *Keystone Chronicle,* March 15, 1930, p. 5; PRP, Box 1, Folder 3.
36. "The Keystone Chroniclers," *Big Farmer* 1 (1928), p. 40.
37. "The Busy-man Program," August 29, 1930, p. 3; PRP, Box 35, Folder 8.

38. Ibid., p. 4.
39. Ibid.
40. *The Three Doctors* continuity script, October 22, 1931, p. 1; PRP, Box 40, Folder 1.
41. *The Three Doctors* continuity script, October 31, 1931, p. 1; PRP, Box 40, Folder 1.
42. "Getting up Story for the Gownies," undated continuity script; PRP, Box 40, Folder 1.
43. Jerry Franken, "Soap Opera," *P.M. New York Sunday*, September 26, 1943, p. 19.
44. John Gihon to Paul Rhymer, March 20, 1933; PRP, Box 36, Folder 1.
45. *Vic and Sade*, November 23, 1933, p. 1; PRP, Box 4, Folder 4.
46. Ibid., p. 8.
47. *Barbershop Philosophers*, April 25, 1931, p. 1; PRP, Box 35, Folder 8.
48. John Dunning, *On the Air: The Encyclopedia of Old-Time Radio* (Oxford: Oxford University Press, 1998), p. 480.
49. "Death Bed Romance," September 19, 1933, p. 4; PRP, Box 35, Folder 8.
50. Ibid., p. 10.
51. Ibid.
52. "Mickey Mouse Theater," undated script, p. 10; PRP, Box 35, Folder 8.
53. John C. Rose to Paul Rhymer, July 21, 1938; PRP, Box 36, Folder 1.

Chapter Two

1. Esther Shultz, "Vic and Sade Author Forced into Success," *Chicago American*, March 2, 1937.
2. "It Might Be Your Home," *Radio Stars*, September 1936, p. 79.
3. "Arthur H. Van Berschot," *Chicago Sun-Times*, July 8, 1957.
4. "*Vic and Sade* in Living Portraits," *Radio and Television Mirror*, April 1942, p. 23.
5. Ibid., p. 22.
6. "Meet Vic and Sade," *Radio Stars*, March 1935, p. 78.
7. Ibid.
8. Ibid.
9. *Vic and Sade*, March 28, 1932, p. 2; PRP, Box 2, Folder 2.
10. Ibid., p. 3.
11. *Vic and Sade*, June 30, 1932, p. 2; PRP, Box 2, Folder 2.
12. Ibid., pp. 7–8.
13. *Vic and Sade*, July 1, 1932, p. 1; PRP, Box 2, Folder 2.
14. Ibid., p. 7.
15. Ibid., pp. 11–12.
16. *Vic and Sade*, July 4, 1932, p. 2; PRP, Box 2, Folder 2.
17. Ibid., p. 3.
18. Ibid.
19. Ibid.
20. Ibid., p. 4.
21. Ibid., p. 7.
22. Ibid.
23. Ibid., pp. 8–9.
24. Ibid., p. 9.
25. Ibid., p. 10.
26. *Vic and Sade*, July 5, 1932, p. 3; PRP, Box 2, Folder 2.
27. *Vic and Sade*, July 7, 1932, p. 2; PRP, Box 2, Folder 2.
28. Ibid., p. 5.
29. David E. Kyvig, *Daily Life in the United States, 1920–1939: Decades of Promise and Pain* (Westport, CT: Greenwood Press, 2002), p. 21.
30. *Vic and Sade*, July 7, 1932, p. 7.
31. John Alfred Heitmann, *The Automobile and American Life* (Jefferson, NC: McFarland, 2009), chapters 3 and 6.
32. *Vic and Sade*, July 7, 1932, p. 10.
33. Raymond William Stedman, *The Serials: Suspense and Drama by Installment* (Norman: University of Oklahoma Press, 1971), pp. 240, 250n.
34. *Vic and Sade*, July 7, 1932, p. 10.
35. Bill Idelson, *The Story of Vic & Sade* (Albany, GA: BearManor Media, 2007), p. 18.
36. Damian McElrath, *Dan Anderson: A Biography* (Center City, MN: Hazelton, 1999), p. 7.
37. William E. Leuchtenberg, *Herbert Hoover*, American Presidents Series (New York: Henry Holt, 2009), pp. 3–5.
38. *Vic and Sade*, July 15, 1932; reprinted in *Friends of Vic and Sade*, no. 17.
39. Ibid.
40. Stedman, *The Serials*, p. 242.
41. Ibid.
42. "Meet Vic and Sade," p. 78.
43. Fred Schroeder asserted in 1978 that the town was Crooper, forty miles from Peoria ("Radio's Home Folks, *Vic and Sade*: A Study in Aural Artistry," *Journal of Popular Culture* 12, no. 2 [1978]: p. 255), apparently based on one humorous reference to Sade's gowns being provided by Yamilton's of Crooper in the 1957 television revival (Dunning, *On the Air*, 701). His claim has given rise to many subsequent descriptions of the town as Crooper.
44. Paul Rhymer, *Vic and Sade: The Best Radio Plays of Paul Rhymer*, ed. Mary Frances Rhymer (New York: Seabury Press, 1976), p. 161.
45. George S. Masnick, "Home Ownership and Social Inequality in the United States," *Home Ownership and Social Inequality in Comparative Perspective*, eds. Karin Kurz and Hans-Peter Blossfeld (Stanford: Stanford University Press, 2004), p. 307.
46. Ibid.
47. Ibid.
48. Robert S. Lynd and Helen Merrell Lynd, *Middletown in Transition* (New York: Harcourt, Brace, 1937), p. 187.
49. Ibid., p. 188.
50. *Vic and Sade*, January 14, 1942; PRP, Box 23, Folder 4.
51. *Vic and Sade*, February 3, 1941, audio recording.
52. *Vic and Sade*, undated audio recording c. mid–1941.
53. "Too Many Serials on Air, Say Women," *Chicago Times*, October 6, 1940.
54. "Meet Vic and Sade," p. 78.
55. Darrell Ware, "Kicked Around," *Tower Radio*, July 1935, p. 24.

56. *100 Prize Winning Hints* (Chicago: John F. Jelke, undated), pp. 3, 9.
57. Franken, "Soap Opera," p. 19.
58. Mary Rhymer, "Introduction," xxi; Richard A. Bellamy, "Radio's Rhymer, a Fabulous Chap," *Milwaukee Journal*, January 24, 1943, p. 10.
59. Franken, "Soap Opera," p. 19.
60. Ward, "Kicked Around," pp. 24, 56.
61. "Radio Tattler," *Radio Guide*, October 22, 1938.

Chapter Three

1. Orrin E. Dunlap, Jr., "Listening In," *New York Times*, December 27, 1931, p. 109.
2. William Peck Banning, *Commercial Broadcasting Pioneer: The WEAF Experiment, 1922–1926* (Cambridge: Harvard University Press, 1946), p. 110.
3. Morleen Getz Rouse, "Daytime Radio Programming for the Homemaker," *Journal of Popular Culture* 12, no. 2 (1978): 316.
4. Ibid., 317.
5. Ruth Van Deman and Fanny Walker Yeatman, *Aunt Sammy's Radio Recipes: The Great Depression Cookbook*, ed. Martin Greif (New York: Universe Books, 1975), p. 45.
6. Dunlap, "Listening In"; "The Hopes of a New Year," *New York Times*, December 27, 1931, p. 109.
7. James Thurber, "Soapland," in *The Beast in Me and Other Animals* (San Diego: Harcourt, Brace, 1974), pp. 191–192.
8. *Dictionary of American Slang* quoted in Robert C. Allen, *Speaking of Soap Operas* (Chapel Hill: University of North Carolina Press, 1985), p. 9.
9. *Vic and Sade*, June 28, 1935.
10. "The Cecil and Sally Radio Program," *The Digital Deli Too*, http://www.digitaldeliftp.com/Digital DeliToo/dd2jb-Cecil-and-Sally.html.
11. Program epigraph.
12. Fred J. MacDonald, *Don't Touch That Dial!: Radio Programming in American Life, 1920–1960* (Chicago: Nelson-Hall, 1979), p. 241.
13. Jim Cox, *The Great Radio Soap Operas* (Jefferson, NC: McFarland, 1999), p. 79.
14. Dunning, *On the Air*, p. 420.
15. Larry Wolters, "The Most Memorable Moments of 30 Years of Radio," *Chicago Tribune*, August 30, 1959, N12.
16. "Life with Ma," *Time*, August 26, 1957.
17. Dunning, *On the Air*, p. 81.
18. James S. Olson, *Historical Dictionary of the Great Depression: 1929–1940* (Westport, CT: Greenwood Press, 2001), p. 34.
19. Stedman, *The Serials*, p. 249.
20. "Hummerts' Mill," *Time*, January 23, 1939.
21. Dunning, *On the Air*, p. 539.
22. Ibid., p. 540.
23. Stedman, *The Serials*, p. 258.
24. Dunning, *On the Air*, p. 666.
25. Stedman, *The Serials*, p. 280.
26. Stedman, *The Serials*, p. 281.
27. Dunning, *On the Air*, p. 635.
28. Stedman, *The Serials*, p. 313.
29. Cox, *The Great Radio Soap Operas*, p. 106.
30. Ibid., p. 107.
31. Morleen Getz Rouse, "Daytime Radio Programming for the Homemaker," *Journal of Popular Culture* 12, no. 2 (1978): 315.
32. Marilyn Levin, "Creating Consumers in the 1930s: Irna Phillips and the Radio Soap Opera," *Journal of Consumer Research* 22, no. 1 (1995): 75–89.
33. Michelle Hilmes, *Radio Voices: American Broadcasting, 1922–1952* (Minneapolis: University of Minnesota, 1997), p. 151.
34. Lavin, "Creating Consumers," pp. 75–89.
35. Bruce Lenthall, *Radio's America: The Great Depression and the Rise of Mass Culture* (Chicago: University of Chicago Press, 2007), p. 71.
36. MacDonald, *Don't Touch That Dial!*, p. 238.
37. Lenthall, *Radio's America*, p. 73.
38. Norman Brokenshire, *This Is Norman Brokenshire: An Unvarnished Self-Portrait* (New York: David McKay, 1954), p. 95.
39. Ibid., p. 96.
40. Kenneth Burke, *A Rhetoric of Motives* (Berkeley: University of California Press, 1969), p. 21.
41. Rudolf Arnheim, "The World of the Daytime Serial," in *Radio Research 1942–1943*, ed. Paul F. Lazarsfeld and Frank N. Stanton (New York: Duell, Sloan and Pearce, 1944), p. 56.
42. Arnheim, "The World of the Daytime Serial," p. 56.
43. August 5, 1933, p. 1; PRP, Box 4, Folder 2.
44. February 22, 1935, p. 7; PRP, Box 8, Folder 2.
45. MacDonald, *Don't Touch That Dial!*, p. 238.
46. Stedman, *The Serials*, p. 306.
47. Ibid., p. 307.
48. "Mail from the Listeners," *New York Times*, March 13, 1938, p. 176.
49. "Women to Boycott Radio Love Dramas," *New York Times*, January 11, 1940, p. 17.
50. Ruth Millett, "We, the Women," *Telegraph-Herald*, January 18, 1940, p. 6.
51. "FCC Head Hits Big Network Soap Operas," *Daily Kennebec Journal*, November 12, 1943, p. 7.
52. "Radio 'Love' Held Vital to Profits," *New York Times*, March 16, 1940, p. 17.
53. "Mutual System Chief Defends Soap Operas" *Montreal Gazette*, June 23, 1947, p. 6.
54. "Radio 'Love,'" p. 17.
55. Paul F. Lazarsfeld and Frank N. Stanton, eds., *Radio Research 1942–1943* (New York: Duell, Sloan and Pearce, 1944), appendix A, pp. 551, 555.
56. Hilmes, *Radio Voices*, 154.
57. Ibid.
58. Quoted in Thurber, *The Beast in Me*, pp. 251–252.
59. "Suppurating Serials," *Time*, March 23, 1942.
60. MacDonald, *Don't Touch That Dial!*, p. 232.
61. Robert C. Allen, *Speaking of Soap Operas* (Chapel Hill: University of North Carolina Press, 1985), pp. 18–29.
62. Lenthall, *Radio's America*, p. 55.
63. "Soap Operas Beneficial," *Science News Letter*, July 3, 1948, 13.
64. Ibid.
65. Stedman, *The Serials*, p. 315.
66. Ibid., 314–315.

67. Ibid., 320.
68. Ibid.
69. "Meet Vic and Sade," *Radio Stars*, March 1935, pp. 43–79.
70. M. Denison, "Soap Opera," *Harper's Monthly*, April 1940, p. 503.
71. Max Horkheimer and Theodor W. Adorno, *Dialectic of Enlightenment: Philosophical Fragments*, ed. Gunzelin Schmid Noerr, trans. Edmund Jephcott (Stanford: Stanford University Press, 2002), p. 95.
72. Jack Gould, "Soap Factory: Something About the Hummerts, Frank and Anne, and 6,000,000 Words a Year," *New York Times* February 14, 1943, p. 9.
73. Richard Pheatt, "Famed Serial Writer Celebrates Ten Years of Writing," *Toledo Blade*, June 3, 1940.
74. May 6, 1936, p. 1; PRP, Box 11, Folder 3.
75. Eugene Burr, "Comment," *Billboard*, October 3, 1942, p. 57.
76. January 23, 1939, p. 5; PRP, Box 17, Folder 4.
77. *Vic and Sade*, June 13, 1944, audio recording.
78. *Vic and Sade*, September 28, 1942, audio recording; Marr Sound Archives (Arthur B. Church Collection), University of Missouri–Kansas City Library, call number KMBC 241.

Chapter Four

1. Harry Quilter, "The Gospel of Intensity," *Contemporary Review*, June 1895, pp. 761–782.
2. Herbert J. Gans, *Popular Culture and High Culture: An Analysis and Evaluation of Taste* (New York: Basic Books, 1975), p. 10.
3. John Hetherington, "Critiquing Culture in the 'Small House': How *Vic and Sade* Brought the Mass Culture Critique to the Masses," *Journal of Radio & Audio Media* 15, no. 1 (2008): 77.
4. John Storey, *Inventing Popular Culture: From Folklore to Globalization* (Malden, MA: Blackwell, 2003).
5. Bruce Lenthall, "Critical Reception: Public Intellectuals Decry Depression-Era Radio, Mass Culture, and Modern America," in *Radio Reader: Essays in the Cultural History of Radio*, eds. Michelle Hilmes and Jason Loviglio (New York: Routledge, 2002), p. 42.
6. William Aylott Orton, *America in Search of Culture* (Boston: Little, Brown, 1933), p. 216.
7. Orton, *America in Search of Culture*, 219.
8. See discussion in Ben Urwand, *The Collaboration: Hollywood's Pact with Hitler* (Cambridge: Harvard University Press, 2013).
9. Christopher H. Sterling and John Michael Kittross, *Stay Tuned: A Concise History of American Broadcasting*, second edition (Belmont, CA: Wadsworth, 1990), p. 656.
10. Orton, *America in Search of Culture*, 246.
11. *Standard Market Data and New Information about KSTP: Northwest's Leading Radio Station* (KSTP, 1936), p. 12.
12. "The Press: Ink v. Air," *Time*, May 4, 1931.
13. *Standard Market Data*, p. 21.
14. Orton, *America in Search of Culture*, p. 246.
15. Ibid., p. 251.
16. Ibid., pp. 254–255.
17. Ibid., p. 309.
18. Frederick H. Lumley, *Measurement in Radio* (Columbus: Ohio State University, 1934), pp. 188–189, 191, 198–199.
19. James Rorty, *Our Master's Voice: Advertising* (New York: John Day, 1934), p. 269.
20. "Education: Bringing Up Radio," *Time*, June 1, 1931.
21. Hugh Richard Slotten, *Radio's Hidden Voice: The Origins of Public Broadcasting in the United States* (Urbana: University of Illinois, 2009), p. 152.
22. Lumley, *Measurement in Radio*, p. 201.
23. Ibid., pp. 203–205.
24. Lenthall, "Critical Reception," p. 46.
25. Ibid., 49.
26. Slotten, *Radio's Hidden Voice*, pp. 42–50.
27. David Manning White, "Mass Culture in America: Another Point of View," in *Mass Culture: The Popular Arts in America*, eds. Bernard Rosenberg and David Manning White (New York: Free Press, 1957), pp. 19–20.
28. "Education: Bringing up Radio," *Time*, June 1, 1931.
29. Orton, *America in Search of Culture*, p. 246.
30. H. V. Kaltenborn, "The Future of Radio," *Education by Radio* 1 (1931): 53.
31. "Why Educational Broadcasting Stations?" *Education by Radio* 1 (1931): 52.
32. Rorty, *Our Master's Voice*, p. 266.
33. Ibid., p. 278.
34. Gerd Horten, *Radio Goes to War: The Cultural Politics of Propaganda during World War II* (Berkeley: University of California Press, 2003), p. 138.

Chapter Five

1. Paul R. Gorman, *Left Intellectuals and Popular Culture in Twentieth Century America* (Chapel Hill, NC: University of North Carolina Press, 1996), p. 94.
2. Ibid., quoting Alfred H. Lloyd.
3. Kenneth R. Cunningham, "The Meaning of 'Leisure': An Analysis of Community Studies," *The Family Life Coordinator* 10, no. 1 (January 1961): 3–16.
4. Ibid., p. 3.
5. Ibid.
6. Robert N. Wilson, "The Courage to Be Leisured," *Social Forces* 60, no. 2 (1981): 282.
7. Mihaly Csikszentmihalyi, "Leisure and Socialization," *Social Forces* 60, no. 2 (1981): 332.
8. Margaret Mead, "The Pattern of Leisure in Contemporary American Culture," *Annals of the American Academy of Political and Social Science* 313 (1957): 13.
9. John R. Kelly, "Life Styles and Leisure Choices," *The Family Coordinator* 24, no. 2 (1975): 186, citing John R. Kelly, "Work and Leisure: A Simplified Paradigm," *Journal of Leisure Research* 4 (1972): 50–63.
10. *Vic and Sade*, August 3, 1932, p. 5; PRP, Box 2, Folder 3.
11. Ramon B. Zabriske and Bryan C. McCormick, "The Influences of Family Leisure Patterns on Perceptions of Family Functioning," *Family Relations* 50, no. 3 (2001): 282, citing R. V. Russell.
12. Susan Arai and Alison Pedlar, "Moving Beyond

Individualism in Leisure Theory: A Critical Analysis of Concepts of Community and Social Engagement," *Leisure Studies* 22 (2003): 188.

13. *Vic and Sade*, September 3, 1934, p. 1; PRP, Box 6, Folder 4.
14. Ibid., p. 2.
15. Wilson, "Courage to Be Leisured," p. 297.
16. *Vic and Sade*, June 15, 1936, p. 1; PRP, Box 11, Folder 4.
17. *Vic and Sade*, June 3, 1941, audio recording.
18. Ibid.
19. *Vic and Sade*, July 25, 1944, audio recording.
20. William H. Young and Nancy Young, eds., *The Great Depression in America: A Cultural History*, vol. 2 (Westport, CT: Greenwood Press, 2007), pp. 563–4.
21. *Vic and Sade*, May 11, 1938, p. 1; PRP, Box 15, Folder 6.
22. Young and Young, *Great Depression*, p. 563.
23. Kyvig, *Daily Life in the United States*, p. 27.
24. Young and Young, *Great Depression*, vol. 1, p. 34.
25. Rhymer, *Small House*, p. 190.
26. On social interests, see Arai and Pedlar, "Moving Beyond Individualism in Leisure Theory," p. 188.
27. *Vic and Sade*, November 2, 1933, p. 7; PRP, Box 4, Folder 4.
28. *Vic and Sade*, July 18, 1944, audio recording.
29. Kathy L. Piess, "American Women and the Making of Modern Consumer Culture," *The Journal for Modern Multi-Media History* 1, no. 1 (1998), http://www.albany.edu/jmmh/vol1no1/peiss-text.html.
30. *Vic and Sade*, November 16, 1941, p. 1; PRP, Box 23, Folder 3.
31. *Vic and Sade*, August 3, 1938, audio recording.
32. *Vic and Sade*, June 1, 1939, audio recording.
33. *Vic and Sade*, February 25, 1937, p. 9; PRP, Box 13, Folder 1.
34. *Vic and Sade*, October 21, 1942, audio recording; Marr Sound Archives (Arthur B. Church Collection), University of Missouri–Kansas City Library, call number KMBC 428.
35. *Vic and Sade*, December 29, 1939, audio recording.
36. *Vic and Sade*, October 10, 1941, audio recording.
37. Ibid.
38. Vic and Sade, November 12, 1937, p. 2; PRP, Box 14, Folder 6.
39. Ibid., p. 3.
40. Ibid., pp. 6, 9–10.
41. *Vic and Sade*, May 16, 1941, audio recording.
42. Ibid.
43. Ibid.
44. *Vic and Sade*, December 31, 1940, audio recording.
45. *Vic and Sade*, July 4, 1940, audio recording.
46. Jean Shepherd, "Foreword," in *Vic and Sade: The Best Radio Plays of Paul Rhymer*, ed. Mary Frances Rhymer (New York: Seabury Press, 1976), xii.
47. *Vic and Sade*, May 11, 1938, p. 10; PRP, Box 15, Folder 6.
48. *Vic and Sade*, January 27, 1944, p. 4; PRP, Box 26, Folder 3.
49. *Vic and Sade*, August 1, 1938, p. 1; PRP, Box 16, Folder 3.
50. Ibid., p. 2.
51. Ibid., p. 5. The actual lines of Longfellow are as follows: "Truly a wonderful man was Caius Julius Caesar! / Better be first, he said, in a little Iberian village, / Than be second in Rome..." (2.13–15).
52. "Growth of the Telephone Service," *New York Times*, December 3, 1901.
53. Jean-Guy Rens, *The Invisible Empire: A History of the Telecommunications Industry in Canada*, vol. 1 (McGill-Queen's University Press, 2001), p. 324.
54. Claude S. Fischer, "Gender and the Residential Telephone, 1890–1940," *Sociological Forum* 3, no. 2 (1988): 212; see also Claude S. Fischer, *America Calling: A Social History of the Telephone to 1940* (Berkeley: University of California Press, 1992), p. 231.
55. Ibid., p. 225.
56. Ibid., p. 226.
57. Ibid., pp. 221–222.
58. *Vic and Sade*, January 28, 1943, p. 5; PRP, Box 23, Folder 5.
59. *Vic and Sade*, November 7, 1941, p. 4; PRP, Box 22, Folder 3.
60. S. T. Joshi and David E. Schultz, *An H. P. Lovecraft Encyclopedia* (Westport, CT: Greenwood Press, 2001), p. 144.
61. Emily Post, *Etiquette in Society, in Business, in Politics, and at Home* (New York: Funk & Wagnalls, 1922), p. 491.
62. Claude S. Fischer, "Changes in Leisure Activities, 1890–1940," *Journal of Social History* 27, no. 3 (1994): 453.
63. Post, *Etiquette*, p. 492.
64. *Vic and Sade*, February 9, 1944, p. 7; PRP, Box 26, Folder 4.
65. *Vic and Sade*, June 9, 1941, audio recording.
66. Post, *Etiquette*, p. 491.
67. *Vic and Sade*, March 19, 1940, audio recording.
68. Gary Dean Best, *The Nickel and Dime Decade: American Popular Culture During the 1930s* (Westport, CT: Praeger, 1993), p. 15.
69. *Vic and Sade*, April 18, 1934, p. 3; PRP, Box 5, Folder 4.
70. Ibid., pp. 6–10.
71. Ibid., p. 8.
72. *Vic and Sade*, March 27, 1940, audio recording.
73. *Vic and Sade*, October 14, 1941, audio recording.
74. Ibid.
75. *Vic and Sade*, May 18, 1944; PRP, Box 27, Folder 4.
76. Best, *Nickel and Dime*, p. 20.
77. Ibid.
78. Young and Young, *The Great Depression*, vol. 1, p. 270.
79. *Vic and Sade*, April 25, 1933, pp. 6–7; PRP, Box 3, Folder 4.
80. Young and Young, *The Great Depression*, vol. 1, p. 193.
81. *Vic and Sade*, July 4, 1944, audio recording.
82. Irving Crespi, "Card Playing as Mass Culture," in *Mass Culture: The Popular Arts in America*, eds. Bernard Rosenberg and David Manning White (New York: Free Press, 1957), p. 420.
83. Ibid.

84. *Vic and Sade,* December 4, 1934; PRP, Box 7, Folder 4.
85. Crespi, "Card Playing as Mass Culture," p. 418.
86. Ibid., p. 420.
87. *Vic and Sade,* December 4, 1934, p. 1.
88. *Vic and Sade,* April 21, 1943, audio recording (originally broadcast March 4, 1936).
89. Ibid.
90. Clifford Putney, "Service over Secrecy: How Lodge-Style Fraternalism Yielded to Men's Service Clubs," *The Journal of Popular Culture* 27, no. 1 (1993): 179.
91. *Vic and Sade,* June 13, 1940, audio recording.
92. Willard C. Sutherland, "A Philosophy of Leisure," *Annals of the American Academy of Political and Social Science* 313 (1957): 2.
93. Arai and Pedlar, "Moving Beyond Individualism in Leisure Theory," p. 192.
94. Putney, "Service over Secrecy," p. 185; Robert S. Lynd and Helen Merrell Lynd, *Middletown: A Study in Modern American Culture* (San Diego: Harcourt, Brace, Jovanovich, 1956), pp. 277, 304–8; Robert S. Lynd and Helen Merrell Lynd, *Middletown in Transition* (New York: Harcourt, Brace, 1937), pp. 275, 285–6.
95. Lynd and Lynd, *Middletown in Transition,* pp. 285–6.
96. Putney, "Service over Secrecy," p. 186.
97. *Vic and Sade,* February 1, 1936, p. 6; PRP, Box 10, Folder 5.
98. Putney, "Service over Secrecy," p. 180.
99. *Vic and Sade,* January 2, 1940, audio recording.
100. *Vic and Sade,* January 19, 1943, pp. 4, 7; PRP, Box 23, Folder 5.
101. Ibid., p. 8.
102. *Vic and Sade,* January 22, 1940, audio recording.
103. Quoted in LeRoy Ashby, *With Amusement for All: A History of American Popular Culture Since 1830* (Lexington: University of Kentucky Press, 2006), p. 43.
104. Ibid.
105. *Vic and Sade,* February 16, 1941, audio recording.
106. Putney, "Service over Secrecy," p. 183.
107. *Vic and Sade,* May 12, 1941, audio recording.
108. *Vic and Sade,* January 23, 1939, p. 9; PRP, Box 17, Folder 4.
109. *Vic and Sade,* May 11, 1937, p. 7; PRP, Box 13, Folder 5.
110. Ibid.
111. *Vic and Sade,* September 15, 1933, reprinted in *Friends of Vic and Sade,* p. 20.
112. Lynd and Lynd, *Middletown in Transition,* p. 270.
113. "The Dempsey-Tunney Fight," *Chicago Tribune,* September 22, 1927.
114. Quoted in Bruce J. Evensen, *When Dempsey Fought Tunney: Heroes, Hokum, and Storytelling in the Jazz Age* (Knoxville: University of Tennessee Press, 1996), p. xv.
115. *Vic and Sade,* December 9, 1935, p. 3; PRP, Box 10, Folder 3.
116. *Vic and Sade,* June 4, 1941, audio recording.
117. Ashby, *With Amusement for All,* p. 33.
118. Jeffrey Stanton, "Coney Island Freaks," 1997, http://www.westland.net/coneyisland/articles/freaks.htm.
119. Ashby, *With Amusement for All,* pp. 33–34.
120. Ibid., p. 34.
121. *Vic and Sade,* July 7, 1937, p. 4; PRP, Box 14, Folder 2.
122. Ashby, *With Amusement for All,* pp. 30–31.
123. *Vic and Sade,* May 10, 1938, p. 1; PRP, Box 15, Folder 6.
124. *Vic and Sade,* July 23, 1940, audio recording.
125. *Vic and Sade,* August 3, 1936, p. 1; PRP, Box 12, Folder 1.
126. Ibid.
127. Ibid., p. 2.
128. Ibid., p. 3.
129. Ibid., p. 7.
130. Ibid., p. 4.
131. Paul Rhymer, *Vic and Sade: The Best Radio Plays of Paul Rhymer,* p. 4.
132. *Vic and Sade,* July 4, 1944, audio recording.
133. Alice Bertha Gomme, *The Traditional Games of England, Scotland, and Ireland,* vol. 1 (London: David Nutt, 1894), pp. 229–31.
134. George Barton Cutten, *The Threat of Leisure* (New Haven: Yale University Press, 1926), p. 6.
135. Susan Currell, *The March of Spare Time: The Problem and Promise of Leisure in the Great Depression* (Philadelphia: University of Pennsylvania Press, 2005), pp. 23–24.
136. Ibid., p. 28.
137. Ibid., p. 58.
138. Cutten, *The Threat of Leisure,* p. 67.
139. Frederick Lewis Allen, *Since Yesterday: The 1930s in America, September 3, 1929–September 3, 1939* (New York: Harper and Row, 1986), pp. 268–9.
140. Allen, *Since Yesterday,* p. 271.
141. Kyvig, *Daily Life in the United States,* p. 79.
142. Allen, *Since Yesterday,* p. 271; Kyvig, *Daily Life in the United States,* p. 79.

Chapter Six

1. Tim Dirks, *The Great Train Robbery* (1903), http://www.filmsite.org/grea.html.
2. American Film Institute, "The Hollywood System and the Golden Age of Silents, 1915–1920," http://www.fathom.com/course/21701779/session3.html.
3. Richard Butsch, "American Movie Audiences of the 1930s," *International Labor and Working Class History* no. 59, Workers and Film: As Subject and Audience (Spring 2001): 109.
4. Ibid.
5. Robert Sklar, *Movie-Made America: A Cultural History of American Movies,* revised edition (New York: Vintage, 1994), p. 153.
6. Lauren Boegen, "Reality Bites: Social Implications of the Early Twentieth-Century Movie," *Constructing the Past* 4, no. 1 (2003): 38.
7. Ibid.
8. Ibid., p. 39.
9. Ibid., p. 40.
10. Ibid., p. 41.
11. Sklar, *Movie-Made America,* p. 162.

12. "Hollywood and the Great Depression," http://www.digitalhistory.uh.edu/historyonline/hollywood_great_depression.cfm.
13. Best, *Nickel and Dime Decade*, p. 84.
14. Boegen, "Reality Bites," p. 42.
15. Tim Dirks, "The History of Film: The 1930s."
16. Jay Haley, "The Appeal of the Moving Picture," *The Quarterly of Film Radio and Television* 6, no. 4 (1952): 366.
17. Ibid., p. 365.
18. Ibid.
19. Ibid., p. 373.
20. Richard Koszarski, *An Evening's Entertainment: The Age of the Silent Feature Picture 1915–1928*, vol. 3, History of American Cinema Series, series ed. Charles Harpole (New York: Scribner's, 1990), p. 25.
21. Haley, "The Appeal of the Moving Picture," p. 361.
22. *Vic and Sade*, June 4, 1941, audio recording.
23. *Vic and Sade*, March 22, 1933, pp. 1, 3; PRP, Box 3, Folder 4.
24. *Vic and Sade*, March 19, 1940, audio recording.
25. *Vic and Sade*, November 8, 1943, audio recording.
26. *Vic and Sade*, April 16, 1934 (AM), p. 9; PRP, Box 5, Folder 4.
27. Ibid., p. 5.
28. Eric A. Johnston, "The Motion Picture as a Stimulus to Culture," *Annals of the American Academy of Social and Political Science* 254 (1947): 101.
29. Irving Howe, "Notes on Mass Culture," in *Mass Culture: The Popular Arts in America*, eds. Bernard Rosenberg and David Manning White (New York: Free Press, 1957), p. 497.
30. Ibid.
31. *Vic and Sade*, April 4, 1940, p. 4; PRP, Box 20, Folder 1.
32. *Vic and Sade*, August 4, 1944, audio recording.
33. *Vic and Sade*, July 26, 1944, audio recording.
34. *Vic and Sade*, May 9, 1938, p. 10; PRP, Box 15, Folder 6.
35. Ibid., p. 6.
36. Ibid., p. 5, quoting Tennyson, *Idylls of the King*, "Lancelot and Elaine," lines 1–2. Rhymer misspells Astolat in his script, replacing the final "a" with an "o."
37. Ibid., p. 8.
38. *Vic and Sade*, April 4, 1940, audio recording.
39. Crespi, "Card Playing," p. 418.
40. *Vic and Sade*, August 9, 1942, audio recording.
41. Leo C. Rosten, "A 'Middletown' Study of Hollywood," *Public Opinion Quarterly* 3, no. 2 (1939): 315.
42. *Vic and Sade*, September 17, 1940, reprinted in *Friends of Vic and Sade*, no. 27.
43. *Vic and Sade*, March 25, 1940, audio recording.
44. *Vic and Sade*, July 4, 1935, p. 4; PRP, Box 9, Folder 2.
45. Hetherington, "Critiquing Culture in the 'Small House': How *Vic and Sade* Brought the Mass Culture Critique to the Masses," pp. 76–89.
46. Crespi, "Card Playing," 420.
47. Horkheimer and Adorno, *Dialectic of Enlightenment*, pp. 108–09.
48. Rhymer, *Small House*, p. 221.
49. Ibid., p. 222.
50. Ibid., p. 224.
51. Dirks, "Crime & Gangster Films," http://www.filmsite.org/crimefilms.html.
52. Rosten, "A 'Middletown' Study of Hollywood," p. 316.
53. Karina Wilson, "Horror Begins to Talk … and Scream," *Horror Film History*, http://www.horrorfilmhistory.com/index.php?pageID=1930s.
54. John Kenrick, "The 1930s, Part I: 'Hip, Hooray and Ballyhoo,'" *Musicals 101*, 2003, http://www.musicals101.com/1930film.htm.
55. Ibid.
56. Horkheimer and Adorno, *Dialectic of Enlightenment*, p. 109.
57. *Vic and Sade*, July 26, 1944, audio recording.
58. *Vic and Sade*, January 1, 1935, p. 2; PRP, Box 7, Folder 6.
59. *Vic and Sade*, August 9, 1944, audio recording.
60. Mark Weinstein, "Movie Contracts: Is 'Net' 'Gross?'" in *An Economic History of Film*, eds. John Sedgwick and Michael Pokorny (New York: Routledge, 2005), p. 243.
61. Dirks, "History of Film: The 1930s."
62. Johnston, "The Motion Picture as a Stimulus to Culture," p. 98.
63. Ibid.
64. Ibid., p. 100.
65. Ibid., p. 101.
66. Samantha Barbas, *Movie Crazy: Fans, Stars, and the Cult of Celebrity* (New York: Palgrave Macmillan, 2002), p. 78.
67. Kathryn H. Fuller, *At the Picture Show: Small-Town Audiences and the Creation of Movie Fan Culture* (Washington: Smithsonian Institution Press, 1996), p. 148.
68. Rhymer, *The Small House*, pp. 81–2.
69. *Vic and Sade*, July 4, 1944, audio recording.
70. Joe Waldo Finler, *The Hollywood Story* (London: Wallflower Press, 2003), p. 156.
71. Rosten, "A 'Middletown' Study of Hollywood," p. 316.
72. *Vic and Sade*, December 5, 1935, p. 9; PRP, Box 10, Folder 3.
73. *Vic and Sade*, September 20, 1944, audio recording.
74. Johnston, "The Motion Picture as Stimulus to Culture," p. 101.
75. *Vic and Sade*, April 4, 1940, p. 4; PRP, Box 20, Folder 1.
76. Howe, "Notes on Mass Culture," p. 497.

Chapter Seven

1. "120 Years of Adult Literacy," National Assessment of Adult Literacy, http://nces.ed.gov/naal/lit_history.asp.
2. Douglas Waples, *Research Memorandum on Social Aspects of Reading in the Depression* (New York: Social Sciences Research Council, 1937), p. 93.
3. Waples, *People and Print*, p. 85.
4. Michael Kammen, *American Culture, American Tastes: Social Change and the Twentieth Century* (New York: Knopf, 1999), p. 83.

5. Young and Young, *The Great Depression in America*, p. 58.
6. Maureen Corrigan, "What People Were Reading During the Depression," *Fresh Air*, WHYY (Philadelphia, PA: WHYY, June 15, 2009).
7. Faith Baldwin, "White Collar Girl," *Deseret News*, August 6, 1934, p. 11.
8. Corrigan, "What People Were Reading During the Depression."
9. Young and Young, *The Great Depression in America*, p. 59.
10. "Ely Culbertson, 1891–1955," http://www.acbl.org/about/hall-of-fame/biography.php?id=11.
11. Gans, *Popular Culture and High Culture*, chapter 2.
12. Peter Swirski, "Popular and Highbrow Literature: A Comparative View," CLCWeb: *Comparative Literature and Culture* 1, no. 4 (1999): 6.
13. Swirski, "Popular and Highbrow Literature," p. 6.
14. Ibid., p. 8.
15. Gans, *Popular Culture and High Culture*, p. 22.
16. Swirski, "Popular and Highbrow Literature," p. 10.
17. Ibid., p. 11.
18. Kammen, *American Culture, American Taste*, p. 84; Janice A. Radway, *A Feeling for Books: The Book-of-the-Month Club, Literary Taste, and Middle-Class Desire* (Chapel Hill: University of North Carolina Press, 1997), p. 227.
19. Paul F. Lazarsfeld, *Radio and the Printed Page* (New York: Duell, Sloane, and Pearce, 1940), p. 136.
20. Ibid., p. 304.
21. Ibid., p. 136–37.
22. Ibid., p. 140.
23. Ibid., p. 145.
24. Ibid., p. 174.
25. Edmund Pearson, *Dime Novels; or, Following an Old Trail in Popular Literature* (New York: Little, Brown, 1929), part I, chapter 1, available at http://gaslight.mtroyal.ab.ca/dimex01.htm.
26. *Dime Novels and Penny Dreadfuls*, http://www-sul.stanford.edu/depts/dp/pennies/cover.html.
27. "Beadle and Adam," *The American Women's Dime Novel Project: Dime Novels for Women, 1870–1920* http://chnm.gmu.edu/dimenovels/publishers/beadle.html.
28. Pearson, *Dime Novels*, part I, chapter 2.
29. Ibid., chapter 1.
30. Christine Bold, "Malaeska's Revenge; or, The Dime Novel Tradition in Popular Fiction," in *Wanted Dead or Alive: The American West in Popular Culture*, ed. Richard Aquila (Urbana: University of Illinois Press, 1996), p. 23; Emory Elliot (ed.), *The Columbia Literary History of the United States* (New York: Columbia University Press, 1988), p. 533.
31. *Dime Novels and Penny Dreadfuls.*
32. J. Randolph Cox, "Dime Novels," *The Oxford History of Popular Print Culture*, Vol. 6: U.S. Popular Print Culture: 1860–1920, ed. Christine Bold (Oxford: Oxford University Press, 2012), p. 64.
33. Pearson, *Dime Novels*, part I, chapter 5.
34. Ibid.
35. *Vic and Sade*, January 22, 1940, audio recording, and February 15, 1938, p. 5; PRP, Box 15, Folder 3.
36. *Vic and Sade*, January 22, 1940, audio recording.
37. *Vic and Sade*, June 13, 1939, audio recording.
38. Paul Rhymer, *Vic and Sade: The Best Radio Plays of Paul Rhymer*, p. 38.
39. *Vic and Sade*, March 19, 1940, audio recording.
40. *Vic and Sade*, February 8, 1938, p. 2; PRP, Box 15, Folder 3.
41. Paul Rhymer, *Vic and Sade: The Best Radio Plays of Paul Rhymer*, p. 115.
42. Pearson, *Dime Novels*, part I, chapter 7.
43. *Vic and Sade*, January 22, 1940, audio recording.
44. Paul Rhymer, *The Small House*, p. 170.
45. Paul Rhymer, *The Small House*, p. 174–75.
46. Pearson, *Dime Novels*, part I, chapter 4.
47. *Vic and Sade*, December 31, 1940, audio recording.
48. *Vic and Sade*, July 20, 1944, p. 2; PRP, Box 27, Folder 5.
49. *Vic and Sade*, March 19, 1940, audio recording.
50. *Vic and Sade*, July 20, 1944, p. 2.
51. *Vic and Sade*, June 30, 1941, audio recording.
52. Pearson, *Dime Novels*, part I, chapter 1.
53. William McCormick, "The Dime Novel Nuisance," *Lend a Hand*, April 1890, p. 254.
54. Ibid., p. 255.
55. Ruth Strang, "Reading Interests, 1946," *The English Journal* 35, no. 9 (1946): 477.
56. Joe Jennings, "Leisure Reading of Junior High School Boys and Girls," *Peabody Journal of Education* 6, no. 6 (1929): 333–47.
57. William G. Brink, "Reading Interests of High School Pupils," *The School Review* 47, no. 8 (1939): 613–21.
58. Geraldine E. White, "Surveying Reading in a High-School Community," *The English Journal* 31, no. 9 (1942): 669–72.
59. Esther M. Andersen, "A Study of Leisure-Time Reading of Pupils in Junior High School," *The Elementary School Journal* 48, no. 5 (1948): 260.
60. Ibid., p. 262.
61. *Vic and Sade*, June 26, 1932, p. 1.
62. Waples, *Research Memorandum*, p. 79.
63. Ibid., p. 81.
64. Ibid., pp. 85, 175.
65. Robert E. Park, "The Natural History of the Newspaper," *American Journal of Sociology* 29, no. 3 (1923): 277–78.
66. Ibid., p. 278.
67. *Vic and Sade,* October 9, 1933, p. 6; PRP, Box 4, Folder 3.
68. *Vic and Sade,* October 19, 1933, p. 2; PRP, Box 4, Folder 3.
69. *Vic and Sade*, September 21, 1933, p. 1; PRP, Box 4, Folder 3.
70. Park, "Natural History of the Newspaper," p. 278.
71. *Vic and Sade*, October 19, 1933, p. 4.
72. *Vic and Sade*, January 1, 1935, p. 9; PRP, Box 7, Folder 5.
73. *Vic and Sade*, December 23, 1937; PRP, Box 15, Folder 1.
74. Park, "Natural History of the Newspaper," p. 286.
75. Ibid., p. 275.
76. *Vic and Sade*, May 26, 1933, p. 1; PRP, Box 3, Folder 5.

77. *Vic and Sade*, April 25, 1933, p. 6; PRP, Box 3, Folder 4.
78. *Vic and Sade*, January 4, 1943, audio recording.
79. *Vic and Sade*, 21, 1933, p. 2.
80. *Vic and Sade*, May 7, 1937, p. 1; PRP, Box 13, Folder 5.
81. William H. Young and Nancy K. Young, *The 1930s* (Westport, CT: Greenwood Press, 2002), p. 264.
82. Ibid.
83. *Vic and Sade*, December 22, 1933, p. 4; PRP, Box 15, Folder 1.
84. Waples, *Research Memorandum*, p. 176.
85. Karen Majewski, *Traitors & True Poles: Narrating a Polish-American Identity, 1880–1939* (Athens: Ohio University Press, 2003), p. 50.
86. Bill V. Mullen, *Popular Fronts: Chicago and African-American Cultural Politics, 1935–1946* (Urbana: University of Illinois, 1999), p. 129.
87. Ibid.
88. Charles Johanningsmeier, *Fiction and the American Literary Marketplace: The Role of Newspaper Syndicates in America, 1860–1900* (Cambridge: Cambridge University Press, 1997), p. 208, quoting *The American Magazine*.
89. Ibid.
90. Hugh E. Agnew, "Home Newspaper ... Reading Habits: A Study of 22,456 New York City Families," *National Marketing Review* 1, no. 3 (1936): 216–24.
91. Johanningsmeier, *Fiction and the American Literary Marketplace*, pp. 209–27.
92. Mary Anne de Forest, "Thrill Chaser," *Street & Smith's Love Story Magazine*, October 20, 1934, p. 19.
93. *Vic and Sade*, April 8, 1940, audio recording.
94. L. P. Holmes, "Heritage of Conflict," *Ranch Romance*, September 8, 1933, p. 5.
95. Paul Rhymer, *The Best Radio Plays*, p. 185.
96. *Vic and Sade*, August 16, 1944, audio recording.
97. *Vic and Sade*, June 13, 1944, audio recording. (Art Van Harvey apparently misspoke before correcting himself.)
98. Bruce B. Berger, "Employee/Organizational Communications," *Institute for Public Relations*, November 17, 2008, http://www.instituteforpr.org/topics/employee-organizational-communications.
99. "The Human Relations Approach," http://comminfo.rutgers.edu/~whitew/357lecture_3.htm.
100. *Vic and Sade*, undated audio recording, c. December 1940.

Chapter Eight

1. "Nineteenth-Century Education," http://www.chesapeake.edu/Library/EDU_101/eduhist_19thC.asp.
2. Diane Ravtich, "American Traditions of Education," in *A Primer on America's Schools*, ed. Terry M. Moe (Stanford, CA: Hoover Institution Press, 2001), p. 9.
3. "Immigration," *The Massachusetts Teacher*, October 1851, pp. 290–91.
4. "Twentieth-Century Education," http://www.chesapeake.edu/Library/EDU_101/eduhist_20thC.asp.
5. See Paul E. Petersen, *The Politics of School Reform, 1870–1940* (Chicago: University of Chicago Press, 1985) for further discussion.
6. H. Clay Tate, *The Way It Was in McLean County, 1972–1822* (Bloomington, IL: McLean County Historical Association, 1972), p. 199.
7. *Child-Welfare Magazine* 11 (1917): 208.
8. *Vic and Sade*, September 4, 1934, p. 3; PRP, Box 6, Folder 4.
9. Tate, *The Way It Was*, p. 203.
10. "Nineteenth-Century Education."
11. *Vic and Sade*, December 31, 1943, p. 4; PRP, Box 26, Folder 2.
12. Ibid., p. 8.
13. Ibid., p. 9.
14. Ibid., p. 11.
15. Ibid., p. 12.
16. Ibid.
17. *Vic and Sade*, September 21, 1933, p. 5; PRP, Box 4, Folder 3.
18. September 21, 1933, p. 6.
19. Ibid., p. 10.
20. *Vic and Sade*, February 27, 1940, audio recording.
21. *Vic and Sade*, January 9, 1935, pp. 5, 9; PRP, Box 7, Folder 6.
22. Ibid., p. 10.
23. Plato, *Republic* 536e, trans. Benjamin Jowett.
24. *Vic and Sade*, January 3, 1935, p. 2; PRP, Box 7, Folder 6.
25. Ibid., p. 3. The Latin phrase, "Non disputandum esse nihil omnibus hoc," is roughly translated as, "This is not to be discussed by anybody."
26. Ibid., pp. 11–12.
27. *Vic and Sade*, undated audio recording c. 1939.
28. *Vic and Sade*, June 5, 1940, p. 4; PRP, Box 20, Folder 3.
29. Ibid.
30. *Vic and Sade*, February 2, 1938, p. 1; PRP, Box 15, Folder 3.
31. *Vic and Sade*, July 11, 1938, p. 4; PRP, Box 28, Folder 1.
32. Petersen, *The Politics of School Reform*, p. 75.
33. Tate, *The Way It Was*, p. 208.
34. Young and Young, *Great Depression in America*, p. 19.
35. Ibid., p. 139.
36. David Angus and Jeffrey Mirel, *The Failed Promise of the American High School, 1890–1995* (New York: Teachers College Press, 1999), p. 84.
37. Takashi Yamashita, "The Effects of the Great Depression on Educational Attainment," p. 8, http://www.sole-jole.org/7274.pdf.
38. *Vic and Sade*, June 15, 1933, p. 4; PRP, Box 3, Folder 6.
39. Rhymer, *The Small House*, p. 106.
40. David O. Levine, *The American College and the American Culture of Aspiration, 1915–1940* (Ithaca: Cornell University Press, 1986), pp. 146–50.
41. Levine, *The American College*, pp. 117–18.
42. Lynd and Lynd, *Middletown in Transition*, pp. 209–11.
43. Ibid., pp. 208–09.
44. "Surviving the Crash," http://www.lincolnhall.illinois.edu/history/crash/enrollment/.

45. "Chickens for Tuition," *Illinois Wesleyan Magazine* 18, no. 2 (Summer 2009), http://digitalcommons.iwu.edu/iwumag/vol18/iss2/5.
46. *Vic and Sade*, April 12, 1935, p. 11; PRP, Box 8, Folder 4.
47. Paul Rhymer, *The Small House*, p. 94.
48. Ibid., p. 95.
49. Ibid., p. 96.
50. *Vic and Sade*, June 2, 1936, p. 5; PRP, Box 11, Folder 4.
51. Dunning, *On the Air*, p. 560.
52. "The Quiz Kids: 50 Years Ago a Bunch of Educated Upstarts Became a Radio Smash Hit," *The Chicago Tribune*, December 2, 1990, http://articles.chicagotribune.com/1990-12-02/features/9004100175_1_quiz-kids-quiz-program-show-business.
53. "Radio: Benny & the Masterminds, *Time*, April 21, 1941.
54. Dunning, *On the Air*, p. 561.
55. *Quiz Kids*, March 20, 1949, audio recording.
56. "Radio: Quiz Kids Eclipsed," *Time*, September 14, 1942.
57. Ibid.
58. Dunning, *On the Air*, p. 562.
59. Ibid., 561.
60. "The Quiz Kids: 50 Years Ago ..."
61. Dunning, *On the Air*, p. 341.
62. Ibid., p. 344.
63. Ibid., p. 341.
64. *Information, Please*, February 20, 1942, audio recording.
65. "Radio: The Midget Euclid," *Time*, March 29, 1943.
66. Dunning, *On the Air*, p. 561.
67. *Vic and Sade*, July 4, 1932, p. 2; PRP, Box 2, Folder 2.
68. *Vic and Sade*, March 7, 1933, p. 4; PRP, Box 3, Folder 4.
69. *Vic and Sade*, February 4, 1937, p. 6; PRP, Box 13, Folder 1.
70. *Vic and Sade*, October 18, 1932, p. 3; PRP, Box 4, Folder 3. (The script is dated "October 18," but the date is crossed out and a March date penciled in.)
71. *Vic and Sade*, February 25, 1937, p. 3; PRP, Box 13, Folder 1.
72. *Vic and Sade*, June 1, 1943, p. 2; PRP, Box 24, Folder 4.
73. Vic and Sade, June 5, 1944, p. 2; PRP, Box 27, Folder 5.
74. Walter J. Beaupre, "The Easy Aces: Radio's Original Comedy Couple," http://www.otrsite.com/articles/artwb011.html.
75. Richard Hofstadter, *Anti-Intellectualism in American Life* (New York: Vintage, 1963), p. 7.
76. Donald Clark Hodges, "Anti-Intellectualism in a Society of Eggheads," *American Journal of Economics and Sociology* 25, no. 4 (1966): 427.
77. "Anti-Intellectualism," *The Science News-Letter* 69, no. 10 (March 10, 1956): 149.
78. Wertheim, *Radio Comedy*, p. 517.
79. "Meet Vic and Sade," p. 78.
80. *Vic and Sade*, November 28, 1937, audio recording.
81. *Vic and Sade*, July 5, 1932, p. 3.
82. *Vic and Sade*, July 11, 1944, pp. 7–8.
83. July 11, 1944, p. 9.
84. *Vic and Sade*, July 16, 1942, audio recording.
85. *Vic and Sade*, July 11, 1944, p. 10.
86. Ibid., p. 12.
87. *Vic and Sade*, May 11, 1938, p. 1; PRP, Box 15, Folder 6.
88. Ibid., p. 4.
89. *Vic and Sade*, September 22, 1939, audio recording.
90. *Vic and Sade*, July 4, 1932, p. 2.
91. *Vic and Sade*, February 21, 1936; PRP, Box 10, Folder 5. (Rhymer's script states that it was intended for the "Saint Louis Educational Congress," to follow remarks by Bob Brown. I can find no record of such a congress, but the date of the script coincides with the NEA's superintendents' conferences in St. Louis that year, which *Time* condemned as a "left-wing" gathering poised between liberalism and socialism ("Superintendents in St. Louis," *Time*, March 9, 1936).
92. Ibid., p. 5.
93. Ibid., p. 6.
94. Ibid., pp. 7, 9.

Chapter Nine

1. Lenthall, *Radio's America*, p. 42.
2. *Standard Market Data and New Information About KSTP: Northwest's Leading Radio Station* (KSTP, 1936).
3. Alexis de Tocqueville, *Democracy in America*, vol. II, trans. Henry Reeve (New York: D. Appleton, 1899), p. 584.
4. Tocqueville, *Democracy in America*, vol. II, p. 4.
5. Roger J. Williams, "Individuality and Its Significance in Human Life," in *Essays on Individualism*, ed. Felix Morley (Philadelphia: University of Pennsylvania Press, 1958), p. 127.
6. *Vic and Sade*, June 26, 1936, p. 5; PRP, Box 11, Folder 4.
7. *Vic and Sade*, December 18, 1936, p. 10; PRP, Box 12, Folder 5.
8. "Children's Nicknames Merely Lead to Fights," *Science News Letter*, March 2, 1935, pp. 142–43.
9. *Vic and Sade*, December 18, 1936, p. 10.
10. *Vic and Sade*, February 11, 1938, p. 8; PRP, Box 15, Folder 3.
11. James K. Skipper, Jr., Paul Leslie, and Brenda S. Wilson, "A Teaching Technique Revisited: Family Names, Nicknames, and Social Class," *Teaching Sociology* 18, no. 2 (1990): 210–11.
12. *Vic and Sade*, April 17, 1940, audio recording.
13. Undated 1936 script, http://www.otrr.org/jimbo/vicandsade/Rhymer-scripts/xx-xx-xxRushBringsHomeaDog.html.
14. *Vic and Sade*, October 1, 1942, audio recording.
15. Williams, "Individuality," p. 131.
16. Bellamy, "Radio's Rhymer," p. 10.
17. Putney, "Service over Secrecy," p. 182.
18. *Vic and Sade*, July 5, 1944, audio recording.
19. *Vic and Sade*, May 7, 1937, audio recording.
20. *Vic and Sade*, November 28, 1937, audio recording.

21. Paul Rhymer, *Small House*, p. 170.
22. Ibid., p. 171.
23. Ibid., p. 172.
24. "Fibber McGee and Molly: The War Years—Home Front of Wistful Vista," http://www.fibbermcgeeandmolly.com/wwii-broadcasts-homefront-of-wistful-vista.html.
25. Bellamy, "Radio's Rhymer," p. 10.
26. Robert John Landry, *This Fascinating Radio Business* (Indianapolis: Bobbs-Merrill, 1946), p. 248.
27. Christopher Sterling, ed., *The Concise Encyclopedia of American Radio* (New York: Routledge, 2010), p. 536.
28. Gerd Horten, *Radio Goes to War: The Cultural Politics of Propaganda during World War II* (Berkeley: University of California Press, 2003), p. 138.
29. *Vic and Sade*, September 9, 1941, audio recording.
30. *Vic and Sade*, June 29, 1944, audio recording.
31. *Vic and Sade*, June 4, 1942, audio recording.
32. Ibid.
33. Ibid.
34. Ibid.
35. "Text of Hoover's Speech on Relation of Government to Industry," *New York Times*, October 23, 1928, p. 2.
36. Don Martindale, "Timidity, Conformity, and the Search for Personal Identity," *Annals of the American Academy of Political and Social Science* 378 (1968): 84.
37. *Vic and Sade*, June 2, 1943, p. 7; PRP, Box 24, Folder 4.
38. Ibid., p. 8.
39. Ibid., 1943, p. 13.
40. *Vic and Sade*, January 15, 1943, pp. 3–4; PRP, Box 23, Folder 5.
41. *Vic and Sade*, August 13, 1943, p. 5; PRP, Box 25, Folder 2.
42. Martindale, "Timidity, Conformity," p. 83.
43. Ibid., p. 84.
44. Ibid., p. 85.
45. John Dewey, *Individualism Old and New* (Amherst, NY: Prometheus, 1999), p. 41.
46. *Vic and Sade*, November 15, 1941, audio recording.
47. *Vic and Sade*, April 3, 1939, audio recording.
48. Dewey, *Individualism Old and New*, pp. 12, 26.
49. Ibid., p. 27.
50. R. F. Swift, "Individualism and Fellowship," *The Philosophical Review* 35 (1926): 546.
51. *Vic and Sade*, May 1, 1944, audio recording.
52. *Vic and Sade*, February 11, 1941, audio recording.
53. *Vic and Sade*, September 3, 1934, p. 1; PRP, Box 6, Folder 4.
54. Ibid., p. 5.
55. *Vic and Sade*, January 23, 1941, audio recording.
56. Ibid.
57. Swift, "Individualism and Fellowship," pp. 545–46.
58. *Vic and Sade*, January 4, 1937, p. 10; PRP, Box 10, Folder 6.
59. *Vic and Sade*, January 4, 1943, audio recording. (The fictional Caribbean islands are spelled phonetically.)
60. Robert W. Hodge, Paul M. Siegel, and Peter H. Rossi, "Occupational Prestige in the United States, 1925–63," *American Journal of Sociology* 7, no. 3 (1964): 295.
61. *Vic and Sade*, November 7, 1939, audio recording.
62. *Vic and Sade*, February 27, 1940, audio recording.
63. *Vic and Sade*, June 2, 1942, audio recording.
64. *Vic and Sade*, January 3, 1941, p. 1; PRP, Box 21, Folder 5.
65. *Vic and Sade*, July 23, 1943, audio recording.
66. *Vic and Sade*, undated audio recording, c. 1940.
67. Rhymer, *Vic and Sade: The Best Radio Plays of Paul Rhymer*, pp. 233–34.
68. *Vic and Sade*, December 21, 1942, p. 3; PRP, Box 23, Folder 4.
69. Ibid., p. 6.
70. *Vic and Sade*, January 15, 1943, p. 3; PRP, Box 23, Folder 5.
71. Ibid., p. 3.
72. Ibid., p. 12.
73. *Vic and Sade*, August 13, 1943, p. 8; PRP, Box 25, Folder 2.
74. Ibid., p. 11.
75. *Vic and Sade*, April 5, 1944, audio recording.
76. *Vic and Sade*, August 11, 1943, audio recording.
77. *Vic and Sade*, August 11, 1944, audio recording.
78. Paul Rhymer, *The Small House*, p. 300.

Conclusion

1. *Vic and Sade*, September 29, 1944, audio recording.
2. Paul Rhymer to Irene (no last name given), September 22, 1945; PRP, Box 36, Folder 1.
3. Quoted in "Refreshing Comedy," *Knickerbocker News*, July 25, 1946.
4. "'Vic and Sade' Goes TV for Colgate; Debuts in July," *Billboard*, June 18, 1949, p. 7; "Esty Uses 'Colgate Theater' as New Idea Try-Out," *Billboard*, November 19, 1949, p. 5.
5. John Crosby, "Vic and Sade Fine on Video Tryout," *Pittsburgh Post-Gazette*, August 7, 1949; "'Vic and Sade' Goes TV," p. 7; "There'll Be Some Changes," *Time*, August 29, 1949.
6. Cy Wagner, "Vic and Sade," *Billboard*, July 30, 1949, p. 12.
7. Studs Terkel, *Touch and Go: A Memoir* (New York: New Press, 2007), p. 119.
8. "Paul Rhymer's Vic and Sade Returns to TV ... In Color," *Bloomington Pantagraph*, January 17, 1957.
9. Bea Pepan, "The Private Life of Cliff Norton," *Milwaukee Journal*, May 20, 1951.
10. *The Public Life of Cliff Norton* #14, May 11, 1950; PRP, Box 33, Folder 2.
11. Bea J. Pepan, "'Sade' Does Her Newest Chore Without 'Vic,'" *Milwaukee Journal*, February 9, 1947.
12. "Former Radio Star Dies," *The Leader-Post*, March 14, 1977.
13. Tim Brooks and Earle F. Marsh, *The Complete Directory to Prime-Time Network and Cable TV Shows, 1946–Present*, ninth edition (New York: Ballantine Books, 2007), p. 593.

14. Walter Pierce Sheppard, "*One Man's Family*: A History 1932 to 1959 and a Script Analysis 1932 to 1944" (Ph.D. diss., University of Wisconsin, 1964), 184.
15. Tim Hollis, Clarence Hartzell biography, http://www.otrr.org/jimbo/vicandsade/web/bio-hartzell.jpg.
16. Ibid.
17. Bob Leszczak, *Single-Season Sitcoms, 1948–1979: A Complete Guide* (Jefferson, NC: McFarland, 2012), p. 184.
18. Hollis, biography.
19. Ibid.
20. Personal communication, October 2013.
21. Gans, *Popular Culture and High Culture*, p. 32.
22. *Vic and Sade*, July 4, 1944, audio recording.

Selected Bibliography

Agnew, Hugh E. "Home Newspaper ... Reading Habits: A Study of 22,456 New York City Families." *National Marketing Review* 1, no. 3 (1936): 216–24.

Allen, Frederick Lewis. *Since Yesterday: The 1930s in America, September 3, 1929–September 3, 1939.* New York: Harper and Row, 1986.

Allen, Robert C. *Speaking of Soap Operas.* Chapel Hill: University of North Carolina Press, 1985.

Andersen, Esther M. "A Study of Leisure-Time Reading of Pupils in Junior High School." *The Elementary School Journal* 48, no. 5 (1948): 258–67.

Angus, David, and Jeffrey Mirel. *The Failed Promise of the American High School, 1890–1995.* New York: Teachers College Press, 1999.

"Anti-Intellectualism." *The Science News-Letter* 69, no. 10 (March 10, 1956): 149.

Aquila, Richard, ed. *Wanted Dead or Alive: The American West in Popular Culture.* Urbana: University of Illinois Press, 1996.

Arai, Susan, and Alison Pedlar. "Moving Beyond Individualism in Leisure Theory: A Critical Analysis of Concepts of Community and Social Engagement." *Leisure Studies* 22 (2003): 185–202.

Ashby, LeRoy. *With Amusement for All: A History of American Popular Culture Since 1830.* Lexington: University of Kentucky Press, 2006.

Banning, William Peck. *Commercial Broadcasting Pioneer: The WEAF Experiment, 1922–1926.* Cambridge: Harvard University Press, 1946.

Barbas, Samantha. *Movie Crazy: Fans, Stars, and the Cult of Celebrity.* New York: Palgrave Macmillan, 2002.

Best, Gary Dean. *The Nickel and Dime Decade: American Popular Culture During the 1930s.* Westport, CT: Praeger, 1993.

Boegen, Lauren. "Reality Bites: Social Implications of the Early Twentieth Century Movie." *Constructing the Past* 4, no. 1 (2003): 38–45.

Bold, Christine, ed. *The Oxford History of Popular Print Culture.* Vol. 6: U.S. Popular Print Culture: 1860–1920. Oxford: Oxford University Press, 2012.

Brink, William G. "Reading Interests of High School Pupils." *The School Review* 47, no. 8 (1939): 613–21.

Brokenshire, Norman. *This Is Norman Brokenshire: An Unvarnished Self-Portrait.* New York: David McKay, 1954.

Brooks, Tim, and Earle F. Marsh. *The Complete Directory to Prime-Time Network and Cable TV Shows, 1946–Present.* 9th ed. New York: Ballantine Books, 2007.

Butsch, Richard. "American Movie Audiences of the 1930s." *International Labor and Working Class History* no. 59, "Workers and Film: As Subject and Audience" (Spring 2001): 106–20.

"Children's Nicknames Merely Lead to Fights." *Science News Letter*, March 2, 1935, 142–43.

Cox, Jim. *The Great Radio Soap Operas.* Jefferson, NC: McFarland, 1999.

Csikszentmihalyi, Mihaly. "Leisure and Socialization." *Social Forces* 60, no. 2 (1981): 332–40.

Cunningham, Kenneth R. "The Meaning of 'Leisure': An Analysis of Community Studies," *The Family Life Coordinator* 10, no. 1 (January 1961): 3–16.

Currell, Susan. *The March of Spare Time: The Problem and Promise of Leisure in the Great Depression.* Philadelphia: University of Pennsylvania Press, 2005.

Cutten, George Barton. *The Threat of Leisure.* New Haven: Yale University Press, 1926.

Dewey, John. *Individualism Old and New.* Amherst, NY: Prometheus Books, 1999.

Dunning, John. *On the Air: The Encyclopedia of Old-Time Radio.* Oxford: Oxford University Press, 1998.

Elliot, Emory, ed. *The Columbia Literary History of the United States.* New York: Columbia University Press, 1988.

Evensen, Bruce J. *When Dempsey Fought Tunney: Heroes, Hokum, and Storytelling in the Jazz Age.* Knoxville: University of Tennessee Press, 1996.

Finler, Joe Waldo. *The Hollywood Story.* London: Wallflower Press, 2003.

Fischer, Claude S. *America Calling: A Social History of the Telephone to 1940.* Berkeley: University of California Press, 1992.

———. "Changes in Leisure Activities, 1890–1940." *Journal of Social History* 27, no. 3 (1994): 453–75.

———. "Gender and the Residential Telephone, 1890–1940." *Sociological Forum* 3, no. 2 (1988): 211–33.

Foster, Jack (producer). *A Tribute to Vic and Sade*. Radio documentary. June 24, 1973. Available from http://vicandsade.net/interviews.cgi.

Fuller, Kathryn H. *At the Picture Show: Small-Town Audiences and the Creation of Movie Fan Culture*. Washington: Smithsonian Institution Press, 1996.

Gans, Herbert J. *Popular Culture and High Culture: An Analysis and Evaluation of Taste*. New York: Basic Books, 1974.

Gomme, Alice Bertha. *The Traditional Games of England, Scotland, and Ireland*. Vol. 1. London: David Nutt, 1894.

Gorman, Paul R. *Left Intellectuals and Popular Culture in Twentieth Century America*. Chapel Hill: University of North Carolina Press, 1996.

Haley, Jay. "The Appeal of the Moving Picture." *The Quarterly of Film Radio and Television* 6, no. 4 (1952): 361–74.

Heitmann, John. *The Automobile and American Life*. Jefferson, NC: McFarland, 2009.

Hetherington, John. "Critiquing Culture in the 'Small House': How *Vic and Sade* Brought the Mass Culture Critique to the Masses." *Journal of Radio & Audio Media* 15, no. 1 (2008): 76–89.

Hilmes, Michele. *Only Connect: A Cultural History of Broadcasting in the United States*. Belmont, CA: Wadsworth, 2002.

———. *Radio Voices: American Broadcasting, 1922–1952*. Minneapolis: University of Minnesota, 1997.

———, and Jason Loviglio, eds. *Radio Reader: Essays in the Cultural History of Radio*. New York: Routledge, 2002.

Hodge, Robert W., Paul M. Siegel, and Peter H. Rossi. "Occupational Prestige in the United States, 1925–1963," *American Journal of Sociology* 7, no. 3 (1964): 286–302.

Hodges, Donald Clark. "Anti-Intellectualism in a Society of Eggheads." *American Journal of Economics and Sociology* 25, no. 4 (1966): 427–37.

Hofstadter, Richard. *Anti-Intellectualism in American Life*. New York: Vintage, 1963.

Horkheimer, Max, and Theodor W. Adorno. *Dialectic of Enlightenment: Philosophical Fragments*. Edited by Gunzelin Schmid Noerr. Translated by Edmund Jephcott. Stanford: Stanford University Press, 2002.

Horten, Gerd. *Radio Goes to War: The Cultural Politics of Propaganda During World War II*. Berkeley: University of California Press, 2003.

Idelson, Bill. *The Story of Vic & Sade*. Albany, GA: BearManor Media, 2007.

Jennings, Joe. "Leisure Reading of Junior High School Boys and Girls." *Peabody Journal of Education* 6, no. 6 (1929): 333–47.

Johanningsmeier, Charles. *Fiction and the American Literary Marketplace: The Role of Newspaper Syndicates in America, 1860–1900*. Cambridge: Cambridge University Press, 1997.

Johnson, Eric. "The Motion Picture as a Stimulus to Culture." *Annals of the American Academy of Social and Political Science* 254 (1947): 98–102.

Joshi, S. T., and David E. Schultz. *An H. P. Lovecraft Encyclopedia*. Westport, CT: Greenwood Press, 2001.

Kaltenborn, H. V. "The Future of Radio," *Education by Radio* 1 (1931): 53–54.

Kammen, Michael. *American Culture, American Tastes: Social Change and the 20th Century*. New York: Knopf, 1999.

Kelly, John R. "Life Styles and Leisure Choices." *The Family Coordinator* 24, no. 2 (1975): 185–90.

Koszarski, Richard. *An Evening's Entertainment: The Age of the Silent Feature Picture, 1915–1928*. Volume 3. History of American Cinema Series. Series edited by Charles Harpole. New York: Scribner's, 1990.

Kurz, Karin, and Hans-Peter Blossfeld, eds. *Home Ownership and Social Inequality in Comparative Perspective*. Stanford, CA: Stanford University Press, 2004.

Kyvig, David E. *Daily Life in the United States, 1920–1939: Decades of Promise and Pain*. Westport, CT: Greenwood Press, 2002.

Landry, Robert John. *This Fascinating Radio Business*. Indianapolis: Bobbs-Merrill, 1946.

Lazarsfeld, Paul F. *Radio and the Printed Page*. New York: Duell, Sloane, and Pearce, 1940.

———, and Frank N. Stanton, eds. *Radio Research, 1942–1943*. New York: Duell, Sloan and Pearce, 1944.

Lenthall, Bruce. *Radio's America: The Great Depression and the Rise of Mass Culture*. Chicago: University of Chicago Press, 2007.

Leszczak, Bob. *Single Season Sitcoms, 1948–1979: A Complete Guide*. Jefferson, NC: McFarland, 2012.

Levin, Marilyn. "Creating Consumers in the 1930s: Irna Phillips and the Radio Soap Opera." *Journal of Consumer Research* 22, no. 1 (1995): 75–89.

Levine, David O. *The American College and the American Culture of Aspiration, 1915–1940*. Ithaca: Cornell University Press, 1986.

Lumley, Frederick H. *Measurement in Radio*. Columbus: Ohio State University, 1934.

Lynd, Robert S., and Helen Merrell Lynd. *Middletown: A Study in Modern American Culture*. San Diego: Harcourt, Brace, Jovanovich, 1956.

———. *Middletown in Transition*. New York: Harcourt, Brace, 1937.

MacDonald, J. Fred. *Don't Touch That Dial!: Radio Programming in American Life, 1920–1960*. Chicago: Nelson-Hall, 1979.

Majewski, Karen. *Traitors & True Poles: Narrating a Polish-American Identity, 1880–1939*. Athens: Ohio University Press, 2003.

Martindale, Don. "Timidity, Conformity, and the Search for Personal Identity." *Annals of the American Academy of Political and Social Science* 378 (1968): 83–89.

McElrath, Damian. *Dan Anderson: A Biography*. Center City, MN: Hazelton, 1999.

Mead, Margaret. "The Pattern of Leisure in Contemporary American Culture." *Annals of the American Academy of Political and Social Science* 313 (1957): 11–15.

Moe, Terry M., ed. *A Primer on America's Schools*. Stanford, CA: Hoover Institution Press, 2001.

Morley, Felix, ed. *Essays on Individualism*. Philadelphia: University of Pennsylvania Press, 1958.

Mullen, Bill V. *Popular Fronts: Chicago and African-American Cultural Politics, 1935–1946*. Urbana: University of Illinois, 1999.

Olson, James S. *Historical Dictionary of the Great Depression: 1929–1940*. Westport, CT: Greenwood Press, 2001.

Orton, William Aylott. *America in Search of Culture*. Boston: Little, Brown, 1933.

Park, Robert E. "The Natural History of the Newspaper." *American Journal of Sociology* 29, no. 3 (1923): 273–89.

Pearson, Edmund. *Dime Novels; or, Following an Old Trail in Popular Literature*. New York: Little, Brown, 1929. Available at http://gaslight.mtroyal.ab.ca/dimex01.htm.

Petersen, Paul E. *The Politics of School Reform, 1870–1940*. Chicago: University of Chicago Press, 1985.

Piess, Kathy L. "American Women and the Making of Modern Consumer Culture." *The Journal for Modern Multi-Media History* 1, no. 1 (1998). http://www.albany.edu/jmmh/vol1no1/peiss-text.html.

Post, Emily. *Etiquette in Society, in Business, in Politics, and at Home*. New York: Funk & Wagnalls, 1922.

Putney, Clifford. "Service over Secrecy: How Lodge-Style Fraternalism Yielded to Men's Service Clubs." *The Journal of Popular Culture* 27, no. 1 (1993): 179–190.

Quilter, Harry. "The Gospel of Intensity." *Contemporary Review*, June 1895.

Radway, Janice A. *A Feeling for Books: The Book-of-the-Month Club, Literary Taste, and Middle-Class Desire*. Chapel Hill: University of North Carolina Press, 1997.

Rens, Jean-Guy. *The Invisible Empire: A History of the Telecommunications Industry in Canada*. Vol. 1. McGill-Queen's University Press, 2001.

Rhymer, Paul. "Adjustment." *College Life*, October 1931.

———. "Hen." *College Humor*, September 1928.

———. Paul Rhymer Papers, 1928–1972. Wisconsin Historical Society, Library-Archives Division, University of Wisconsin-Madison, Madison, Wisconsin.

———. *The Small House Halfway up in the Next Block: Paul Rhymer's Vic and Sade*. New York: McGraw-Hill, 1972.

———. *Vic and Sade: The Best Radio Plays of Paul Rhymer*. Edited by Mary Frances Rhymer. New York: Seabury Press, 1976.

Rorty, James. *Our Master's Voice: Advertising*. New York: John Day, 1934.

Rosenberg, Bernard, and David Manning White, eds. *Mass Culture: The Popular Arts in America*. New York: Free Press, 1957.

Rosten, Leo C. "A 'Middletown' Study of Hollywood." *Public Opinion Quarterly* 3, no. 2 (1939): 314–20.

Rouse, Morleen Getz. "Daytime Radio Programming for the Homemaker." *Journal of Popular Culture* 12, no. 2 (1978): 315–27.

Schroeder, Fred E. H. "Radio's Home Folks, *Vic and Sade*: A Study in Aural Artistry." *Journal of Popular Culture* 12, no. 2 (1978): 253–64.

Sedgwick, John, and Michael Pokorny, eds. *An Economic History of Film*. New York: Routledge, 2005.

Sheppard, Walter Pierce. "*One Man's Family*: A History 1932 to 1959 and a Script Analysis 1932 to 1944." Ph.D. diss., University of Wisconsin, 1964.

Skipper, James K., Jr., Paul Leslie, and Brenda S. Wilson. "A Teaching Technique Revisited: Family Names, Nicknames, and Social Class." *Teaching Sociology* 18, no. 2 (1990): 209–13.

Sklar, Robert. *Movie-Made America: A Cultural History of American Movies* (revised edition). New York: Vintage, 1994.

Slotten, Hugh Richard. *Radio's Hidden Voice: The Origins of Public Broadcasting in the United States*. Urbana: University of Illinois, 2009.

Stedman, Raymond William. *The Serials: Suspense and Drama by Installment*. Norman: University of Oklahoma Press, 1971.

Sterling, Christopher, ed. *The Concise Encyclopedia of American Radio*. New York: Routledge, 2010.

Sterling, Christopher H., and John Michael Kittross. *Stay Tuned: A Concise History of American Broadcasting* (Second edition). Belmont, CA: Wadsworth, 1990.

Storey, John. *Inventing Popular Culture: From Folklore to Globalization*. Malden, MA: Blackwell, 2003.

Strang, Ruth. "Reading Interests, 1946." *The English Journal* 35, no. 9 (1946): 477–82.

Sutherland, Willard C. "A Philosophy of Leisure." *Annals of the American Academy of Political and Social Science* 313 (1957): 1–3.

Swift, R. F. "Individualism and Fellowship." *The Philosophical Review* 35 (1926): 539–52.

Swirski, Peter. "Popular and Highbrow Literature: A Comparative View," *CLCWeb: Comparative Literature and Culture* 1, no. 4 (1999). http://docs.lib.purdue.edu/clcweb/vol1/iss4/4/.

Tate, H. Clay. *The Way It Was in McLean County, 1972–1822*. Bloomington, IL: McLean County Historical Association, 1972.

Terkel, Studs. *Touch and Go: A Memoir*. New York: New Press, 2007.

Thurber, James. *The Beast in Me and Other Animals*. San Diego: Harcourt, Brace, 1974.

Time-Life Books. *This Fabulous Century: 1920–1930*. New York: Time-Life, 1988.

Tocqueville, Alexis de. *Democracy in America*. Vol. II. Translated by Henry Reeve. New York: D. Appleton, 1899.

Urwand, Ben. *The Collaboration: Hollywood's Pact with Hitler*. Cambridge: Harvard University Press, 2013.

Van Deman, Ruth, and Fanny Walker Yeatman. *Aunt Sammy's Radio Recipes: The Great Depression Cookbook*. Edited by Martin Greif. New York: Universe Books, 1975.

Waples, Douglas. *Research Memorandum on Social Aspects of Reading in the Depression*. New York: Social Sciences Research Council, 1937.

Wertheim, Arthur Frank. *Radio Comedy*. New York: Oxford University Press, 1979.

White, Geraldine E. "Surveying Reading in a High-School Community." *The English Journal* 31, no. 9 (1942): 669–72.

Wilson, Robert N. "The Courage to Be Leisured." *Social Forces* 60, no. 2 (1981): 282–303.

Young, William H., and Nancy Young, eds. *The Great Depression in America: A Cultural History*. Vols. 1 and 2. Westport, CT: Greenwood Press, 2007.

———. *The 1930s*. Westport, CT: Greenwood Press, 2002.

Zabriske, Ramon B., and Bryan C. McCormick. "The Influences of Family Leisure Patterns on Perceptions of Family Functioning." *Family Relations* 50, no. 3 (2001): 281–89.

Index

Numbers in ***bold italics*** indicate pages with photographs.

Adams, Franklin P. 153, 154
"Adjustment" 14
Adorno, Theodor 57
advertising 5, 15, 18, 19, 58, 65, 67, 68, 70, 119
Aepix 10, 146
Ainsworth, Annabelle 106, 114, 118, 119
Allen, Melvin 58
Anderson, Dan 32
anti-intellectualism 28, 151, 155–159
Applerot, Mis' 52, 61, 97, 130, 156, 158, 166, 176, 179
Argus 9, 10, 150
Arnheim, Rudolf 50
Arnold Grimm's Daughter 56
audition episodes 15, 23
Aunt Sammy 43
automobiles 11, 14, 20, 30, 32, 35, 39, 40, 48, ***77***, 78, 79, 82, 119, 142, 160, 186; accidents 99; as class symbol 78
Aylesworth, M.H. 43

Backstage Wife 46, 47
Barbas, Samantha 119
"Barbershop Boys" 20
"Barbershop Philosophers" 20, 22, 45
Barnum, P.T. 100, 101
Beach, Isabella 58, 59
Beadle and Adams 127
Beadle Dime Novels 127
Berg, Lewis 55, 56
Berkeley, Busby 110, 116
Bernard, Mrs. Everett L. 53
Bernice (horse) 7, 85
Bess (sister of Sade) 78, 81, 88, 89, 111
Best, Gary Dean 89
Betty and Bob 26, 30, 34, 45–47
Bijou Theater 8, 25, 92, 106, 109, 111, 113, 114, 118, 120, 129, 144, 161

Bloomington, Illinois 3, 5, 10, 13, 15, 24, 34, ***35***, 107, 109, 132, 142, 143, 145, 146
Blue Network 45; *see also* NBC; Red Network
Book-of-the-Month Club 125
books 16, 21, 28, 34, 49, 68, 85, 109, 111, 121–123, 125–127, 129, 131, 132, 136, 137, 138, 145, 146, 154, 158, 159
Boston Blackie 1
Bradbury, Ray 3, 7, 8
Bright Kentucky Hotel 6, 36, 97, 113, 130, 166
Brokenshire, Norm 49
Brown, Bob 37
Browning, Robert 155
Browning, Tod 100, 116
Burke, Kenneth 50, 51
Burns, Robert 145
Busyman Program 17, 22, 125
Butsch, Richard 106

Cactus Jim 186
Call, Mr. 184
Call, Sydney 34
Carberry 78, 89
card games 91, 92
Carnegie, Dale 123
Carradine, John 153
CBS 38–40, 45, 68, 70, 104, 183
Cecil and Sally 44, 45
celebrity culture 119
Chicago 3, 9, 18, 19, 23, 37, 38, 44, 56, 60, 63, 67, 83, 90, 95, 99, 102, 114, 134, 136, 152, 166, 184–186
Chinbunny, Mr. 178, 179
Christmas 79, 80, 81, 82, 83, 134, 173, 180
Christmas cards 81
citizenship 90
Clara, Lu, and Em 26, 44, 45, 55
Clark, Smelly 33, 34, 81, 82, 99, 101, 112, 114, 161, 162, 178, 179

Cohen, Richard 2
Colgate Comedy Hour 184
collectivism 161, 170, 171, 173–175
college education 149–151
College Humor 11, 14
College Life 14
commercialism 18, 55, 63, 66, 73, 80–83, 92, 99, 103, 105, 106, 180, 187, 188
Common School Movement 141, 142
community 6, 15, 36, 45, 62, 64, 71, 79, 85, 87–90, 92, 93, 101, 105, 114, 120, 133, 134, 135, 141, 149, 160, 161, 164, 165, 166, 167, 170, 174, 175, 176, 178, 182, 189
community organizations 92–98
Conan, Dick 184
Consolidated Kitchenware 24, 29, 35, 61, 84, 92, 139, 140, 148, 163, 173, 174, 175
continuity writing 3, 9, 10, 14, 15, 18–20
conversation 83–86
Cordova, Pom Pom 61, 111, 134
Corrigan, Maureen 122
Cousin Willy 186
Cox, Jim 48
"Crilotte and the Engineer" 10, 11
Crisco 38, 39, 58, 59
critics and criticism 7, 8, 22, 38, 52, 54, 57, 59, 61–66, 68, 70, 71, 78, 88, 98, 99, 104, 105, 112, 114, 118, 119, 123–125, 131, 141, 151, 159, 160, 170, 187, 188
Crooper, Illinois 192*n*43
culture industry 57
Cunningham, Kenneth R. 73
Cutten, George Barton 104

Dane, Frank 184
Darrow, Gerard 152, 154

Dave Garraway at Large 185
davenport 26, 27, 84, 121–123, 125, 127, 129, 131, 133, 135, 137, 139
Davis, Rooster 7, 34, 114, 115, 145, 149, 161, 162
Davis, Rotten 92, 161, 163
daytime radio 3, 5, 7, 8, 22, 26, 30, 34, 35, 37, 41–61, 69, 160, 162, 183, 185
Deathbed Romance 21, 22
De Forest, Lee 56, 70
Dempsey-Tunney fights 99
Department of Agriculture 43
department stores 80
DeRienzi, Lolita 61, 139, 162
Dewey, John 173–175
Dick Van Dyke Show 186
Dickens, Charles 6
dime novels 126–129, 131
Disney Productions 22, 107
Donahue, Mis' 76
Donahue, Mr. 76
Dreamerson, Donna 106, 118, 119
Drummond, Bulldog 145

Easy Aces 1, 155
education 68, *69*, 71, 97, 98, 141–159
Edwards School 141, 142, *143*, 146, 151
electricity 103, 104, 157
Erickson, Mr. 36, 37, 182

Fadiman, Clifton 153
Federal Communications Commission 53, 54
Federal Radio Commission 67
Fibber McGee and Molly 1, 15, 18, 49, 156, 167, 184, 186
Fineman, Irving 68
Fisher, Mis' 28, 59, 74, 158
Fishigan, Rishigan 36
Fly, James L. 53, 54
Flynn, Bernadine *4*, 5–7, 23, *25*, 38, 75, *117*, *147*, 184, 185
Forbes, Skinny 145
Ford, Henry 78
Forum 13, 136
fraternal organizations 93, 165, 166, 175, 179
freak shows *100*, 101
Freaks 100, 116
Freemasons 93, *94*, *165*
Friends of *Vic and Sade* 2
Fuddleman, Four-Fisted Frank 106, 111, 118, 119, 187

Gans, Herbert J. 62, 124, 125, 188
Gasoline Alley 6, 31
gender roles 95–97
gifts 81–83, 173
Gillian, Eddie 184
Goldbergs 37, 48, 55, 184

Golden, Gloria 106, 109, 111–114, 117–120, 187
Golden Gloves Story 185
Golenpaul, Dan 152, 153
Gook, Rush 1, 6, 7, 19, *31*, 36, 38, 51, 52, *54*, 59, 61, 62, 74, 75, 79, 81–83, 85, 88, 90, *91*, *96*, 99, 101, 103, 104, 111, 113, 114, *122*, 129, 130, *138*, 140, 144–151, 159, 161, 162, *164*, *168*, 169, 170, 178
Gook, Sade 1, 3, *4*, 5–7, 11, 23, 24, *25*, 26–30, *31*, 35, 36, 38, 51, 52, *54*, 57–59, 61, 62, 74–76, 78–85, 87–90, *91*, 92, 94, *96*, 97, 104, 111–113, 120, *122*, *128*, 129, 130, 133, 134, 135, *138*, 139, 140, 145, 148, 156–159, *164*, 166, *168*, 176, 179, 180, 183
Gook, Vic 1, 3, *4*, 5, 6, 19, 23, 24, *25*, 26–30, *31*, 33–36, 49, 51, 52, *54*, 58, 59, 61, 74–76, 78, 79, 81–86, 89, 90, *91*, 92–94, *96*, 103, 104, 111, 112, *122*, *128*, 129, 130, 134, 135, *138*, 139, 140, 144, 146, 154, 155, 157, 162, 163, *164*, 165, 166, *168*, 173–176, 180, 183
gossip 15, 28, 83–85, 87, 97, 119, 134
Great Depression 7, 8, 10, 14, 32, 36, 46, 73, 78, 86, 89, 92, 94, 100, 107, 110, 111, 113, 121–123, 125, 132, 133, 136, 141, 148–151, 156, 161, 171, 173, 181
Great Train Robbery 106
Griffith, D.W. 106
Gumpox, James 6, 7, 28, 79, 83, 85, 86, 113, 131, 180
Gutstop, Hank 36, 75, 81, 93, 103, 114, 181

Hackfram, Hunter 172
Haggin, B.H. 68
Haley, Jay 110
handball 98, 99, 101, 183, 188
Harris, Mis' Florence 84, 174, 184
Hartzell, Clarence 32, *33*, 185, 185, 186
Hawaii 51, 76, 84, 158
Hawkins Falls 185
"Hen" 11–13
Henry, William D. 56
Heth, Joice 101
high(brow) culture 63, 64, 67–69, 99, 114, 118, 124–126, 155, 159
Hilmes, Michelle 5, 8, 55
Hodges, Donald Clark 156
Hofstadter, Richard 156
Hollywood 65, 101, 106, 107, 109, 110, 112, 115, 116, 118–120, 153
home ownership 35, 36

Hoover, Herbert 32, 50, 70, 170, *171*, 173, *177*, 181
Horkheimer, Max 57
"Hot Cockles" 104
Housekeeper's Chats 43
housewives 1, 3, 5, 43, 44, 49, 51–53, 56, 57, 81, 86, 87, 97, 125, 138, 162, 187; *see also* women
Howard (horse) 7, 83, 85
Hummert, Frank and Anne 26, 46, 48, 57
humor 1, 5, 6, 10, 11, 13, 14, 17, 18, 20, 21, 22, 24–26, 36, 44, 45, 49, 74, 99, 101, 110, 116, 152, 155, 160, 162, 163, 172, 182
Humor of Vic and Sade 184
Hutchinson, Paul 70
Hutton, Richard 2
Hyena Grease 181

"I Won't Listen" 52, 53, 55, 61
Idelson, Bill 6, *31*, 32, 33, 38, 39, *40*, 75, *147*, *168*, 186
identification 50–52
Illinois Wesleyan University 3, 9, 10, 13, 149, 150
individualism 7, 64, 161, 163, 165, 166, 170–174, 176, 181
individuality 6, 7, 64, 135, 160, 161, 163–165, 170, 172, 173, 176, 178, 180, 182
Information, Please 151–154
Inner Sanctum 1
intellectualism 28, 99, 151, 155–159
Ironized Yeast 37
Ivory Flakes 58

Jack Armstrong, the All-American Boy 52
Jelke's Good Lukc Margarine 37, 38
jigsaw puzzles 89–91
Johnson, Blue-Tooth 34, 85, 129, 162, 178
Johnson, Mr. Albert (dog) 34, 145, 163
Johnson and Johnson 5, 15, 18
Johnston, Eric 112, 118–120
Judy and Jane 46
Just Plain Bill 45, 46, 48, 55

Kaltenborn, H.V. 70
Keats, John 155
Keller, Mis' 83, 87, 163, 172, 181, 182
Kelly, Joe 152
Keystone Chronicle 3, 5, 9, 15–18, 20, 23
Keystone Steel and Wire Company 3, 15
Kieran, John 153, 154
Kitchenware Dealers' Quarterly 121, 139, 140, 175

Klank, Stella 88
Kneesuffer, Ike 184
Kobak, Edgar 53
Konk, R.J. 95
Kupperman, Joel 154

Lady Margaret 130, 131
Lancaster, Mark 2
Lardner, Ring 68
Lazarsfeld, Paul 125, 126
leisure 73–105, 107, 155, 188; defined 73–74
Lenthall, Bruce 64, 160
letters 87, 88, 111
Levine, David O. 149
Life of Mary Southern 51
literature 86
Little Orphan Annie 46
lodges 61, 73, 75, 93–97, 111, 121, 134, 146, 165, 166, 175, 176, 178, 179, 181, 183
Longfellow, Henry Wadsworth 155, 195n51
Lora Lawton 59
Lorenzo Jones 48, 49
Lovecraft, H.P. 87
low(brow) culture 99, 105, 119, 125
Lum and Abner 20, 156, 186
Lumley, Frederick J. 67
Lynd, Helen 36, 94, 98, 149
Lynd, Robert 36, 94, 98, 149

Ma Perkins 45
MacDonald, Dwight 68
magazines 11–14, 17, 22, 23, 42, 55, 59, 86, 103, 119, 121, 122, 125, 126, 128, 129, 136–139, 142, 154, 156, 176, 185
malapropisms 155
management 139, 140
marching team 175, 176
Martin, Raymond "Skinny" 148
Martindale, Don 173
mass culture 62–71, 118, 124, 159, 160, 187, 188
mass media 62
materialism 81, 95, 97
McCormick, William 131
McFlongalotch, Herman 172
McLean County 107, 142, 143, 148, 186
McNamee, Graham 17
Mead, Margaret 74
Meadows, Victor *see* Gook, Rush
Mencken, H.L. 161
Merchandise Mart 39, 40, **60**
Merwin Cup 10
Mesner, Clarence 5, 6, 23, 26, 37
Mickey Mouse 21, 22
Mickey Mouse Theater of the Air 21
middle class 30, 34, 35, 104, 106, 124, 125, 151

Middletown 36, 98, 149
Miller, Russell 8, 32, *33*, 34, 61, 84, 85, 111, 120, *128*, 144, 146, 147, 157, 166, *168*, 183
Millikan, Robert Andrews 70
Mills, C. Wright 68
Morse, Carlton E. 186
Motion Picture Association of America 112
movie theaters 107, *108*, *109*, *113*, as social spaces 114, 115
movies 7–9, 62, *63*, 64–66, 68, 71, 88, 89, 100, 103, 104, 106–120, 136, 152, 158, 183; as escape 110, 111
Mullen, Frank 20
music 90, 104, 105
musicals 116, 117
Mutual Network 53
My Son and I 56

National Allocation Plan 167
National Committee on Education by Radio 70
National Education Association 158, 200n91
National Farm and Home Hour 18, 20
Nazis 65, 126
NBC 2–5, 9, 10, 14, 15, 17–23, 26, 31–33, 37, 38, 40, 43, 45, 48, 60, 65, 66, 70, 91, 96, 104, 121, 125, 147, 151, 160, 164, 167, 184–186, 188; *see also* Blue Network; Red Network
New York Times 43, 53
newspapers 5, 9–11, 15, 16, 23–25, 28, 35, 49, 65, 76, 85, 88, 104, 112, 121, 122, 127, 132–139, 153, 159, 166, 179, 185, 186; and community 134; and fiction 136, 137
nicknames 161, 162
Normal, Illinois 3, 107, 142, 143
novels 89, 122, 123, 126–129, 131, 136

Office of War Information 71, 167, 168
Oglesby, Mis' 169
One Man's Family 34, 184, 186
Orange Crush 18, *19*
organizational communication 140
Orton, William 7, 63–68, 71, 188

Painted Dreams 17
Pantagraph 3, 5, 15, 35, 107, 109, 132, 134, 135
parades 74, 75, 116, 166, 175, 184, 186
patriotism 169, 170, 178
Pearson, Edmund 127, 131
Pepper Young's Family 37, 46, 47, 51, 57

Phillips, Irna 17, 57
poetry 154, 155, 158, 159
popular culture 62, 63, 124, 125
Post, Emily 88, 95
prestige 9, 13, 51, 56, 124, 137, 142, 143, 149, 151, 154, 177, 178, 181
Procter & Gamble 5, 6, 8, 23, 25, 37–39, 41, 43, 49, 58, 167
propaganda 70, 71, 126, 167, 169, 170
Public Life of Cliff Norton 185
pulp fiction 128, 129, 137, 139

Quiz Kids 151–154

radio (medium) 1–10, 14, 15, 17–19, 21–24, 28, 30, 31, 34, 37, 41–53, 55–58, 60–62, 64–71, 73, 74, 79, 84–86, 89, 94, 97, 99, 104, 105, 116, 125, 126, 136, 137, 147, 151–156, 160, 167–169, 183–188; and education 69–71, 126; and government control 71; and mass culture 64
radio (technology) 7, 49, **50**, 65, 160
Radio and Television Mirror 24
Radio Stars 23, 34, 37, 156
railroad 14, 36, 83, 103
Ramsey, William 5, 23
Ranch Romance 138
Razorscum, Mr. Charley 6, 84, 103
Razorscum, Mis' 6
reading 121–140
records 90
recreation 3, 74–78, 84, 92, 99, 100, 101, 103, 104, 105, 132, 136, 142
Red Barn Fencing 15
Red Network 26; *see also* Blue Network; NBC
Redman, George 9, 10
"Reflections Marvelous" 10
Rhymer, Mary Frances 6, 9, 10
Rhymer, Paul 1–3, 5–24, 26–30, 32, 34–36, 38, 41, 57, 59, 71, 76, 80–84, 88, 93, 95, 99, 101, 105, 107, 118, 120, 121, 125, 127, 129, 136, 139, 140, 143, 145–151, 155, 156, 158, 159, 163, 164, 167, 168, 170, 173, 175, 182–185, 187, **188**, 189; continuity writing 9, 10, 18–20; *Pantagraph* writer 3, 5, 15; scriptwriting 15, 16, 18–22, 38; short stories 10, 11–14; television career 184, 185
Richards, Leland 145
Right to Happiness 55, 57
romance fiction 135–139
Romance of Helen Trent 46, 47
Roosevelt, Eleanor 153

Roosevelt, Franklin 3, 71, 170, *171*
Rorty, James 7, 64, 70, 71, 189
Rosenberg, Bernard 68
Rosten, Leo C. 113, 120
"rube" style 20
Ruebush, Mr. 29, 52, 111, 157
Rush, Uncle Fletcher 13, 32, *33*, 49, 74, 76, 82–84, 87, 111, 131, 163, 164, 169, 172, 173, 179–183, 186

Sacred Star Searchlight 176
Sacred Stars of the Milky Way 36, 61, 76, 89, 90, 92, 93, 95–97, 111, 165, 166, 173–175, 179
sadism 99
Saltzman, Charles McKinley 67
schools 8–11, 28, 30, 35, 46, 52, 55, 70, 73, 75, 87, 90, 105, 126, 129, 131, 141–152, 154, 156, 161, 174, 178, 179, 187
Schwarz, Barbara 2
Scott, Mis' 101, 188
Scott, Nicer 34, 76, 161, 162, 169, 170, 173, 178
serials 1, 8, 15, 17, 26, 27, 30, 37, 42, 44–47, 49–53, 55–58, 61, 69, 110, 128, 129, 137, 160, 167, 185
Seth Jones 127
Shakespeare, William 17, 20, 146, 153, 154
Shaw, Donald S. 53
Shepherd, Jean 84
shopping 8, 27, 37, 73, 79–83, 134, 156, 180
short stories 10, 12, *13*, 14
Simon, A.L. 55
Sisters of the Shining Sea 89
Sklar, Robert 107
Sludge, Mr. Harry 79, 84, 119, 163
Smokey Rogers: Fire Chief 19, 23
soap operas 17, 26, 42, 44–59, 61, 162, 185

sponsorship 15, 18, 19, 37, 38, 42, 43, 46, 49, 154
Spoonerisms 155
Stanley, J. Clinton 121
Stanley, Third Lieutenant Clinton 61, 89, 103, 121, 126, 127, 129–132, 145
Starbright, Mr. and Mrs. 184
Stedman, Raymond William 1, 30, 34, 47
Stella Dallas 46, 48, 61
Stembottom, Fred 78, 82, 84, 92, 93, 104, 188
Stembottom, Ruthie 35, 51, 78–80, 85, 87, 92, 97, 114, 163, 174, 180
Stoopnagle and Budd 1, 155
Strang, Ruth 132
studio system 118–120
sustaining programs 6, 26, 37, 66, 154
Swift, R.F. 174
Swirski, Peter 124, 125

tall tales 172
Taylor, Frederick 139
telephone 35, 86, 87
television 4, 8, 19, 23, 68, 184–187
Terkel, Studs 184
theater 64
Thimble Club 52, 61, 84, 97, 113, 114, 156–158, 166, 169, 176
This Is Nora Drake 47
Those Endearing Young Charms 186
Three Doctors 18, 19
Thurber, James 3, 7, 43, 46, 58, 59, 61
Tiers, Van Dyke 152
Tisdel, Mildred 141–143, 146, 151
titles (honorary) 176–178
Tocqueville, Alexis de 64, 161, 164, 166

trains *see* railroad
travel 76–79

University of the Air 125

vacations 34, 76–79, 84, 134, 181
Van Harvey, Art 2, *4*, 5, 6, 23, *25*, 32, *33*, 38, *117*, *147*, 184, 185
Van Loon, Hendrik Wilhelm 7
Virginia Avenue 3, 24, 35, 36, 169, 170
Virginia Avenue Area Sons of Patriotism Salvage Indemnity 169, 170

Waples, Douglas 121, 136
Warner, W. Lloyd 56
washrags 1, 79, 80
WEAF 42
White, David Manning 68
Whitehouse, David 8, 32, *33*, 147, *168*, 186, 187
Whittier, John Greenleaf 154, 155
Wilbur, Ray Lyman 70
Williams, Roger J. 161, 163
Woman in White 55–57
women 5, 11, 51–53, 55, 56, 79–80, 95, 136; as audience 5, 49, 55, 56, 119; and shopping 79–80; and writing 136; *see also* housewives
women's clubs 97, **98**
Women's National Radio Committee 51
WOR 68, 69
World War II 110, 118, 126, 132, 167, 168

Yamilton's 36, 79, 157, 161, 192n43
"Yella" 13, 14
YMCA 99
Young Widder Brown 46, 60

www.ingramcontent.com/pod-product-compliance
Lightning Source LLC
Chambersburg PA
CBHW060300240426
43661CB00060B/2845